A COGNITIVE HISTORICAL APPROACH TO CREATIVITY

At the heart of creativity is the practice of bringing something new into existence, whether it be a material object or abstract idea, thereby making history and enriching the creative tradition.

A Cognitive Historical Approach to Creativity explores the idea that creativity is both a cognitive phenomenon and a historical process. Blending insights and theories of cognitive science with the skills, mentality and investigative tools of the historian, this book considers diverse issues including: the role of the unconscious in creativity, the creative process, creating history with a new object or idea, and the relationship between creators and consumers. Drawing on a plethora of real-life examples from the eighteenth century through to the present day, and from distinct fields including the arts, literature, science and engineering, Subrata Dasgupta emphasizes historicity as a fundamental feature of creativity.

Providing a unified, integrative, interdisciplinary treatment of cognitive history and its application to understanding and explaining creativity in its multiple domains, *A Cognitive Historical Approach to Creativity* is essential reading for all researchers of creativity.

Subrata Dasgupta is Professor Emeritus in the School of Computing and Informatics, University of Louisiana at Lafayette where, from 1993 to 2018, he held the Computer Science Trust Fund Eminent Scholar Chair. From 1999 to 2013 he was also Director of the Institute of Cognitive Science. He has authored numerous works on the cognitive, historical and computational aspects of creativity.

A COGNITIVE HISTORICAL APPROACH TO CREATIVITY

Subrata Dasgupta

Routledge
Taylor & Francis Group

LONDON AND NEW YORK

First published 2019
by Routledge
2 Park Square, Milton Park, Abingdon, Oxon OX14 4RN

and by Routledge
52 Vanderbilt Avenue, New York, NY 10017

Routledge is an imprint of the Taylor & Francis Group, an informa business

© 2019 Subrata Dasgupta

British Library Cataloguing-in-Publication Data
A catalogue record for this book is available from the British Library

Library of Congress Cataloging-in-Publication Data
A catalog record has been requested for this book

ISBN: 978-0-367-14569-9 (hbk)
ISBN: 978-0-367-14571-2 (pbk)
ISBN: 978-0-429-03236-3 (ebk)

Typeset in Bembo
by Wearset Ltd, Boldon, Tyne and Wear

Printed and bound in Great Britain by
TJ International Ltd, Padstow, Cornwall

CONTENTS

PROLOGUE

I The creative tradition and its mentality

This book begins with the proposition that to be creative is to *make history*. And, in the spirit of historian Eric Hobsbawm's (1983) definition of "tradition," we will speak of the *creative tradition* to mean the practice found through the whole of human prehistory and recorded history of *bringing into being significantly new and valuable things*—both material objects and abstract ones. The creative tradition almost certainly came into being out of necessity, for the sake of survival, at the very dawn of human prehistory with the invention of the first stone tools. It is arguably humanity's oldest living tradition.

The creative tradition is rendered visible in all those ways we have come to associate with the word "creativity": in material forms as art objects, tools, weapons, machines, structures, books, textiles and so on; and in symbolic or abstract forms as theories, theorems, laws, plans, designs, doctrines, ideas and concepts, procedures, algorithms, etc. These are the visible and perceptible expressions of this tradition. And underpinning this tradition is a certain kind of mentality: one with the propensity to think in ways others do not, to paraphrase art historian E.H. Gombrich (1993).

II The "magical realism" of the creative tradition

Literary scholar John Livingstone Lowes (1930) ended his magnificent study of the poet Samuel Taylor Coleridge admitting the mysterious nature of creativity (p. 428). Nobel laureate Peter Medawar (1990, p. 98), a consummate essayist as well as a brilliant biologist, quoted Lowes approvingly, concluding that there was nothing more one could add to Lowes's assertion. But he failed to mention Lowes's caveat that the poetic imagination is the consequence of normal and discernible powers and that our understanding of this will only enrich rather than diminish the beauty of poetry (pp. 428–429).

I happen to be one of those who agree with Lowes. The magicality of the creative tradition—of its constituent, individual, myriad, inventive processes—never diminishes even when we succeed in shedding light on them. The charm of creativity does not "fly/At the mere touch of cold philosophy" as John Keats lamented. We are constantly surprised, amazed and enchanted by the emanations from the minds of writers, poets, scientists, inventors, craftspersons, engineers, philosophers, musicians, artists, mathematicians and the like.

So we might say that the creative tradition is also a magical tradition as much as it is a timeless one. But like the magic practiced by magicians there is nothing supernatural or transcendental about it. Creativity is not the fruit of "divine dispensations" as Plato insisted. Rather—and this is at the heart of our discussion in this book—the products of the creative tradition are *extraordinary products of ordinary cognitive operations combined in unordinary ways*. We are reminded of the literary genre termed "magical realism" practiced by such writers as Gabriel Garcia Marquez and Salman Rushdie, described by Rushdie as the fusion of the improbable and the quotidian (Bowers 2004, p. 3). We are tempted to view the creative tradition as also bestowed with a kind of magical realism—the emergence of the improbable out of the mundane. How so we will see.

III   Artifact and artificer

At this point let me introduce two terms that will be central to this whole discussion. By *artifact* we will mean anything produced by human effort and whose existence is defined by *purpose* or *intent*. Thus, an artifact is a non-natural thing. This may be of a material kind—and, thus, subject to or constrained by the physical laws of nature (for example, a piece of pottery, a scientific instrument, a bridge, a sculpture or a building)—or it may be of an abstract kind, intrinsically independent of the physical laws of nature (e.g., a mathematical theorem, a literary style, a philosophical doctrine or an algorithm); or possibly a hybrid of the two.

By *artificer* we will mean the producer of an artifact. While it is the case that some non-human living beings (such as chimps) are perceived as artificers in a limited sense, and even certain artifacts (specifically, artificial intelligence-based computer systems) are increasingly regarded as artificers, the artificers of interest in this book will be human beings. It is human creativity that interests us here, not animal or computational creativity.

As we will see, the concepts "artifact" and "artificer" are not nearly as straightforward as this brief introduction suggests; furthermore the *relationship* between artifacts and artificers is crucial to any discussion of creativity and will certainly merit further discussion.

IV   Creative phenomena

So what are the *constituents* of the creative tradition? Consider the following scenarios:

One. There is a specific, highly original individual artifact (material or abstract); for example, a machine, a painting, a scientific concept or a philosophical idea. Usually the artificer is an individual but there is also the possibility of a cluster of cooperating individual artificers. We want to understand the nature of the *singular act of creation* that gave birth to the artifact in question.

Two. There is a specific individual artificer: a painter, sculptor, scientist, poet, novelist, playwright, engineer, composer, inventor, philosopher, craftsperson, designer, scholar, social thinker and so on. Such an artificer may devote his or her entire life to the creation of artifacts that in one way or another made history. In this case, we may wish to understand the nature of this artificer's *creative life*.

Three. There is a specific creative *movement* in some region of the world spread over a period of time—a few years perhaps, or decades, or even a century: an artistic movement, a technological revolution, an intellectual or cultural transformation, etc. In such a scenario we may wish to understand the nature and development of a resulting *shared mentality* among the artificers characterizing the movement.

Collectively, we will call such particular acts of creation, creative lives and creative movements, *creative phenomena*. They constitute the ingredients of the creative tradition. More precisely, individual creative phenomena are the weft and warp of the creative tradition. And, as we will see, they share a vital attribute: *creative phenomena are manifestations of minds (individually or collectively) making history*. Each such phenomenon has contributed to the propagation of the creative tradition and, thus, to the history of the world.

V   The historicity of creativity

By making history, creative phenomena become part of history. There is, thus, an inherent existential *historicity* to creative phenomena.

For one thing, when a creative phenomenon comes into being, the process that gave rise to it has already occurred; it belongs to the past. This is true for the invention of an individual artifact as it is for the shaping of an artificer's creative life or the making of a creative movement. Whether we are speaking of Picasso's creation of the painting *Les Demoiselles d'Avignon* (Rubins, Seckel and Cousins 1994; Green 2001), the life of multidisciplinary scientist Herbert Simon (Dasgupta 2003a, 2003b) or the techno-economic movement called the Industrial Revolution (Ashton 1969; Hardy 2014), by the time these creative phenomena are so recognized, they are part of the past.

This means that to understand the nature of a creative phenomenon the creativity researcher cannot normally resort to the laboratory; most times they cannot devise experiments that will (re)produce such phenomena in a controlled environment. Rather, these problems are of the nature of historical problems; we must treat them as historical events. To explain or interpret such phenomena is to engage in *historical explanation*. Thus the investigator of a phenomenon drawn from the creative tradition becomes necessarily a historian.

But such historical explanations must be of a specific kind, for the historian needs to recognize that creative phenomena are, at their core, *cognitive* phenomena. The artificers are the history makers, and loci of their history-making are their minds. The most fundamental issues that the creativity researcher-as-historian will have to address are of a cognitive nature. What kinds of beliefs and knowledge participate in some given creative phenomenon? What aims and goals stimulate it? What new beliefs, knowledge and goals are generated by the underlying processes? Does affect play a part and if so how? What styles of reasoning can be elicited? What cognitive acts are involved? What roles do the conscious and the unconscious play in the process? What of random thoughts and chance events? What place does the irrational have in creative thinking? In other words the creativity researcher-as-historian must enter the business of *mentalization* (Fotopolou and Tsakiris 2017): constructing stories of how other minds (those of the artificers) work in the realm of creativity.

The mind, of course, is not an island of its own. Every creative phenomenon has a cultural and social backdrop that must be taken into account. Indeed the interplay of culture and cognition is bidirectional: while some scholars have argued that culture shapes cognition (Tomasello 1999; Sørensen 2011), others insist that cognition has shaped culture (Tooby and Cosmides 1992). Our position on this is along the lines advocated eloquently and persuasively by the pioneer cognitive scientist Jerome Bruner (1990): that cognition—the process by which we *make meaning* out of our experiences in the world—is immersed *in* culture hence any cognitive explanation of a creative phenomenon must be culturally grounded.

Creative phenomena manifest historicity in yet another way: the relevant cognitive explanation itself will contain a strong historical component. To make sense of a creative phenomenon one must delve into *its* past, its prehistory. "The past survives in the present" as the English philosopher R.G. Collingwood (1946, p. 225) once put it.

Consider, for example, the three kinds of creative phenomena mentioned earlier. In the first, the creativity researcher is to offer an explanation of how a singular act of creation came about. To do this she must reach back to the artificer's personal past and to the cultural, social and epistemic states of the world in which the act of creation began. The researcher must enter the archives. Or, in the case of investigating the nature of an artificer's creative life, the creativity researcher must enter into a biographical engagement with the artificer—and what is biography but the history of the individual—life history as it is often called nowadays.

Moreover the artifact produced by the artificer itself usually has a "back story." The researcher may well have to unveil *its* prehistory. Shakespearean theater scholar Evelyn Tribble and cognitive scientist John Sutton (2011) have referred to artifacts as "saturated with the imprints of many other times" (p. 100). To take an example from the history of metallurgy, the form and functioning of the modern blast furnace (which produces iron from its ores) can only be understood as an act of creation when one has traced its complicated *evolution* from its origins in antiquity (Aitchison 1960; Forbes 1964, pp. 111–129).

In the case of a creative movement, it is virtually axiomatic that any explanation of the characteristic mentality governing the movement entails the intrusion of history. Creative movements—the seventeenth century Scientific Revolution, the eighteenth century Industrial Revolution, the Impressionist movement of the nineteenth century, the modernist movements in twentieth century literature and architecture, to take some well-known examples—are almost invariably responses or reactions to some historical situation. Here, the researcher must invoke social and cultural dimensions as much as cognitive ones.

Perhaps most significantly, we can only recognize that something has "made history" by acknowledging that *nothing quite like it* had existed prior to its existence and/or that it had *consequences* in time after it came into existence. In other words, a phenomenon such as the invention of an artifact, the living of a creative life or a movement is viewed as a creative phenomenon because of its significance to the creative tradition as it was before the phenomenon or as it became after it.

VI   Thus ... cognitive history

The historicity of creative phenomenon makes a historian out of the creativity researcher and a cognitive scientist out of the historian. The creativity researcher metamorphoses into a *cognitive historian*. If the aim of history (including historical biography) is to uncover hitherto hidden or unknown or neglected aspects of the past (Collingwood 1946; Evans 2000) or to compose narratives about the past (Jenkins 2003), *cognitive history* strives to render visible and narrate the hitherto hidden or unknown cognitive nature of creative phenomena.

To the best of my knowledge, cognitive scientist Nancy Nersessian (1995) first proposed this term as an approach to understanding the "thinking practices" of scientists. But the scope of cognitive history can be enlarged to encompass the whole of the creative tradition: to embrace not just science but art, technology, engineering, design, literary production, music, scholarship, craft and so on. Here, then, is an expanded "definition":

> Cognitive history is the symbiosis of the methods of historical (including biographical) and cognitive (including cultural) inquiries. Its aim is to describe, understand and explain the making of creative phenomena.

Like other kinds of historians (political, economic, social, cultural, intellectual) the cognitive historian must draw upon the kinds of evidence available in the archives. If an artificer is still living the cognitive historian may add the results of interviews (oral history) to the evidence. At the same time her investigation and story telling will be shaped—and contained—by a theoretical framework derived from cognitive science (or one or more of its contributing disciplines (Barsalou 2010)) rather as the economic historian is guided by economic theory. Cognitive history is a multidisciplinary mode of inquiry.

VII The case study (or idiographic) method

A principal reason why creativity compels our attention (and admiration) is that creative phenomena are relatively *rare* events. In the felicitous words of art historian George Kubler (1962), invention is largely the prerogative of the few who inhabit the "crumbling edge of convention" (p. 68). They are the ones who make history, and events that make history are usually singular and unique, so distinctive that they are known by names: the Italian Renaissance, the Industrial Revolution, the theory of natural selection, the poem "The Waste Land" are a few examples. And, of course, the artificers themselves become identifiable historical figures. Milton and Shakespeare, Newton and Galileo, Marx and Comte, Watt and Edison, Cézanne and Gaughin, Tagore and Yeats are not just exemplars of the supreme artificer; they are unique in and of themselves, so their particular creative lives become singular creative phenomena.

The cognitive historian in this respect is very much like the humanities scholar. Like some kinds of historians, biographers and literary scholars, his domain is the individual: a particular creative phenomenon—be it an act of creation, a creative life or a creative movement. He must espouse the *case study* method as a means of inquiry.

As psychologist Doris Wallace (1989) has pointed out the case study has been, and is, used as a strategy in many disciplinary traditions. We are all familiar with their presence in medical, legal and psychoanalytical literatures and in the writings of literary scholars and critics. To these we can add engineering and design wherein the engineer's or the designer's focus is usually the individual utilitarian artifact. Even academic psychologists recognize the importance of the individual case study. They call it the *idiographic* problem situation in contrast to their more familiar search for general principles that they call the *nomothetic* problem situation (Runyon 1982).

As for the natural sciences, many scientists study particular phenomena: a particular organism for example, or a particular family of chemical compounds. Thomas Kuhn's (2012) celebrated (and controversial) concept of "normal science" referred to scientists solving particular *problems* (or "puzzles" as he also called them). But even in doing normal science there always hovers in the background a larger ambition: to test universal/nomothetic principles or even, more ambitiously, to discover universal/nomothetic laws. The study of the individual in the natural sciences, and also in the artificial sciences (such as computer science and engineering theory), is thus an idiographic means to a nomothetic end.

In contrast, cognitive history, as both a discipline and a subject matter, draws on nomothetic principles (of cognitive science) to describe and explain idiographic creative phenomena taken from the creative tradition. The case study of a particular creative phenomenon is thus the unit of inquiry in cognitive history.

VIII   This book

And so, this book. My goal here is to present and explore *cognitive history as an approach to creativity studies*. It takes the historicity of creativity as a starting point and explores how minds—mostly individually, sometimes collectively—make history. The focus is on individual creative phenomena—individual acts of creation, individual creative lives and individual creative movements—taken, plucked out so to speak, from the annals of the creative tradition. We will be navigating the *artifactual world*.

Most of the creative phenomena discussed here belong to the so-called modern era (nineteenth and twentieth centuries, with one episode from the eighteenth century) though I will have occasion to refer to earlier times. The domains of these individual creative phenomena are manifold: painting, fiction and poetry writing, and filmmaking from the arts; physics and biophysics from the natural sciences; computer science, administrative science, economics, metallurgy, structural engineering and mechanical engineering from the artificial sciences and technology; boat making from the craft tradition; and the philosophy of science from the humanities. Culturally, this work spans both West and East: the protagonists who appear and reappear throughout the book are mostly from America, Britain and India—the three countries and their cultures with which I am most familiar—with a few from other countries in Western Europe. For the reader's convenience a "dramatis personae" is provided following this Prologue.

IX   This author

While my profound intellectual debt to others, before my time and in my time, who have thought long and deep and hard on creativity, cognition and history will be obvious from the citations and the bibliography, this book is itself the culmination of my own learning, reading, thinking, discussing, teaching and writing on the topic of creativity and the creative tradition over the past twenty-five years in the course of which I metamorphosed from computer scientist to cognitive historian. This metamorphosis, in retrospect, seems entirely natural: as a computer scientist my interest lay in how computer scientists, mathematicians, programmers and engineers brought computational artifacts into being, mostly in the course of the twentieth century; an interest that led me into the cognitive history of computational artifacts (Dasgupta 2014a, 2018a). But along the way and almost insidiously (it now seems to me), this interest in computational artifacts and their artificers per se expanded to a larger artifactual world ranging over science, engineering, art, filmmaking, literature in particular; and a span of time reaching back to prehistory. The creative tradition as a whole, in fact.

ACKNOWLEDGMENTS

In writing this book my intellectual debt to scores of scholars will be evident from the citations and the bibliography. More proximately, I have had the benefit of discussions and debates with a number of people who, in one way or another, have helped shape some of the ideas found in this book. Some of them were my immediate colleagues, some my students, some fellow adventurers in the domain of creativity and related studies. Their respective disciplines ranged over philosophy of science, art, computer science, psychology, linguistics, history of science, sociology of science, design theory, literary studies and cognitive science—all of which contribute in one way or another to the study of creativity.

And so, thank you: Robert S. Anderson, Istvan Berkeley, Tirthankar Bose, Evangeline Boudreaux, Donald S.L. Cardwell, Claude Cech, Carmen Comeaux, Deepanwita Dasgupta, Janet Elias, Jonathan S. Feinstein, Michelle Feist, Liane Gabora, John S. Gero, Wenceslao J. Gonzalez, Richard Hills, Norman N. Holland, Deepak Kumar, Anthony S. Maida, Thomas Nickles, David N. Perkins, Lewis Pyenson, Arnab Rai Choudhuri, George Rodrigue, Herbert A. Simon, Dean Keith Simonton, Abha Sur, Naresh Vempala, Robert S. Weber and Maurice V. Wilkes.

Three anonymous reviewers made invaluable comments and suggestions on the initial proposal for this book on behalf of the publisher. I thank them, though I would have preferred to acknowledge them by name.

My thanks to Ceri McLardy, my editor at Routledge who embraced this work from the time she received my proposal. It has been a pleasure working with her.

I thank Claire Toal and her production team for their professionalism; and Charlotte Parkins for her meticulous copy-editing.

For over twenty-five years my work in creativity studies, history of science, and cognitive history has been supported by the Computer Science Trust Fund Eminent Scholar Endowed Chair in the University of Louisiana at Lafayette. Appointment to this chair has afforded me the freedom to wander at will amidst the curious lanes and alleys of creativity.

Last but not the least, my thanks to my family for always being there.

DRAMATIS PERSONAE

The following artificers appear as protagonists in this work. Some of them appear as "principal characters." They are indicated by asterisks.

Prehistoric Technologists and Artists.
Crawfish Boat-makers of South Louisiana. (*)
Kenneth Appel (1932–2013). American mathematician.
Jagadis Chandra Bose (1858–1937). Indian physicist and biophysicist. (*)
Per Brinch Hansen (1938–2007). Danish computer scientist.
Lewis Carroll (Charles Ludwig Dodgson) **(1832–1898).** English logician and fantasy writer.
Paul Cézanne (1839–1906). French painter.
Nirad C. Chaudhuri (1897–1999). Indian autobiographer and historian. (*)
Samuel Taylor Coleridge (1772–1834). English poet and essayist.
John Constable (1776–1837). English painter.
Camille Corot (1796–1875). French painter.
Charles Darwin (1809–1882). English naturalist and evolutionary biologist.
Leonardo da Vinci (1452–1519). Italian painter, engineer and scientist. (*)
Emily Dickinson (1830–1886). American poet.
Edsger J. Dijkstra (1930–2002). Dutch computer scientist. (*)
Albert Einstein (1879–1955). German-born, Swiss–American theoretical physicist. (*)
Francis Galton (1822–1911). English polymath scientist.
Mohandas Gandhi (1869–1948). Indian nationalist, and political and social activist.
James Joyce (1882–1941). Irish novelist and short story writer.
Wolfgang Haken (1928–). German mathematician.
Godfrey Harold (G.H.) Hardy (1877–1947). English mathematician.

Donald E. Knuth (1938–). American computer scientist.

Thomas S. Kuhn (1922–1996). American philosopher and historian of science. (*)

Robert Maillart (1872–1940). Swiss structural engineer.

Édouard Manet (1832–1883). French painter. (*)

Gregor Mendel (1822–1884). Austrian monk and botanist.

Claude Monet (1840–1926). French painter.

Henry Moore (1898–1986). English sculptor.

Pier Luigi Nervi (1891–1979). Italian structural engineer and architect. (*)

Robert S. Nichols (1893–1944). English poet and playwright. (*)

Flannery O'Connor (1925–1964). American short story writer and novelist. (*)

Pablo Picasso (1881–1973). Spanish painter and sculptor. (*)

Chandrasekara Venkata (C.V.) Raman (1888–1970). Indian experimental physicist. (*)

Satyajit Ray (1921–1992). Indian filmmaker and writer. (*)

George Rodrigue (1944–2013). American painter. (*)

Rammohun Roy (1772–1833). Indian social, religious and educational reformer. (*)

Amrita Sher-Gil (1913–1941). Indian–Hungarian painter. (*)

Herbert A. Simon (1916–2001). American social, cognitive and computer scientist. (*)

Stephen Spender (1909–1995). English poet and essayist.

Philippe Starck (1949–). French industrial/product designer.

Robert Stephenson (1803–1859). English engineer. (*)

Rabindranath Tagore (1861–1941). Indian poet, composer, playwright and philosopher. (*)

Alan Turing (1912–1954). English mathematician and computer pioneer.

Joseph Mallard William (J.M.W.) Turner (1775–1851). English landscape painter.

John von Neumann (1903–1957). Hungarian-born American mathematician and computer pioneer.

James Watt (1736–1819). Scottish inventor, craftsman, engineer and entrepreneur. (*)

Maurice V. Wilkes (1913–2010). English computer pioneer. (*)

Frederick C. Williams (1911–1977). English electronics engineer and computer pioneer.

Terry Winograd (1946–). American computer scientist.

Robert Burns Woodward (1917–1979). American organic chemist.

William Butler (W.B.) Yeats (1865–1939). Irish poet.

1

THE COGNITIVE–HISTORICAL SPACE

I What is cognition?

If we wish to make sense of creative phenomena of the kind mentioned in the Prologue we need some sort of broad background within which we can both frame and understand such phenomena. For our purposes I will call this the *cognitive–historical space*.

But what *is* cognition? Some writers answer by simply giving examples of what they think are its instances. For example, cognitive scientist Zenon Pylyshyn (1984) introduced his book *Computation and Cognition* by identifying a "vocabulary" of cognitive terms: perception, recognition, classification of experiences, inferencing, decision making, remembering and knowledge processing (p. 15).

But what connects these terms and concepts? What is common to them that we may call them instances of cognition? Some writers have offered working definitions. For example, for neuropsychologist Richard Gregory (1987) cognition is the means for "handling knowledge" (p. 149). So knowledge is at the center of this view of cognition, a view that psychologist Howard Gardner (1985) concurred with. And so, by extension, the discipline of cognitive science is concerned with the origins, nature, development, and uses of knowledge (p. 6). In her textbook on cognition Margaret Matlin (2009) reiterates this centrality of knowledge (p. 2).

Most writers, of course, equate cognition with mental activity. Thus *mind* and cognition become one; for the knowledge-centered advocates the mind is a knowledge processor. But is knowledge processing all that there is to cognition? Is this what is common to the various cognitive terms mentioned by Pylyshyn? And if so, what is the nature of this knowledge processing that Howard Gardner called "cognitive science?"

We find one explicit answer to these questions in cognitive scientist and philosopher Margaret Boden's (2006) two-volume, 1500-page history of cognitive science titled, significantly, *Mind as Machine*. Cognitive science, she tells us, is concerned with mental processes and the workings of the mind/brain system (p. xxxv). But then she adds that such mental processes are best perceived as the workings of a *machine* (ibid.). Yet, she cautions, there is more to cognitive science than just cognition. She refers to psychologist George Miller, one of the founders of cognitive science, and his colleagues, notably Jerome Bruner, who included *volition*, *conation* (that is, motivation) and *emotion* within the scope of cognitive science (Boden 2006, p. 10).

Unfortunately, this eclecticism did not last: As Boden explained, because of the inconvenience of such matters as motivation and emotion as subjects of empirical study, they were soon put aside (p. 11).

When Boden spoke of cognitive science as the study of the mind as a "machine" she was, of course, referring to the computer: she recognized cognitive science as the interdisciplinary science of mind wherein the central theoretical concepts were founded in computer science (p. 12).

Just how or why the computer entered the picture has its own history reaching back to the 1940s and the work and ideas of some remarkable scientists such as psychologist Kenneth Craik, mathematician/computer theorist Alan Turing, neurophysiologist Warren McCulloch, mathematical logician Walter Pitts and mathematician/computer theorist John von Neumann (Craik 1943; McCulloch and Pitts 1943; Turing 1950; von Neumann 1945, 1951, 1958). By the late 1970s, when the journal *Cognitive Science* was inaugurated (in 1977) and the Cognitive Science Society was instituted at a conference in La Jolla, California (in 1979), computer science in the form of one of its subdisciplines, *artificial intelligence* (AI) was firmly in place as an influential contributory discipline of cognitive science. In defining cognitive science as the study of "mind as machine," Boden was giving voice to just how influential this view (which we may call *computationalism*) is.

II Cognition as meaning-making

Not everyone in the cognitive science community accepts the computational perspective. In particular Jerome Bruner became in later life very vocal in his opposition to computationalism. In his book *Acts of Meaning* Bruner pointed out that the intent of the "cognitive revolution" was to bring "mind" back into psychology after its fifty-year exile (at least in America) under the insidious influence of behaviorism (Bruner 1990, p. 1). The irony, he lamented, was that this desire was soon overtaken by the influence of computationalism as the "ruling metaphor" and, indeed, ideology for achieving this end. But this was *not* what he and his colleagues intended the "revolution" to be: their intention had been to locate *meaning* as the core idea in psychology (p. 2). For Bruner, then, cognition is a *meaning-making* enterprise. But in order to construct such meaning, cognition is not only constituted of actions located within a being. Meaning-making also entails the active participation of *culture*—as an inherent constituent of mind (p. 33). Thus, Bruner believed, it was his and his collaborators' hope that cognitive science would be the systematic study of how humans (and, possibly, other animals) make meaning out of their interactions with the world.

III Cognitive science as the science of meaning-making

Our starting point in this book is Bruner's position. More precisely, we will take as axiomatic the following propositions.

Proposition 1: There exists an entity called *mind* possessed by human beings (and possibly to a lesser extent by other living forms). Let us call such beings *conscious agents*.

Proposition 2: The function of mind is to enable conscious agents to *make meaning out of their experiences with, and in, the world at large*—both the external world outside their physical extent and the internal world within their physical extent. Such meaning-making processes constitute *cognition*.

Proposition 3: Cognitive processes involve the participation of *culture*.

Proposition 4: The aim of *cognitive science* is to construct or propose *empirically plausible* models and hypotheses about such meaning-making (that is, cognitive) processes.

By "empirically plausible" we mean that the models/hypotheses of cognitive processes must meet two kinds of constraints.

The behavioral constraint: All explanatory models or hypotheses about cognition must be consistent with the observed behavior of conscious agents and how they interact with one another and with the world beyond.

The physical or biological constraint: All explanatory models or hypotheses about cognition must be consistent with the constraints imposed on the mind by the known physical and/or biological attributes of conscious agents.

The latter, of course, refers to observable or known neuronal and sensory-motor constraints.

The significance of the word "conscious" should be noted. *Consciousness* is, of course, a much studied and debated concept among philosophers of mind (see, e.g., Chalmers 1996), and its place (and that of its counter-concept, *unconsciousness*) in the study of creativity will be the subjects of a later chapter. In speaking of "conscious agent," I use the word in the psychological sense of the agent being *aware* of its environment and of itself (*self-aware*) and whose behavior takes into account such awareness.

Computationalism is, thus, not intrinsic to these propositions. But this is not to discount the language and concepts of computer science as modes of, or as metaphors in, explanation. Notice that proposition 2, "Bruner's proposition," suggests what cognition *is*, not how it may be realized; and the "empirically plausible models" of proposition 4 leaves open the possibility for empirically plausible computational models We will have some occasion in the course of this book when *computational thinking* (Dasgupta 2016a, pp. 119–128) will be a fruitful tool of explanation.

IV   Elements of a cognitive–historical space

This brings us back to our central concern: human creativity. Having clarified the concepts of cognition and cognitive science for our purposes we can now consider in some depth the various elements constituting our cognitive–historical space. We postulate that the individual human agents who participate in creative phenomena can be characterized in terms of the elements of the cognitive–historical space. Thus, the cognitive historian's own understanding, analysis and explanation of a creative phenomenon will be articulated in terms of this same space. In other words we will theorize about creative phenomena in general by referring to this framework.

Community

The creative being—the artificer—is not an island of her own (despite the myth of the "lonely genius"). She belongs to a community—or society—that in different ways nourishes her. Psychologist Mihalyi Csikzentmihalyi (1988) called such a social entity a "field," rather like a field of force in physics.

For one thing, the artificer needs one or more target *consumers* of her artifacts. The consumer's role is to experience the artifact, to judge it, criticize it, interpret it and, in some situations, use it. The consumer may also serve as an *agent of transmission* and *dissemination* of information about the artifact to other members of the artificer's immediate community, or even to members of other communities, possibly across generations. This is where the teacher, the textbook writer, the synthesizer, the scholar, the critic and the "popular" expositor become important players in the making of creative phenomena.

Community is also the *source of stimuli* for the artificer. She may glean ideas and knowledge from other members of the community to which she belongs or perhaps from other distant societies. In other words the artificer is as much the consumer of other people's artifacts as the producer of artifacts.

It is not for nothing that Paris became the epicenter of new movements in art in the nineteenth and early twentieth centuries. Nor that Calcutta (now Kolkata) became, through the course of the nineteenth century, the locus of a creative movement called the Bengal Renaissance. Nor that the Cavendish Laboratory in Cambridge became an amazingly fertile place for the development of nuclear physics in the first half of the twentieth century. Nor that a part of Northern California—"Silicon Valley"—emerged as the epicenter of the development of computer and information technology in the fourth quarter of the twentieth century. In each case artificers within a community—painters in the first situation, writers, poets, social reformers, theologians, and scientists in the second, physicists in the third, and computer scientists, solid state physicists and digital engineers in the last—stimulated and "fed off" one another's works and ideas.

Culture

The poet/playwright T.S. Eliot in his classic essay *Notes on the Definition of Culture* wrote of "three senses" of this term: as associated with the individual, a group (or class) or an entire society (Eliot 1962, p. 21). But, Eliot said, there is a hierarchical relationship between them: a society's culture is the most fundamental, then that of the group or class, and then that of the individual. If I have understood him correctly, culture "flows" from society to group/class to individual. In more recent times, such scholars as the anthropologist Michael Tomasello (1999) would agree with Eliot, while others, notably psychologists John Tooby and Leda Cosmides (1992) have opined the reverse: that culture is the product of (individual) psychology.

But what *is* culture? Literary scholar Raymond Williams (1963) presented four distinct interpretations of the term (p. 16): (a) The state or habit of the mind, as when we say that a person is "cultured." (This is consonant with Matthew Arnold's idea of culture as a person's "*inward* condition of mind and spirit" (Arnold 1970, p. 209).) (b) The state of the intellectual development of a society. (c) The corpus of activity known as "art." (d) An entire way of life.

This last seems particularly relevant to creativity. It approximates the anthropologist's sense of the term as when Clifford Geertz (1973) described culture as "webs of significance" humans themselves have "spun" (p. 5). For the anthropologist a society's culture comprises of whatever a person belonging to that society needs to know or believe in order to function within that society (D'Andrade 1995, p. xii). But that culture must be *meaningful* ("webs of significance") to the society that subscribes to it. To follow Bruner's thinking, culture is the *public* ingredient of the meaning-making process. And in turn, it is itself the product of cognition, a human creation, a gigantic artifact, a product of human collective creativity.

To my mind, a particularly useful and insightful characterization of culture is offered by anthropologist Dan Sperber (1996). He distinguished between *mental representations* and *public representations*. The former are the symbol structures that reside within individual agents; the latter inhabit *populations* of agents (p. 25)—communities. Public representations are (to use a term with a computational flavor), *distributed* representations—and such representations, when relatively stable over a long period, Sperber suggested, constitute culture (p. 57). And so, following this line, we will take culture to mean a body of *public, widely-distributed, and temporally stable symbolic representations* of things in the world inhabiting particular communities.

As for the relationship between mental (cognitive) and cultural representations, Sperber takes a decidedly eclectic view that straddles both camps of the cognition–culture debate mentioned above. Each is the cause and effect of the other: cognitive representations are interpretations of public representations, which in turn emanate from other individual mental representations (p. 26). Otherwise, Sperber suggests, there are no boundaries separating one from the other (p. 49).

In concrete terms, the elements of culture include (representations of) customs, traditions, mores and manners, symbol structures, shared beliefs and knowledge, values, perceptions, language, art objects, utilitarian objects and world views. While anthropologists study these phenomena in particular societies, the cultural historian traces and tracks the course of some particular cultural element (for example, the ideal of chivalry or the practice of table manners) through some historical period (Burke 2008). In any case, such cultural elements *are all artifacts*. And significantly, culture being an attribute of some particular community, it is a shared public entity distributed within that community. Hence we talk of many different cultures: scientific, African-American, corporate, Jewish, print, digital, academic and so on. Literary scholar and historian Edward Said (1994) noted that this sense of "culture" is "a source of identity" (p. xiii), a fact that is of importance (as we will see) in the realm of creativity.

Nature

The natural environment may, and usually does, play a vital role in most creative realms. Its presence is usually in the form of experiencing the natural world or observing its manifold forms, and its influence in initiating or executing creative phenomena. The poet's observation of a natural phenomenon evokes the onset of a poem's composition; the painter's contemplation of a momentous vista leads to his composition of a picture. Natural scientists begin their investigations by asking questions about nature, whether the observed variations of species or the detection of a signal from the outer reaches of the cosmos or the radiation emanating from a chunk of some matter. Structural engineers who design bridges may be inspired by the natural environment in which their bridges will be situated, as was the Swiss engineer Robert Maillart (Billington 1979).

Ecological space

Community, culture and nature constitute the individual artificer's environment. They shape, stimulate and goad the artificer in different ways. And, in turn, the artificer may modify culture and, thereby, community—and even, perhaps negatively, nature (as the current climate warming phenomenon exemplifies). Following the notion of "cognitive ecology" explored by Evelyn Tribble and John Sutton (2011), we can argue that collectively, community, culture and nature constitute the *ecological* component of the total cognitive–historical space.

Beliefs and knowledge

Ultimately it is the artificer's *mind* wherein creative work begins and occurs. And every individual, creative or otherwise, possesses a symbolic representation of one or more networks of values, beliefs, facts, doctrines, dogmas, ideologies, rules, laws, percepts, theories—about the natural world, about the artificial world, about other individuals and about one's own self. Let us call this representational structure the person's *belief/knowledge space*. Our cognitive–historical space—the theoretical framework which the cognitive historian will appeal to—will include beliefs/ knowledge as a vital subspace.

A part of the contents of one's belief/knowledge space is shared by that individual with other individuals subscribing to a common culture. As an Indian–American certain elements of my belief/knowledge space are shared with other Indians on the one hand, and with other Americans on the other. As a scientist I share certain beliefs and knowledge with other scientists; as a cognitive historian with other historians; as a soccer fan with other soccer fans; and so on. But a person will also hold certain beliefs, values and percepts that are *private* to her—about others, about herself, about the world at large: her standards of beauty or ethics, or her un/belief in God, for example. Moreover, when an individual *internalizes* elements of her shared culture(s) she may *transform* them so that her interpretation of such cultural elements and their representation in her belief/knowledge space may be entirely idiosyncratic. So, while (apropos Sperber) there is no boundary between cultural representations and individual representations, the act of making an individual representation out of a cultural one may transform or *mutate* the latter—a characteristic phenomenon of cultural transmission which Sperber (1996, p. 58) explicitly recognizes.

If we accept (as I do) Jerome Bruner's (1990) view that cognition is the brain/ mind process by which we make meaning out of our experiences (pp. 43–50), then an individual's belief/knowledge space lies at the very core of cognition. Generally speaking, one's belief/knowledge space is not a fixed thing; it is not a "closed system." It is continuously *revised* in the course of one's life in the light of new experiences, new elements of the ecological subspace. This process begins in infancy and ends with death (or with some serious neurological malfunction perhaps). Sometimes—most times—the changes are tiny, barely perceptible; sometimes they may be emphatic. On occasion a change may be powerful, so profound as to constitute a *gestalt* switch or epiphany.

The idea of the belief/knowledge space as an integrated space of *symbolic representations* has computational implications. A well-trodden subdiscipline of computer science is the design, analysis and understanding of *data structures*. These are formal rules for representing "data objects" (such as an array of numbers or a file of information about a company's employees) in computer memory (Dasgupta 2016a, pp. 10–11). Here is a situation wherein computationalism offers a formal way of thinking about a cognitive concept: the belief/knowledge space as a collection of data structures.

Affects

We will call a person's collection of emotional sensibilities her *affect space*. We do not claim that this is a representational space as is the belief/knowledge space.

Rather, following the lead of cognitive neuroscientist Antonio Damasio (1994), we take affects as abstractions of *bodily* states under control of the neuronal (brain) system (p. 139).

As we noted, many cognitive scientists exclude emotion from the realm of cognition (Newell 1990, p. 16; von Eckardt 1993, p. 6). But, again following Bruner's position, affect is inextricably entwined with cognition, indeed is *part of* cognition since meaning-making is profoundly shaped by one's emotional states (see, e.g., Hogan 2003, Chapter 6; Matlin 2009, pp. 131ff.). For Keith Oatley (1992, p. 3), a cognitive theorist who has explored the relation between art and emotion, emotions are one of the means for organizing knowledge and action in dealing with an imperfectly understood world.

In the realm of creativity emotions are integral to the creative process, not only in the production of artifacts but also in their consumption. Moreover, as Damasio (1994, p. 133) notes, emotions are not only characterized by changes of bodily states; they can be, and are, *consciously felt*. One is not just afraid, one may be consciously aware of being afraid. Thus, Damasio makes a distinction between an emotion and the *feeling* of that emotion (p. 132). This is important in the context of creativity, for an emotion in the form of a conscious feeling in response to some personal experience or encounters, or observing some situation is often the *beginning* of the creative process. Wordsworth's (1916) celebrated dictum that poetry is "emotion recollected in tranquillity" is a particularly vivid and well-known expression of this connection between felt emotion and creativity. The feeling of *interest* is another kind of feeling that serves as a source of creative work as economist and creativity researcher Jonathan Feinstein (2006) has documented extensively.

Needs, drives, desires, goals

In psychoanalysis, the sexual (libidinous) and aggressive drives are at its very center (Gay 1985, p. 89) and are taken to be instinctual or innate (Brenner 1974). But there are, of course, other drives such as hunger, ambition and curiosity. Such drives are elements of a person's repertoire of needs, drives, desires, intentions and goals which collectively constitute what we shall call here his *need/goal space*.

Some needs and desires may be fundamental to a person's very existence. Regardless of whether they are innate in origin or are acquired by way of sociocultural encounters, they are so strong that the person's identity is defined by them, especially in the case of creative people. I will call these *superneeds*, and they may vary in how they shape the creative being. A writer is impelled to write, the inventor to invent, the scholar to make sense of human thought and behavior. Generically superneeds embody the *need to create*. The American short story writer Flannery O'Connor, for instance, felt that she could not be other than a writer: To not write was far worse than to write (Fitzgerald 1979, p. 342; Comeaux 2006, p. 99). Masura Ibeka, co-founder of Sony Corporation and prolific inventor of electronic artifacts, has talked of his passion for inventing originating in curiosity and the desire to satisfy that curiosity (Watson 1991).

Of course, needs are not always of such existential significance. They may *develop* by way of particular training or experience cultivated by individuals. Tendencies to "map" new experiences and problems into one's domain of special knowledge, skill and training and thereby attempt to address them are instances of needs that, though less compulsive than superneeds, may become almost as compelling. Such *learnt* needs become "second nature."

In order for needs and desires to be satisfied they must be transformed into tractable or achievable intentions or *goals*. A poet's need to respond to some experienced emotion—Wordsworth's "emotion recollected in tranquility" but also, poetry as "the spontaneous overflow of powerful feelings" (Wordsworth 1916, pp. 6, 26)—might be transformed into a goal to compose a poem in response. Sometimes the satisfaction of a goal may require the generation of still more tractable *subgoals* as the means of its achievement. And while needs and desires are not taken to be symbolic representations, we assume that goals *are* representations, so that the *goal space*, like the belief/knowledge space is a space of representations of needs and desires. As we will argue later, needs and goals are where creative work begins.

Cognitive operations

Consider Pylyshyn's cognitive terms (Section I above): "recognition," "inference," "deduction," "recollection." These are *operations* whereby things happen in the cognitive domain. *Retrieval* of a piece of knowledge from the belief/knowledge subspace is such an operation. *Drawing an analogy* between a given problem situation and some phenomenon already understood is another. *Generalizing* a conclusion based on particular instances is yet another. *Deducing* a particular conclusion from known or observed phenomena is a fourth. *Interpreting* an experience or an observation is a fifth.

Collectively, they constitute elements of what we will call here the *operational space*. Some of these operations cause transformations in the belief/knowledge space, others may link elements of the affect, need/goal and belief/knowledge spaces; some operations may be entirely confined to the cognitive realm of an individual while the actions of others may depend on elements of the ecological space as sensory inputs or may effect transformations in the ecological space by way of motor outputs.

It is important to note that cognitive operations can be identified at different levels of abstraction. The operational space as a component of the cognitive–historical space, comprising of operations such as deduction, generalization, analogical inference and so on, are at a level of abstraction that are appropriate for making meaning of creative phenomena; such operations will be at a higher abstraction level than the operations one may envision at (say) the brain (or neuronal) level (such as the propagation of electrical signals along an axon or the passage of chemical transmitters across a synaptic junction). We also note that computationalism (or what computer scientist Jeanette Wing (2006, 2008) first called "computational thinking") offers some insights into certain possible kinds of cognitive operations: the most ubiquitous operations in computing are *algorithms* but, as AI has revealed, there are less exact kinds of operations known collectively as *heuristics* (Dasgupta 2016a, pp. 33–61, 104–118).

Bounded rationality

A tacit assumption creativity researchers make about their subjects' behavior accord to what Allen Newell (1990, pp. 150–152) termed the *principal of rationality*. That is:

> If an agent has knowledge or believes that one of her operations will lead to the achievement of one of her goals, then she will select and execute that operation.

Thus *intendedly* rational action begins with goals and the selection of operations that the agent believes will satisfy such goals.

But appearances may be deceptive. Suppose a creativity researcher (cognitive historian) obtains evidence that an artificer has performed some particular operation in response to a goal. According to the principle of rationality the researcher might infer that the artificer has acted rationally; that she does, in fact, possess the requisite knowledge or belief that the operation will lead to the desired goal.

This inference on the cognitive historian's part may, however, be quite unwarranted. For instance, the artificer's belief or knowledge may be incorrect; or it may be incomplete. Even more problematically, there may be the possibility that selecting the correct operation (or a sequence of operations) from one's operational space in response to a goal may be beyond the artificer's cognitive capability.

In other words, the rationality principle may be more the ideal than the actual. Well before he began his long collaboration with Newell in the realm of AI, Herbert Simon recognized this. Based on his studies of how people in organizations actually make administrative decisions, Simon suggested that human decision making occurs under conditions of limited or *bounded* rationality (Simon 1976). This insight—which he later extended into the realm of economic decision making (Simon 1982, 1987), earning him a Nobel Prize in economics, and then into the realm of human problem solving in general (Simon 1996)—can be stated concisely as:

> *The principle of bounded rationality*: Given a goal, a conscious agent may not possess correct or complete beliefs/knowledge of, or be able to economically select, the correct operation(s) that will lead to the satisfaction of that goal.

Ideally then, in the context of creativity, an artificer's behavior is assumed to be governed by the principle of rationality. In practice it is *constrained* according to the principle of bounded rationality. This implies that, in general, any operation (or sequence of operations) an artificer chooses in the pursuit of a goal represents at best a *hypothesis* that the operation(s) will lead successfully to the attainment of the goal.

Cognitive space

While community, culture and nature together constitute the ecological space within the cognitive–historical space, beliefs/knowledge, affects, needs/goals, operations and bounded rationality collective constitute its *cognitive* component. The individual agent participating in a creative phenomenon—whether as artificer or consumer—is considered to be *internally* characterized by a cognitive space. The agent's behavior over time is the outcome of the interaction between his cognitive and ecological spaces.

Historicity

This is manifested by the *presence of the past* in a person's mind: in "remembrance of things past." One's belief/knowledge space will contain not only current beliefs and knowledge but also past beliefs and knowledge; it will contain linkages showing evolutionary pathways between beliefs/knowledge at different points of historical and personal time. One's mental representation of, say, Newton's laws of motion may be linked with Aristotle's theory of motion. Observing an Amrita Sher-Gill painting (we will consider her later in this book) in an art museum, an observer may be reminded of Gaughin's paintings. In other words, historicity may be manifested in one's cognitive space by a diachronic schema that connects beliefs and knowledge pertaining to different moments of historical time—the presence in one's belief/knowledge space of temporally variant "versions" of particular beliefs and knowledge.

Historicity is also reflected in what cognitive psychologists call "episodic memory" or "autobiographical memory"—representations of events, episodes and persons that one experienced or knew in the past. Autobiographers and memoirists retrieve the contents of their episodic memory as do novelists and poets—witness Wordsworth's autobiographical poem "The Prelude."

Of course, one does not have to create in order to be conscious of historicity. Anyone who revisits one's childhood place after a gap of some years will recall events, occasions, people and experiences related to that place as it was in her childhood; or may feel an emotion rooted in remembrances of that place in earlier time.

Historicity is also manifested in the fact that community, culture and nature—an individual's ecological space—all *evolve* over time, across different time scales. The physical/natural world has evolved over *cosmological* and *geological* time, and even over (recorded) *historical* time. Material and abstract artifacts also have evolved over prehistorical and (recorded) historical times but, more spectacularly, over what we may call *cultural* time—that is, over the period in which individual cultures are born, live and die. Individual lives evolve over *biographical* or *life–historical* time. These various evolutionary changes contribute to our sense of historicity and there will be representations of such evolutionary pathways.

Moreover, as we have noted, creative phenomena *make* history and thus become part of history: they alter the structure of history itself. In the words of art historian George Kubler (1962) they shape historical time. And community, culture and belief/knowledge spaces are enriched in one way or another over time by creative phenomena.

Historicity is, thus, a shared feature that straddles both the ecological and cognitive spaces and renders a cognitive–*historical* space.

2

ARTIFACTS

The very "stuff" of creativity

I Creativity as a pluralistic concept

What do we mean by the word *creativity*? Despite its ubiquity in ordinary discourse the concept is remarkably elusive to pin down. One psychologist, Calvin Taylor (1988), after reviewing the literature, came to the conclusion that the many different interpretations fell broadly into one or another of a number of perspective classes.

One was the *gestalt* view, according to which creativity refers to a *process* involving the recombination of ideas or on the restructuring of holistic ("gestalt") patterns of entities. Another view associated creativity with *novelty* or *originality* of the *product* of some process. Yet a third laid emphasis on *self-expression*: whenever one expresses oneself in a unique or individualistic way one is being creative. A fourth orientation claims that creativity demands a particular kind of *cognition* or pattern of thinking. Finally, there is the *psychoanalytic* view wherein creativity is explicable in terms of the interaction of the id, ego and superego.

Only the most dogmatic would take exception to any one of these perceptions. We can easily find examples of situations that seem to cohere with one or the other of these interpretations. For instance, self-expression seems the most apposite when we observe small children playing with wooden blocks or in the context of someone who paints or makes things as a hobby. On the other hand, a technological invention or a scientific discovery, according to our common intuition at least, would allow us to describe the inventor or scientist as creative because of the originality of what he or she has produced.

But again, only the most dogmatic would insist that just one of these perceptions is "correct" and no other. Rather, we might recognize that these perceptions are not mutually exclusive. A scientist may be deemed creative not only because he or she has discovered something new but also because this discovery has effected a radical restructuring of an entire branch of science, a "gestalt switch." Or we may recognize situations in which two or more of these views are *complementary* to one another. A psychoanalytical interpretation of an artist's work may offer an insight into her creativity; exploring her self-expressiveness another. The two complement each other.

In contrast to these views, there are those who attribute creativity to some "divine dispensation." Writing in the fourth century BCE Plato was a particularly prominent begetter of this view. In *Ion*, speaking through the mouth of his dead teacher Socrates, Plato described creativity as a "divine power." When the poet composes, he said, the verses that emanate are not of his own making; he is possessed by a "heaven sent madness." The poet is only the agent through whom the gods speak (Rouse 1984).

Twenty-two hundred years later, the eighteenth century poet, painter and engraver, William Blake, recorded how his poem on Milton came without prior thought and almost against his will (Harding 1942, p. 14). On the other side of the world two centuries later, the Nobel Prize winning poet, philosopher and composer, Rabindranath Tagore, would refer to his *jiban debatã* (life spirit), a universal divine force as the fount of his creative being. It was this deity that presided over the poet's life, his inner self (Tagore 1972).

If we take the "divine origin" position then, of course, there is no more to be said about creativity. We simply shake our heads, clap our hands in wonder and marvel at it. Mercifully, the serious student of creativity summarily dismisses this position if only because, as the Nobel laureate biologist Peter Medawar (1990) wryly observed, that whatever be the nature of creativity, it is an error-prone process that goes against the idea of a divine origin. He pointed out that scientists frequently propose wrong hypotheses; one would surely expect the gods to be reasonably infallible rather than boundedly rational (Chapter 1, IV). The creativity researcher, thus, seeks secular explanations of creativity. And, as Calvin Taylor's rough classification suggests, it is likely that any "theory of creativity" is likely to be not only secular but also pluralistic in nature. But where should we begin?

II   Artifacts

We can start with the indubitable fact that *artifacts* constitute the very "stuff" of creativity. *No artifact, no creativity*. To understand creativity we must begin by understanding the nature of artifacts.

In everyday parlance we often associate the word "artifact" with what we see in museums. Arrowheads, pots, bowls and containers of all shapes and sizes, coins, glassware, spears, swords and armor, jewelry made of bone or beaten metal, fragments of buildings and monuments—they assault our eyes and minds in archeological and anthropological museums. In an art museum we encounter paintings, drawings, etchings, frescoes, murals and sculptures in marble and bronze. In a museum of technology we witness artifacts of a more opaque kind: orreries and astrolabes, clocks, telescopes, code breaking machines, steam engines, calculating devices and computers, aircraft, rockets and space ships.

Of course artifacts do not only belong to museums. They are all around us, we live among them, we are engulfed in them. The feminist scholar Donna Haraway (1991, p. 291) writes of the "cyborg"—a "cybernetic organism" that is a hybrid of machine and organism—which is what many humans are, with our prosthetics and implanted devices and our ubiquitous smart phones and other mobile devices without which so many of us are utterly incapacitated.

But what *is* an artifact? Our natural tendency to call all those denizens of museums artifacts stems from the assumption or knowledge that they are all *made* things. Likewise, our assumption about our prosthetics and personal digital devices. We also unthinkingly assume that all those "museum pieces" are not accidentally produced; that whoever created them did so *intentionally*. Suppose then we begin with the following "working" definition:

> An artifact is anything that is consciously conceived or produced by a conscious being (artificer) in response to some want, need, desire or goal.

The artificer is overwhelmingly a human being but some non-human living beings (e.g., chimpanzees) have shown clear evidence of a capacity to make simple artifacts.

III Artifacts *versus* natural things

Is this "definition" sufficient to distinguish artifacts from natural things? In fact, the distinction between the natural and the artificial have exercised thinkers since antiquity.

In *Physics*, Aristotle distinguished between the natural and the artifactual by observing that natural things have within them their own source of motion and energy whereas artifacts—"products of art"—have no such intrinsic attribute (Bambrough, n.d.). Yet he admits that artificial things may manifest impulses "accidentally" if, for instance, they are made of natural things (e.g., stone or earth) and the latter are the cause of the things' "natural impulses." And he goes on to say that in the realm of art, matter *is made to* serve a purpose, whereas in the realm of nature matter is its inherent constituent (p. 214).

Aristotle was deploying the word "art" (*ars*) in its original sense to mean *technē*, the practice of making or craftsmanship. And his insight, that in the realm of artifacts, matter serves a purpose, whereas in nature, matter just *is*, appears in our "working" definition above (Section II).

Historian Heinrich von Staden (2007), discussing the writings on Greek medicine known as the Hippocratic Corpus, tells us that the physicians of the fifth and fourth centuries BCE had to distinguish between *physis*—the intrinsic "nature" of the bodily constituents, diseases and drugs that they needed to know—and *technē*—the practice of their art of healing. *Physis* ("nature") and *technē* (art) thus were the ancient Greeks' terms for distinguishing between the natural and the artifactual.

Yet, in our own times, many thinkers have come to the conclusion that there really is no sharp divide between the natural and the artifactual. Philosopher Bernadette Bensaude-Vincent and historian of science William Newman (2007) give as examples the fact that many manufacturing processes begin with materials extracted from nature, so that in some sense, the resulting artifacts are not quite entirely artificial (p. 2). Conversely, they note, that by way of agriculture and industry even the "natural wild" is, in our technological times, scarcely purely natural.

The puzzle of the natural/artifactual distinction may be illustrated by a specific example taken from metallurgy:

> A blast furnace is a gigantic chimney-like machine in which iron ore, limestone and coke (fuel) are introduced at the top and a blast of air injected near the bottom. The limestone serves as a "flux" that reduces the melting temperature of the ore. As the input charge moves down the furnace the ore is chemically "reduced" to relatively pure iron (called "pig iron") by removing the impurities in the ore. The outputs of the blast furnace, extracted separately near its bottom, are molten pig iron and the impurities ("slag").

So here we see a complicated confluence of the natural and the artificial. The iron ore (containing iron oxide along with other matter) was extracted from the ground and we would unhesitatingly think of it as a natural thing. The same applies to limestone. On the other hand, the fuel, coke, is not raw coal but coal that has been processed and refined into a purer form of carbon. So coke is an artifact. The main product of the blast furnace is a relatively pure iron (called "pig iron" because the molten iron flowing out through a channel near the bottom of the blast furnace is poured into molds called "pigs"). This being the product of the blast furnace (itself an artifact) is *not natural*. It is the product of human intention, thus must be considered an artifact. Yet, as philosopher Richard Grandy (2007) pointed out, iron is a chemical element and would seem a "prototypical natural kind" (p. 19). Moreover, the metallurgical *process* whereby pig iron is produced is a physico-chemical—thus *natural*—process: metallurgists have discovered the complex set of chemical reactions that go on as the input charge descends the furnace; they have ascertained the thermodynamics attending the chemical changes. So while metallurgists through the course of centuries *invented* not only the blast furnace but also the iron-making process, other metallurgists, of much more recent times, *discovered* the chemical processes underlying these inventions. For the latter, iron-making could be assumed *as if it is a natural process*, whose characteristics could be discovered in laboratory settings. Such metallurgists were not in the business of *making* artifacts but rather in the business of *understanding*. Likewise, metallurgists in the laboratory can study the chemical and physical characteristics of pig iron—its precise chemical composition, its strength, hardness, malleability, brittleness, etc.—as if it is a natural thing. In these activities, the metallurgist may adopt the persona of the *natural scientist* who can study these properties of pig iron without invoking purpose.

Suppose someone comes upon a lump of some matter lying in a field in the countryside and sends it to a laboratory. Chemists and physicists investigate its properties; they can do so by treating the matter *as is*. Suppose the chemists determine that the lump of matter is almost pure iron with a small amount of carbon and still smaller amounts of other elements. What might they conclude? If they have knowledge that iron of such purity is not found in nature they might infer it is an artifact, the product of a blast furnace or some other iron-making furnace. On the other hand they may also tentatively infer that this is an instance of natural iron of such and such composition and characteristics and add it to the corpus of knowledge concerning the chemical element iron.

So whether or not a lump of iron is a natural thing or an artifact becomes a *cognitive* matter: a matter of prior knowledge and of decision making on the part of the investigating scientists. *Given* a lump of iron, one can study its properties *as if* it is a natural thing. In that case the lump is ontologically (if not chemically) indistinguishable from an iron-based mineral such as hematite or limonite: *it just is*; they *just are*. On the other hand, if the lump of iron was known to have been produced in a blast furnace, one can obviously study it as an artifact; it is not something that just is, but a product of human *purpose*. And the questions asked about it must address both what the purpose is, and whether the iron will serve this purpose—questions that would not be asked if the lump of matter is viewed as if it is a natural thing.

There should be no ambivalence, however, in the case of the blast furnace itself. No one should doubt that this is an artifact. And yet, there seems no absolute criterion by which such a firm conclusion can be reached. Our certainty that this is an artifact rather than a natural thing must rest on our acquired and experiential knowledge about the kind of thing that is unequivocally artifactual and about the kind of thing that is unequivocally natural. For instance, a layperson, observing a blast furnace for the first time, may infer that this object is an artifact perhaps because she has stored in her belief/knowledge space a *schema* (a prototypical representation) for a certain kind of chemical processing artifact (based on prior observation or being told so), and the blast furnace "matches" this schema. (Schemas play an important role in the realm of creativity as we will see in a later chapter.) Or perhaps there is nothing in the observer's belief/knowledge space of schemas of natural things that comes anywhere close to a match with the blast furnace, in which case the observer hypothesizes that this is an artifact.

IV "True" and "false" artifacts

Despite such ambivalences, most people who professionally think about these matters (engineers, designers, computer scientists, psychologists, clinicians, artists, craftspersons, creativity researchers, etc.) harbor little doubt that there is a distinction between artifacts and natural things; between artifactual kinds and natural kinds. And purpose is the all-important criterion dividing the artificial from the natural. Aristotle recognized this. But purpose does not simply mean a *causal* relationship between human agency and the artifact. Notice the clause "consciously conceived or produced" in the "working" definition in Section II above.

For example, the majority of climatologists agree that global climate warming is a consequence of human action: the emission of carbon dioxide and other chemicals into the atmosphere by human-made industrial processes and machines. Recently there have been arguments put forth that the process called "fracking" to extract oil has caused earthquakes in some places. One might argue then that such climatic trends and geological phenomena (including rising sea levels, receding wetlands, tsunamis, etc.) are artifacts because they are the results of human agency.

But such phenomena are not the intended consequences of goals and needs but rather *unintended* consequences of human intentions. Likewise, consider a faulty computer program. It contains a bug. If the programmer did not intentionally insert the bug into the program it is not an intended consequence of the program design process, in contrast to a computer virus deliberately inserted into a piece of software.

So climate warming, receding wetlands, raised sea levels and bug-infested programs, though consequences of human thought and action, and thus artifactual in nature, should not count as *true* artifacts since they are not produced in response to needs and goals. Rather they might be termed *false* artifacts. A similar qualification was made by philosopher Amie Thomasson (2007, p. 57) who notes that an artifact's function must be an intended function.

Even with this caveat is the above working definition sufficient for our purposes? Thomasson raised the issue of reproduction (p. 52). A couple *decides* to have a child; a baby is *consciously* conceived. Does that make the baby a true artifact? And what if a child is conceived unintentionally? Would that baby be a false artifact?

Intuitively we must reject both these conclusions. So our working definition must be revised:

> A *true* artifact is something that (a) is consciously conceived or produced by a conscious being (artificer) in response to some want, need, desire or goal; and (b) its structure, function and behavior can be understood if and only if one takes into account the artificer's needs or goals.

Thus, the structure, behavior or function of a natural entity, even when produced consciously by human agency, can be comprehended in terms of its natural features; one does not need to take into account the artificer's needs or goals for such comprehension. The phenomenon of global warming, though an unintended consequence of human agency, can itself be explained in terms of other natural processes (carbon dioxide emission, etc.). The behavior of babies (or their anatomy or physiology) is not a function of its parents' desire or need to have a child.

In other words, the artificer's needs or goals are an integral part of an artifact. Amie Thomasson arrived at a similar conclusion (p. 53). The implication of this view is clear though surprising: since needs and goals are cognitive features, *artifacts are endowed with cognitive attributes*. To make sense of a digital device, one must begin with asking what its maker's intention was in making this device. Constitutional lawyers and justices of the American Supreme Court, in interpreting the U.S. Constitution (as much an artifact as is a digital device), desire to understand what the intentions (goals) of the Founding Fathers were in framing the constitution.

There remains a further problem. Suppose a person consciously conceives the design of a machine or composes a poem but *it remains inside her head*. For example, Samuel Taylor Coleridge claimed that he *dreamt* "up" the poem he would call "Kubla Khan" during a deep, opium-induced sleep. As he narrated it, in the summer of 1797, while living in a lonely farmhouse in South West England, Coleridge woke from a sleep during which he claimed to have composed some two or three hundred lines of the poem. On waking, he began to write it, believing that he could recollect the poem in its entirety; but after some fifty-four lines he was interrupted by a visitor and when the latter left he found to his chagrin that he could no longer recollect the rest of the poem. And so "Kubla Khan" (published in 1816)—a poem, an artifact—as it presently exists is just these fifty-four lines. (Coleridge's account is quoted in full by literary scholar John Livingstone Lowes in *The Road to Xanadu* (1930, p. 356), his brilliant study of Coleridge's "ways of the imagination.")

But could we claim that the part Coleridge dreamt but never recorded on paper was also part of the artifact known as "Kubla Khan?" Intuitively this seems problematic. This dilemma is resolved if we insist that for something to count as a true artifact *it must exist in the public domain.* So a further revision of our working definition leads to what will be our "final" version:

> A true artifact is something (a) that is consciously conceived or produced by a conscious being (artificer) in response to some want, need, desire or goal; (b) that is in the public domain; and (c) whose structure, function and behavior can be understood if and only if one takes into account the artificer's need, want or goal.

V Classifying artifacts

Whenever a particular population of entities manifests diversity the need to *classify* arises. The most venerable instance is in biology—the universe of living things—in which the development of classification schemes (taxonomies) reach back to Greek antiquity (if not earlier) and taken to a highly developed state by the eighteenth century Swedish naturalist Carl Linnaeus. Another mature classification scheme from the natural world is the periodic table of chemical elements co-pioneered in the nineteenth century by the German Lothar Meyer and the Russian Dimitri Mendeleev.

But the instinct to classify is also much evident in the artifactual world—perhaps most familiarly for the purpose of classifying books as used by libraries. My intention here is to identify distinct classes of artifacts. This, we will see, will have a bearing in our attempt to make sense of creativity.

VI Material artifacts: utilitarian and affective

We generally tend to think of artifacts as *material* entities. Our examples of iron and the blast furnace are material artifacts. The historian George Basalla (1988) concluded, after examining the patent literature of the United States, that the diversity of technological material artifacts was of the same order of magnitude as that of biological species. Leaving aside Basalla's actual estimate, the point to take in is the astonishing range of material artifacts since the birth of stone tools some 2.5 million years ago in East Africa (Schick and Toth 1993).

Basalla was thinking of *utilitarian* artifacts—things made by humans to satisfy *practical* needs, wants or desires. Collectively, utilitarian artifacts fall under the rubric of technology.

But not all material artifacts are utilitarian. There are things whose creation is driven by aesthetic, emotional or spiritual needs. Let us call these collectively *affective artifacts*. Art objects such as paintings, sculptures, jewelry and religious icons are obvious examples. Though apparently not as ancient as technology the need to make art objects—a defining cultural characteristic of "modern" *Homo sapiens*—still has an impressive antiquity. The archeologist Steven Mithen (1996) has referred to a mammoth tusk ivory statuette of a man with a lion's head, pieces of which were discovered in Southern Germany, believed to be made some 33,000–30,000 years ago.

Perhaps the most spectacular manifestations of prehistoric art objects are the cave paintings and engravings found mostly in Southern France and Northern Spain. The discovery of the Chauvet Caves in December 1994 and analysis of the art in these caves using radiocarbon dating indicates that some of the Chauvet paintings are as old as 30,000 years BP ("before the present") (Chauvet, Deschamps and Hillaire 1996). More recently (in October 2014) paintings have been discovered in caves in the Indonesian island of Sulawesi, believed to be at least 40,000 years old.

Indeed, the origin of art and affective artifacts appears to be continually receding into farther reaches of prehistory: at the time of this writing (September 2018), archeologists have discovered in a site near Cape Town, a small stone flake on which were drawn six, almost parallel, lines in red ochre (a natural pigment), crossed by three diagonal lines. The flake was found in a cave site dated from between 70,000 and 100,000 years ago and so, if the archeologists' interpretation holds true, it is the oldest affective artifact found so far (St. Fleur, 2018).

Technology (broadly conceived) and art (broadly conceived) are thus the twin pillars of the realm of material artifacts—one utilitarian, the other affective. When art historian George Kubler meditated on "the history of things" in his book *The Shape of Time* (1962) he was referring to material artifacts both utilitarian and affective. However, he made a clear distinction between the two. Aesthetic artifacts are intrinsically useless while utilitarian artifacts (tools, in his language) are intrinsically useful (p. 16). This, as we see below, is not always the case.

Material artifacts by their very nature must obey physico-chemical laws—the laws of nature. They might consume energy and, in turn, produce energy, they may decay physically and chemically over time, they occupy physical space and, in some cases, their activities consume physical (measurable) time. They can be seen, touched and sometimes smelt. Thus the artificer of material artifacts—potter, painter, engineer, sculptor, etc.—will need to take account of the laws of nature in both framing goals and creating artifacts in response to goals. More precisely, such artificers may both exploit and be constrained by the laws of physics and chemistry. For instance, the architect's design of an auditorium intended for musical performances—an exemplar of a material artifact which, contra Kubler, is both utilitarian and affective—will appeal to the laws of mechanics in designing the structure but must also be respectful to and constrained by the laws of acoustics.

It is because of the material artifact's relationship with the laws of nature that the ambivalence of their identity as natural or artifactual enters the debate.

VII   Abstract artifacts: utilitarian and affective

Material artifacts, represented by technology and the visual arts, are tangible and even palpable. But there is also a vast universe of intangible, non-material artifacts. Procedures, plans, methods, designs, mathematical concepts and theorems, artistic styles, musical genres, literary styles, rules, laws, algorithms and, above all, ideas (including the idea of creativity!) are all instances of *abstract artifacts* (Dasgupta 1996, pp. 11–12).

Like material artifacts they are products of human minds, invention and creativity, originating in conscious needs, goals and desires. But they are abstract in that *they are not governed by physico-chemical laws*. Mathematical theorems, philosophical ideas, military strategies, painterly styles and musical compositions are all artifactual but they are *intrinsically* immune to the ravages of nature. The laws of thermodynamics or of genetics do not apply to Pythagoras's theorem, or to the First Amendment of the U.S. Constitution, or to the literary style called magical realism. For that matter, such laws *themselves* are not susceptible to the laws of nature. A particular physical *embodiment* of an abstract artifact is a slave to the laws of nature but not the abstract artifact itself. The characteristic architecture of Gothic cathedrals—a design, thus an abstract artifact—will not be physically altered by nature even though any one of its physical embodiments, the Notre Dame in Paris for example, or Canterbury Cathedral, is constantly subject to the ravages of nature's laws. *They* have to be repaired to counter the effects of nature's laws but not their architectural design. Thus the confluence of the natural and the artifactual characteristic of material artifacts is not an issue in the realm of abstract artifacts; the latter are unequivocally *un*-natural.

Yet abstract artifacts, like their material counterparts, are *objectively real*. Once created and made public they are no longer in the subjective world of their artificers' minds. An artistic style, a literary genre, a mathematical theorem, an engineering design can be passed from one mind to another, they can be analyzed, criticized, deconstructed, replicated and mutated by anyone else. Philosopher of science Karl Popper (1972) described these abstract yet objective and public products of human thought as "World 3" objects in contrast to the physical "World 1" and mental "World 2" entities.

Abstract artifacts thus bear a certain resemblance in this regard to (material) genes, which is why biologist Richard Dawkins (1976) coined the word *meme* to mean a unit of *cultural* transmission. Dawkins's examples of memes included such things as ideas, fashions, methods of making things (p. 206)—all, in fact, abstract artifacts. Later in this book we will consider the implication of this analogy between abstract artifacts (memes) and (material) genes for analyzing creativity.

Like material artifacts, abstract artifacts can be utilitarian or affective: economic plans, military strategies, a nation's laws and a political doctrine are almost unequivocally utilitarian, whereas a symphonic composition, a sonnet and a painterly style are as unequivocally affective. (There are, however, artifacts that are both utilitarian and affective which are discussed later in this chapter.)

VIII   Durable and transient artifacts

Most compellingly, because of their non-materiality, as long as there are people interested in them and are willing to worry about them, abstract artifacts are potentially *indestructible*. Material artifacts, being governed by nature's laws, are potentially destructible. The Britannia Bridge, built in Wales in the 1840s by Scottish engineer Robert Stephenson, was damaged by fire in 1970 and thus no longer exists. Engineers and engineering students can, however, still study its underlying—and very distinctive—*idea* (a tubular, wrought-iron structure) and its *design* from their various descriptions in the historical literature (Rosenberg and Vincent 1978). Of course, it is quite possible for an abstract artifact, such as a philosophical doctrine, to be lost through the vicissitudes of history, just as it is possible for a material artifact, such as the monoliths of Stonehenge, to have been preserved. So we can say, at the very least, that the life of an artifact, material or abstract has at the very least a certain *durability*. (There is, however, a notable class of exceptions to this, discussed below.)

Since for something to be an artifact it must be in the public domain, even abstract artifacts need a *material expression*. Engineering drawings represent designs, magical realism is expressed through written texts, Cubism by actual canvases and so on. But the *fundamental* characteristics of an abstract artifact are independent of their material representations; Gabriel Garcia Marquez and Salman Rushdie expressed magical realism through their various novels but the idea of magical realism has its own permanent, independent existence. The reader might link abstract artifacts to Platonic forms. The crucial difference is that abstract artifacts are human inventions, products of human thought.

As we have noted, material artifacts—a lathe for example, a building, a kitchen knife, a vase, a painting or a scientific instrument—though potentially destructible, have a certain durability. Once produced, they have a life span. And as potentially indestructible artifacts, abstract artifacts such as theorems and their proofs, algorithms, poems, stories and musical compositions are more or less guaranteed indestructible durability. Once invented they have an indefinite life span.

But there is a class of abstract affective artifacts that by their very nature are *transient*. Consider a concert pianist's performance of Beethoven's "Moonlight Sonata"; or an actor's interpretation of the character of Lear; or a soprano's rendition of the aria "Voi Che Sapete" from Mozart's *The Marriage of Figaro*. These events become lost the moment they are over. And yet in their occurrences, who would deny their artifactual nature, as human creations, and that their performers are artificers? The life spans of transient artifacts are only as long as their fleeting occurrences.

IX Intellectual artifacts

There is also a particular subclass of abstract artifacts that are neither intrinsically utilitarian nor affective. I will call them *intellectual* artifacts in the sense that their appeal is *primarily* to logic and reason; their prime function is to stimulate the intellect rather than emotions. *Ideas* are the most obvious examples of intellectual artifacts: political ("liberty," "democracy," "revolution"), scientific ("atom," "entropy," "evolution," "computation"), psychological ("mind," "subconscious," "ego"), mathematical ("proof," "infinity," "prime number"), literary ("deconstruction," "metaphor," "meter"), technological ("machine," "engine," "architecture"), philosophical ("truth," "moral law," "knowledge," "justice") and so on.

I should point out that not all creativity researchers think of ideas as artifacts: Margaret Boden (2010a), for example, talks of "ideas and artifacts" as outputs of the creative process, thus implying a distinction between them.

But intellectual artifacts may be more "down to earth" though still abstract: Heisenberg's uncertainty principle refers to quantum phenomena, Turing's thesis refers to the realm of computing, the bending moment refers to engineering structures: they are a few examples of such kinds of intellectual artifacts.

X Hybrid artifacts

Sometimes these distinctions between different kinds of artifacts (material/abstract, utilitarian/affective/intellectual) are not that sharp. There are artifacts that are both material *and* abstract, or utilitarian *and* affective, or utilitarian *and* intellectual. Computer programs (software) are an especially intriguing example. A program is, after all, a very precisely defined procedure expressed in a particular artificial language to perform some computation. In this respect it is entirely abstract, for it is made of *symbols*. Yet, though symbol structures, they *cause physical events to occur*: electrical signals are transmitted, the physical states of circuits are changed, physical devices are set in motion and so on. In my book *It Began with Babbage* (Dasgupta 2014a) I introduced the term *liminal* to characterize this dual aspect of certain artifacts. ("Liminality" refers to a state of ambiguity, of between and betwixt, a twilight state.)

Liminality is just one kind of *hybridity*. Another important kind is when an artifact is both utilitarian and affective. The most obvious examples are found in the realm of architecture: in his book *Art and Technics* (1952), historian and cultural critic Lewis Mumford (1952) speaks of this domain as exemplifying a rare conjoining of beauty and practical function (p. 111). Medieval cathedrals such as Notre Dame in Paris and Canterbury Cathedral in England appeal to people for their aesthetics, as works of art. Yet they are also places of worship; they must satisfy the practical needs of congregational worship and other religious rituals such as weddings, baptisms and funerals. In this sense they are utilitarian. They also embody important engineering *ideas* and in this sense constitute intellectual artifacts. The campus of Simon Fraser University lodged atop Burnaby Mountain in Vancouver, Canada, can take away a visitor's breath because of its beauty, both in design and situation. But it is a university, a locus of the practical task of higher education and research. This university campus is both an affective and a utilitarian artifact and its designer, Canadian architect Arthur Erikson, had to balance and fuse both these aspects in creating this design.

The artifacts of civil engineering are often of this hybrid nature. Engineering scientist and professor David Billington (1979) described the work of Swiss bridge engineer Robert Maillart in which art, science and engineering were fused into one. Maillart's bridges were hybrid artifacts that were composites of utility, affect and ideas. In more recent times the Millennium Bridge in London, as a footbridge, is (like all bridges) utilitarian. But this suspension bridge designed by the British engineering firm Arup has a strong aesthetic appeal. Such hybridity in civil engineering structures, this resolution of the tension between (or fusion of) utility and beauty, was described by Italian structural engineer and architect Pier Luigi Nervi (1966) in his Charles Eliot Lectures on *poetry* at Harvard University and published as a book titled, significantly, *Aesthetics and Technology in Building*. These are prime examples that refute George Kubler's dichotomy between useful and aesthetic artifacts.

As yet another example, from the realm of computing, computer scientists Donald Knuth and Edsgar Dijkstra have both explored and discussed the place of beauty in the construction of computer programs and algorithms. Knuth (1992a, 1992b) in particular has insisted that programs (liminal artifacts) must be works of art and manifest literary quality (that is, should be as pleasurable to read as literary writings are) as well as satisfy severely utilitarian functions as efficiency. Dijkstra (1980) titled one of his papers "Some Beautiful Arguments using Mathematical Induction."

One of the most striking instances of the hybridity of the intellectual and the affective was discussed by the English mathematician G.H. Hardy in his book *A Mathematician's Apology* (1969), a kind of elegy on his life as a mathematician. Mathematical theorems (and their proofs) are abstract artifacts that are about as intellectual as one can imagine. But, Hardy insisted, a mathematician makes patterns, as do artists and poets, except that the mathematician's patterns are made out of ideas (p. 84). But like the artist's patterns, the mathematician's must exhibit beauty. There is no place, in mathematics, Hardy declared famously, for ugliness (p. 85). In more recent times science writer David Stipp (2017) devotes an entire book to exploring and elucidating the beauty of a single equation due to the eighteenth century mathematician Leonhard Euler and, in particular, what aesthetics mean in the context of mathematical ideas.

In her collection of essays *Creativity and Art*, cognitive scientist and philosopher Margaret Boden (2010b) distinguishes between artwork and craftwork: the primary purpose of craft, she believes, unlike that of art, is to satisfy some practical need, though it may also be aesthetically satisfying (p. 52). At first blush this characterization of "craftwork" seems reasonable. We have no problem in applying it to something like fine china tea and dinner sets. But what of the Millennium Bridge or Notre Dame Cathedral? By Boden's definition they must also count as "craftwork!"

XI Affordance

As we have noted, artifacts are created for a purpose. This demarcates the artifactual from the natural (organic or inorganic), for *natural things have no purpose*. They just *are*. In describing and explaining natural objects such as plants and animals, rocks and minerals, oceans and mountains, planets, stars and black holes, atoms, molecules and subatomic particles, the natural scientist may, in certain circumstances, ascribe *function* to them. For instance one might say that the function of the nuclear force is to bind the constituents of a subatomic nucleus together, or that the function of the heart is to pump blood through the body. But to assign function is not to ascribe purpose, for purpose originates in the artificer's mind as the precondition of creation.

However, purpose can transform a natural object into an artifact at a moment's notice. A large rock becomes a place to sit on, a stone becomes a missile, a thick branch lying on the ground becomes a cane or walking stick for a hiker, a twig becomes a tool for chimpanzees to extract termites from a mound or hole.

In the context of biological systems such opportunities offered by an organism's *environment* to shape the organism's behavior along certain directions was first identified by psychologist James Gibson (1966). He called this characteristic of the environment *affordance*. Since then the term has been assimilated into the psychologist's vocabulary (Boden 2006, pp. 466–469).

Affordances may also be offered by artifacts as cognitive scientist Donald Norman (1989) has pointed out. An artifact's affordance refers to the possible ways it can be used not only to meet an intended purpose but also to serve other, possibly unexpected purposes.

Picasso's famous sculpture of a bull's head was made out of a bicycle seat (for the head) and handlebars (for the horns). Such artifacts intended for one set of purposes afforded an altogether different pair of purposes. However *all artifactual affordances are created in the artificer's mind*. The ability to perceive affordances in objects—natural or artifactual—and thereby produce artifacts is a marker of the artificer's creativity.

XII   The creative tradition: making the artifactual world

As we noted early in this discussion, creativity has to do with the making of artifacts. This is what binds the artist, the scientist, the engineer, the novelist, the poet, the composer, the philosopher, the critic, the historian, the planner, the musician, the actor and the craftsperson. They are all in the business of making artifacts. They are all artificers. And what binds them together is that they are all participants in a tradition that reaches back to the very beginnings of humanity, to *Homo habilis* some 2.5 million years ago when technology was born. I am referring to the *creative tradition* by which I mean the propensity to bring into the world ideas, symbols, things and thoughts that have altered people's ways of thinking, doing, living and perceiving the world (see Prologue, I).

This creative tradition is the common ground. Or rather *a* common ground because there are others, as we will see.

But there is more to this idea of the creative tradition. The "world" to which it contributes is itself a creation of the creative tradition: what we may justifiably call the *artifactual world*. With the invention of the first stone tools—the very dawn of the creative tradition—the natural world began to be populated, albeit ever so slowly, by artifacts. The beginning of the creative tradition marked the beginning of the *colonization* of the natural world by artifacts; the colonization of the natural world by culture (Chapter 1, IV).

And over the course of history this artifactual world has never looked back. On the contrary. The process by which this world grew was painfully slow to begin with; stone tools dominating its landscape for most of the 2.5 million years since the emergence of the genus *Homo*. But then with the appearance of modern *Homo sapiens* it "took off" so to speak. Archeologists have discovered non-utilitarian artifacts dating to the beginning of the Upper Paleolithic age, dated to some 40,000 years ago: beads and pendants—body ornaments (White 1992, 2003). As I have previously mentioned, the discovery of a mammoth ivory statuette dated to about 33,000–30,000 years BP (Mithen 1996) and the cave art now considered almost as old. Very recently, as also noted (VI above), an affective artifact believed to be some 70,000 years old has been excavated. For some scholars this proliferation of artistic activity defined the transition from the Middle to the Upper Paleolithic age. One writer called this the "creative explosion" (Pfeiffer 1982). Archeologist Steven Mithen (1996) evocatively called the origin of art at that time the "big bang of human culture."

All those who create are adding something to the artifactual world. Creativity engages with it. Even the natural scientists whose domain is the natural world, even their laws, theories, explanations and models, though pertaining to the natural world, are artifacts. They belong to the artifactual world, as do the products created by the musician, the engineer, the philosopher, the writer and the artist.

But the fact that making artifacts is a common ground between these diverse kinds of artificers does not mean they are all alike as creative beings. There are differences that lie in the nature of their respective artifacts to begin with: not just because a bridge or a computer is a material artifact while a poem or a mathematical theorem is an abstract one, but also because of differences *within* the class of material artifacts (between computers and bridges, say) or *within* the class of abstract artifacts (between poems and theorems, say). And, of course, because of differences between the purposes of the artifacts created by the scientist and novelist, engineers and composers, poets and craftspersons.

XIII   Elites of the artifactual world

Not all artifacts excite us. Many are dreary, many ugly, many that seem pointless: walk into a "gift shop" and witness some of its wares. Others are positively repulsive as, for example, the idea of racial or sexual superiority. But then there are those that, one way or another, capture our attention, captivate us, ensnare our imagination or touch our nerves. They alter our ways of thinking, our very perception, the way we live, even reshape our identity. They surprise us, penetrate our consciousness and perhaps lodge in our unconscious. They are the special ones. They are the "elites" of the artifactual world that we usually associate with creativity. But what is it that makes them the elites of the artifactual world? Who decides?

3

ARTIFICERS AND CONSUMERS

I The historicist theory

Despite the many interpretations of the idea of creativity (Chapter 2, I) we have seen that it has at least one invariant: the artifact. Without an artifact there is no creativity.

But artifacts themselves are not creative. Creativity is a characteristic of the *artificer*—one who brings into existence artifacts of a certain kind or quality. The artificer is a second invariant of the idea of creativity. And, as proposed in the Prologue, the artificer is deemed creative when in making an artifact she makes history. Let us call this the *historicist* theory of creativity.

This scenario associates creativity with *individual* artifacts. For instance we may believe that a writer is creative on the merits of a particular novel she has written because that novel has made history (in some sense)—a case in point is Margaret Mitchell and *Gone With the Wind*. But if she writes nothing else or she is prolific in her output yet these other works are not deemed to have made history, we would not be able to say that the author was creative in these other acts of production. In other words, an act of production is not necessarily an act of creation.

II Varieties of history-making

But what does "making history" entail in the context of creativity? Cognitive scientist Margaret Boden (1991) identified two kinds of history-making. One is when an artificer produces an artifact that is *original with reference to the artificer's personal history*. In Boden's terminology such an artifact would be deemed *P-original* ("P" for personal or psychological) and the artificer *P-creative*. Others may well have created the same artifact before our protagonist but this does not dilute or diminish her personal *cognitive* achievement. Each time a high-school student solves a back-of-the chapter mathematical problem, each time a chemistry graduate student successfully completes an intricate and delicate laboratory experiment, each time a programmer correctly implements a complex algorithm he has never programmed before, each time an actor first performs the role of Hamlet, each time an engineer executes a project he has no prior experience of, he or she is a P-creative artificer.

Boden's second sort of history-making is when the artifact is original with respect to *all of past history*—that is, with all of time preceding the time when the artifact was produced. The artifact is accordingly deemed *H-original* ("H" for historical) and the artificer *H-creative*. As we will see, establishing an artifact's H-originality and the artificer's H-creativity is by no means an easy task. But there are some situations when proof of H-creativity is quite easily obtained. When Maurice Wilkes and his collaborators designed and implemented the EDSAC computer in 1949 (Dasgupta 2014a, pp. 122–126), Wilkes et al. were not only collectively and individually P-creative—neither he nor his students had ever built a digital computer before—but they were unequivocally H-creative: EDSAC became the first ever fully operational electronic-stored program digital computer in the history of the world. Picasso's *Les Demoiselles d'Avignon* (1907) was a kind of painting Picasso had never painted before—one art historian describes it as a "turning point in Picasso's development" (Cox 2000, p. 37)—hence his P-creativity in creating this work; but he was H-creative in that in the history of Western painting no one had created an image in this style before Picasso (Green 2001).

P-creativity thus refers to an individual's past lifetime—more broadly, to *biographical* time. In contrast, H-creativity relates to the past *world–historical* time.

Most creativity researchers are not satisfied by just the notion of an artifact's originality. Novelty per se does not satisfy the idea of making history. It must be also *valuable* in some significant sense. This may be because the artifact is surprising in its characteristics or behavior; or in the way it is a derivative of prior artifacts; or because the artifact represents a solution to a long-held problem (an "open problem" as mathematicians would say); or because the artifact is instrumental in falsifying or corroborating a current theory or belief; or because it improved on existing artifacts of a similar nature; or because it presents to a culture, a society or the world a new way of looking at things. Making H-creative history, thus, entails often deep and expert *judgment*, as we will see.

But in addition to producing an artifact that is original and significant with reference to past history, there are also two other situations that may prevail relating to *future* time.

Consider the situation in which an artifact produced at some point of historical time T has an *epistemic consequence* for one or more artifacts produced at some future time $T' > T$. By "epistemic consequence" I mean that the knowledge embedded in the artifact produced at time T served, in part at least, as an input to the production of artifacts at time T'. We will call this *C-creativity* ("C" for consequential) (Dasgupta 2011). *Les Demoiselles d'Avignon* was not only H-original; it was one of the most influential shapers of Cubism (Cox 2000, p. 37)—a style or a genre of painting Picasso himself co-invented (with Georges Braque) and which, in the work of many other painters (such as Juan Gris), became a painterly (that is, creative) movement. *Les Demoiselle d'Avignon* was profoundly consequential in the history of art. In painting it Picasso, by all art-historical accounts, was *C-creative*.

There is a further possibility. An artifact is produced at some point of historical time T and it is discovered that at some (possibly *much*) later time $T^* > T$ an artifact was created bearing a marked similarity to the earlier artifact, though there may be no evidence of an epistemic consequence of the former artifact on the latter. In other words the artifact produced at time T anticipated the artifact produced at time T^*. We will call this situation *A-creativity* ("A" for anticipatory) (Dasgupta 2018b). Charles Babbage's conception and design of the Analytical Engine in the mid-nineteenth century was certainly an expression of his H-creativity; he was also, to some extent, C-creative in that at least one later inventor, Percy Ludgate, was influenced in part by his design principles (Dasgupta 2014a, pp. 35–38). But Babbage also anticipated by almost a century the principle and conception of the stored program digital computer by a group of pioneers in the late 1940s (Dasgupta 2014a, pp. 17 *et seq*) even though the latter were not influenced by Babbage's design principles. With respect to these pioneers of the 1940s, Babbage was thus also A-creative.

So from a historicist standpoint we can identify three ways in which creativity is history-making in the world–historical sense: H-creativity, referring to the time before the act of creation, and C-creativity and A-creativity referring to times after the act of creation. For convenience we will collectively refer to them as *world–historical* creativity.

There is a hierarchical relationship between these kinds of creativity. An H-creative artificer is also P-creative; an A-creative artificer is also, very likely, H-creative. However, there is no logical relationship between C- and A-creativity: an artificer can be A-creative but not C-creative and *vice versa*. For example, as just noted, while the Analytical Engine anticipated the modern stored program computer, the latter was never an epistemic consequence of the former. In this sense, in relation to the development of the stored program digital computer, though Babbage was A-creative he was not C-creative. On the other hand, Freud's creation of psychoanalysis as a branch of psychology—an abstract artifact—was epistemically linked to the invention of Surrealism in art—thus (among other ways) Freud was C-creative in relation to Surrealism but he did not anticipate Surrealism, hence Freud cannot be deemed A-creative in relation to this genre of art.

III The case for and against P-creativity

For Margaret Boden, as for some other thinkers on creativity such as psychologist Philip Johnson-Laird (1988) and philosopher Robert Nozick (1989), P-creativity is what really matters. Boden rightly noted that H-creativity interests those concerned with the history of the creative tradition such as art and literary historians, and historians of science, technology and design. But for her, as a cognitive scientist, to understand an artificer's P-creativity is to understand the act of creation in its most pristine state, the "thing in itself" as it were. P-creativity seems also most relevant to those who see creativity-as-self-expression—one of Calvin Taylor's (1988) types of creativity (see Chapter 2, I). An investigator in exploring the self-expressiveness in children, for example, would clearly espouse P-creativity as the relevant domain of interest.

On the other hand, another creativity theorist, psychologist Mihalyi Csikzentmihalyi (1996) finds H-creativity more intriguing (p. 26). But we can go further. H-, C- and A-creativity are the types that make and relate to world history in a way P-creativity does not. This is what makes a cognitive historian out of a creativity researcher. If we wish to understand how specific, creative phenomena—the creation of individual artifacts, the cognitive style undergirding individual artificers, the mentality of creative movements—contribute to the creative tradition (Prologue, I, IV) then P-creativity is only of interest if it sheds light on instances of world–historical creativity.

There are other reasons, as we will see later in this chapter, why P-creativity does not appeal to the cognitive historian.

Thus, our concern in this book will be unabashedly on world–historical creativity, for it is H-, C- and A-creativity that contribute to the grandeur of history as we normally understand the term. Yet, we will have occasion to speak of P-creativity in certain situations of the world–historical kind.

IV Enter the consumer

Thus far, this symbiotic coupling of artifact and artificer appears to dominate the scene. But there is another essential actor on the stage, a third element in this drama. For every artificer and her artifact there is someone *for* whom the artifact is made: a reader for the novel or poem, a listener for the symphony, a fellow scientists for the theory, a viewer for the painting, a fellow scholar for the critical insight, a user for the machine, etc.

For every created artifact then, there is a *consumer*. In fact every artificer has a consumer in mind, an "ideal" one, when she embarks on her act of production. This ideal consumer may well be herself but that is a special case of the general situation of the artificer's imagining *some* ideal consumer on whom she projects her vision of the artifact. Thus any discussion of creativity must go beyond the artificer–artifact coupling. It must recognize the presence of the consumer. Properly speaking creativity entails a *ménage a trois*: artificer/artifact/consumer.

In the realm of art this threesome aspect of creativity has long been recognized in some fashion. Psychoanalyst Ernst Kris (1952) wrote that art entails a form of communication involving a sender, one or more receivers, and a message (p. 16). (Kris was writing not long after the new mathematical science of information theory had been invented by engineers such as Claude Shannon, and was exciting the attention of psychologists (Shannon and Weaver 1949). Kris's terminology reflects this influence.) But this *ménage a trois* has a presence in all realms of creativity, not just art. Artifacts form a *via media* between the artificer and the consumer. So in any account of the act of creation the consumer's presence is as significant as that of the artificer.

V The consumer as judge

For one thing, it leads to a *consumer-centered* view of originality: an artifact is deemed original if one or more consumers *judge* it so. An artifact's originality and the artificer's creativity are thus matters of public judgment.

This also poses problems. What if the consumer lacks the knowledge, the perceptiveness, the sensibility to comprehend the artifact's originality? This suggests that the artificer's creativity is held hostage to the consumer's in/competence or in/ability or even dis/inclination to judge an artifact's originality.

Sometimes, originality itself may not be in doubt but its *value* may be the determining factor for the consumer-as-judge to turn away from an artifact. This is why (as noted earlier) some thinkers insist that it is not enough that an artifact be original, it must be original in a valuable sort of way. Margaret Boden (2010b, p. 29, 2014, p. 227) is among the most prominent theorists who emphasize the value-laden character of creativity. Artificers themselves hold a similar view. The theoretical physicist David Bohm (2004) meditating on why scientists do what they do and why their work so consumes them, makes the point that the scientist seeks not only to discover something hitherto unknown but also to learn something significantly new about the natural world (p. 3). For G.H. Hardy (1969), the mathematician seeks to discover "patterns" that manifest beauty (p. 85). Aesthetic appeal is what lends value to mathematical invention. For the synthetic chemist and Nobel laureate Robert Burns Woodward, as told by his daughter Crystal Woodward (1989), the technical practice of successfully synthesizing new organic molecules—a craft of which he was a master—was made especially meaningful when his aesthetic sensibility was satisfied, not only in the structural forms of the chemical molecules he created but also in the ways in which he designed the steps of his syntheses (p. 234). Woodward's contemporary, theoretical chemist and superb "chemical essayist" Roald Hoffman, also a Nobel laureate, has meditated in detail on "molecular beauty." Molecules have structure and thus shape. Hoffman offers examples of synthesized molecules—artifacts—both inorganic and organic, and explains the subtleties of their structures; he speaks of one particular molecule as an "aesthetic object" in the way it manifested dimensionality (Kovac and Weinerg 2012, p. 277): one-dimensional structures are assembled into two-dimensional ones, which are linked to form the complete three-dimensional molecule.

But structural beauty is not the only criterion of molecular beauty. It may be manifest in the nature of some chemical transformation (Kovac and Weinerg 2012, p. 279). Hoffman illustrates this with examples of synthesized molecules, the processes designed by their chemist–artificers to bring about this synthesis and in what sense these processes manifest aesthetic qualities.

For an artifact to be judged original in a "valuable" sort of way places a severe load on those who do the judging. The rejection of Eduard Manet's painting *Le Dejeuner sur l'Herbe* (1863) by the jury of the Paris Salon was precisely because the jury—consumers-as-judges—could not accept the particular nature of its originality, both in its subject matter and its painterly style. Yet when this painting was exhibited the same year in the "alternative" Salon des Refuses its reception by critics and connoisseurs was not unfavorable (McCauley 1998). Likewise, every one of the "palette knife paintings" Manet's contemporary Paul Cézanne submitted to the Paris Salon in the 1860s was rejected. Here again, Cézanne's radicallly new style, his use of the palette knife as brush, was rejected by the Salon jury (Lewis 2000, pp. 44–64).

No single work of art serves more dramatically as an example of the originality paradox than Pablo Picasso's *Les Demoiselles d'Avignon*. Picasso began preliminary work on this painting in the winter of 1906–1907 and it was completed some time in the summer, probably June–July 1907 (Green 2001). During this time several people were witness to the work-in-progress, mostly Picasso's friends, including the art critic and poet Guillaume Appolinaire, artists André Derain, Henri Matisse and Georges Braque, and the collectors Leo and Gertrude Stein. Without exception their responses to the work were strongly negative. Yet ten years later the critic and pioneer of the Surrealist movement André Breton was calling *Les Demoiselles* a "sacred image." And in 1937 Alfred Barr, then director of New York's Museum of Modern Art, described the work as the century's "most important painting" (Seckel 1994). The point of its initial rejection and later acceptance was not originality itself, but the quality of this originality, its *significance*: insignificant in the eyes of its original judges and enormously significant in the eyes of Breton and Barr.

One might object that art poses this problem with the consumer-as-judge because judgment of a work of art is an aesthetic, hence subjective matter. But other domains of the artificial may also be susceptible to this problem, not least in the realm of science.

Consider, for example, Galileo's situation in the Florence of the Medicis. In his remarkable study *Galileo, Courtier* (1993), historian of science Mario Biagioli describes how Galileo could not convince the followers of Aristotle of the validity of his theory of buoyancy, or of the "new," Copernican astronomy. Here, Galileo was an artificer in several senses: first in the invention of new observational *instruments* (his telescopes), second in his production of *facts* about the heavens (the sunspots and the moons of Jupiter observed with his telescopes), and third, in his *arguments* in support of his buoyancy theory and of Copernicanism. The Aristotelian "philosophers" were the consumer–judges. Biagioli's explanation is long and complex and it is impossible to do his explanation justice here, but stripped to its barest essence the problem lay in that the Aristotelians did not (or refused to) *understand* Galileo because their "socio-professional" *identity* forbade them to do so. Put simply, their identity-based Aristotelian worldview was (to use a celebrated term due to philosopher–historian of science Thomas Kuhn (2012)) *incommensurate* with the Galilean worldview.

In the case of the social sciences, the announcement of the Nobel Memorial Prize in economics for Herbert Simon in 1978 caused considerable puzzlement amid the economists' community. The official Nobel Foundation citation tells us that the prize was awarded for Simon's original researches into economic decision making processes (Carlson 1979)—work that he had done primarily in the 1940s and 1950s. Yet the originality of Simon's work, though thus sanctified by the award of a Nobel, remained a matter of uncertainty even into the 1990s, depending on who the consumer-as-judge was. This was due to the fact that Simon had invented a new research tradition—cognitivism—for analyzing economic and other forms of decision making, a tradition that stood far apart from the dominant research tradition in economics (known as the "neoclassical" tradition) (Dasgupta 2003b).

VI Of peer consumers and lay consumers

In the preceding discussion the consumers-as-judges were intellectually, culturally and cognitively at par with the artificers they were judging. Picasso's friends belonged to Picasso's world. The Aristotelian philosophers of seventeenth century Florence were of the same intellectual, cultural and social milieu as was Galileo. The people who chose Simon for the Nobel Prize were themselves—or at least some of them—economists and at the same intellectual level as was Simon.

The scientist who judges another scientist, the connoisseur or artist who judges another artist, the musician or music critic who judges a musician, the scholar who judges another scholar are all consumers of a special kind. They usually have (one hopes) the knowledge, training, sensibility and expertise to make responsible judgments. Only a physicist of a certain quality can comprehend fully the significance of a new physical theory or discovery; only a mathematician of a certain caliber can grasp the significance of a new mathematical result; only an engineer of a certain level of expertise and experience can judge the structural quality of a new tower building or a bridge; only the highly trained musical ear can properly judge the aesthetics and technicalities of a new musical composition. In the realm of art and literature, however, such consumers may not themselves be the same kind of artificer as those whose works they are judging. (The art connoisseur Bernard Berenson, the literary critic F.R. Leavis and the theater critic Kenneth Tynan come to mind.) Yet we may call them all *peer* consumers.

Not all consumers, however, are of this kind. The viewer in an art exhibition, the lover and avid reader of literature, the listener at a classical concert, the filmgoer or theatergoer, the driver of a motor car or the user of a laptop computer—they too judge artifacts and their artificers, except that their judgment may be based on criteria different from those of peer consumers. Let us call them *lay* consumers.

The voices of peer consumers may dominate judgment of creativity in some domains but for many artificers—novelists, musicians, painters, filmmakers, stage directors, inventors and designers, even political philosophers—lay consumers matter as much as (sometimes more than) the peers. They judge in numbers. (In contemporary parlance they serve as "crowd" consumer–judges.) They may be relatively anonymous, even voiceless, but they are not powerless for it is they who buy the books, pay at the box office, attend the concerts and flock to exhibitions. Their judgment as consumers will also have to be reckoned with.

So in judging in what manner an artificer makes history, we run into the problem of who the "right" judge is. Should it be the artificer, the peer consumers or the lay consumer? In the case of an artifact's P-originality, the artificer is likely to be the "proper" judge: after all, who knows the artificer's personal history better than herself? But even this may pose problems: for instance, it is possible that the artificer *thinks* she has created a particular artifact for the first time, but she may have forgotten an earlier similar experience.

In the case of H-originality the only kind of judge that can properly assess this would have to be a peer consumer. It is unlikely that a lay consumer will have the requisite knowledge to make such judgment.

VII Artificers: elite and subaltern

The distinction between P-creativity and the three kinds of world–historical creativity is also to some extent the distinction between what we may call *elite* and *subaltern artificers*: between those who have dominated history and those who have been largely ignored, between the powerful and the powerless. (I have appropriated this meaning of the word "subaltern" from the Subaltern school of historians (Ludden 2002)). World–historical creativity (it might be argued) relates to those who have been recognized by history as *the* creative ones—the brilliant and extraordinary, mostly male, usually white, usually Western. Such creativity brings to mind the "great men theory of history." It brings to mind the idea of the genius, and since the very idea of genius is closely linked to the Romanticism of the late eighteenth–early nineteenth centuries it is tempting to associate world–historical creativity with the spirit of the Romantic Age (Roe 2005).

Yet throughout history there have been men *and* women whose voices have not been heard, whose thoughts have not been recorded, for they have scarcely appeared in the historical narrative. P-creativity is thus *ideologically* more in line with the subaltern perspective. While anyone who is world-historically creative is also P-creative, there are countless people who are or have been P-creative but not H-, C- or A-creative. Their creativity is a very personal matter but history may be quite oblivious to it.

Yet, as Margaret Boden has pointed out, P-creativity is more *universal*. We are all potentially P-creative. This very universality and its subaltern slant lends the study of P-creativity a different kind of appeal for the creativity researcher.

VIII The unnaturalness attending personal creativity

The problem is how does one go about *studying* P-creative artificers? Ideally one should observe them in their "natural" state, *in vivo*, as they go about their tasks. Ideally one should have access to their thought processes by ways of jottings, note taking, audible comments and so on. I have done this kind of observation. My subject was George Rodrigue, an American painter known mainly for his "Blue Dog" and "Cajun" paintings. Rodrigue's place in contemporary American art was, I think, consolidated when the prestigious art book publisher Harry N. Abrams produced a substantial book on his art (Rodrigue 2003).

One December afternoon in 2002 I sat in his studio and observed him as he painted, while my assistant (my son) videotaped him as he worked. Occasionally Rodrigue would pause to explain something to me.

The picture that resulted after about an hour (it was a first version which he would further develop later) was no doubt original in the sense that he had never painted *this* picture before. What I had observed, and what I reported (Dasgupta 2005) was *in vivo* P-creativity. But was it creativity in the "natural state?" For the artist was surely conscious of my presence and of the video camera focused on him. To what extent our presence affected his process of painting is impossible to say, but surely it must have had some effect. A version of Heisenberg's uncertainty principle kicking in, so to speak.

Even more problematic is to study P-creativity in a controlled laboratory setting, wherein a subject is *assigned* tasks intended to elicit "data" concerning P-creativity. The psychological literature on creativity is full of experimental studies of this sort.

A classic study of this sort was performed by psychologist Catherine Patrick (1937) with a group of artists. As she stated it, her objective was to study the thought process of artists given the task of sketching pictures in a laboratory-like setting, complete with a "control group" of "non-artists." The experiment also entailed individual interviews with the experimental subjects and their answers to questionnaires about their method of work.

The main problem with this *in vitro* form of investigation is its *unnaturalness*—even more than that of *in vivo* observations. The artists were commanded to produce paintings "on tap" so to speak: they were given a poem and asked to draw a picture inspired by it (Patrick 1937, p. 39).

Catherine Patrick argued that the resulting pictures composed by the artists typified their usual work (pp. 58, 59). Her evidence was the opinions expressed by the artists themselves some 80 percent of whom claimed there was no "essential difference" between these pictures and those they normally painted. Thus the *in vitro* study was justified on the ground that the experimental conditions *replicated* the natural conditions under which the artists normally work; that Patrick's observations were conducted *as if* the study was done *in vivo*. But of course the conditions were *not* natural. Controlled experiments with human subjects are not the same as experiments with animals or nonliving things. Just as my observation of George Rodrigue could well have disturbed his act of production so also Patrick's wholly artificial conditions could well have intruded upon her subjects.

The dilemma of P-creativity then lies in that its observation under quasi-natural conditions (as in my observation of Rodrigue at work) or experimental conditions (as in Patrick's study of her artists) do not contribute directly to the study of natural creativity.

IX The naturalness attending world–historical creativity

Examination of world–historical creativity is much less vulnerable to the frailties that attend P-creativity. A world-historically creative artificer has produced an artifact (material, abstract or hybrid) that is already part of history. No amount of probing can influence the act of creation itself. H-, C- or A-creativity is an historical phenomenon, meaning that not only is it something that has already happened but it has happened in the natural course of things and that it has made history. To take the most exalted examples, the discovery of penicillin, the identification of DNA as the molecular basis of life, the design of the first wrought-iron railway bridge, the invention of Cubism, the blending of magic and realism in writing fiction, the conceiving of a machine that computes were not events that were artificially induced on command. They constitute the very stuff of *natural creativity*—whereby, paradoxically, the artifactual world is made and shaped— "creativity in the wild," subject to all the trials and tribulations, the triumphs and exaltations, the vicissitudes and disappointments that attend human history. Moreover (and this is important) because world-historically creative artificers make history in some sliver of the artifactual world (in some significant sense, no matter how tiny that sliver is) there is always the likelihood of the availability of "data" surrounding such creators: archival material including published books and articles, diaries, notebooks, correspondence, memoirs, recorded interviews and so on.

X   The trickiness of historical judgment

By Margaret Boden's definition, an artificer's H-creativity relates to the production of an artifact that had never previously existed in human history. This determination might itself be a daunting task: to claim something about the *whole* of human history embracing all time and all space. This might be a problem even in relation to the time of production itself since the judge must guarantee that the same artifact has not been produced in some other part of the world at about the same time or just before.

In 1837 the English naturalist Charles Darwin had arrived at a theory that, he believed, explained biological evolution and the formation of new species. The theory involved a mechanism he named "natural selection." This theory of evolution by natural selection was the abstract artifact he had invented.

For various reasons Darwin chose not to publish his theory at the time. In fact, save for a few intimate scientific friends it remained his secret for over twenty years and for all this time he had no reason to suppose that he was not the inventor of the theory. Then to his chagrin, in 1858, he learnt by way of a letter and an accompanying manuscript sent to him from the other side of the world by one Alfred Russel Wallace that the latter had arrived at exactly the same theory. Darwin's personal belief that he was the sole inventor of the theory of natural selection was demolished virtually overnight (Mayr 1982, pp. 408–425). The outcome was a joint announcement of Wallace's and Darwin's work at a meeting of the Linnean Society in London on July 1, 1858.

If ascertaining the historical *newness* can be problematic, even more so is the judgment that an artifact is *valuable* or *significant*. In fact the really hard part is that this valuation will depend, not only on the nature and complexity of the artifact, but also the field to which it belongs as well as the acumen, knowledge, experience and sensibility of those who judge, whether the artificer himself or consumers. If the judge is wanting in one or more of these aspects then the identification of originality may easily be missed.

In the case of the Darwin–Wallace episode, we learn that the president of the Linnean Society regretted in the Society's annual report of 1858 that no "striking discoveries" had been made in the Society's scientific domains that year (Mayr 1982, p. 423).

Indeed, at the Linnean Society meeting itself the presentation of the Darwin–Wallace theory (by two of Darwin's friends, the *doyen* of British geology Charles Lyell and the distinguished naturalist Joseph Hooker) was greeted by the audience with bemused silence (Desmond and Moore 1992, p. 470). What was patently significant about the idea of natural selection to Darwin's closest scientific friends, Lyell, Hooker and the biologist Thomas Henry Huxley, was evidently not so to others, at least for some time.

Sometimes the problem for which an artifact is created as a solution may itself be not comprehended by others. In a personal conversation with this author (in December 1991 at the Olivetti Research Laboratory in Cambridge, England), computer pioneer Maurice Wilkes would recall that when he presented his idea of microprogramming—a novel technique for designing a computer's control unit which would be enormously consequential—to an audience of engineers and scientists at a conference in Manchester, U.K. in 1951, the problem for which microprogramming was a solution was not appreciated by the audience. His problem, he told this author, was essentially a *private* problem.

On the other hand, in scientific and technological arenas the value of an artifact may be directly related to the acknowledged difficulty of the problem for which the artifact was a solution. For example a long-standing unsolved problem in mathematics was the "four-color problem": can a two-dimensional ("planar") map be colored with no more than four colors so that no two adjacent regions have the same color?

This problem was stated as a mathematical conjecture in 1852. That five colors suffice to color any planar map had been proved in the late nineteenth century but despite many attempts the solution to the four-color problem remained a conjecture for a century and a quarter (Davis and Hersch 1981, pp. 380–382). For mathematicians the solution to long-standing "open" problems (in the mathematicians' jargon) is a high-stakes affair and the four-color problem was no exception. Thus the excitement in 1977 when two Americans, Wolfgang Haken and Kenneth Appel (assisted by John Koch) produced a *computer-generated* proof for the conjecture (Haken, Appel and Koch 1977). The proof itself was the (abstract) artifact. The value of this act of production lay not only in the solution of a century-old problem but also in the strategy used to arrive at the proof. This was the first instance, in the venerable mathematical tradition, of a computer-generated proof. Haken and Appel's H-creativity was twofold: in the proof itself, and in presenting a new *concept* of a mathematical proof. (Unsurprisingly this proof strategy turned out to be hugely controversial in the mathematical world (Appel 1984)).

XI Epistemic judgment

We have noted that an artificer's act of production becomes an act of creation only if the artifact is original in some significant sense. As we have also seen, judging what that "significant sense" is, is a matter that can be highly subjective.

Yet there is a sense in which judgment of an artifact's originality may be made relatively objective: by judgment based on the richness *of* the knowledge embedded in the artifact—to what we may call the artifact's *epistemic complexity* (Dasgupta 2013).

Epistemic complexity consists of the unusual or surprising knowledge that both contributes both (as input) to the creation of an artifact and the quality of the knowledge that is generated (as output) by the artifact's creation. (In the case of an abstract artifact such as a scientific theory or a design method or a philosophical doctrine or an algorithm the artifact is itself a piece of knowledge. In the case of a material or liminal artifact such as a computer or a piece of software or a bridge the knowledge is encoded in the artifact.)

The making of an artifact is a knowledge-rich process. The artificer brings to the act of production a rich network of knowledge (including beliefs and values). The act of conceiving and bringing into being an artifact entails the deployment, by the artificer, of this network of knowledge. Knowledge thus serves as an input to the artificer's act.

But this act of production also produces knowledge: new facts, new theories, new concepts and ideas, and new insights. Knowledge is thus also an output of the artificer's act. The originality of an artifact will lie in the quality or significance of the new knowledge encoded in the artifact as input and as output. We may call judgment based on assessment of epistemic complexity *epistemic judgment*.

As an example, consider the engineer–architect Pier Luigi Nervi who, in 1936, designed and built aircraft hangars for the Italian Air Force (Nervi 1966). There were "several traditional solutions" to build such structures—designing aircraft hangars could be seen as exercises in routine design, entailing established input knowledge to the design process with little new or significant knowledge generated as output, that is with low epistemic complexity. But Nervi eschewed the normal path. Instead he created an "organism" that transmitted the loads to the supports and columns at the sides and thus provide a large, uninterrupted volume of space for the aircrafts. The huge dome-like vault was composed of a curved, intersecting network of ribs. This was old knowledge invented 800 years earlier by master masons who built the Gothic cathedrals—but adapted to a radically different type of structure. The sublimity of medieval houses of worship was transposed to the most plebeian of buildings—with arresting aesthetic effect. Here was a structure that was epistemically complex because it deployed old knowledge in a wholly surprising context. Epistemic complexity, then, is a marker of an artifact's H-originality, and of the artificer's H-creativity.

XII "Whiggish" interpretation of creativity

The *time* at which creativity is judged is of the essence. As we have seen, H-creativity relates a moment of time in history, when an artifact was produced, to all the times that preceded that moment. The judge, so to speak, places himself at that moment of production: that moment becomes the "present" in his mind.

If judging is actually done at roughly the time when the artifact is produced, this is not a problematic matter. Picasso's friends were very much "in the moment" when they witnessed *Les Demoiselles d'Avignon*. The mathematical community who passed judgment on Haken and Appel's proof of the four-color theorem were their contemporaries.

But what if the judging is done long after the moment of production has passed? What if the judging is done a decade later or even a century after? To what extent should the consumer-as-judge allow her *present-situatedness* affect her judgment of the creative worth of an artificer of the past, someone who may be long dead?

This is a question faced by historians in general. To what extent do we allow our present circumstances, our present values and tastes influence our judgment, assessment and understanding of the past? This question was first raised in 1931 by the historian Herbert Butterfield (1973) in a now classic book called *The Whig Interpretation of History*. Referring to the so-called English "Whig" historians of the nineteenth century ("Whigs" were the liberals or progressives in contrast to the "Tories" or conservatives), Butterfield scorned these historians who, he said, valorized or demonized historical actors according to whether their thoughts and actions cohered with the historians' contemporary values. This viewing of the past through the lens of the historians' present came to be called, derisively, "whiggism" or "present-centeredness."

Ever since Butterfield conventional wisdom has dictated that present-centeredness must be eschewed at all cost. The past is to be judged according to the context of that time, not of the historian's own time. Yet, in practice, historians *select* events and people of the past as their objects of inquiry in the light of concerns, values and events of their own time. What the historian must do is to walk a narrow path avoiding *judging* the past according to present contexts yet *selecting* from the past according to present concerns (Harrington 1987).

In judging past creativity, however, there is certainly a sense in which *it pays to be Whiggish*. The value or significance of an artifact may lie in its later *consequences*—that is, in the judgment of C-creativity.

XIII C-originality revisited

An artifact's H-originality may be ascertained as early as the time the artifact is produced whereas the consequences of a new artifact may not always be so evident until some appreciable elapse of time. Thus C-originality may entail *more* of an historical judgment than H-originality. Moreover, when we consider the role of *value* as an ingredient of creativity, clearly an artifact that is C-original is likely to be of greater value than one that is "just" H-original.

Picasso's *Les Demoiselles d'Avignon*, for example, manifests both these aspects. Nothing in the history of painting before its appearance had ever been quite like it. It was unequivocally H-original. But, as we have noted (Section II above) it also gave rise to the style of painting called Cubism; it influenced the future course of art history (Golding 2001; Green 2001).

Eduard Manet's painting *Le Déjeuner sur l'herbe* (1863) is another case in point. We have seen that the Paris Salon jury rejected this work though it was then exhibited at the alternative Salon des Refuses, an exhibition created by Emperor Napoleon III to display paintings rejected by the main Salon. Even then the critics and other viewers of the time struggled to make sense of the painting (Hayes Tucker 1998). This was certainly in part because of the enigmatic quality of its subject matter. It shows an outdoor scene in a wooded area, occupied by two women and two men. The men are fully, even dandily, clothed. One of the women in the foreground is naked, sitting sideways, her face turned toward the viewer, her gaze bold, impudent. The second woman, slightly in the background, scantily dressed, stands in a body of water, a pond perhaps. The two men sit by the naked woman but seem quite oblivious of her presence. Besides them are a basket, fruits and other accoutrement of a picnic.

The very content of this picture perplexed the viewers of the time and has continued to intrigue viewers ever since. The painting was H-original in that its consumers of the time—peer and lay—had not seen such a painting in a *contemporary* setting. The theme itself was not new: There hung in the Louvre a painting originally attributed to the Renaissance artist Georgione (Hayes Tucker 1998, p. 13) but more recently attributed to Titian (Lewis 2000, p. 82). This work also shows two women, both naked, in the company of two fully dressed men. As in the Manet they sit in sylvan surroundings; as in the Manet the men seem oblivious to the women's presence.

Manet, of course, was aware of the Titian/Georgione painting: for one thing it hung in the Louvre, a museum he much frequented (Hayes Tucker 1998, p. 14); for another, he had a copy of this painting made by a friend hanging in his studio at the time. Painters, of course, frequently appropriate their great predecessors' themes and then reinterpret them in their own style.

Manet's H-creativity no doubt lay in *how* he had taken Titian's theme and created his own vision of the theme. Its originality lay in some large part in its "shock value," the *surprise* it evoked in the viewer's mind—surprise being, as Margaret Boden (2010b) has pointed out, one of the ways whereby the originality of an artifact impresses itself on the consumer's mind. (Indeed, for cognitive psychologist Jerome Bruner (1979, p. 18), "effective surprise" *is* the hallmark of a creative enterprise.)

But Manet's creativity also lay in its consequences. The painting turned out to be C-original; Manet was, in the context of this painting, C-creative. In the words of art historian Paul Hayes Tucker, *Le Déjeuner* "became a touchstone for avant garde painters of that time and after" (p. 7). Two years after the painting caused such a stir, his younger contemporary Claude Monet produced his own version.

Paul Cézanne painted several versions of it including one (in 1869–1870) bearing the same title (Lewis 2000, p. 83). More than thirty years after the Manet, Paul Gaughin's *Where Do We Come From? Who Are We? Where Are We Going?* (1897) paid tribute to *Le Dejeuner.* Even later, Henri Matisse appropriated Manet's theme in painting *Luxe, Calme, et Volupte* (1904–1905). And a century later we find the aged Picasso creating a spate of pictures along Manet's theme, all titled *Luncheon in the Grass after Manet*: in oil on canvas (1960), in pencil and colored pencil (1961), and in ink (1970) (Hayes Tucker 1998, p. 7).

Manet's *Le Déjeuner sur l'herbe* illustrates well the way C–creativity comes into being, at least in the realm of art.

XIV   Science and C-creativity

The situation in science is somewhat different since science thrives on predictive capabilities in a way art or literature does not. In many (but not all) sciences an assertion becomes credible (or at least plausible) *as* a scientific proposition if it leads to predictions that can be independently observed or experimentally examined. Such propositions, almost by definition, have consequences.

These consequences may take different forms. The proposition may open up a whole new field of exploration that had never before existed—it may lead to possible practical applications, most exclusively it may alter the very worldview of an entire scientific community or, still more exaltedly, of human society. Thus judgment of a scientist's creativity with respect to a scientific discovery is intrinsically entwined with both the H–originality and the C–originality of the discovery.

Consider the discovery of a hitherto unknown natural phenomenon, e.g., the discovery of a new fundamental (subatomic) particle. In what sense is such a discovery of a natural phenomenon an *artifact*?

The answer is that the discovery produces a *new piece of knowledge (or belief)* about the phenomenon. Philosophers and cognitive scientists sometimes call this propositional (or declarative) knowledge—because it takes the form of propositions about nature, e.g., "The Higgs boson exists" or "global warming is the effect of carbon dioxide emission into the atmosphere."

A new piece of scientific knowledge about the natural world is produced in the mind of a scientist. It is then communicated through publications, correspondence or lectures to other scientists and thereby becomes, in the form of a symbol structure, shared knowledge. In the words of philosopher of science Karl Popper (1972) it becomes *objective* knowledge—knowledge that is independent of an individual possessing that knowledge subjectively. In Popper's words, "knowledge without a knower" (pp. 108–109). Yet it is the product of human thinking, thus an abstract artifact.

In fact a piece of objective propositional knowledge is an abstract artifact in exactly the same sense that a poem, the proof of a theorem, a computer algorithm or the design of a bridge (but not the bridge itself which is a material artifact) is so. And the scientist who produces such knowledge is its artificer.

To return to C-creativity in science, the knowledge that a scientist produces about some natural phenomenon may not only be H-original but by its predictive nature, it is almost immediately *potentially* C-original since the consequences of this knowledge may be evident almost at the time of its production. In other words, one may be able to judge the scientist's C-creativity at the same time her H-creativity can be judged.

In February 1928 the physicist C.V. Raman and his associates (notably, K.S. Krishnan), working in a laboratory in Kolkata (formerly Calcutta), India, were convinced that they had discovered a new phenomenon about light. It was already known that a beam of light is scattered by molecules of a liquid or gas, producing a diffuse radiation having the same frequency (and thus same wave length) as of the original ("incidental") light beam. Raman et al. discovered that the scattering they observed was accompanied by a modified scattered radiation of a different frequency and wave length—"a new type of secondary radiation" as Raman and his co-discoverer K.S. Krishnan described it (Raman and Krishnan 1928). This phenomenon came to be called the Raman effect.

The H-originality of the discovery was beyond doubt; it was epistemically judgable and so judged. The Raman effect was new knowledge. But it was also consequential and was so realized by other scientists-as-consumers almost immediately. By August 1929, less than eighteen months after the first communication of the Raman effect in the British journal *Nature*, some 150 papers on the Raman effect had been published, authored by physicists in Britain, Europe, America and elsewhere (Venkataraman 1988, p. 215). In November 1929, Ernest Rutherford, twice Nobel laureate and director of Cambridge's Cavendish Laboratory, delivered his presidential address to the Royal Society and made mention of this discovery which, he said, was not only intrinsically "of great interest" as a physical phenomenon, but also promised the unfolding of "a new field of experimental inquiry" that would shed "valuable light" on the structure of chemical knowledge (quoted by Venkataraman 1988, p. 215).

Such was the realization by the global physics community, honors were showered upon Raman almost immediately: a gold medal from Italy, knighthood from the British government and King George V, honorary doctorates from German and Scottish universities, a coveted medal from the Royal Society, and the biggest plum of all, from Sweden, the Nobel Prize for physics in 1930—incredibly, within two years of the discovery itself.

Raman's C-creativity (and, in fact, that of his principal collaborator K.S. Krishnan who, many believed, should have shared the Nobel) was thus recognized (and how!) at almost the same time his H-creativity was evident. This judgment, unequivocally epistemic, not subjective, has not abated with the passage of time. According to one estimate some 12,000 papers on the Raman effect and its application (as Raman spectroscopy) had appeared by 1980 (Keswani 1980, p. 5).

Perhaps Raman's example is exceptional. As noted above, there is a certain asymmetry between the judgment of H-originality/H-creativity and C-originality/C-creativity. The former can often be judged almost immediately after the artifact has been created since only the antecedents of that artifact need be considered. But while judgment of C-originality might be *anticipated* at the time of an artifact's production (for example, the consequences of the stored program computer concept was grasped by many computer pioneers almost as soon as it emerged in the mid-1940s), more often than not, assessment of C-originality demands the eclipse of some time after the birth of the artifact. A striking example from the realm of computing was the invention of microprogramming, a technique for designing a computer's control unit, in 1951: its influence and effect were not felt till over a decade later (Dasgupta 2014a, pp. 185–186, 250–251).

The computer scientist Per Brinch Hansen, a significant figure in the fields of programming methodology and programming languages, reflecting on his invention of the programming language Concurrent Pascal in 1993, almost two decades after its creation (Brinch Hansen 1975), wrote that what gave him most pride was that by way of this language he had demonstrated something no one had before him, that it was possible to write serious concurrent programs—programs that evoked concurrent, interacting computations (Brinch Hansen 1996, p. 392).

Thus he clearly believed in the H-originality of his programming language. And most observers (including this writer) would agree with him. Concurrent Pascal's H-originality—and Brinch Hansen's H-creativity—cannot be contested. But, he also pointed out that a key concept embedded in Concurrent Pascal, called the "monitor," had been co-invented by him. Concurrent Pascal was, in his terms, a "monitor language." And he made the point that between 1976 and 1990, several "monitor languages" came into existence. Not all were influenced by Concurrent Pascal, he noted, but several were. In this regard Concurrent Pascal had consequences for the development of parallel programming languages; it was C-original in this regard. In designing Concurrent Pascal, Per Brinch Hansen had every reason to be judged not only H-creative but also C-creative.

In the history of artificial intelligence (AI) a seminal work was a computer program called SHRDLU created by computer scientist Terry Winograd (1972). SHRDLU was a fully operational simulated robot; a liminal computational artifact with a capacity for understanding sentences (commands, declarations and questions) in English and performing simulated actions in a very limited world of toy blocks of different shapes, sizes and colors. At the time of its invention SHRDLU was widely judged by the AI research community as a landmark in the development of natural language understanding systems. It was H-original without question. (For a recent historical discussion of this work see Dasgupta 2018a, pp. 193–199.)

Consequentially, SHRDLU's value lay not in the artifact itself—it would prove to be disappointing in that it did not lead to other, more general natural language understanding systems—but in the richness of new kinds of knowledge embedded in the artifact, as assessed by Winograd (1980) writing eight years later. In other words, its value as an original contribution to AI lay in its epistemic complexity, in the sense described earlier in this chapter. If not the artifact itself, this knowledge became available to future researchers. Given the kinds of knowledge embedded in SHRDLU—this included knowledge represented widely in the form of procedures, its systemic quality (components of closely and "busily" interacting subsystems), its ability to carry out realistic conversations with a human user and to carry out realistic tasks, its ability to make inferences about the toy blocks world it resided in—one can certainly claim that SHRDLU was unequivocally C-original and, by the same token, Terry Winograd was C-creative.

XV   Overlooking originality

Whether or not an artifact is deemed original (and its artificer is judged creative) evidently depends on the latter's personal history and on his or her cognitive capacity and performance; but it also depends on the artificer's private beliefs about the worth of the artifact *and* on the beliefs, knowledge, perception, sensibilities and actions of denizens of the relevant community of consumers.

These factors are especially important in the case of C-creativity, for this judgment may depend on matters that may be totally unrelated to the factors that go into establishing H-creativity.

To take an example from the realm of technology, an invention is granted a patent: a recognition of H-originality. It is also favorably received by the relevant technological community. But it fails to make inroads into the commercial market because of some other manufacturer's powerful influence on the market. The invention languishes and never makes the transition from H-originality to C-originality because of factors (political, say) having nothing to do with the "intrinsic" worth of the invention. The hapless inventor, at least in respect to that particular invention, cannot be said to be C-creative.

In fact, generally speaking, the matter of identifying C-creativity is fraught with problems. Ideas, scientific discoveries, technological inventions or literary works may be overlooked by the community or may be ignored; the significance of the artifact may be missed altogether. Or what was once believed to be C-original may be no longer so regarded in the light of new evidence. The artifact is "demoted" from the realm of C-originality and the artificer's reputation as a C-creative person may correspondingly diminish. Or it may be that one's C-creativity is recognized or even enhanced in one place but negated in another.

This elusiveness in the very idea of creativity seems to lie in the quality of originality itself. For *originality is not an "objective" attribute of an artifact.* There is the artificer's judgment and there is the consumer's judgment—and the two may be at odds with each other. The artificer may be too "close" to the artifact to make a rational determination of its originality. The consumer may not be psychologically or intellectually able to grasp the significance of the artifact; or he may be ignorant of the past. Both artificer and consumer may have distorted views of the former's creativity.

A celebrated case in point is the discovery of the laws of heredity in 1866 by Gregor Mendel, an Austrian monk by vocation though educated as a scientist in the University of Vienna.

We may assume that Mendel himself understood the significance of his work: from his perspective—that of the artificer-as-judge—his discovery was no doubt

H-original. And the fact that a journal accepted and published a paper describing his findings suggest that this work was judged H-original by at least one consumer, the journal's editor. Although this journal, the *Proceedings of the Natural History Society of Brunn* (Brno) was a relatively minor one, libraries of most of the major scientific institutions of the time subscribed to it. Moreover, Mendel's paper was known to at least two influential European botanists who either failed to grasp its significance or, more distressingly, chose to ignore the work. (Mendel's experiments involved a species of peas; thus they fell within the realm of botany.)

At any rate, Mendel's laws were ignored and lay forgotten for some thirty years. The issue of the originality of the laws and its discoverer's creativity did not even arise until his paper was "discovered" independently by two botanists in the final years of the nineteenth century and their significance realized. By then Mendel was long dead. (This account is based on Mayr 1982, pp. 722–726.) The laws of heredity entered the canon of biological knowledge, not only as something H-original but also because of its profound consequences. The science of genetics that flowered in the first half of the twentieth century was called "Mendelian genetics" (Ruse 1973; Mayr 1982; Huxley 2010). Mendel's C-creativity was thus recognized and till now it remains intact.

XVI   Being ahead of one's time: A-creativity revisited

If the botanists who knew about Gregor Mendel's work chose to ignore it deliberately, such an action was reprehensible to say the least. Others may have overlooked his paper because of Mendel's obscurity, tucked away as he was in a monastery, or because of the minor status of the journal concerned. But sometimes even distinguished artificers may be vulnerable to the cognitive frailty of consumers. An example is that of the Englishman Alan Turing.

In the annals of mathematics, logic and computing Turing stands *very* tall. By the end of the 1940s Turing's reputation in these realms was massive on both sides of the Atlantic (Hodges 1983; Dasgupta 2014a). In particular, the consequences of a paper he published in 1936 established the fundamental nature of *computability* (that is, what it means to compute something) and laid the groundwork for much of theoretical computer science (Dasgupta 2014a, pp. 44–59, 245). He is an incontrovertible, epistemically judgable instance of a C-creative scientist many times over. *Yet recognition of his creativity in another situation failed.*

At Britain's first ever conference on computers, held in Cambridge in 1949, Turing presented a short paper in which he discussed the germinal idea underlying what computer scientists later called "proofs of program correctness" (Turing 1949). The main idea was that checking whether a computer program is correct or not can be done much as one proves the correctness of theorems.

There is little doubt that Turing had identified the essential *idea* of proving program correctness even though the word "proof" does not appear in the text. In fact he had *anticipated* much work that would follow almost twenty years later. But there is no published evidence that his paper evoked any interest among the 140 odd participants at this conference, including some of the most formidable mathematical, scientific and engineering minds in Europe who were pioneering the development of electronic computing. Like Mendel's paper it was ignored or forgotten; nor was it belatedly "discovered" as Mendel's paper was, and its significance recognized. Some twenty years later, the American Robert Floyd (in 1967) and the Englishman C.A.R. Hoare (in 1969)—both, ironically, recipients of the Turing Award, computer science's most prestigious honor—developed between them a theory of program correctness as it is now known. Neither referred to Turing's 1949 paper. Clearly they were unaware of it, and so it had no influence on their thinking. Turing's H-creativity in this context was only established in the early 1980s (Morris and Jones 1984). And if his paper had no consequences in the development of the theory of program correctness it was because he was "ahead of his times" in this regard: his paper proposed an idea (an abstract artifact) that would anticipate something which would be reinvented some two decades later. Turing's 1949 paper described a procedure, an abstract artifact, that was A-original. In producing this artifact Turing was *A-creative*.

XVII   The (super)need to be original

Whether or not an artifact is P-original, H-original, C-original or A-original is a matter of historical judgment, as we have seen from the various examples. That is, such judgment—and that of the creativity of the artificer—can only be made after the artifact comes into existence, and in the context of what is known about the personal history of the artificer (in the case of P-creativity) and the "global" history of the creative tradition (in the case of H-, C- and A-creativity).

Regardless of this, though, there is a further quality of the artificer that is noteworthy. No artificer who *in fact* becomes creative is simply content to produce an artifact that is commonplace, that has been already produced before or elsewhere. Rather she desires to produce artifacts that are distinctive—that expresses her uniqueness, her individuality, her originality. The potentially creative being *aspires to be original*. Even the textbook writer must convince himself (and his publisher) that his book is distinctive in such and such ways, that it says something no other "competitor" does.

In other words, the artificer *seeks to break away from the past*. Cognitive scientist Howard Gruber (1989) described this trait as "deviation amplification." This is more than an aspiration, it is a compelling need, so compelling that we may call it a *superneed*. And it is a superneed that seems to be shared by most highly creative people.

For instance, the scientist who devises a crucial experiment to corroborate or falsify a theory is not only driven by a feeling of dissatisfaction about the uncertain status of the theory, but he may also desire to design and execute an experiment that has not been performed before. The experiment itself is the artifact being created. Many of the great scientific experiments in history bear this stamp of originality, reflecting the scientist's superneed to be original (Harré 1981). Likewise the artist may seek to create a new genre or painting or a new style, create a niche for herself never known to exist. For the mathematician G.H. Hardy (1969), the most sublime goal one can aspire to is to leave for posterity something of permanent value (p. 77).

In the annals of modern Indian art the painter Amrita Sher-Gil has a particularly prominent place. For one thing she was a woman, and her work in the 1930s proclaimed that the woman artist in India must be reckoned with. For another, as we will recount later, there was the originality of her work: she invented her own distinctive style that made her paintings distinctly recognizable. But what interests us here is her superneed to be original. Born in 1913 to a Hungarian mother and an Indian Sikh father, she spent 1929–1934 in Paris receiving her training at the famed École des Beaux Art. In that period she produced over sixty works mainly in charcoal and oil. Her work was accepted by and exhibited at the Grand Salon, the same Salon that had once rejected Manet and Cézanne.

Her Paris period was an exploration in Post-Impressionism. Some of her paintings were distinctly Cézannesque and at least one was a tribute to Gaughin. By her own account (Sher-Gil 2002) her work in the Paris period was entirely Western in substance and style.

But then she chose to return to India because she felt that her destiny as an artist lay in India. And there was something else. In Paris she was one of many gifted artists embedded in a vibrant network of painting styles and movements. She was in a world inhabited by the likes of Matisse and Picasso, André Breton and the Surrealists, the abstract art of Joan Miro, and the afterglow of the Post-Impressionists. But she wanted to make history, and to do that in Paris, in Europe, in the West, meant the invention of a painterly style within the European tradition, yet one that would stand apart from all else. But she had no desire to be labeled "Cézannesque" or "Gaughinesque." When one of her pictures was exhibited in the Grand Salon in 1933, one of her professors compared her to Gustav Courbet. She acknowledged the compliment but she had no desire to paint like Courbet. *She had* to *be herself.* Her decision to return to India facilitated this aspiration, this superneed to be original. For her, India was *terra incognita* as far as painting was concerned, a vast empty canvas at her disposal to be filled by her as she pleased. And only *she* had ownership of this canvas: witness her brazen statement in 1938: "Europe belongs to Picasso, Matisse and many others, India belongs only to me" (Sher-Gil 1936). By 1935, within a year of her return to India from Paris, she had produced four paintings that proclaimed her new style, her invention of what would become the quintessential Sher-Gil style.

4

A COGNITIVE *PAS DE DEUX*

I   A special case of C-creativity

This book rests on the proposition that to be creative is to make history. A particularly long-ranging way of making history is, as we have discussed, when the artificer is C-creative: she creates an artifact that is epistemically consequential in the creation of later artifacts.

But there is yet another, more powerful, way in which C-creativity may be manifest: in its cognitive effect on (both peer and lay) *consumers* who are not necessarily serving as judges.

Consider the following experiences: I read W.B. Yeats's poem "He Wishes for the Cloths of Heaven"; I listen to the first movement of Beethoven's Sixth Symphony; I watch Satyajit Ray's film *Charulata*; I view Botticelli's *Primavera*.

The point is this. Whether I undergo these experiences, once, twice or a dozen times, *I never fail to experience a strong emotion of some kind*. Indeed, it seems that I repeatedly seek these experiences in order to evoke these emotions. The emotions may differ from one experience to another—from reading Yeats's poem to listening to Beethoven's Sixth to looking at the Botticelli to watching the Ray film. But in all cases, the artifact in question affects my state of mind. So here is a different scenario to the one we considered in the previous chapter.

There is an artificer who experiences a state of mind we will call her *goal state*: a need, desire or want. In response to this goal state she brings into existence an artifact intended to satisfy her goal state. This in turn leads to the artificer experiencing another mental state we will call the *artificer's response state*. This total act—from goal state to artifact production to response state—constitutes the act of production. There is also a consumer who experiences a mental state in response to the artifact. We call this the *consumer's response state*. The act itself—from perceiving the artifact to experiencing a response state—constitutes the act of consumption.

These two acts, that of production and of consumption, may engage with each other in a certain way as follows:

> A *creative encounter* occurs between artificer and consumer in the event the consumer *identifies* with the artificer in the sense, and to the extent, the consumer believes her response state is identical to the artificer's response state.

Here I have borrowed the idea of "identification" from psychoanalytic theory—according to which "identification" is a process whereby one adopts the behavior or mentality of someone else (Brenner 1974).

In other words, the consumer is not a judge of the artificer as we have stated in the preceding chapter. Rather, creativity is the outcome of a kind of interactive phenomenon we will call the creative encounter between artificer and consumer by way of the produced artifact. This encounter not only entails the artificer's own capacity to transform his goal state into an artifact in response to that state but to do this in a way that the resulting artifact evokes in the consumer a response state which the consumer *believes* is identical to the artificer's response state. *The artificer's creativity lies in her capacity to evoke in a consumer such a response state*; one in which the latter identifies with the former. The artificer's creativity lies in its consequences for one or more consumers' state of mind. It is in this sense that the creative encounter is a manifestation of C-creativity.

Creativity, in this scenario, engages both artificer and consumer as actors. It suggests that creativity entails a *private relationship* between the two, that they are engaged in a kind of cognitive *pas de deux*.

This idea of the creative encounter, if not the term, is a known theme in the realm of the psychology and philosophy of art. Thus the psychoanalyst Ernst Kris (1952) wrote that the study of art entails the study of communication in which a sender sends a message to one or more receivers (p. 16). Another psychoanalyst, Daniel Schneider (1962) spoke of the artist inducing, through his art, the viewer to identify with the artist (pp. 85–86). And philosopher of art Richard Wollheim (1987) described the meaning of a picture being determined by the mental state of the artist, and the mental state evoked by the picture in the viewer (p. 22).

The psychologist Rollo May (1994, pp. 77 *et seq*) actually used the term "creative encounter," especially in the context of art, but with a different meaning. For May, the encounter is between the artificer and some particular experience in the world that leads her to create. He speaks for instance of an encounter between a painter and the "objective reality" of a tree which leads the painter to paint the tree in a particular way; the consumer, in May's formulation, enters the situation *after* this encounter is over: he is privileged to experience the picture resulting from the earlier encounter.

But the creative encounter idea as I have suggested (and along the lines articulated by Schneider and Wollheim) need not be restricted to the realm of art, though it certainly seems specially relevant to art and literature. For instance, the present author deployed it in a study of a creative movement in nineteenth century India called the Bengal Renaissance (Dasgupta 2007). In particular circumstances (as we will see) it can inform our understanding of creativity in science, engineering and scholarship.

Let us consider the ingredients of the creative encounter—the elements of this *pas de deux* in more detail.

II The act of production as a cognitive act

We begin by expanding and framing the act of production in cognitive terms. It begins in a goal state identified or felt by the artificer as a result of some experience or emotion. For example, a scientist feels the need to *satisfy his curiosity* about some novel or unexpected physical phenomenon; a poet feels the need to *respond* to the melancholic sight of an abandoned village; a painter enchanted by the vista of sunlight reflected on the ocean surface wishes *to express his emotion* in paint; a technological inventor dissatisfied by the performance of a particular machine *seeks to improve* its design; a novelist feeling nostalgic about her childhood *desires to capture* her past by writing a story that captures aspects of that childhood.

Acts of production originate in such goal states. The act itself results in an actual artifact intended to satisfy this state of mind that in turn leads to the artificer's experience of a response state. That is, the artificer behaves according to the principle of rationality but constrained by the reality of bounded rationality (see Chapter 1, IV). Thus, when the scientist arrives at an explanation for a puzzling phenomenon, or the poet composes a poem, or the painter paints a landscape, or the inventor designs and builds a new machine, or the writer writes a novel—in each case there is an artificer's response state. For the scientist it may be the conviction that his theory or hypothesis correctly explains the phenomenon of interest. For the artist it may be a hybrid of aesthetic pleasure and the release of tension at having expressed her emotion. And so on.

For this act of production to have any chance of becoming an act of creation the artificer must imagine a "target" consumer *other than herself* and identify with that consumer. In performing her act of production she is as much this hypothetical target consumer as the producer.

Of course, the artificer may well be totally solipsistic: she eschews any consumer other than herself. She produces for herself—in which case *there is no possibility of a creative encounter*, merely an act of production. It is also possible for a creative encounter to occur without the artificer intending it to happen. For instance, according to the psychiatrist Albert Rothenberg (1990) the poet Emily Dickinson, who never made public her poems, appeared to have written poetry for herself as the reader (p. 79). Yet within years off her passing, when her poetry was published, the response of the poetry-reading public (the consumers' collective response) was huge. Hers was a case where the creative encounter emerged long after her acts of production had occurred; this is how C-creativity may often happen.

The *schizoid* personality, according to psychiatrist Anthony Storr (1972) is prominently characterized by detachment and self-sufficiency. The schizoid being avoids intimacy and emotional involvement. He is introverted and concerned with his own inner world rather than his social environment. Storr's archetype of the schizoid character was Albert Einstein and there is much biographical and anecdotal evidence in support of this view. Einstein's detachment is widely documented in the "Einstein literature"—as, e.g., in Philip Frank's (1965) biography.

One would suppose that the creative schizoid being can engage in acts of production but with scant concern for a creative encounter with any consumer other than himself. Yet even Einstein sought consumers for his ideas. He discussed physics with colleagues, he wrote up his ideas as papers and sent them for publication, he wrote books. If Storr was correct Einstein may well have possessed a schizoid personality but he nonetheless sought and actively engaged in creative encounters.

Not every act of production, of course, leads to a creative encounter. In the worst possible scenario, if I paint a picture or write a poem that appears to have no effect on *anyone* (other than on me or my idealized, imaginary consumer) there *is* no creative encounter.

III   The consumer's responsive sensibility

An act of consumption ends in a consumer's responsive state. The same artifact might induce one consumer to identify with the artificer, yet have no effect on another consumer. In the former case a creative encounter occurs, in the latter it does not.

To participate in a creative encounter, however, a consumer must have the *capacity* to respond to a produced artifact. In the particular realms of art, literature, music and even mathematics, and sometimes natural science, she must possess a certain *responsive sensibility*. In the realm of painting Richard Wollheim (1987) used the term "expressive perception"—meaning our capacity to see a painting as expressing a certain kind of feeling (p. 80). This is an instance of what I mean by the consumer's responsive sensibility. The art historian E.H. Gombrich (1969) used the phrase "the beholder's share" to mean something similar: the viewer of a painting has a role to play in the reading of an image (p. 182). And philosopher Noël Carroll (2014) has emphasized the reader's "constructive imagination"—the capacity the reader must bring to bear to a work of fiction (pp. 75–76, 80). For all these writers, the consumer's contribution is as vital as that of the artificer to make meaning of the artifact.

We have noted (in Chapter 3, V) that to judge an artifact's originality the consumer must have the requisite *knowledge*. This knowledge—as well as *imagination*—is necessary for the consumer's possession of a responsive sensibility to, say, a mathematical, scientific or technological artifact. The computer pioneer Maurice Wilkes, designer and lead builder of the world's first fully operational stored program computer in 1949 (this history is told in Dasgupta 2014a, pp. 115–126), has recorded in his memoir his immediate reaction to the celebrated memorandum written by John von Neumann on the idea of the stored program computer. He immediately recognized that the principles laid out by von Neumann were "the real thing" and his own subsequent design followed along these lines (Wilkes 1986, pp. 108–109). This was responsive sensibility at work in a technological realm, a sensibility that was rooted in Wilkes's knowledge, intuition and imagination. It was a particularly fateful creative encounter between Wilkes the consumer and von Neumann the artificer by way of a set of principles of design, an abstract artifact.

Of course, not all responses are equal in strength. Some may be fleeting, others may linger appreciably, or are so strong that they become a part of the consumer's memory. This is especially true when the artifact happens to be *transient*, as an actor's or a musician's performance is, and the consumer happens to be a member of the audience (see Chapter 2, VIII). There is then a *depth* and *duration* of the creative encounter that can vary widely across acts of production and consumption.

IV The consumer's identification with the artificer

As indicated earlier, it is not enough for the consumer to respond to an artifact in any old way. For a creative encounter to occur the response must be such that the consumer identifies with the artificer.

Such identification will demand that the consumer believes that *her* response to the artifact is identical to a greater or lesser extent to what she believes the artificer's response state is to that artifact. When I read Yeats's poem "He Wishes for the Cloths of Heaven" I experience a certain emotion; that is my response state. And I identify with Yeats in that I believe that Yeats must have responded similarly to the poem; more importantly it was his goal to *induce* in his reader such an emotion. This is the creative encounter between Yeats the artificer in 1899 and myself, a twenty-first century consumer. And Yeats's creativity in composing this poem lay in *his ability to evoke in me the emotion I experience* whenever I read the poem. In the realm of art, Ernst Kris spoke of the spectator (the consumer) *recreating* a work of art in his mind in a manner bearing some similarity to the artist's experience (Kris 1952, p. 59). For a creative encounter to occur the consumer has also to give some effort. Of course, except under exceptional circumstances the consumer can never really *know* the process experienced by the artificer. (A substantial reason for this is that the process itself may have been occurred in the *unconscious*—an issue we will consider later in this book.) She may at best construct a *plausible* account of the process.

Of course, identification is not a binary quality, not something that "is" or "is not"; it can *vary* in extent or depth, depending on the nature of the mediating artifact, on the consumer's responsive sensibility, and on the nature, quality and depth of her actual response. Furthermore, the quality of the creative encounter may vary with *time*: a consumer's response to an artifact may well *change* over time, in which case the quality or intensity of the creative encounter can vary with time. A listener's response to a new musical composition, a viewer's response to a new film, a critic's response to a new novel may metamorphose from an initial indifference (a case of a "null" creative encounter) to one of profound comprehension of, and at one with, what the artificer was intending. Or conversely, what was once a creative encounter may fade away with time.

In the case of Picasso's *Demoiselles d'Avignon* (mentioned in Chapter 3, IV), as we noted, Matisse evidently responded to the painting, but his response state was surely not one that led him to identify with Picasso. We cannot say that Picasso and Matisse in this particular instance engaged in a creative encounter. In contrast André Breton spoke of the paintings as "a sacred image" and wrote that one can only speak of it in a "mystical manner" (Seckel 1994, pp. 213 *et seq*). We do not know whether Picasso actually felt the way Breton did or whether he projected such emotions onto his imaginary target viewer as he went about this work. But we can plausibly claim that Breton held some belief that Picasso's *intention* in painting this picture—his goal state—reflected this kind of emotion, and that he also believed that the painting did indeed satisfy this intention. There was an unmistakable creative encounter between Breton and Picasso over *Les Demoiselles d'Avignon* just as surely there was no such encounter between Matisse and Picasso.

The relationship between W.B. Yeats and the poet, philosopher and composer Rabindranath Tagore offers a particularly striking example of the creative encounter, in this case between two future Nobel laureates. Here, Tagore was the artificer and Yeats the consumer. The artifact was a collection of Tagore's English prose translations of his own poems written in Bangla, his native language (Tagore was an Indian Bengali). Tagore called this English collection *Gitanjali* (*Song Offerings*), which was first published in 1912 in limited edition (Tagore 1912). A year later he was awarded the Nobel Prize for literature for this work. He was Asia's first Nobel laureate.

Yeats first came upon *Gitanjali* when a mutual friend (the artist William Rothenstein) sent him the typed manuscript of the English translation in June 1912. Yeats would write of the emotion these prose poems evoked in him, as he read them everywhere, on the train, in restaurants, on buses (Yeats 1912, p. vii). It was not so much their "strangeness" that moved him but rather that it was as if he was encountering in literature, perhaps for the first time, "our voice as in a dream" (pp. xii–xiii).

We have here a profound record of a creative encounter, between two exceptional poets. Tagore's act of creation lay in his power to evoke such emotion in Yeats through the poems of *Gitanjali*; yet no such power would have succeeded without Yeats's responsive sensibility that accorded within him his emotional response to the poems. Yeats was very much a peer consumer and this no doubt made a difference. This *emotional* identification of the poet–consumer with the poet–artificer was unequivocal, as Yeats confessed.

V   The role of originality in the creative encounter

While originality may not be the *sine qua non* of creativity in the realm of the creative encounter, the *desire to be original* is undoubtedly one of the dominant goal states characterizing the act of production. We have noted (in Chapter 3, XVII) the artificer's compelling superneed to separate himself from the past—and (paraphrasing Howard Gruber (1989, p. 8)), add to the sum of human knowledge: *to make history*.

To take an example, the polymath scientist Herbert Simon began a lifetime in research in the social, behavioral and computer sciences with a desire to write a doctoral dissertation on the "[l]ogical structure of a science of administration" that would be concerned as much with the logical structure in Newton's *Principia* and Aristotle's *Ethics*, and with economic price theory as with the logic of administrative science (Simon 1937).

This was a breathtakingly ambitious dissertation project (he was then a graduate student in political science in the University of Chicago). We might shrug it off as the voice of youth if we did not know how his future career would embrace with spectacular success this early desire for a multidisciplinary intellectual life (Dasgupta 2003a, 2003b). In any case, his announced choice of a research topic leaves one in no doubt that here was a mind which sought to do something no one had done before; he desired, at the very least, to be H-original.

As another example, consider the late twentieth century artist George Rodrigue (mentioned in Chapter 3, VIII) who is best known for his "blue dog" paintings and prints. In America, following the Second World War, there had emerged a succession of artistic styles and outlooks. They included Abstract Expressionism in which the emphasis was on the spontaneous freedom of expression, often by way of non-representational shapes and forms, and Pop Art, a prominent feature of which was the use of hard edges and near-photographic techniques.

Rodrigue received his training in the Art Center College of Design in Los Angeles in such an artistic milieu. But when he returned from Los Angeles to South Louisiana, his birthplace, he knew what he would *not* paint. He would *not* pursue the styles of either Abstract Expressionism or Pop Art, for he felt he could not contribute anything new by painting in these styles. Rather, he said, "my own direction must go elsewhere, lest it appear I could not find my original way" (audiotaped interview by this writer of George Rodrigue, September 30, 2002). The similarity with Amrita Sher-Gil's determination to forge her own style (mentioned in Chapter 3, XVII) is striking.

VI   Aesthetics as a factor in the creative encounter

Desire for originality is one vital factor entering into the artificer's goal state, but it is not the only one. *Aesthetics* is another.

We have already touched on the place of aesthetics in creativity (Chapter 2, X). As a source of emotion, both in artificer and consumer, aesthetics is present not only in the realms of art, music, film and literature but also in science and even technology. In all spheres of the creative tradition we find, repeatedly, the act of production being driven, sometimes consciously but as often unconsciously, by the desire, the *need*, to create something beautiful. Aesthetic pleasure and the desire to experience it and invoke it in the consumer, thus, very often constitute an artificer's goal state. Conversely, the consumer's response itself may be dictated by an aesthetic sensibility and taste, elements of her responsive sensibility.

Among mathematicians, Henri Poincaré (1985), G.H. Hardy (1969) and Jacques Hadamard (1954) have all written on the place of aesthetics in mathematical discovery, as has artificial intelligence (AI) pioneer Seymour Papert (1978) who has empirically studied the nature of mathematical thinking in both adults and children. For Hardy, in particular, beauty—the harmonious fitting together into a pattern—is the litmus test of the validity of a mathematical theorem or proof (p. 85). Such beauty was not just a matter of *form*. It also demanded, Hardy insisted, *seriousness* of the theorem or proof (p. 90).

Poincaré famously made the point that what distinguishes the mathematical mind from other kinds of minds is the presence in the former of an "aesthetic" mathematical sensibility which others may not possess (Poincaré 1985, p. 29). The elements of "mathematical aesthetics" include the "harmony" of numbers, and geometrical elegance. Hadamard, echoing Poincaré, writes that "the intervention of the sense of beauty" plays an essential role in the act of mathematical discovery itself (p. 31).

Very recently, science writer David Stipp (2017) has devoted an entire book to exploring the aesthetic nature of mathematics and, in particular, the mathematicians' perennial search for beauty in mathematical solutions. His principal protagonist was the eighteenth century mathematician Leonhard Euler and his discovery of the equation known as Euler's formula which relates the quantities e, pi, and the imaginary number i by the equation $e^{**} (pi^*i) + 1 = 0$.

The computer scientist Donald Knuth is a particularly well-known proponent of what we might call the "programming aesthetic." He wrote of computer programming as an art form (Knuth 1992a). Programming should be aesthetically satisfying; programs should be beautiful. The experience of writing a program should be akin to composing poetry or music. Toward this end he proposed that programs should be *works of literature*, that one gains pleasure in writing them so that others may gain pleasure in reading them as a form of literature. He called this philosophy "literate programming" (Knuth 1992b). Practicing what he preached, Knuth designed and implemented a remarkable digital typesetting system (consisting of two programs called TEX and METAFONT), which were written as literate programs and published as a series of books under the collective title *Computers and Typesetting* (Knuth 1986). As it happened TEX and METAFONT were highly consequential in the domain of mathematical typesetting (thus C-original). More strikingly, the volumes of *Computers and Typesetting* were collectively a "literary" artifact which Knuth the artificer created with the intention of evoking in its readers (consumers) a certain kind of aesthetic response.

The history of utilitarian material artifacts—physical technology—reveals a very definite tendency on the part of those who invent, design and make useful things to be driven by desires or goals that are unmistakably aesthetic in nature (Pye 1978; Billington 1983). Of course, one might argue that bridges, buildings, automobiles and the artifacts produced by industrial designers are intended to *be* beautiful (as well as practical), whereas in other technological domains the aim of invention is strictly utility and economy. Yet even in severely technical and practical domains, aesthetics can serve as a compelling source of the inventor–engineer's goal state. A striking example from the history of computers is the invention by Maurice Wilkes (in 1951) of a method of designing the control unit of a computer. This method is called microprogramming (Wilkes 1986). Wilkes has recorded that he was led to this invention by a very personal perspective that valued regularity and orderliness—both aesthetic issues. Moreover, his concern with such aesthetics was essentially a *private* problem (M.V. Wilkes, in an interview with the author, Cambridge, December 19, 1991). Initially his invention hardly elicited any response from his fellow computer pioneers; as a creative encounter it had to wait for several years (Chapter 3, X).

Finally, we mention aesthetics as a creative force in the natural sciences. Harmony, symmetry, coherence, simplicity and unity are, almost universally, values that arouse feelings of beauty across cultures and worldviews. They constitute what we may call the "natural aesthetic." To the natural scientist, such as the Nobel laureate organic chemist Robert Burns Woodward, whose synthesis of organic compounds was a melding of chemical attributes and structural form into a harmonious whole, these were precisely the attributes forming the essence of physical nature (Woodward 1989). For the physicist–plant biophysicist Jagadis Chandra Bose, his attempts to show how both organic and inorganic matter respond similarly to electrical stimuli were motivated by his idea of *monism*—the principle of unity of all things (Dasgupta 2009). This is an idea that many past thinkers on aesthetics have taken to be a central aesthetic principle (Beardley 1966). The Nobel laureate astrophysicist Subramanium Chandrasekhar (1987) has suggested—in a book called, significantly, *Truth and Beauty: Aesthetics and Motivation in Science*—that elements of the natural aesthetic are values that drive and motivate scientists in their search for understanding physical reality.

VII   Emotions recollected in tranquility

The poet William Wordsworth (1916) famously wrote that poetry is "emotion recollected in tranquility." In fact, emotions—sadness, joy, tranquility, excitement, anger, horror—are as much sources of the artificer's goal state in the realm of literature, music, art, even scholarship, as are feelings induced by aesthetic values or the desire for originality. Likewise, the consumer's identification with the artificer, and the completion of a creative encounter between the two often demand the consumer to *emotionally* identify with the artificer. The biographical, autobiographical and critical literature on poets, musicians and artists are rich in evidence of the variety of emotions that serve as elements of the artificer's goal state. Psychologist and musicologist Rosamund Harding (1942) cited many instances of this. Thus when W.B. Yeats was asked about the impulse that gave rise to his poems he replied that his poems all began in some emotional experience, in some moment of "personal excitement" (quoted, p. 65). And in a statement strikingly Wordsworthian, the Russian composer Pyotr Tchaikovsky noted that the composer, like all artists, is moved by some emotion but expresses his feelings not at that moment but *retrospectively* (p. 72).

VIII   Fluidity of the creative encounter

The principle of the creative encounter leaves ample scope for *disagreement* and *controversy* about the act of creation. There is always room for critical argument.

This raises a question. The same act of production may elicit quite different response states in different consumers. In some cases there may be no evidence of a creative encounter at all; in other cases the creative encounter may be muted; in still other situations, it may be very strong. *Apropos* the latter two situations should we take all creative encounters to be equally valid? *Not necessarily.* For example, the consumer's identification with an artificer may be based on false assumptions about the act of production itself, or it may be rooted in wrong reasoning on the consumer's part, or in his incomplete knowledge; on a kind of "false consciousness." But, in some situations, it may be possible to *test* the validity of a creative encounter.

An example of this was an act of production by Jagadis Chandra Bose (mentioned earlier), India's first "modern" scientist. Between 1894 and 1900 Bose was studying the optical properties of millimeter-length radio waves and in the course of this work he invented a radio wave receiver (called at the time a "coherer").

Even in his lifetime it was believed by some of his compatriots that this invention by Bose was "appropriated" and utilized (without acknowledgment) by the radio pioneer Guigielmo Marconi in his first historic transatlantic radio transmission of 1901; and that Bose never received the credit rightfully due to him. Almost a century later this idea was revived by a NASA engineer (Bondyopadhyay 1998). One can claim that the latter engaged in a creative encounter with Bose. However, based on both historical and logical evidence this claim on Bose's behalf was shown to be false (Dasgupta 2009, pp. 250–254); and so that particular creative encounter was, in fact, false.

There is another point worth noting about the fluidity of the creative encounter. A consumer's responsive sensibility may well develop over time. It can be acquired. Responsiveness is at least in part a *cultural trait*. Clearly someone who is tone deaf is unlikely to ever overcome this cognitive deficiency but a "normal," sensitive listener from an Eastern culture (such as India) who is initially quite unresponsive to Western classical music can gradually learn to respond to it. Thus, her responsive sensibility to a Mozart concerto (say) or a Verdi opera may well *develop* over time.

Here lies yet another aspect of the fluidity of the creative encounter. The latter demands hard work on the part of the consumer as it more evidently does on the part of the artificer. Creative encounters may be deep or shallow and the depth is certainly dependent on the knowledge, sensibility, responsiveness and the amount of mental effort the consumer brings to the act of consumption. The viewer who "knows something about art," the listener who is musically trained, the reader who is poetically sensitive, the moviegoer who understands something about the nuances of filmmaking—their creative encounters with artificers will likely be deeper than for those who are subaltern consumers.

IX   Genetical potential and cultural development

Whether an artificer is deemed creative by virtue of being judged so because of the historical originality of her artifacts or because her artifacts result in a creative encounter with consumers, the idea held by some that creativity is an innate trait of some people—that some artists, musicians, mathematicians, inventors, for example, are "born creative"—is seriously challenged. For someone to *be* creative there must be an act of creation; so to claim that such-an-such person is "born creative" is an unwarranted assumption.

A person may, of course, be genetically endowed with a *potential* for creativity. Reviewing the literature on the genetics of creativity neuropsychologists Baptiste Barbot, Mei Tan and Elena Grigorenko (2013) have pointed to a significant body of evidence indicating that intelligence is highly heritable—though no specific genes have been definitively linked with intelligence. Rather, the evidence suggests that multiple genes additively influence intelligence (p. 73). And the creativity-related cognitive attribute commonly called *divergent thinking*—the ability to explore a problem situation along different directions and postulate possible solutions that differ from one another (Csikszentmihalyi 1996, pp. 368–369)—has also been linked with certain genetic features (Barbot, Tan and Grigorenko 2013, p. 74). There is also evidence that certain creativity-related personality traits have genetical roots. For instance, Barbot et al. have noted that *novelty-seeking*—a trait which we can associate with the superneed to be original (see Chapter 3, XVII), which Howard Gruber (1989) called "deviation-amplification"—has been linked with the action of the neurotransmitter dopamine whose transmission is associated with specific genes (p. 75).

But just as we accept, based on empirical evidence, that the mind *develops* by way of *cultural* means, as cognitive scientist Michael Tomasello (1999) has forcefully argued, so also there is nothing startling in the idea that an individual's potential for creativity may *develop* by way of cultural forces, for example by way of observing, imitating or learning. Of course, there may be a wide variation in the nature and rate of this deployment process, and so we have "early developers" (of whom child prodigies are extreme exemplars) or "late developers."

At the same time to speak of "development" suggests development *toward* something—some adult or mature form, as biological development connotes. Does a person's potential for creativity develop toward such a mature form? Probably. One cannot be creative unless one's potential for creativity has developed to some level of maturity.

How do we know when the potential for creativity has reached maturation? As the saying goes, the proof of the pudding lies in the eating: simply when the artificer is observed or judged to *be* creative; when, for example he is judged as H-creative, C-creative or A-creative; or when he is observed, as a special case of C-creativity, to engage with one or more consumers in creative encounters.

It is important, here, to not confuse the development of one's creative potential with what creativity researcher and management theorist Jonathan Feinstein (2006) called *creative development*. If I have understood him correctly, his notion of creative development refers to the actual *processes* by which artificers produce artifacts deemed original.

5

KNOWLEDGE SCHEMAS IN CREATIVE THOUGHT

I   The case of the Greek–Lebanese restaurant

Consider the following scenario. Driving into a new city and realizing I'm hungry I search for a restaurant. Eventually I come upon a place that announces itself as offering "Greek–Lebanese" cuisine. If I have never experienced Greek–Lebanese food I may hesitate. I have received a piece of *information* that I cannot put to use. I don't *know* what this kind of food is like. On the other hand the very word "Greek" may cause a certain set of impressions to surface in my conscious mind. For example, an image of a very blue Mediterranean Sea, white sundrenched houses, the Acropolis, the names of Plato and Aristotle, *The Republic*, Euclid, the Olympic Games, Raphael's fresco *The School of Athens*....

On the other hand, if I've eaten Middle Eastern food before an entirely different set of impressions may surface in my consciousness: images of kabobs and chicken shawarma, grapeleaves, hummus and babaganouche, tabuli salad and pita bread; recollections of their tastes; image of tearing pieces of pita bread and using them to scoop up chunks of hummus....

Regardless of whether I've eaten "Greek–Lebanese" food or not, the sign that here is a restaurant may also precipitate in my conscious mind a certain kind of *narrative*:

> There will be small tables with chairs or booths with benches. I will be ushered to a table. I'll be shown a menu by a waiter. There will be silverware and napkins lid out on the table. The server will take my order, and soon after I will get my food and drink.

The sign at the front of the restaurant proclaiming it as a "Greek–Lebanese" restaurant is a piece of information that *triggered* these separate sets of facts, images, events, stories, rules and remembered sense impressions. Each such set (whether of Greece or of Middle Eastern food or of a restaurant) is an integrated entity that defines a set of particular *prototypical concepts*. One is a certain concept of Greece, another of Middle Eastern food, a third of a restaurant.

In fact, these concepts constitute fragments of larger *symbol structures* that form my personal *knowledge* of Greece, Middle Eastern food and restaurants, respectively. As knowledge they are constituted of pieces of information; but the power of knowledge is vastly more than the power of information, for my knowledge of these matters promotes certain expectations about the experience of eating such food or being in a restaurant; this knowledge facilitates certain predictions and certain kinds of inferences I can make about this particular cuisine and this particular restaurant. (For example, that the food will not be spicy and will be relatively healthy; or that this restaurant will be playing Middle Eastern music; and that it will *not* be playing Bollywood songs, or rap or R&B.)

We do not think with information per se. They are, so to speak, building blocks that we integrate into new conceptual structures, or assimilate into existing conceptual structures, and it is these structures that become the knowledge that enters into thinking.

II Schemas and schema theory

Cognitive scientists have another term for such complex conceptual symbol structures that represent a restaurant, Middle Eastern cuisine or Greece. They call them *schemas* (or *schemata*).

Although the idea of a schema can be traced back to at least Immanuel Kant, the modern psychological notion is usually attributed to the British psychologist Frederick Bartlett's (1932) classic work *Remembering*. Bartlett himself admitted that his source for the notion was his mentor Henry Head but that he shaped it to his own purpose (pp. 198–200).

By "schema" Bartlett meant an organized structure of past experiences which a person brings to bear in any given situation (p. 201). This notion has been adopted in more recent times by certain psychologists and computer scientists into a "schema theory" (also called "frame theory"). However, I should caution that there is no unequivocally accepted, universal schema theory. People concerned with the workings of the mind seem to be in agreement on the general concept of the schema and its place in thinking, but their interpretations are not identical.

For Bartlett, as we have just seen, a schema is an organization of past experiences that participate in responding to a new situation. Thus the responses of my imaginary self in the Greek–Lebanese restaurant scenario above. For the Swiss development psychologist Jean Piaget (1976), in describing the cognitive development of children a schema (or *scheme* as he preferred to call it), is a kind of "general structure" for some action which can be applied to situations that vary under environmental conditions; moreover, a new experience is assimilated into an existing schema thus enlarging or enriching the latter (p. 66). Piaget goes on to explain that when confronted with an object never seen before a child will attempt to *assimilate* it into his or her available stock of schemas (p. 114). Anyone who has watched a child trying to construct something with toy building blocks will understand what Piaget meant.

In more recent decades the construction of schemas by small children very early in their cognitive development has been further studied by psychologists and linguists. The development psychologist Margaret Donaldson (1992) has noted that schematic representation presents no problem for children of three or more. She cited as an example a study carried out by another investigator in which children aged between three and seven, given paper and pencil and shown a number of bricks, were asked to put down on paper "something" to indicate how many bricks there were. About a third of the three- and four-year olds used some distinct mark, usually a simple line, to represent each brick (p. 128). Here, Donaldson was pointing to the children's ability to abstract from the individuality of things to a schematic representation (p. 127).

Cognitive scientist Michael Tomasello (1999) has discussed extensively the role of schemas in language development in children. Children, he tells us, build abstract linguistic constructs from the actual utterances they hear (p. 135). These abstract constructs are initially simple schemas. He describes a study of his own daughter's language development in which he found simple schemas involving verbs (p. 138). For example, using the verb *Draw* his daughter constructed a number of schemas such as "*Draw* —-," "*Draw*—*on* —-," and so on. He offered what he called the "verb island hypothesis" which claimed that children's early linguistic competence entails the construction of such schemas that are filled in or *instantiated* in individual cases (p. 139).

Psychologist George Mandler (1985) saw schemas as organizations of experience (*à la* Bartlett) that may be as concrete as the representation of a particular object (e.g., the interior of a favorite café) or as broad as the representation of a general concept (such as that we call "restaurant"). Moreover, according to Mandler, schemas are *hierarchically* organized: my restaurant schema has as *subschemas* representations of different kinds of restaurants ("posh" ones, diners, fast food places, etc.) and any one of these subschemas may have as subschemas representations of particular restaurants I may be familiar with. Conversely, perceiving a particular chair will not only activate in one's mind the "chair schema" but also more general *superschemas* such as "furniture schema" (pp. 36–38).

Cognitive/brain/computer scientist Michael Arbib and philosopher of science Mary Hesse situated schema theory as the "heart" of cognitive science (Arbib and Hesse 1986, p. 13). Partly influenced by Piaget they suggested that *all* cognitive phenomena involve activations of schemas (p. 13).

They made the important distinction between *synchronic* and *diachronic* schemas. The former refers to situations at any particular point of time, when an individual mind holds in long-term memory a stock of schemas that collectively form the individual's beliefs and knowledge: a "snapshot" as it were of the *state* of the individual's beliefs and knowledge at any moment of time. The term "diachronic" refers to the fact that one's assemblage of schemas change over time—a representation of the succession of states of one's beliefs and knowledge across some time duration. (This corresponds to the presence of historicity discussed in the Chapter 1, IV in the form of temporally variant versions of a person's past belief/knowledge space coexisting with current beliefs and knowledge.)

Artificial intelligence (AI) pioneer Marvin Minsky in a highly influential paper called "A Framework for Representing Knowledge" (1975) imported the language of computer science into this discussion. He adopted Bartlett's concept but described schemas as elaborate *data structures*—a precise concept in computer science, meaning the ways of representing data objects in computer memory. He called these data structures *frames*—a "remembered framework" which is summoned to consciousness in response to a new situation or experience and then appropriately adapted to fit the given experience (p. 212).

Like Mandler, Minsky viewed schemas as hierarchically organized and linked together to form schema (or frame) *systems* (p. 218). Consider the following example:

> I am presently writing these words with a Mont Blanc fountain pen. I claim to possess a hierarchical schema system for my beliefs and knowledge concerning this kind of object. At the highest, most general level, my schema represents the general nature of all fountain pens: their form or shape, their main components (top, body, nib, clip), how they are used, what to do when the ink runs out (unscrew the nib part from the rest of the body, remove the cartridge, insert a new cartridge), what action to take if the ink does not flow smoothly (shake the pen).

That part of the schema describing what to do when the ink runs out may be the "default" description, since most times this is what one should do. But it is possible that I may have an alternative to this procedure in my fountain pen schema since the ink can also be held in long tubes, siphoned from ink bottles. If I have this alternative element in my fountain pen schema then on encountering such a pen I won't be unduly surprised. In fact, for a person of a certain age this siphon mechanism would be the default in an older version of the fountain pen schema that I certainly once held, though the "current" schema will show the cartridge principle. Both versions will be present in a diachronic representation of my fountain pen schema.

At a lower level there are subschemas corresponding to my experiences with a number of different brands of fountain pens I happen to currently own and use. The subschemas are *instantiations* of the top-level schema, for they represent actual forms and colors and characteristics of the nibs (fine, medium) of each pen. These subschemas also contain representations of their respective idiosyncrasies that cause me to change, however slightly and subtly, my writing mode and my expectations if and when I change pens.

Finally, when I'm using a particular pen (as I now am) it becomes *an extension of my body*; a part of what psychologist Ulrich Neisser (1988) called the "ecological self." The schema representing my *self-knowledge* is, thus, *linked* to my fountain pen schema whenever I am using a pen.

We may add to the various interpretations of the schema concept mentioned above others offered not only by experimental psychologists (Alba and Hasher 1983) but also computationally influenced cognitive scientists (Holland, Holyoak, Nisbett and Thagard 1986, pp. 12–13, 287–319), anthropologists (D'Andrade 1995, pp. 122–149), and even literary scholars (Holland 1989; Turner 1996).

An especially striking schema-based hypothesis about how humans come to interpret a piece of text was advanced by linguist Charles Fillimore (1975). He suggested that in reading a text, the reader first creates a partial schema with many unfilled "slots." Further reading of the text helps in filling in the slots, thereby adding details to this "world picture." In the course of this process expectations are built up which are later either "fulfilled or thwarted," and so it goes (quoted by D'Andrade 1995, p. 123).

Clearly, schemas have appealed to a wide range of investigators in a variety of disciplines whose common interest is the mind. Yet, as is obvious, their interpretations are not identical; rather they bear a family resemblance. It is then more appropriate to view schema theory as a *meta-theory*—a schema as it were for interpreting specific schema theories—Bartlett's, Piaget's, Minsky's, Arbib and Hesse's, Mandler's and so on.

III Everyday schemas

Regardless of their respective perspectives, schema theorists generally agree that human beings are constantly constructing, using, instantiating and modifying their mental stock of schemas which, as symbol structures holding their beliefs and knowledge, facilitate their living, making sense of, and acting in, the everyday world. We may call these *everyday schemas*. My fountain pen schema is an example. The restaurant schema (with a Middle Eastern food subschema) is another.

Of course, in everyday life, under benign circumstances we do not *consciously* think we are using schemas. Under normal circumstances schemas become part of what cognitive scientists call the *cognitive unconscious* (Kihlstrom 1987). It is only under abnormal or disruptive situations or (to borrow from W.B. Yeats) when things fall apart that we become aware of the schematic nature of our thoughts, perceptions, beliefs, knowledge and procedures.

Let me use, as an example, the use of a hammer. Computer scientist Terry Winograd and social theorist Fernando Flores (influenced by philosopher Martin Heidegger) noted that when one is hammering the hammer is not recognized as an independent entity. It is part of the "readiness-to-hand" background, taken for granted, an element of the "hammerer's world" as integral to it as is the hammerer's arm. The hammerer only becomes conscious of the hammer *as a hammer* when there is a breakdown of some sort. When it becomes "unready-to-hand," for example, when the head becomes loose or the tool slips from one's grasp, or is too large (or too small) for the job at hand (Winograd and Flores 1987, p. 36).

A particular hammer conforms to a hammer schema, but as long as it does its job the hammerer loses sight of that schema, just as when I'm writing my fountain pen schema is lost to my consciousness. Under normal circumstances the hammer is just an extension of the hammerer's arm—a part of his ecological self. It is only when a breakdown occurs that its schematic nature surfaces to the hammerer's awareness.

IV Cultural schemas

Certain everyday schemas are of course universal. But others, of more interest to our exploration of creativity, are culture-specific. Weddings may be universal and at a very abstract level all weddings (presumably) follow a shared schema. But wedding ceremonies in detail vary from one religion to another, in fact within a religion from one culture to another. (Among Christians, Catholic and Protestant ceremonies differ. And in India, different Hindu communities from different regions practice differing ceremonies.)

It is then unsurprising that students of culture pay close attention to schemas as an analytical tool in their studies of cultures and societies. Anthropologist Roy D'Andrade (1995), for example, cites several examples of ethnographic studies of Western cultural schemas: the Western "romance schema," the "germ schema" (characterizing American beliefs about illness), including the "folk belief" that exposure to cold weather increases the likelihood of catching cold, schemas characterizing the American concepts of "family" and "friendship," and so on (pp. 124–132). Psychobiologist Henry Plotkin (2003), among those who have attempted to construct relationships between cognition and culture, refers to schemas as structures constituting what psychologists call "semantic memory" and which serve as "mental centers of gravity which attract to themselves particular experiences which they then shape" (p. 175). Plotkin, citing the work of psychologist David Rubin (1995) on the role of memory in oral traditions, writes of schema theory as providing a source of understanding how preliterate cultures might work in preserving and propagating their rituals and beliefs (p. 177) by way of schemas held in memory.

V Plasticity and elasticity of schemas

An important and highly desirable property of schemas for them to be effective is that they are "loose," flexible. They need to be both elastic and plastic so that they may be modified or adapted, often in surprising ways. *Rigid* schemas lead to dogmatic beliefs and prejudiced perceptions, to stereotyped notions that, of course, are sources of cultural misunderstanding and antipathies or, worse, of racial, ethnic and sexual prejudices. (As I write this the Internet is full of reports of a billionaire African-American media celebrity who was refused to be shown a very expensive handbag in a Zurich shop, the shop-assistant telling her that she couldn't afford it. The fact that the shop assistant did not recognize the face is unimportant; what is, is the rigid schema this person held about Black people.)

A far more harmless (and more amusing) example I was witness to was when two American guests attending a Hindu wedding manifested bemusement, even indignation, at what they perceived to be disrespect being shown to the bride and groom at the wedding. Unlike Christian weddings which are highly structured, formal, sequential affairs, Hindu weddings might seem somewhat chaotic to the newcomer, wherein while the religious ritual is in progress guests may choose to socialize, with audible chatter that may even drown the *mantras* chanted by the priest. Hence the two guests' umbrage. Presumably, their wedding schema was plastic enough to be suitably modified by this experience: a subschema would probably have been constructed to accommodate the nature of Hindu weddings.

VI Intellectual schemas

What has all this to do with creativity? Creative people, of course, act, understand and perceive according to their stock of everyday and cultural schemas as everyone else does. But in addition *as creative beings* they invent, borrow from, discover and in general accumulate their own assemblage of schemas that allow them to produce within their particular, specialized domains. I will call these *intellectual schemas*.

When confronted with a new situation, e.g., the desire to write a poem in response to some emotional experience, the artificer *selects one or another of her stored schemas as a starting point*. This is the core of the act of production (and potential act of creation) and later we will see how this might work.

The art historian E.H. Gombrich (1969) related the place of schemas in the realm of art when he wrote of art making as a process of beginning with a schema then gradually "correcting" or modifying it. It is helpful if the starting point selected by the artist is "loose" or even a bit vague or abstract for then it can be easily modified according to the artist's goal. Thus an artificer not only adapts her external stimulus, her situation or goals to a pertinent schema, *she also adapts her schema to her needs or goals*.

The Bengali–Indian filmmaker Satyajit Ray made a strikingly similar observation in a recorded interview with actor Dhritiman Chatterji (personal communication). In searching for a literary work to adapt for the screen, Ray remarked that he much preferred the short story or novella to the novel. The short story or novella, being concise in the way they necessarily are, leaves much more room for instantiating into a film script than does the novel. In Ray's case the short story or novella afforded much more plasticity and elasticity for adaptation than did the novel; they served as more effective schemas.

The *consumer* is also beholden to his repertoire of schemas. When he encounters a new produced artifact, say a novel or a new mathematical theorem, he will attempt to interpret that artifact guided by some relevant schema. His reaction to the artifact will depend on the extent to which he can assimilate the artifact into an existing schema. The hostility that Manet's *Le Déjeuner sur l'herbe* evoked within the Paris Salon jury in 1863 (see Chapter 2, IV) was likely because the jury members' stock of painterly schemas could not be matched against this work or because it seriously violated their shared stock of schemas about artistic subjects and styles. And just as the artificer must adapt her schema to the needs of a goal or need so also the consumer, when engaging with an artifact, may need to adapt one or more of her schemas to the artifact at hand. In general, then, whether artificer or consumer, a person's stock of intellectual schemas will *evolve* over time. Hence the relevance of diachronic schemas.

Philosopher Noël Carroll (2014) has emphasized this aspect of the consumer's role in the realm of fiction: the reader's role. He suggestively calls such consumers "the creative audience," and he postulates that in reading a work of fiction the reader brings to the task, as a "default assumption," a general schema Carroll calls the "realistic heuristic" which will usually work for the reader's understanding of the story but not always, since fiction has the option from deviating from realism (p. 70)—as in fantasy or magical realism fiction.

In such cases the realistic heuristic must be put in abeyance and replaced by some other schema, for example a schema pertaining to the particular genre of fiction—in Carroll's term a "genre heuristic" (pp. 70–71). And if neither the realistic nor the genre heuristic allows the reader to make sense of the fictional work some other schema may be appealed to, for instance a "culture heuristic," a schema pertaining to the cultural background in which the story is set (p. 71). The reader who has never encountered magical realism fiction will not be able to assimilate the novels of Gabriel Garcia Marquez or Salman Rushdie into a "realist heuristic" schema. In fact, one who encounters a magical realist novel for the first time will not possess *any* schema within which such novels as Marquez's *One Hundred Years of Solitude* or Rushdie's *Midnight's Children* can be meaningfully interpreted.

Such situations are faced by both artificer and consumer. There are times when a new experience, situation, need or goal is so seriously at odds with an artificer's stock of schemas, she may have to *restructure* an existing schema or, even more radically, *invent* a new one. We might say that world–historical creativity (H-, C- or A-) occurs when an artificer *invents a new schema*. And to comprehend how artificers' invented schemas are brought into being is to gain insight into the highest level of creativity.

In the case of the first-time reader of magical realist fiction something similar will occur: the reader-as-consumer must construct a new schema around the novel she is reading, just as the Western listener hearing Indian classical music for the first time must invent a new schema around this experience. But once the schema for (say) magical realism is constructed, a new reading of a work of fiction that the reader *knows* to be of this genre will pose no serious problem.

VII   An intellectual schema model

We have noted that the term "schema theory" really means a meta-theory of schemas. We have also just considered the fact that artificers construct and use particular schemas—which I have called "intellectual schemas"—for their own creative ends. At this stage, it might be worthwhile to instantiate the meta-theory and compose an *intellectual schema model* that can serve as an analytical framework for furthering our inquiry into the cognitive–historical nature of creativity.

A schema is a hierarchical structure of beliefs and knowledge and their interrelations that serve as a means of representing in the person's mind some prototypical or archetypal concept. When that person encounters an external stimulus (a new experience or situation or problem) she attempts to respond to it by appealing to an existing schema in her mental schema space. Thereby the schema guides her in responding to the stimulus.

In interpreting and responding to the stimulus with respect to some existing schema some *adjustments* may have to be made to the schema. It may have to be *refined* or *expanded* to assimilate the stimulus without seriously affecting the overall structure of the schema. But there may be occasions when the nature of the stimulus is seriously at odds with one's entire repertoire of schemas, in which case either the closest matching schema may have to be *radically altered* or restuctured or may even necessitate the *invention* of an entirely new schema.

Just as a schema possesses an internal, possibly hierarchical structure so also it may be a component of a larger *superschema* of which it is a *subschema*. Moreover, schemas may be connected in a *non-hierarchical* way, some intimately, others less so forming a *schema network* that occupies the person's memory space. A modification in a schema may have an effect "upwards" (on its containing superschema) or "downward" (on one or more of its constitutive subschemas) or "laterally" (or schemas connected to it non-hierarchically). The lateral effect will be strong or weak depending on how strong the links are between schemas.

When a new schema is invented it will be assimilated into and integrated with the schema network.

We noted earlier George Mandler's distinction between synchronic and diachronic schemas. The former is a *static* entity representing a person's state of beliefs and knowledge of some domain at a particular point in his personal history. The latter is a *dynamic* entity representing the evolution of the person's states of belief and knowledge over some period of his personal history. Thus, a person's intellectual biography will, in some manner, describe her diachronic schema network. In the case of an act of creation synchronic schemas will show the artificer's (and consumer's) states of beliefs and knowledge before and after the creative process. Diachronic schemas will characterize the *process* itself, linking the "before" and "after" states of beliefs and knowledge.

How schemas participate in the dynamic situation will be discussed in a later chapter. For the present let us "flesh in" our picture of synchronous schemas with some examples.

VIII   Inventing a religious schema

All people hold to a belief system concerning God. This is as true for agnostics and atheists as for people of faith. We all tell stories to ourselves (and to others if they care to listen) about God or the absence thereof. The great religious systems of the world and all the innumerable "local" religious belief systems are abstract artifacts, created and evolved by prophets and priests, apostles and disciples, scholars and shamans over the centuries. We each possess a schema (or perhaps a schema system) concerning God and religion.

To take an example from the realms of antiquity and more recent "primitive" societies, the scholar Mircea Eliade (1978) in *The Forge and the Crucible* writes of the mythologies surrounding ancient metallurgy and the rites they gave rise to. Artisans such as those who extract iron from the ores would perform certain rituals in preparation for their task performed in sites considered sacred. These rituals included fasting, meditating, praying and states of cleanliness (p. 56). In other words, these iron workers of old and even of some more recent societies possessed not only schemas representing religo-magical beliefs concerning the ores buried within the Earth–Mother; but also their preparation before going about the task of extracting the iron from the ores entailed certain schemas guided by such beliefs.

To take a completely different example, Albert Einstein lost his belief in the stories told in the Bible. He abandoned his Jewish faith, indeed became indifferent to all religious affiliations at an early age (Jammer 1999, pp. 25–26). But Einstein possessed a belief of a kind concerning God. His God was the seventeenth century Dutch philosopher Baruch Spinoza's God. Not the personal God of the Judeo-Christian tradition but rather a God manifest in the impersonal order in the physical universe. There are no divine laws according to Spinoza, only the laws of nature, and it is these that Spinoza identified as God's will (Armstrong 1993, p. 312). Einstein admired Spinoza and in response to the question of whether he believed in God (posed to him in a telegram, fifty-word, pre-paid, by a New York rabbi), he answered (by return cable) that the God he believed in was Spinoza's God as revealed in the lawful order of nature, and not in a God who engages in the fates of human lives (Jammer 1999, p. 49).

I have strayed into the subject of God and religion for two reasons: one is that religious beliefs/unbeliefs offer examples of cultural, even everyday, schemas since all humans possess them and abide by them in their daily lives whether as the faithful or the faithless. The other reason is that in the course of history religious belief/unbelief systems have been *invented* and thus are eminently relevant to any discussion of creativity. To repeat, religious belief/unbelief systems are abstract artifacts with artificers on the one hand and consumers on the other. They begin as intellectual schemas but they are then assimilated by communities of (largely subaltern) consumers and become cultural and, to many, everyday schemas.

Most of the great world religions of course have a very long history. Some, like Judaism and Hinduism reach back to well over three millennia before the present, others like Christianity and Islam are somewhat younger in age. Yet to explore their inventions and the creation of their associated schemas is, to say the least, forbiddingly formidable because of their long and bewilderingly complex evolutionary histories.

As it happens, though, in the nineteenth century, just before Queen Victoria began her reign, something like a reformation of Hinduism occurred in the Eastern region of Bengal whose main city, Calcutta (now Kolkata), was the capital of the Raj (the British reign in India). A reformed Unitarian offshoot, a "satellite" religion called *Brahmoism* (from "Brahmo" or "Brahman" = Supreme Being) was invented around 1828.

Its prime artificer was a remarkable and colorful intellectual, a religious, social and educational reformer named Rammohun Roy. Brahmoism remains a relatively minor faith in India in terms of the size of its congregation. But in the nineteenth century and after, its cultural, intellectual, social, educational and creative influences were profound. Its practitioners have been at the vanguard of Indian modernism. It played a major role in a nineteenth century-long intellectual, social and creative *movement* called the Bengal Renaissance with influences that spread across India in the twentieth century (Kopf 1969, 1979; Dasgupta 2007, 2010).

My aim here is to describe the two belief systems, Hinduism and Brahmoism in terms of their respective (but *very* partial) schemas and thereby offer a concrete sense of the structure of schemas.

Let us begin with a partial schema for the concept of *religion*.

> **NAME** *Religion*
>
> **TYPE** *Faith-Based-Belief*
>
> **INSTANCES** *Deism; Christianity; Judaism; Islam; Hinduism; Confucianism; Buddhism; Zoroastrianism; Mormonism; Brahmoism; Jainism; Pantheism....*
>
> **ATTRIBUTES** *Primary Scriptures; Objects of Worship; Means of Worship; Metaphysics; Social Schemes; Social Practices*

Though not shown here, the schema for TYPE *Faith-Based-Belief* may itself be a subschema of another schema called (say) *Belief* which will contain as other subschemas, in addition to *Faith-Based-Belief*, other kinds of beliefs, e.g., *Rational-Belief* and *Evidence-Based-Belief*.

Consider now the schema for *Hinduism*, an instance of *Religion*.

> **NAME** *Hinduism*
>
> **TYPE** *Religion*
>
> **PRIMARY SCRIPTURES** *Vedas; Upanishads; Puranas; Bhagavada Gita; Dharmasastra; Vedanta*
>
> **OBJECTS OF WORSHIP** *Ishwara/Brahmo/Brahman/Supreme Being; Trinity/Brahma, Vishnu, Siva; Mother Goddess/Kali/Durga; Lakshmi; Saraswati; Hanuman; Ganesha....*

MEANS OF WORSHIP Individualistic; Idols and Images

METAPHYSICS Polytheism; Monistic Idealism; Intuition-as-Source-of-Knowing; Moksha/Liberation; Non-Attachment; Karma; Rebirth; Dharma/Moral Law

SOCIAL SCHEMES Caste/Varna

SOCIAL PRACTICES Casteism; Law of Inheritance; Exclusion of Beef Eating

This schema is based on texts by Radhakrishnan and Moore (1957) and Sen (1961). As can be seen, *Hinduism* being of TYPE *Religion* has inherited all the ATTRIBUTES of the *Religion* schema. These ATTRIBUTES are *instantiated* here to indicate what they are in the particular case of *Hinduism*.

Compare this schema with that of *Brahmoism* (based on Ghose 1885; Collette 1988; Kopf 1979; Biswas 1992).

NAME Brahmoism

TYPE Religion

PRIMARY SCRIPTURES Vedas; Upanishads; Vedanta

OBJECTS OF WORSHIP Ishwara/Brahmo/Supreme Being

MEANS OF WORSHIP Congregational; Non-Idolatry

METAPHYSICS Monotheism; Monistic Idealism

SOCIAL PRACTICES Anti-Casteism; Anti-Law of Inheritance

As one can see there are common elements in these two schemas. Both, for example, use as primary scriptures, the *Vedas*, the *Upanishads*, and *Vedanta*; both espouse a metaphysic of monistic idealism. In other respects they differ sharply, most notably in the espousal, in Brahmoism, of monotheism in contrast to the polytheism in Hinduism. As I have pointed out elsewhere (Dasgupta 2007), Rammohiun Roy and his close associates *invented* Brahmoism by excluding certain features of Hinduism, retaining others and adding new features (such as *Non-Idolatry* and *Anti-Casteism*). The founders of Brahmoism began with the schema of Hinduism and *modified* it to create a new religion.

In the schemas for both Hinduism and Brahmoism, the instantiations of various parts will also be linked to schemas that characterize these entities. Looking at the three schemas depicted here we see how they are connected into a partly hierarchical and partly non-hierarchical *schema network* that will be constitutive of a well-informed Bengali–Indian's religious belief/knowledge space.

IX Representing schemas

The fundamental assumption undergirding schema theory is that they are structures that reside in our physical (long-term) memory. How they are encoded at the neuronal level is a matter for cognitive neuroscientists. (One hypothesis is described later in this section.) For the purpose of understanding their role in everyday thinking and creative thinking we need to represent schemas externally. How we do so is a matter of personal preference or convenience. Perhaps the most compelling factor is *clarity*: the representation must allow us to make sense of its place in thinking.

So there is no generally accepted language for expressing schemas. In the case of the fountain pen and restaurant examples I used ordinary prose as a mode of expression. In the case of the religious schemas I employed a slightly more structured notation rather in the style of (and, indeed, influenced by) computer program module descriptions. But the language was still *textual*. Other authors have used *graphical* notations. For example, in his book *Conceptual Revolutions* (1992) philosopher and cognitive scientist Paul Thagard (1992) presented schemas for a variety of complex scientific concepts graphically. For engineers, architects and designers, graphical representations (such as engineering drawings, architectural drawings and sketches) are the preferred mode not only for external representations but for thinking about designs (Jones 1980; Ferguson 1992; Cross 2011). On the other hand, if we are trying to represent a schema for *doing* something (what cognitive scientists and some computer scientists call procedural knowledge) or wish to depict how *change* occurs, the representation must capture its *dynamical* aspect; the schema must not be about structure but *process*.

One of the major achievements in chemistry, for example, was the invention in the late eighteenth and early nineteenth centuries of a notational system to express *chemical reactions*—chemical processes, in fact. The general schema for such reactions is

$$Molecule + Molecule + \ldots + Molecule = Molecule + Molecule + \ldots + Molecule$$

Here, the "+" on the left side of the "=" signifies combination or *interaction*; the "+" on the right side denotes *conjunction* ("and"); the symbol "=" itself signifies *transformation*. So for instance, an instantiation of this schema would be

$$Zn + H2SO4 = ZnSO4 + H2$$

— meaning that Zinc and Sulphuric Acid interact to form Zinc Sulphate and Hydrogen. Note that the symbols "Zn," "H2SO4," "ZnSo4" and "H2" are also instantiations of schemas invented to denote the nature of chemical elements and compounds.

In the case of some kinds of complex processes (for example, involved in human thinking) schemas may be representable in the manner of *computer programs*. That is, we might have to appeal to computational representations. But processes are tricky things. For example, certain processes occur in sequential form: *A1* begins and ends before *A2* begins, *A2* ends before *A3* begins, and so on. Other kinds of processes entail concurrency or parallelism. For example (as we will consider later) unconscious thinking seems to contain a great deal of concurrency within it, while conscious thinking demands sequentiality. Or there may be an interleaving of sequential and concurrent actions forming what mathematicians would call a "partially ordered" process. Because of the ubiquity of sequential and parallel processes in computational systems computer scientists have devoted a great deal of attention to the invention of notation and languages based on such notation to depict the dynamic, interactive nature of computational processes involving sequential and parallel components. Thus, using the symbols ";" to denoted sequentiality and "II" to denote concurrency, a schema for a sequential process involving several subprocesses P1, P2, ..., Pn might be represented as "P1; P2; ...; Pn" while a schema for a concurrent process involving subprocesses P1, P2, ..., Pn would be represented as "P1 II P2 II ... II Pn." A partially ordered interleaving of sequential and concurrent processes can be constructed out of these two schemas. For example, "P1; (P2 II P3); P4; (P5 II P6 II P7); P8" describes a partially ordered process in which P1 preceded the concurrent actions of P2 and P3, and when the latter ends then P4 follows, and upon completion of P4 the concurrent subprocesses P5, P6, P7 occur, followed, finally by P8.

In other words, in the matter of representing schemas, cognitive scientists and creativity researchers can afford to be pragmatic. The objective is clarity and understandability.

X   Schemas as emergent properties of neuronal networks

Our discussion of schemas thus far has assumed that they are *symbol structures*. Symbols *represent* things in the world and a schema is a symbol structure stored in memories that represent our experiences, beliefs and knowledge about the world. Marvin Minsky's reference to schemas (or, in his language, frames) as "data structures" quite explicitly connects schemas to symbol systems as computer scientists think of data structures. Our external representational modes just discussed are, also, symbolic in nature. For example, computational representations of schemas assume that the latter are symbol structures. This symbolic assumption also suggests that schemas impose themselves as symbol structures *on* memory; that when a new schema is constructed, largely unconsciously as the outcome of experiencing and interacting with the world it is stored *in* one's memory, first in what psychologists call working memory and then more permanently in long-term memory. This is entirely consistent with the data structure analogy: computer programmers construct data structures that are *stored* in a computer's memory and then processed.

As it happens, in the 1980s an old model of the mind but revised and recast in a different way came into being which eschewed symbolism altogether. This new theory of cognitive processing came to be *neural network theory* and its philosophical basis came to known as *connectionism*. (The literature of connectionism is vast but for a brief historical narrative from the perspective of artificial intelligence, see Dasgupta 2018a, Chapter 7. For a comprehensive survey from the perspective of human cognition by one of the founders of modern connectionism, see Rumelhart 1989). The idea is that cognition may be modeled as an interconnected network of abstract neurons rather as the brain is an interconnected system of actual neurons. Connectionism thus posits a model or theory of cognition that is *biologically inspired*.

In 1986, David Rumelhart, Paul Smolensky, James McClelland and Geoffrey Hinton, the prime begetters of the "new" connectionism, addressed the problem of schema construction in connectionist terms. They suggested that schemas are not symbolic entities that are explicitly constructed but rather they are implicitly created "in real time" in the very process of interpreting one's environment (Rumelhart, Smolensky, McClelland and Hinton 1986, p. 20). In broad terms they proposed that the way schemas come into being is that the stimulus from the environment activates a set of neurons which form stable sub-patterns that activate one another; these tightly linked sub-patterns form the units we call schemas (p. 20).

So Rumelhart et al. suggest that rather than the symbolist position wherein schemas are data structures stored in memory, a schema is not the *content* of memory at all but is an *emergent property* of an interconnected network of neurons.

The advantage of a computational model (as connectionist models are) is that they can be empirically tested: models can be implemented as programs (as procedural models) and executed on "test data." This is precisely what Rumelhart et al. did. The details of these simulation experiments are not important for our purposes here. Suffice to say that their experiments produced neural networks that characterized schemas for different kinds of rooms, such as for "kitchen," "bathroom" and "living room."

These were impressive results that offer a hypothesis for how new schemas are formed. But the hypothesis does not explain how we accommodate and make sense of new experiences or situations in terms of prior knowledge. How it is, for example, that seeing a particular painting by Picasso for the very first time a viewer recognizes it "as a Picasso" and even identify the "period" in Picasso's long artistic life to which it belongs. Nor how expectations are created, as in the case of the Greek–Lebanese restaurant, in a new experiential everyday circumstance. The symbolist "data structure" model seems far more plausible in such situations.

XI Kuhn's invention of the paradigm schema

Philosophers and historians also invent. For example, historian Norman Cantor (1991) has written how the idea of a period in history termed "The Middle Ages" was invented by some eminent twentieth century medievalist historians. The idea of the Industrial Revolution was also an invention having its own evolutionary history (Hardy 2014).

Thomas Kuhn (2012), who began as a historian of science but evolved into one of the twentieth century's most influential philosophers of science, was certainly an inventor. *The Structure of Scientific Revolution* (2012)—first published in 1962—is about science, and his theory of paradigms provided considerable insight into the nature of scientific creativity. But it is also appropriate in the context of this discussion of schemas as shedding light on Kuhn's own creativity as a historian/philosopher of science.

In writing *Structure* Kuhn as artificer attracted many consumers, both peer (fellow science studies scholars) and lay (non-science studies scholars, students and general readers). Many of the peer consumers have critically judged *Structure*, some positively, some negatively. The book has spawned responses in the form of numerous articles and several books (for example, Lakatos and Musgrave 1970; Laudan 1977; Feyerabend 1978; Lakatos 1978; Nickles 2003b; Richards and Daston 2016). Regardless of the nature of consumer responses, *Structure* was the basis of innumerable creative encounters between Kuhn the artificer and his readers-as-consumers. It has shaped the cognitive identity of a generation of science studies scholars as well as many other kinds of researchers. In writing *Structure* Kuhn was unequivocally C-creative, the reach of his ideas extending to the humanities and social sciences.

Kuhn's creativity lay in the fact that *he invented a schema* for understanding scientific change and creativity.

At the epicenter of Kuhn's schema is his concept of the *paradigm* that, in fact, has its own distinctive schema.

All those who study science "from the outside" (they include philosophers, historians, sociologists, cognitive scientists and computer scientists) are of course aware that much controversy has surrounded Kuhn's concept of the paradigm. In a well-known essay Margaret Masterman (1970) listed no less than twenty-one different ways in which the word was used in the first edition of *Structure*. Responding to Masterman and other critic–consumers Kuhn sought to clarify and distill the concept in a series of publications (Kuhn 1969, 1970, 1977). In what follows I have drawn upon these clarifications and his terminology. And I will represent the *paradigm schema* in ordinary language.

A Kuhnian paradigm comprises of two concepts: a "disciplinary matrix"; and "exemplars."

In general a disciplinary matrix is a network of beliefs, values, "symbolic generalizations," heuristic models and metaphysical assumptions—which collectively establishes a socio-cognitive framework shared by a scientific community and within which scientists of that community identify and solve problems.

Kuhn used the term "symbolic generalizations" to mean general assertions that specify laws, principles, procedures, methods and theories believed to be empirically valid at some given time. Examples include Newton's laws of motion (mechanics), Kepler's laws (planetary physics), Planck's law (quantum physics), Avagadro's hypothesis (physical chemistry), theory of natural selection (evolutionary biology),

Mendel's laws (genetics), Hooke's law (mechanics), the iron-carbon diagram (metallurgy), the Church–Turing thesis (theoretical computer science) and the bending moment diagram (structural engineering).

As for "metaphysical beliefs," these are beliefs in or commitments to abstract principles about a scientific domain that are taken for granted or assumed to be true at some given time. Historical examples include the incorruptibility of the heavens, the immutability of species, the objective reality of the physical world and the absoluteness of space and time.

"Heuristic models" are abstract but useful models to which some relevant aspect of a science is assumed to conform which help give rise to symbolic generalizations. Examples include the idea that molecules of a gas behave like small, perfectly elastic billiard balls in random motion (a model that led to the kinetic theory of gases), that atoms resemble the solar system (giving rise to Niels Bohr's model of the structure of the atom), that the heart is like a pump (William Harvey's discovery of the circulation of blood) and that the mind/brain is an information processing system (giving rise to computational theories of cognition).

"Values" are criteria or conditions used to evaluate and judge the scientific worth of a symbolic generalization. Examples include Occam's principle ("the most preferred hypothesis involves the fewest assumptions"), refutability of scientific theories or laws, predictiveness of scientific hypotheses, the repeatability of experiments.

Finally, "exemplars" are problem–solution complexes students encounter in the course of their studies and training, and are known by scientific practitioners in the course of their professional careers. Historical examples include: analysis of a cantilever beam (engineering mechanics), movement of a frictionless ball down an inclined plane (physics), the Tower of Hanoi problem (computer science/artificial intelligence) and Millikan's oil droplet problem (experimental physics).

XII   Normal science as schema elaboration

Kuhn's aim in creating the paradigm schema was to shed light on scientific creativity: he wished to show how scientific change occurs. The whole of *Structure* is, in fact, nothing less than a kind of narrative theory of scientific creativity, and the paradigm schema is the lynchpin of this theory.

But a caveat: as a theory of scientific creativity it was not concerned with individual artificers or consumers. Rather, his was a *social* theory. Later, I will address this social aspect of creativity in a broader setting.

To repeat, Kuhn invented a paradigm schema—a schema that characterizes all scientific paradigms. Thus the belief/knowledge contents of every *mature* science conforms to this schema and so any particular paradigm pertaining to a particular science is an *instantiation* of this schema. So if Kuhn is right there is a distinct chemical paradigm (for example) whose contents and internal structure will also consist of a disciplinary matrix and a particular set of exemplars which all chemists subscribe to, just as there are also physical, biological, geological, cognitive, computational and other instantiations of the paradigm schema. Notice that these instantiations *are themselves schemas* (or rather *schema systems*) representing a complex entity shared by the practitioners of a particular science. These practitioners have assimilated the paradigm in the course of their scientific development. (In the next chapter I discuss the development aspects of creativity under the rubric of "proactive preparation.")

Here then is a *schema–theoretic* interpretation of Kuhn's theory of scientific change.

A hallmark of a mature science is the presence of a dominant paradigm. "Dominant" means that the majority of the practitioners of that science broadly subscribe to the contents of the paradigm. The paradigm itself constitutes a schema (system). Some key aspects of its contents, such as its metaphysical beliefs, its values, its procedures and methods of inquiry, and its major laws, theories and observations are believed by the scientists to be "true," even unchallengeable.

In the course of development the apprentice–scientist acquires, absorbs and *internalizes* the paradigm; it becomes *her particular* schema. And like all useful schemas this too is flexible and open to change. It can be extended, refined and enriched. As long as its key aspects are not contested elements of the schema can be revised.

There are gaps of ignorance in the paradigm schema that needs to be filled; new problems may be identified; ambiguities need to be disambiguated; vaguenesses need to be clarified; open problems need to be solved. Kuhn called these activities *normal science*, and according to his theory this is what most scientists engage with in the course of their professional lives. Normal science, then, *progressively elaborates, refines and further instantiates the paradigm schema.*

This process of schema elaboration and instantiation is not the sole privilege of some individual scientist. The paradigm being shared, the (approximately) same schema is held in many scientists' minds. The process of normal science involves innumerable alterations and refinements by individual scientists to the shared schema. (Open any comprehensive, advanced textbook for a particular science and you will immediately perceive its normal science content and the rich, dense, elaboration of the schema (system) representing that particular paradigm.) So a science *evolves in a gradualistic manner.* Thus does scientific change occur in the Kuhnian narrative of "normal" science. Normal science is a case of schema elaboration.

XIII   Inventing intellectual schemas

If making history is a superneed that drives creativity (as I have discussed before), *inventing* a brand new intellectual schema is surely one way, perhaps the supreme way, of satisfying that superneed. Assuming the schema is judged valuable as well as original it will guarantee the artificer's H-creativity. If the new schema is so insightful that it results in creative encounters between artificers and consumers—is adapted by others and shapes future thought and/or action—the artificer will have achieved C-creativity. Thomas Kuhn's invention of the paradigm schema is an example. The fact is historians, philosophers and other scholars can be as creative as artists, scientists and technological inventors.

This seems to imply that schema invention is an individual cognitive act. But the production of a recognizably original schema may also be the outcome of a collective effort. For example, in the making of a scientific paradigm, an individual (or a few individuals) may invent the core elements around which the paradigm takes shape but the overall paradigm is usually the outcome of a socio-historical process involving many individuals. As an instance, there's hardly any doubt that what is sometimes called the *Darwinian paradigm* is rooted in the principle of natural selection simultaneously invented by Charles Darwin and Alfred Russel Wallace in the mid-nineteenth century. This principle forms the foundational element of a schema representing a new paradigm. But the Darwinian paradigm is, properly speaking, the outcome of a cognitive–historical process involving many contributors. The paradigm is a schema *system*, the most important of its elements being strictly biological (Ruse 1993; Gould 2002), but others are extra-biological, meandering into a wide range of areas including philosophy, sociology, economics, historiography, psychology, design theory and ethics (Steadman 2008; Basalla 1988; Mokyr 1990). Indeed, as I discuss later, the study of creativity itself has been absorbed by some into the Darwinian paradigm.

In the realms of art, film and literature we might think that inventing schemas is mostly an individual cognitive process. In painting we speak of the "Gauguinesque" or "Cézannesque," in filmmaking we recognize the "Felliniesque," paying homage to the inventors of particular styles. The literary realm has produced such terms as "Kafkaesque," "Orwellian" and "Proustian," terms referring to literary works that are instantiations of schemas invented by Franz Kafka, George Orwell and Marcel Proust respectively.

Yet we cannot generalize and insist that inventing intellectual schemas is always the prerogative of the individual in the realm of the arts for it is easy to find counter-examples. In the literary domain the invention of the narrative mode called magical realism is the result of a diachronic, collective process even though there are key individuals (such as novelists Günter Grass, Gabriel Garcia Marquez, Angela Carter and Salman Rushdie) with which the movement is most intimately associated (Zamora and Faris 1995; Bowers 2004). The great art historian and connoisseur Bernard Berenson (1968)—a peer consumer if ever there was one—discerned in the "Florentine school" of painting certain characteristics that distinguished it from the "Venetian school"; shared characteristics essential to the Florentine artists which yet were the products of extraordinary individuals that made up much of the pantheon of Renaissance artists. In our language Berenson had constructed a personal schema for Florentine painting as a collective enterprise.

XIV   Schemas as affordances

Inventing an intellectual schema is, as mentioned, a means of achieving the highest form of creativity. But a caveat is in order: one does not invent a schema for its sake alone. As with everyday schemas, as with cultural schemas, intellectual schemas are *cognitive tools*. Once invented they must be put to work. So a new schema is only valuable and its invention is a C-creative act if and when it can be gainfully employed.

Kuhn's invention of the paradigm schema is a case in point. It has shaped the way many people think about the structure of the sciences and how scientific change occurs. It provides an *explanatory framework* within which to situate a science, its history or some new discovery in that science. Or it may afford an *analogical framework* within which to make sense of a particular field of inquiry.

Some years ago I was engaged in writing a book on design theory in the context of computer science (Dasgupta 1991). I needed an organizing principle to clarify the various approaches to the design of computational artifacts (algorithms, computer languages, complex software and hardware systems, etc.). The Kuhnian paradigm schema *afforded* me that organizing framework, the *space* I needed. Kuhn's theory was intended to explain the character of change in the natural sciences (most pointedly in physics). There was not a hint throughout *The Structure of Scientific Revolutions* that he was also referring to the artificial sciences (such as computer science or the engineering sciences). But one of the *unintended* consequences of *Structure* (as was the case with Darwin's *The Origin of Species*) was its affordance (Gibson 1966), a property of artifacts I have mentioned previously (Chapter 2, XI).

Kuhn's paradigm schema—an abstract artifact—offered me a certain affordance by way of a partial analogy. Recall that two of the paradigm schema's components are heuristic models and metaphysical assumptions. These concepts afforded by analogy the concept of the *design paradigm*. The analogy was that a design paradigm is to design what heuristic models and metaphysical assumptions are to science (Dasgupta 1991, p. 141). And just as the paradigm schema for natural science can be instantiated to yield actual paradigms for individual natural sciences (the Darwinian paradigm in biology, the cognitive paradigm in psychology) so also the design paradigm *schema* can be instantiated to yield particular design paradigms (consisting of methods, procedures and tools) in specific artificial sciences such as computer science (p. 142). In fact, in the case of computer science the schema was instantiated to yield a number of actual (and alternative) design paradigms for computational artifacts (pp. 142–144).

The property of affordance suggests yet another way of judging creativity. I previously remarked that the invention of a schema must arguably rank at the highest level of creativity. Kuhn's famous concept of a paradigm shift—whereby a dominant paradigm for a science is overthrown and replaced by another paradigm, effecting a scientific *revolution* (Kuhn 2012, especially Chapters VII–XIII)—is an example of this act of schema invention.

But now we can add to this. The richness and power of a schema as an abstract artifact also lies in its *range of possible affordances*. Herein lies a source of a schema inventor's C-creativity, for affordance leads to consequences. The reason why Kuhn should be deemed C-creative rests in large part in that his paradigm schema afforded all kinds of possible uses in directions Kuhn most probably did not anticipate.

At the same time we must note that an artifact's affordances are not always obvious or visible. They may be hidden from view, buried deep in the structure of the artifact. They must be teased out (for example by analogy). The extraction of a schema's (and in general any artifact's) affordances can itself be a creative experience *in which a consumer becomes a creator.*

XV Personal schema (or cognitive style)

Writers talk of "finding one's own voice." By this they mean that an essential element of one's authorial identity is to discover and perfect a distinctive and natural writerly style of one's own. A similar sentiment is expressed by painters, composers, singers (who literally seek voices of their own) and other artists. In the course of their development and training neophyte artificers apprentice themselves to mentors, directly as their pupils, indirectly through the created artifacts that are studied, and learn their craft by modeling themselves on their mentors. (This is part of what I discuss in the next chapter as "proactive preparation.") But sooner or later, like the butterfly emerging out of the chrysalis, they shake off their mentors' influences and invent themselves in their own images.

The concept of individual artistic style has been extensively discussed by art historians and theorists (Robinson 1981; Wollheim 1987; Carney 1991). Indeed, one eminent art historian, Heinrich Wölfflin (1932) viewed the entire history of art as the history of style. Cognitive scientist Margaret Boden (2010) referred to the artist's personal style as "personal signature."

The artists' desire to find their own voices originates in their common superneed to make history. But this need to find one's own style of practicing one's chosen craft is also manifest (though less visibly) by scientists, designers, architects and even some engineers. In other words it is a desire that straddles both sides of the "cultural aisle," the arts/humanities and the sciences/technology.

This aspect of the artificer's identity shared by artificers in many fields has been called *cognitive style* (Dasgupta 2005, 2007). From a cognitive–historical perspective an artificer's cognitive style is perhaps the most significant feature of her creativity because one's cognitive style is a particular *visible trace* of the cognitive processes that occur in her mind, much of which happens in the unconscious. One's cognitive style is a visibly discernible pattern that is an *abstraction* of the different cognitive processes an artificer executes over a long duration (*longue durée*, in the phrase of the influential French historian Fernand Braudel (1980, pp. 25–55)), possibly over the course of her creative life. If we wish to answer the question of creativity, uncovering cognitive style is about as promising a path as any.

Because of this we will explore the phenomenon of cognitive style later in this book. What I wish to impress here is that *a cognitive style is fundamentally a personal schema.* To find a cognitive style of one's own is to invent a personal schema.

6

THE PREPARED MIND

I A "pasteural" maxim

"Where observation is concerned, chance favors the prepared mind." So said Louis Pasteur in 1854. Here is a variation on this maxim: *The prepared mind favors creativity.* But what does a "prepared mind" entail and how does it favor creativity?

One of the first thinkers to address the role of preparation in creativity was the mathematician Henri Poincaré (1985), for whom preparation was a crucial first stage in the act of creation, comprising of a (relatively) short-term bout of intense, *conscious*, *voluntary* work that served as the necessary precondition for productive thinking. The latter itself occurs in the *unconscious*. The whole point of preparation, according to Poincaré, was to set into motion the "unconscious machine."

Poincaré, writing on the eve of the First World War, was interested in mathematical creativity. In 1945, as another World War was about to come to an end, another eminent mathematician, Jacques Hadamard also addressed what he called "the psychology of invention in the mathematical field." And like Poincaré, he too argued that the purpose of preparation was to establish the "general direction" in which the unconscious has to work. The purpose of preparation was to educate the unconscious (Hadamard 1954, pp. 46–55).

Both Poincaré and Hadamard used *introspection* as their mode of inquiry—a method long rejected by academic psychologists. Sometime in between the two mathematicians social scientist Graham Wallas—whose work Hadamard knew of and cited (p. 132) but not in this context—chose to take a longer-sighted view of preparation. To have a prepared mind, Wallas wrote, is to be an educated being. Preparation embraces the process of "intellectual education" as a whole (Wallas 1926, p. 82). The "educated man" acquires knowledge, "thought systems" and rules of thought that he can then draw upon in a way the "uneducated man" cannot. He will also manifest the right "problem attitude," meaning that preparation entails the capacity to frame clear, unambiguous, testable propositions. Only then can the significance of evidence or ideas in proving or disproving propositions be noticed (p. 84).

Like Poincaré before him and Hadamard after, Wallas was not a professional psychologist; he was a professor of political science. But unlike them he based his ideas on "the art of thought" not on his own introspection but rather, as he stated in the preface, on his experience of more than forty years as a teacher and administrator, and on introspective descriptions by other creative beings such as poets of their own thought processes. Wallas also drew widely on the writings of psychologists. His work was a comprehensive, scholarly treatment of the problem of creative thinking along the lines of what I am calling in this book the cognitive–historical approach.

In any case, Wallas on the one hand and Poincaré and Hadamard on the other held different views of the role of preparation in the act of creation. The latter mathematicians envisioned preparation as the conscious activity that sets the stage for some unconscious work—Poincaré and, after him, Wallas called this *incubation*—that will follow immediately in an act of production. This implies that a goal has already been established and conscious preparation is a response or reaction to that goal. Moreover, it is a relatively short-term process. I will call the situation suggested by Poincaré and Hadamard *reactive preparation* insofar as it is a reaction or response to an identified goal.

Wallas in contrast viewed preparation as a kind of intellectual history of the thinking/doing person that prepares him or her to take up creative work in the future. This implies that such preparation entails the construction of a potential for future acts of creation. It is a constituent of what economist and creativity researcher Jonathan Feinstein (2006) called "creative development." I will call this kind of preparation *proactive preparation*.

So when we make the "pasteural" claim that the prepared mind favors creativity we are claiming the relevance both these kinds of preparation—proactive and reactive.

II Proactive preparation

A person's world is a composite of an objective environment—the physical world "out there," the social world of which she is a part, the cultural world of artifacts (material and abstract) she interacts with—and a subjective inner *state*: the contents of her brain/mind complex. In terms of the cognitive–historical framework they constitute the person's *ecological* and *cognitive spaces* respectively (Chapter 1, IV). The beliefs and knowledge (including self-knowledge) a person holds at any given time, her goals, needs, desires, her affects, are constituents of this cognitive space. And these constituents are constantly being revised, with additions, deletions and alterations as a consequence of the person's interactions with her environment. Her cognitive space is as much an "open system" as is her ecological space.

When we say that a person's beliefs and knowledge are constituents of her cognitive space we are implying that the brain/mind complex holds *representations* of one's beliefs and knowledge—as schemas (Chapter 4). Clearly, one must be genetically endowed with the *capacity* to represent or hold such beliefs and knowledge; and to have the capacity to construct, unconsciously or consciously, one's belief/knowledge space. That is, one must possess a *memory system* as a "container" of one's beliefs and knowledge, and the means to store elements in memory, recall them, even forget them. But the evolution of one's belief/knowledge space is an ecologically driven cognitive process of which one is only partly conscious. A person evolves this space throughout her lifetime. This evolutionary process—and by "evolutionary" I mean here nothing more than *gradualistic*—both enriches and revises her belief/knowledge space and also develops fresh means of accessing, retrieving and revising that space. It is this process I have termed proactive preparation and it is *a lifelong process.*

Formal education is obviously one of the means of attaining a prepared mind but it is only one such means. In particular, creative scientists, writers, poets, composers, inventors, scholars and artists usually go well beyond what formal education has to offer. (Indeed, for some, such as the poet–philosopher–writer–songwriter–dramatist Rabindranath Tagore the institution of formal education may well be a prison which they long to break out of (Tagore 2001, p. 40)). Creative artificers saturate themselves not only with knowledge pertaining to what most interests them, including knowledge from other fields. They are often autodidacts. They establish for themselves certain values and goals that formal education alone can rarely induce in them. They observe, read widely, take note of ideas and things, they experience the world.

It is easy to understand why proactive preparation is a prerequisite for creativity. Whether one aspires to be an artist, scientist, musician, writer, inventor or designer, one must master the tools of the trade.

More importantly the creative process is a knowledge-rich enterprise for both the artificer and the consumer. It does not emerge out of ignorance, out of a memory that is a *tabula rasa*, a "blank slate." The potentially creative artificer and the potentially receptive consumer are both inheritors of a shared creative tradition, and they draw on this tradition as sources of ideas and insights. This shared creative tradition is founded on a shared cultural space. A scientist, no matter how original his work is as a scientist, will not *usually* be a consummate poet or literary scholar unless he has also undertaken the kind of preparation that makes a poet a poet of note or a scholar a scholar of distinction. This is the case in any field of endeavor including art. As psychoanalyst Ernst Kris (1952) emphasized, the artists, as much as the scientist and philosopher, is the legatee of a creative tradition; she too stands on the shoulders of giants.

This is why art historians and literary scholars expend so much effort in tracing "sources" of a work of art or a novel or a poem. John Livingstone Lowes's book *The Road to Xanadu* (1930) is a magnificent example of a scholar tracking down in fine detail the origins of various elements of Coleridge's poem "Kubla Khan" first published in 1816. And as noted before, Picasso's *Les Demoiselles d'Avignon* (1907) elicited a huge body of literature concerning its sources as well as its meaning (Rubin, Seckel and Cousins 1994). It is why, in the scientific realm, historian of science Robert Olby's (1974) book *The Path to the Double Helix* compels our attention: James Watson and Francis Crick's discovery of the structure of DNA in 1953 rested on an entire diachronic network of prior work.

In these and other cases the interesting and fascinating issue is not only that the creative process is knowledge-rich but *in what particular way* does a person's proactively prepared mind enter into his work, for the nature of that influence is often exceedingly subtle and nuanced; they may have to be painfully teased out by the creativity researcher, whether he is a psychologist (as was Howard Gruber (1981) in his investigation of the origins of Darwin's great discovery) or a literary scholar (as was John Livingstone Lowes (1930) in his detection of Coleridge's sources). The situation may be aggravated by the (conscious or unconscious) suppression of sources of a creative act.

In his review of James Watson's (1968) controversial (but enormously entertaining) book *The Double Helix*, the Nobel laureate biologist Peter Medawar (1974) tried to explain why Watson was so cheerfully callous of the debts he and Crick owed to their predecessors: the state of science at any point of time, incorporates its own history; the scientist takes for granted that her understanding has been shaped by what others have done before and so one does not therefore have to explicitly acknowledge one's debts to one's scientific ancestors. In Medawar's memorable phrase, the state of understanding of a science is the "integral of a curve of learning" (p. 105).

It lies with the cognitive historian to excavate this history (as did Olby in the case of the double helix) and explicate the workings of the proactive mind. It is why cognitive history is so relevant to the understanding of acts of creation.

III   Aspiring to be original

Proactive preparation also serves a more subtle purpose. Recall from our prior discussion that the act of production begins with an artificer's need, goal or desire, perhaps in response to some emotion or experience (Chapter 4, II). But the artificer who aspires to be a creative being is not simply content to produce an artifact that is commonplace, that has already been produced before, perhaps elsewhere. Rather, she desires to produce an artifact that not only satisfies her need but to do so in a manner that expresses her uniqueness, her individuality and her originality.

So it is not only that the writer has a compelling urge to write, the composer to compose, the scientist to discover, the painter to paint (the superneed to create alluded to in Chapter 1, IV). It is also the case that at the highest level each artificer *seeks* to break away from history; to *make* history. I have earlier (in Chapter 3, XVII) called this the superneed to be original. It is a superneed that seems to be shared by all highly creative people.

But to break away from the past *one must know the past*. This is where proactive preparation enters the stage; for it enables the artificer to know, understand and grasp the current geography of his field. It circumscribes the boundary *beyond* which he must travel.

IV   Chronicle of a renaissance mind foretold[1]

Herbert Simon was that rarest of individuals in the twentieth century: a polymath, a "Renaissance man." His productive life spanned some sixty years and ended only with his death in February 2001. His intellectual reach spread over three distinct areas of empirical science—the social, behavioral and computer sciences—and he also made an important contribution to the philosophy of science. His contribution to economic and administrative decision theory led to a Nobel Prize in economic science; he received the Turing Award, computer science's highest honor for work in co-founding artificial intelligence; and in the behavioral sciences he was one of the progenitors of modern cognitive science. As a creativity researcher and cognitive historian I was as naturally drawn to such a rare instance of *multidisciplinary creativity* (Dasgupta 2003a, 2003b) as natural historians of organic life are captivated by presence of a rare biological species.

Simon was a prodigious writer; his massive corpus of publications included highly technical papers, more discursive essays and articles, and several books. But the work that was probably most widely read and referenced by readers from different disciplines was *The Sciences of the Artificial*, first published in 1969 and republished in two further editions, an elegant and highly influential (C-original) synthesis of his many strands of thought (Simon 1996). The very concept of "artificial science" is certainly his most original and consequential *metascientific* contribution, for in this concept he established connections between the social, behavioral, computer, and systems sciences.

It seems unlikely that Simon intended in his youth or in university *to be* a polymath. Certainly we have no evidence of such intention in his autobiography (Simon 1991). We do have, however, ample evidence of how remarkably varied his intellectual *interests* were from a very early age, in part from formal course work, in part through self-study. (More on the role of interest in creativity later in this chapter.)

We learn early from his autobiography (narrated in part in the third person) that he kept full control of his own education (p. 9). He studied, mostly on his own, mathematics and physics—including the "standard textbooks in mechanics, electricity and magnetism, quantum mechanics and mathematical methods of physics" (Simon, personal communication, April 1, 2000). When he was fifteen he read Dante and Milton and studied ethics. In high school he studied "deeply and widely" economics and the social sciences. He immersed himself in natural history and collected plants and insects. Growing up in Cincinnati, Ohio, he cultivated the local library and museum (pp. 9, 11, 26).

He studied and played chess. At home he observed his engineer father at his workbench making radios and model sailboats. There were engineering books "around" at home and so he had many opportunities to learn about the engineering enterprise (Simon, personal communication, February 16, 2000).

By the end of his second year as an undergraduate at Chicago University in the late 1930s, he had passed his upper division courses in the social sciences, "read widely in the humanities," and "strengthened" his background in physics and biology. He also had a "good introduction" to sociology and anthropology (p. 53). He was a major in political science.

He attended a course offered by the renowned philosopher Rudolf Carnap and drank deep the waters of logical positivism through his encounter with Carnap and, in particular, his reading of English philosopher Alfred J. Ayer's *Language, Truth and Logic* (1971). Ayer's influence on Simon's first and influential book *Administrative Behavior* (1976) would be considerable:

> My later reading of Ayer was, in fact … important in solidifying my ideas …
> and it was certainly his chapter on "is and ought" in LTL [*Language, Truth and Logic*] that I mostly relied upon in my sharp is-ought distinction in AB [*Administrative Behavior*].
>
> *(Simon, personal communication, December 1, 1999)*

An especially striking aspect of Simon's multidisciplinary creativity was his foray into the foundations of physics. One of his papers published in 1947 (the year of the publication of *Administrative Behavior*, his first book) reveals a density of knowledge of physics that went well beyond "textbook knowledge" of facts, concepts and theories. There was evidence of "procedural" (or "operational") knowledge—knowledge of how to draw upon concepts, facts and theories, integrate them, use them, and *create new knowledge*. There is clear evidence of expertise (Simon 1947).

The psychologist Howard Gardner (1997) writes of a common belief held by those who study the development of expertise that it takes about ten years of practice to become a "full-fledged" expert (p. 28). One feature of expertise, according to this view, is the acquisition of several thousand "chunks" of information—a *chunk*, a technical term in cognitive psychology, is a unit of memory comprising of several strongly linked items of information (Matlin 2009, p. 97)—in the course of becoming experts. Herbert Simon (1996, pp. 89–92) has himself argued along these lines. An example cited by both Gardner and Simon is the expert chess player who has been estimated to have at his disposal some 50,000 or more moves. Such expert knowledge develops in the course of long apprenticeship and training, stretching over ten years. For a scientist working in a mature field such as physics, mathematics, chemistry or biology, their expertise accrues through the long grueling years of high school, undergraduate, graduate and post-doctoral training.

Simon's excursion into the foundations of physics seems to refute the ten-year rule. The typical reader (consumer) of or contributor (artificer) to the journal *Philosophical Magazine* (a very prominent and one of the oldest scientific journals, founded in 1798) in which Simon's 1947 paper on Newtonian mechanics appeared would be a natural scientist or mathematician. Such a reader or contributor would have served precisely this kind of long apprenticeship in physics, and he or she would have been astonished to learn that the author of "The Axioms of Newtonian Mechanics" was neither physicist nor mathematician nor a trained philosopher of science but an assistant professor of political science (as Simon then was at the Illinois Institute of Technology).

So whence did this "expert knowledge" of physics originate in Simon's case? Partly through formal course work in high school and university: on completing graduate school the extent of his formal education included "bits and dabs of science" (Simon 1991, p. 85). Even as a fledgling faculty at the Illinois Institute of Technology he continued his formal excursions into physics by attending courses and seminars on theoretical physics, topology and mathematical methods of physics, offered by colleagues at both the Institute and the University of Chicago (p. 100).

But as we have noted, by his own admission Simon was an autodidact. His knowledge space pertaining to physics was created mostly through self-learning. Reflecting on this over fifty years later he would write that by the time of that first paper on Newtonian mechanics he had been, largely through self-study:

> 16 years into serious dabbling in physics and certainly … the equivalent of at least a Master's degree and perhaps more in mechanics.
>
> *(Simon, personal communication, April 1, 2000)*

Thus, he would continue, his 1947 paper "would not be a surprising product coming from a student who had done some graduate study in the philosophy of science with a minor in physics" (ibid.).

The point is that his "serious dabbling in physics" took place during a time he was otherwise engaged in becoming a behaviorally inclined social scientist. As for the ten-year rule, Simon disclaimed that his own work on the foundations of Newtonian mechanics refuted it: "the ten year rule applies to world class experts" which, he said, he was not in physics. He added, deprecatingly and with a touch of irony:

> What it [my experience] exhibits most clearly is that my idea of what constitutes recreation is a little odd by most people's standards.
>
> *(Ibid.)*

V   The entwinement of interest and curiosity

Curiosity and interest are both what philosophers of mind call *intentional* states of mind; a mental state is said to be intentional when it is *about* or *refer to* something in the world other than itself (Searle 1984, p. 16; Chalmers 1996, p. 19). One is curious *about* something in the world; one is interested *in* something in the world. Thus, in this philosophical sense, intentional states are not only intentions (goals) but also beliefs, desires, hopes and fears that are directed toward things in the world outside of the mind itself. For some philosophers, such as John Searle (1992), intentional states are markers of consciousness in that to be conscious of something in the world outside of the mind is to have an intentional state about that something—though not all conscious states are intentional. Searle gives the example of pain: one may be conscious of one's pain but that is not an intentional state since it is not something outside of oneself (p. 84).

Curiosity and interest are entwined intentional states. People pursue at length and thereby acquire deep knowledge about a subject because they are both curious about it and it deeply interests them. All such persons who pursue, sometimes obsessively, a subject are driven by a superneed: the need to know.

Some people read, study and/or experience widely, some phenomenally so. In their cases the superneed to know extends over many subjects, many fields. They are not just content to know one thing well. Simon was clearly such a being. But what distinguishes Simon (and polymaths like him) from others with similar widths of interest and curiosity is that at some point in time the need to *know* does not satiate them. Their multihued interest and curiosity becomes the fount of another superneed: the need to *create*. Simon was not a Renaissance man because he acquired a rich and eclectic belief/knowledge space. He was not just a consumer of knowledge. Rather, as we will see later, he assimilated concepts and ideas from several distinct (and often disparate) areas and *transformed* them into forms that served his particular purpose. His was a Renaissance mind by way of production not just consumption.

In this process of study and learning stretching across his school and university years, Simon was engaged in *multiple* creative encounters as a consumer, with a plethora of artificers, some long dead, some still alive at the time, some proximate (such as Rudolf Carnap) some not so proximate (such as A.J. Ayer). The wide and deep ways and byways of Simon's entwined interest and curiosity resulted in a proactively prepared mind by the time he first ventured into serious research as a doctoral student.

VI   Interest and proactive preparation

But how does interest relate to proactive preparation? On the one hand to *develop* an interest in something one must have engaged in a certain period of proactive preparation. So in this sense proactive preparation *precedes* the formation of interest. On the other hand proactive preparation may itself be directed along a certain path as a result of the germination of interest. So in this situation proactive preparation may *follow* the formation of an interest.

I think it is fair to say that the construction of an interest in—and thus curiosity about—some particular thing or problem or experience and the activity of proactive preparation *in general interleave in time*. They feed off each other. An observation, an experience or an event may cause the preliminary construction of an interest that in turn causes the person to engage in proactive preparation on topics related to and surrounding that interest. This preparation in turn sharpens the interest—or for that matter, may lead to the person in becoming *dis*interested in that topic.

It is worth noting also another view of interest. Creativity researcher and economist Jonathan Feinstein (2006) has documented and discussed extensively the role of interest in the development of the creative mind. Feinstein distinguished between "ordinary" or "casual" interest from what he termed "creative interest." For Feinstein, a "creative interest" is a *topic* or subject one is curious about (p. 36); thus it is objective. It is not an intentional state at all; rather, this topic *engenders* an intentional state of curiosity or fascination. So the objectivity of a creative interest as a topic *à la* Feinstein (if I have understood him correctly) is to be contrasted to the subjective, intentional state of interest as we have discussed above.

VII   The Catholic taste

Music historian and psychologist Rosamund Harding (1942) in a small gem of a book, *An Anatomy of Inspiration*, remarked that creative beings whose creativity is restricted to one particular domain (the usual case) may still cultivate knowledge in areas that are far beyond his own subject (p. 3)—for these more distant shores might bear rich fruits in that person's specialty. As an example she cited the French *savant* Louis Pasteur. In a letter to his father Pasteur mentioned that his research was based on concepts taken from many different branches of science (p. 3). Harding also mentioned the nineteenth century English novelist George Eliot (*nom de plume* of Mary Ann Evans) who, in addition to reading closely the works of other novelists, studied philology and had deep scholarly knowledge of French, German, Italian and Spanish, and read both Greek and Latin. Hebrew was another favorite language of hers; she was also interested, though not well versed in astronomy (p. 4).

We may call this tendency to cultivate a wide span of knowledge regardless of whether one becomes a creative polymath *à la* Herbert Simon or a creative specialist *à la* George Eliot a *Catholic taste*.

VIII   The Holmesian mentality

But there is an opposing mentality. When Dr. Watson first met Sherlock Holmes at the beginning of *A Study in Scarlet* the doctor was bewildered by the nature of the detective's knowledge. Holmes, Watson decided, knew nothing of literature, philosophy or astronomy (not even, to Watson's amazement, the Copernican theory), had the barest of knowledge of politics, "variable" knowledge of botany and some "practical" knowledge of geology. On the other hand Holmes's knowledge of chemistry was "profound," of anatomy was "accurate" if "unsystematic" and of "sensational literature" enormous (Conan Doyle 1984, pp. 21–22).

Watson could discern no pattern in the data. Holmes explained to him that he never acquired any knowledge that was not relevant to his vocation as a "consulting detective." The only knowledge he cultivated was that which would be useful to his "science of detection" (p. 21).

Let us call this the *Holmesian mentality*. It is obviously quite contrary to the Catholic mentality. Holmes's rationale was that our cognitive capacity is severely limited, so why entangle knowledge that is useful in one's vocation with "lumber of every sort" a person may encounter? (Ibid.).

Watson's analysis and Holmes's self-declared epistemic philosophy was, in fact, found wanting in later stories. The reader encounters numerous instances of the unexpected and, sometimes, esoteric nuggets of knowledge tucked away in Holmes's "brain attic," that seemed to have no bearing on his vocation. Indeed, in *The Valley of Fear* we hear him tell an admirer that: all knowledge is useful in detection (Conan Doyle 1984, p. 776). Despite this *volte face* the "Holmesian mentality" is a useful descriptor for the willful, selective retention of knowledge, the antithesis of the Catholic mind.

The Victorian fictional detective's real world contemporary Sir Francis Galton believed in the efficacy of the Homesian mentality. Galton, influenced by his cousin Charles Darwin, is most famous for his infamous founding of eugenics, a highly controversial, once powerfully influential and now discredited pseudo-scientific sciobiological philosophy about the genetical basis of mental fitness and ability and, in the words of evolutionary theorist Stephen Jay Gould (2006), "the [genetical] inheritance of nearly everything" (p. 487). (However, as we have already noted (Chapter 4, IX), modern research indicates that genetics has *a* role in such creativity-related attributes as intelligence and divergent thinking. But it is far from clear what this role is. At this time of writing the prevalent idea is that creativity is related to a synergy of several genetical factors though the role of specific gene actions is still obscure (Barbot, Tan and Grigorenko 2013, pp. 73, 76–77)).

But Galton was a polymath in a characteristically Victorian way. He was a pioneer in theoretical statistics, a passionate seeker of quantification in all things human, an anthropologist, explorer, meteorologist and the inventor of a method of classifying fingerprints that, according to one historian of science, was probably Galton's most practical contribution in the public domain (Sengoopta 2003, p. 98). (Holmes would have approved no doubt: in one of his cases we find fingerprint analysis being used to establish a suspect's identity (Conan Doyle 1984, p. 506)).

Polymath though he was, Galton interests us here because, paradoxically, he apparently held an essentially Holmesian position. No concept or idea that was irrelevant to one's field of interest should be present in the "antechamber" of the mind (Harding 1942, p. 5).

Ultimately, the Holmesian mentality begs the question: how does one know *à priori* what pieces of knowledge will be useful or not in one's creative life?

IX   Portrait of an American artist in preparation

To repeat the Pasteural aphorism: the prepared mind favors creativity. But the relationship between interest/curiosity, preparation and need (especially superneed) can vary between individuals. In some situations "in the beginning" is the interest and this may lead to the forming of a compelling need which in turn leads to proactive preparation. Schematically:

interest/curiosity → superneed → proactive preparation

Or it may be that the interest and need are so intertwined that they are difficult to disentangle, or they may influence each other:

interest/curiosity ↔ superneed → proactive preparation

It is equally plausible that the interest or curiosity leads to the unconscious shaping of a prepared mind and it is only when that preparedness is consciously perceived by the person that a compelling need to create is born:

interest/curiosity → proactive preparation → superneed

In the case of Herbert Simon, discussed earlier in this chapter, this last schematic seems an appropriate descriptor. On the other hand, the late twentieth century painter George Rodrigue, by his own recollection, knew by the time he was about nine that he would be an artist (G. Rodrigue, personal communication, April 17, 2002). Clearly, here a creative interest (in Jonathan Feinstein's sense) and a compelling need to create art went hand in hand. The second of the above schemas seem to describe his situation more closely. Combined with this was his realization that he possessed the gift of art—that he had a creative *potential* in this domain. His preparation began thereafter, encouraged by his parents.

In many ways Rodrigue's formal art education—beginning with art classes in school and private lessons between the ages of ten through fourteen (1954–1958), and ending, at age twenty-three after three years at the Art Center College of Design in Los Angeles (1965–1967)—was not very different from the kind of preparation countless aspiring painters have undertaken through the ages. He honed his skills as a draftsman and in drawing and with paint. In art school he experimented with various techniques, style, media and forms. He learnt to paint in various styles—Impressionism, Primitivism, Cubism and so on (G. Rodrigue, personal communication, April 17, 2002). No single style appears to have dominated his work of the time. He did figure studies, charcoal studies, quasi-naturalistic landscapes, pen-and-ink drawings and oils. He painted people and abstract non-representational works.

A striking aspect of Rodrigue's preparatory years is that his gifts as an artist did not seem to have drawn the attention of any teacher per se, nor any mentor figure. In my interviews and conversations with him I cannot recall hearing him mention a teacher or another artist who had an influential presence in those years. The social *milieux* artists normally thrive in seemed to have eluded him.

These were the 1960s. The art of the era mirrored these tempestuous times. In America, in particular, the movement called Abstract Expressionism had emerged soon after World War II (Chipp 1968, pp. 512–519). Among its most distinguished exponents were Jackson Pollock and Mark Rothko (Golding 2000, p. 116). In the mid-1950s Pop Art brought back figural imagery but in a form quite different from the past. Pop Art was characterized by the use of hard edges and near-photographic techniques. Its immediate forerunners were painters such as Jasper Johns and Robert Rauschenberg, the former noted for his paintings of ordinary two-dimensional objects such as flags (especially the Stars and Stripes), the latter for his inclusion of three-dimensional artifacts into his paintings, such as Coca-Cola bottles, tin cans, and clocks (Bailey 2001, pp. 202, 220).

Pop artists employed techniques gleaned from commercial art. By far the most celebrated of them was Andy Warhol with his silkscreen images of mass-produced objects such as Campbell soup cans, often repeated many times in the same work, and his pictures of celebrities like Marilyn Monroe (Bailey 2001, pp. 208, 210). Among other Pop artists was Roy Lichtenstein noted for his comic strips-inspired works (p. 200).

Rodrigue's preparation was situated against this backdrop. If part of his learning process in Los Angeles was common to all artists of the past two centuries, there was a significant component that was shaped by his time and place: America in the 1960s. By his own account his time in the Art Center College of Design was spent in in intensive study of Pop Art (G. Rodrigue, personal communication, April 17, 2002). As for Abstract Expressionism, this too was taught at the Art Center but "not in terms of art history … but rather as a discipline" (G. Rodrigue, personal communication, April 22, 2002). Rodrigue could not recall that he was aware of artists such as Jasper Johns and Robert Rauschenberg while in art school. His awareness of these artists came later, through visits to museums and reading books on their works.

While in California Rodrigue experimented with Pop Art-as-fine art. He did collages. In one work titled *Pop Goes the Ads* he blended the collage technique with a mix of techniques borrowed from both Pop Art and Op Art (a movement which followed Pop Art in America and which drew its inspiration from optical illusion and other oddities of visual perception) to produce a work showing well-known comic strip characters of the time and comic strip narration techniques (Anon 2003, pp. 48–49). In another work of this preparatory period Rodrigue transferred the collage's cut-and-paste elements entirely to paint, creating a collagesque still-life painting titled *Five Watermelons*.

These paintings were elements of his proactive preparation. Like all artists his personal belief/knowledge and operational spaces were gradually constructed, comprising primarily of skills and techniques: operational knowledge rather than the propositional knowledge characteristic of scientists and scholars such as Herbert Simon. The works he did in his time in Los Angeles can be viewed as *experiments* that tested his mastery of skills and techniques. This is not to say that an artist's preparation entails the acquisition of no other kinds of beliefs and knowledge: they too, in their apprenticeships, visit museums, learn art history, acquire knowledge of specific ("canonical") paintings and of the lives of particular artists. They form opinions about techniques, artworks, artists that become elements of their art-related schemas.

So it was with Rodrigue. Returning to his birthplace, South Louisiana—"Cajun Country"—he had already developed a firm opinion, a firm *self-belief*: he knew what styles he would *not* pursue: neither Abstract Expressionism nor Pop Art, though the nature of the latter style had appealed to him, especially Warhol's work. He needed to find his own path as he wrote to a friend years later (G. Rodrigue to T. Sokolowski, October 6, 2001. Copy in my possession). The need to be original, to deviate from others, to make a history of his own was shaped and sharpened into a more precise (albeit negative) goal: what his style would *not* be.

Rodrigue's own and original way began in a geographic and cultural space as distant as one can imagine from the sophisticated New York-rooted Abstract Expressionism and the glittering pop–celebrity culture of Warholian Pop Art. It began in the landscape of South Louisiana, a geography in which he had been born and bred and which he knew intimately, and in the history and culture of his people, the Cajuns.

This brings us into the realm of a different kind of knowledge altogether, a kind intimately related to the artist's and the writer's proactive preparation and vital to their creative process but perhaps far less so for scientists, scholars, designers or inventors. I am speaking of *self-knowledge*. We will consider this later in this chapter.

X   Portrait of an Indian artist in preparation

In Chapter 3 (XVII), in discussing the superneed to be original we encountered the painter Amrita Sher-Gil. Here was an artist who could not have differed more from George Rodrigue, not only in gender but also in terms of time, place, culture and social background. Of Indian and Hungarian parentage, Sher-Gil's natural habitat was a melting pot of Indian, Hungarian and French *milieux* as they were between the two World Wars. Culturally she was a cosmopolitan in a way Rodrigue was not in their respective formative years. But she was as much a painter of her time and place as Rodrigue was in his. Their visual languages necessarily had a shared vocabulary. Their superneeds were identical: the need to paint. So what was the nature of her proactive preparation and how dis/similar was it from Rodrigue's?

Amrita Sher-Gil's father came from the Sikh nobility (the Sikhs are a religious sect originating in the Northern Indian region of Punjab, and their men are easily recognizable by the turbans and beard they are required to wear.) He was a Sanskrit scholar, a philosopher by inclination and an enthusiastic photographer. Her mother belonged to the Hungarian bourgeoisie with French and Italian ancestry and some Jewish blood. She was trained as an opera singer (Dalmia 2006, p. 6). Both Sher-Gil and her younger sister (by a year) were born in Budapest. Hungarian was her first language (Ananth 2007, p. 13).

Her appallingly short life of twenty-eight years was partitioned into four roughly equal time spans. From 1913 till 1921 the Sher-Gil family lived in Budapest. From 1921 till 1929 they lived in India, mostly in Simla, the Northern hill-station that served as the "winter capital" of the Raj (British India). This was the period in which Sher-Gil's painterly gift became evident. In 1929, urged by Sher-Gil's maternal uncle Ervin Baktay, himself a painter and later a distinguished Indologist, the family moved to Paris so that Sher-Gil, then sixteen, could train as an artist (and her sister Indira as a dancer). She lived in Paris for five years but by 1933, aged twenty, she began to feel an intense desire to return to India where she felt her future lay as an artist (Sher-Gil 1936).

Sher-Gil's last seven years in India were her most creative years when her reputation was established, when she invented a style that was unmistakably her own. (Incidentally, our earlier protagonist George Rodrigue, on returning to South Louisiana from Southern California invented the first of his unmistakably recognizable styles.) The Paris period thus forms the core of her proactive preparation though (as we noted in Chapter 2, and will see further below) even then, precocious as she was, her paintings in Paris were far more than merely "student work." Her Paris period exemplifies how preparation and serious creativity can fuse into one, and why sometimes the prepared and the inventive minds cannot be sharply demarcated.

Sher-Gil's nurture as a painter, if we are to believe her words, was largely a process of discovering on her own. She was the painterly equivalent of the scholarly autodidact, one who did not easily accept advice or suggestions, one who desired to discover for herself (Sher-Gil 1936). Her first formal art lessons, received in Simla in India, after the family's move from Budapest, was from an Englishman, a former teacher in London's Slade School of Art, who was perspicacious enough to recognize her precocious talent (Dalmia 2006, p. 25). Then there was her Hungarian maternal uncle Ervin Baktay who impressed upon her the importance of *plein air* painting and the value of using live models, a practice she would follow for the rest of her short life (p. 25).

In Paris she impressed the Post-Impressionist Lucien Simon with samples of her work and was accepted, underage, as his pupil in the famed École des Beaux Art (p. 27). But Lucien Simon, Sher-Gil tells us, did not actually teach. Rather, he encouraged his pupils to think for themselves, to solve their own artistic problems, to develop their individuality as painters (Sher-Gil 1936). Perhaps this was an important source of her self-nurturing mentality.

Her self-discovery was as much that of a developing adult. In the five years she spent in Paris, Sher-Gil led the life of the bohemian wholly appropriate to the spirit of the city's artistic and intellectual life. She discovered in herself a voracious sexual appetite: she had numerous sexual relationships with both men and women. She wrote with devastating candor to her mother in 1934 that while sexual relations with men were necessary, to meet her sexual needs she must also have encounters with women when opportunity came her way (Sunderam 2010, p. 125). (Sher-Gil's time in Paris overlapped with those of two other celebrated women writers, both older than her: the novelist Colette and the diarist and writer of erotica Anäis Nin, both known for their bohemian lifestyles and many sexual liaisons.)

But Sher-Gil's was never a dissipated life. Her self-discovery was as much intellectual and artistic as psychosexual. She read much, mainly the modernists: the Frenchmen Baudelaire, Verlaine and Proust, the Russian Dostoyevsky, the German Thomas Mann, the Irishman James Joyce, the Englishman D.H. Lawrence, and such Hungarian writers as Endre Any and Dezo Sabo (Sunderam n.d.). She drew, mainly in charcoal, and painted, in oil for the first time. From 1930 through 1932 she produced over sixty works (Dalmia 2006, p. 32). Her charcoals were mainly nudes, male and female. Her oils were mostly portraits, including self-portraits.

Her Paris period of nurture, of discovery and self-discovery, of preparation entailed an exploration of Post-Impressionism. Paul Gauguin, Paul Cézanne, Gustav Courbet beckoned. If *Young Girls* (1932; Anon 2007, plate 24)—which won her an associate membership of the Grand Salon and a gold medal (Dalmia 2006, p. 32)—reminds the viewer of Courbet, even of Cézanne, then *Self Portrait as a Tahitian* (1934), showing her bare-breasted, her long black hair loose down her back (Anon 2007, plate 32), was a tribute to Gaughin. By her own account her work in Paris was "absolutely Western in conception and execution"—though, she hastened to add, it was neither "tame" nor orthodox (Sher-Gil 1936).

XI   The superneed to flout tradition

As we have noted in Chapter 3, departing or deviating from the beaten track appears to be a universal superneed of all creative beings. To repeat, the ambitious artist, like the ambitious scientist or musician, novelist or inventor or poet, wants to *make history*. She can only do this by producing an artifact that is significantly original (rendering her H-creative) and/or creating an artifact that (she hopes) will be consequential to the future history of her field (thus rendering her C-creative). In the latter case this may entail creative encounters with consumers.

Rodrigue's proactive preparation, as we have seen, produced in him a *conscious* superneed to be original after he had completed his apprenticeship in Los Angeles in the mid-1960s. Returning home he didn't know *what* to paint but he knew what he would *not* paint.

Likewise, Sher-Gil's preparation in Paris in the early 1930s produced in her a consciously felt need to deviate from the tradition she had been nurtured in. When she decided in 1933 to return to India it was because she felt that her destiny as a painter lay in India not in Europe (Sher-Gil 1936). This desire may well have been driven by the more fundamental need to make history. In Paris she was one of many gifted artists embedded in a vibrant matrix of painting styles and movements. She was in a world that buzzed with the likes of Matisse and Picasso, Breton and the Surrealists, the afterglow of the Post-Impressionists and the abstract art of Joan Miro. To make history in such a setting, in Europe, in the West, meant the invention of a style *within the European tradition* that would yet stand apart from all else. She did not want to be labeled "Cézannesque" or "Gaughinesque"; she was pleased when, after exhibiting *Young Girls* in the Grand Salon (which had once rejected Manet and Cézanne) in 1933, one of her professors compared her to Courbet. She acknowledged the compliment but she had no desire to paint like Courbet. As she wrote in a letter to a confidant in 1933, she wanted to invent a style—a *painterly schema*—of her own; to be herself (quoted in Dalmia 2006, p. 50).

There are, of course, significant cultural and social differences between the aristocratic, cosmopolitan Amrita Sher-Gil and the Deep South-nurtured George

Rodrigue, my two protagonists here, differences that impacted their respective training as artists. What is striking, though, are their similarities and what they reveal, in general, of the nature of proactive preparation.

If there is a superneed to paint, and this is recognized early by the artificer and his or her mentors, then proactive preparation can begin early in their lives. This is what happened for both Sher-Gil and Rodrigue. But we also see the role the other superneed—the need to deviate from the past, to make history—played in the *outcomes* of their preparatory phases.

Thus we see that proactive preparation is more than a process of constructing belief/knowledge and operational spaces of ideas, concepts, skills, knowledge of other artists' works, cultural knowledge and so on, which the artist can then draw upon. The superneed to be original kicks in. Five years into her life in Paris, Sher-Gil realized that to make history one must part ways with history. Likewise, completing his three-year training in Los Angeles, Rodrigue came to exactly this same realization. For Sher-Gil this meant to part ways with the Post-Impressionists and the great styles and movements she had imbibed in Paris. For Rodrigue this meant to deviate from the Abstract Expressionists, the Pop artists and the Op artists he had studied in Los Angeles. This was their common *goal* when one returned to India and the other to Louisiana. Proactive preparation taught them not only their craft, their tools and their artistic inheritance but also *the path not to be taken*. Though neither, it seems, knew yet just how they would like to fill the empty canvas they had thus created for themselves. In a later chapter we will see how their respective goals to be original came to be satisfied.

The comparison with my other protagonist, the polymath scientist Herbert Simon, is worth noting. Both artists prepared themselves for their chosen vocation as artist. Simon's proactive preparation, in contrast, was driven by intellectual interest and curiosity in almost all things. There is no explicit evidence in his auto/biography that his catholicity in reading and studying was motivated by his eventually chosen vocation, to investigate the scientific nature of rational decision making in humans and machines.

XII   All about *I*

The novelist and teacher of creative writing John Gardner in his influential *The Art of Fiction* admonishes the aspiring writer to evade the common injunction offered to neophyte writers to write what one knows (Gardner 1991, p. 18). He goes on to say that there is nothing more "limiting to the imagination" than when a writer takes this advice. And yet Gardner's own advice is write the sort of story one knows, including stories about one's childhood (ibid.).

But writing on something related to one's childhood *is* to draw upon what the writer knows very well. As psychologists and psychoanalysts have observed, our acutest, most compelling autobiographical memories are about our early lives. Novelists, short story writers, poets and filmmakers commonly (if not inevitably) reach back to their own experiences in creating their first significant artifacts. Wordsworth's *The*

Prelude (1799–1850) is a particularly well-known example from the realm of poetry (Gill and Wu 1994, pp. 157–224). James Joyce's biographer Richard Ellman (1982, pp. 144–149) has shown the autobiographical extent of Joyce's novella "The Dead," published in the story collection *The Dubliners* (published in 1914). This story centers on a woman haunted by the memory of her dead girlhood sweetheart and her confessing this memory to her husband, the story's protagonist. This episode mirrors an event in Joyce's wife Nora's past (Ellman 1982, p. 243).

But there was more. The story unfolds during and in the aftermath of an annual dinner and dance hosted by two unmarried sisters just after the New Year. This event recaptures a Christmas dinner Joyce's great-aunts used to give that he attended as a child. The dinner speech in the story delivered by the story's protagonist was (as recorded by Joyce's brother Stanislaus) a near imitation of their father's "oratorial style" (Ellman 1982, p. 243). The other dinner guests were also based on Joyce's remembrances of these dinners (Ellman 1982, p. 246).

"To write what one knows" is then something that fiction writers (or poets) commonly do. Above all, this knowledge, autobiographical and experiential, is *self-knowledge*. Unlike knowledge acquired formally, the kind we saw as part of Herbert Simon's preparation or those gleaned by artists Rodrigue and Sher-Gil, self-knowledge accrues mostly unconsciously. All humans acquire self-knowledge but writers of fiction and poetry or, more pointedly, autobiographers and memoirists have the privilege of elevating self-knowledge to the level of consciousness for the purpose of their craft.

This is not to say that scientists, inventors or scholars do not *ever* appeal consciously to self-knowledge in their creative encounters. (We will consider later instances of this from the scientific realm.) But what might be relatively less common for these types of creative beings is fairly ubiquitous for the writer.

The prepared mind then is (among other things) *a self-knowing mind*. One's beliefs and knowledge include beliefs and knowledge about oneself. Self-knowledge is thus knowledge about the *I*.

But what does this entail?

XIII Varieties of self-knowledge

According to cognitive psychologist Ulrich Neisser (1988), a person's sense of self can be one of several kinds. One of these originates in his relationship with his physical environment. Neisser called this the "ecological self" (p. 36). My bodily sensation of sitting at my desk in my study, gazing through the window, the movements of my head, eyes, hand and fingers, my sense of grasping my fountain pen, feeling its hard surface as I write these words are all (if I have understood Neisser correctly) aspects of my ecological self. But this self is not confined to the biological body: whatever moves with the body also belongs to the ecological self (p. 39). In my case this would include my eyeglasses and my fountain pen. Furthermore my *agency* in initiating the movements of my arm, hand and fingers and the fountain pen form aspects of my ecological self.

But scholars of various persuasions—philosophers, biologists and psychologists—have come to believe that one's *natural* environment has a place in identity formation (Weingart 1977; Thomasow 1995; Clayton and Opotow 2003). Yet the environment many of us experience in this densely artifactual age is only sparingly natural. Many of us, especially those who live in an urban milieu, are dominated by a built or *artificial* environment; "technoscape" as much as landscape. For convenience let us call the totality of one's Neisserian–ecological, natural, geographical and artificial environment that envelops our body (including the mind/brain) the *environmental self*.

The autobiography scholar John Paul Eakin believes that one cannot conceive of an *I* that is autonomous of the "other" especially what he calls the "proximate other," such as a parent or a sibling (Eakin 1988, 1999, pp. 43ff). Eakin argues that all autobiographies are stories in relation to other selves: one's identity is shaped both by and in contrast to one's parent's identities; Eakin called this the *relational self*.

Not all agree with the universality of this proposition. For example one scholar taking a feminist position asserts that the relational self in autobiography is essentially a characteristic of women autobiographers (Mason 1980).

Ulrich Neisser also identified another kind of self-knowledge pertaining to one's personal memories and experiences. He called this the "extended self." One's identity is in part the outcome of one's experiences. Neisser's extended self is defined by the past as that past is registered in one's autobiographical memory, so I think a more meaningful label for this kind of self-knowledge is what Jerome Bruner (1994) called the *remembered self*. Of course, to be a remembered self implies a capacity *to* remember: a "remembering self."

We each have a certain *concept* of ourselves. Neisser called this the *conceptual* self and I think of all the kinds of self-knowledge this is the tributary into which all other kinds of beliefs and knowledge including other varieties of self-knowledge feed. Personality traits such as introversion and extroversion contribute to one's conceptual self. Various fears and phobias are elements of the conceptual self, as are superneeds, as are interests. For example, Rabindranath Tagore's detestation in childhood of formal, classroom-style education (Tagore 2001, p. 40) was an aspect of his conceptual self. Einstein's suspicion of authoritarianism, acquired in his teens, became a lifelong feature of his conceptual self (Einstein 1970, p. 5).

Self-knowledge then is what we know (or believe we know) about ourselves. It is all about the *I*. And if we accept Neisser's analysis (and that of other psychologists such as Bruner) we can usefully view it as a composite of the knowledge we possess of our environmental, relational, remembered and conceptual selves. These various kinds of self-knowledge bleed into one another. My remembered self will contain elements of my relational self as well as elements of my environmental self. Conversely my present environmental self is shaped by aspects of my remembered self. My conceptual self is shaped by these other kinds of self-knowledge. And, of course, *non*-self-knowledge is fused with self-knowledge. For instance a person may conceive of himself as a socialist (an aspect of his conceptual self) as a result of his knowledge of the history of industrial capitalism (objective non-self-knowledge) and/or reading Karl Marx.

Let us then conceptualize self-knowledge as a "subspace" of one's belief/ knowledge space. But notice that since superneeds can also shape one's conceptual self, elements of one's needs and goals intrude into her self-knowledge subspace.

If I have devoted a rather large amount of *this* (textual) space to the matter of self-knowledge it is because the development of self-knowledge, partly consciously, mostly unselfconsciously, has a prominent presence in the development of the pre- pared mind of a potentially creative being—something not always explicitly recog- nized. Thus Jonathan Feinstein's (2006) lengthy study of what he called creative development frequently touches upon such issues as personal experiences as the beginning of creative development but never actually mentions the *idea* of self- knowledge. The point is that the creative process is often obscured if we ignore the role of self-knowledge in this process.

XIV A writer's self-knowledge

Cognitive scientist and literature teacher Carmen Comeaux (2006), in her study of the fiction writer Flannery O'Connor, dwelt at length on O'Connor's self- knowledge and its role in her craft as one of twentieth century America's preeminent storytellers.

O'Connor was born in Savannah, Georgia in 1925 and died of lupus disease in 1964. Save for five years elsewhere (including attending graduate school in the University of Iowa's famed Iowa Writers Workshop and a stint in the Northeast) she lived in Georgia all her life, a large part in the ancestral farm called Andalusa. Her Southern upbringing profoundly shaped her identity as a writer. As Comeaux noted, the South gave her experiential knowledge that entered into the characters and plots of her stories. She was very much the "Southern writer." But the South also defined her self-knowledge, environmentally, relationally and conceptually, and shaped her worldview all of which entered into her fiction (Comeaux 2006, p. 147). (This was as true for the painter George Rodrigue whose art was born at the confluence of his acquired knowledge of contemporary American art and his profoundly embedded environmental and remembered self-knowledge resulting from his Cajun upbringing in South Louisiana.)

If O'Connor's Southern–ness was integral to her self-knowledge then so was her Catholicism. O'Connor recorded several times in her letters (she "networked" widely through correspondence, including with well-known writers) that her fiction was diffused with her Catholic sensibilities, that her stories couldn't have been written by any other than a Catholic. She referred to her novel (one of two) *Wise Blood* as an example of this sensibility even though it was about a Protestant saint (Comeaux 2006, p. 184). Comeaux remarked that it was probably the inter- action of her Southern–ness and Catholicism, the former an aspect of her environ- mental self, the latter dominating her conceptual self that most strongly influenced her craft (p. 149).

Most strikingly (if not unexpectedly as happens with many writers), O'Connor seemed to have projected aspects of her conceptual self into some of her fictional characters. She admitted her identification with two of the characters in one of her best-known stories, "A Good Man is Hard to Find"; and partly with a character in another story, "Good Country People". A character in her second novel, *The Violent Bear It Away*, though having a setting far removed from O'Connor's world, was (in Comeaux's words) infused with her personality (p. 153).

XV   The remembered *I* of the autobiographer

Autobiography as a literary genre has long been recognized by literary scholars (Olney 1998; Eakin 1999; Anderson 2001). Indeed, the literary reputation of some writers rests considerably or even wholly on their autobiographical writings, for instance in the case Saint Augustine's, *Confessions* (*c.*398–400) and Jean-Jacques Rousseau's, *Confessions* (1781–1789).

Historian and "man of letters" Nirad C. Chaudhuri is a more recent exemplar of such a being. His *Autobiography of an Unknown Indian* (Chaudhuri 2001) was his first book published when he was fifty-four, and he would go on to write many other books. But it was *Autobiography* for which Chaudhuri is still best remembered. For Salman Rushdie (1997) it is "a masterpiece"; Nobel laureate V.S. Naipaul (1984, p. 59) believed that no better work describing the influence of the West on the Indian mind has been written. Journalist and literary editor Ian Jack (2001) remarked that its description of the richness and specificity of everyday life in Indian remains unmatched. Its status as an H-original work in the realm of autobiography was evident to these consumer–judges and many others. Our interest in the present context lies in that it affords an exemplar of the significance of self-knowledge in autobiographical writing.

Most autobiographies begin in one way or another in the first person singular: the *I*. But who is this *I* in autobiography? John Paul Eakin (1999) has pointed out that one needs to distinguish the *I* who is telling the story from the *I* the story is about. The former is the narrator, the latter the protagonist. In the case of Chaudhuri, since *Autobiography of an Unknown Indian* was written when he was fifty-four, and covers the first twenty-four years of his life, we may call the protagonist "Young-NCC" and the narrator "NarrNCC." So it is NarrNCC's voice we are hearing in the autobiography, but the person he is referring to is YoungNCC—who is a *remembered I*. NarrNCC's self-knowledge contains knowledge of the remembered *I*. And this is where the construction of self-knowledge is significant in the act of writing an autobiography.

In writing *Autobiography*, Chaudhuri is a creative being in a particular sense. At the time he wrote it (between 1947 and 1949), NarrNCC has his own belief/knowledge space containing what he believes or knows about his own past (stored in autobiographical memory) and an emotion space containing certain emotions and feelings about his past. He then *builds* a story about himself that draws on this beliefs/knowledge of, and emotions linked to, his remembered *I*. NarrNCC becomes a *story* teller, and like all story tellers he is a creative being. The one important difference between him and other story tellers—fiction writers, poets, balladeers, mythologists and historians—is that the protagonist of his story is himself *as he believed he was*: Young NCC.

In other words, NarrNCC's cognitive–historical space contained as a subspace a cognitive–historical space characterizing the mind and environment of YoungNCC—the remembered *I*. NarrNCC had developed a proactively prepared mind in which the cognitive–historical subspace defining the remembered *I* is a constituent. In other words NarrNCC's self-knowledge—which enabled him to tell his story—contained a representation of the remembered *I*. This, of course, is a manifestation of the historicity dimension of one's cognitive–historical space (Chapter 1, IV).

XVI   Glimpses of a natural scientist in preparation

As I have previously mentioned, perhaps scientists, designers, engineers and inventors are less prone to project their self-knowledge into their creative realms. But this does not mean that self-knowledge is totally absent. At the very least one's conceptual self will find its way, perhaps unconsciously, into the creative process one way or another.

Other than Darwin, few natural scientists of the modern era have been studied more than Einstein. Just as there is a thriving "Darwin industry" so there is an "Einstein industry." Like Darwin, Einstein fascinates not just fellow scientists but philosophers, scholars and intellectuals of all stripes, even the lay person, as such biographies as Ronald Clark's (1971) *Einstein: The Life and Times* (1971) and popular expositions of his physics as Lincoln Barnett's (2005) *The Universe and Dr. Einstein* attest to. My aim here is vastly more modest: I wish to offer a few key glimpses of Einstein in proactive preparation.

Einstein was born in 1879 in the German city of Ulm of Jewish parentage. Though his parents were undogmatic and unobserving in their religion Einstein himself became deeply religious as a small child "by way of the traditional education machine" (Einstein 1970, p. 3). But he underwent a dramatic change at age twelve. Reading books of popular science he concluded that the stories told in the Bible were untrue. Thus was born in the young Einstein an antipathy against every form of authority that became a lifelong stance (Einstein 1970, p. 5). This was an early element of his conceptual self-knowledge. Authority included religious authority and he expressed his newly gotten epiphany by refusing to be bar mitzvahed, the traditional Jewish confirmation ceremony (Pais 1982, p. 38). Thus was also born something more consequential. His loss of religiosity was his first attempt to liberate himself from the shackles of the "merely-personal" (Einstein 1970, p. 5). This meant that for Einstein, private, subjective emotions, needs, desires, even personal relationships were not important. Rather it was the objective world, the world that existed independently of human subjectivity, that reached out to him; he was drawn irresistibly to unravelling the mysteries of this objective world (ibid.). This feeling was reinforced when he realized that other men whom he had come to admire had also been liberated by devoting themselves to this world.

Einstein, writing this at age sixty-seven (in 1946 or 1947), was dipping into his remembered past. This memory itself was part of his remembered self. Thus was born, likely in his early teens, a superneed: the probing of this "beyond the personal" world.

This would be his "road to paradise" (ibid.). Ironically then, Einstein's developing self-knowledge about the *I* included a belief that the *I did not matter*. It was the world "out there" that existed independent of human beings that mattered. Here was a profoundly important *metaphysical belief* that became a core of his belief/knowledge space: the objective reality of the external world.

In a well-known conversation with the poet–philosopher–composer Rabindranath Tagore (whose creative encounter with W.B. Yeats was narrated in Chapter 4, IV) in Einstein's home in Caputh, Germany in 1930 (one of four meetings between the two), Einstein firmly reiterated this belief. For Tagore the world was a human world; there could be no conception of the universe other than a human conception. Truth, Tagore claimed, "is realized through men." Einstein disagreed. He admitted that he could not demonstrate *scientifically* that truth existed independent of humanity. But this was his firm *belief*. For instance, he said, Pythagoras's theorem in geometry stated something that was "approximately true" regardless of the existence of people. (See Das 1966, pp. 911–912, for a transcript of this conversation.)

Einstein's reference to Pythagoras is worth noting for his severing the "chains of the merely-personal" coincided with his discovery, at age twelve, of another "wonder" (Einstein 1970, p. 9). This was Euclidean plane geometry. Here he encountered propositions that could be proved with absolute certainty, beyond any doubt. The clarity and sureness of such proofs cast an indelible impression on him (ibid.).

Looking back at age sixty-seven, Einstein admitted that this idea of obtaining certain knowledge of the objective, experienced world through pure reason was erroneous. As we will see his belief in the relationship of exact mathematics and objective reality was quite complicated. But he could not forget the "wonder" of that experience at age twelve about the nature of geometrical truth.

By the time Einstein discovered the beauty of geometry he was enrolled (in 1888) in the Luitpold Gymnasium in Munich. (The gymnasium system was the highest cadre of secondary school education in Germany at the time.) One of his texts was a book titled *Essentials of Natural Science* by one Joseph Krist, which emphasized that experiments formed the fount of the laws of nature (Pyenson 1985, p. 3). Curiously, in his "Autobiographical Notes" Einstein makes no mention of this book; rather he wrote of his good luck in learning the basic ideas of the natural sciences from a popular book, "Bernstein's *People's Book on Natural Sciences*, a work of 5 or 6 volumes" which he read "with breathless attention" (Einstein 1970, p. 15). As for his discovery of geometry, the probably source of this (according to historian of science Lewis Pyenson (1985, p. 4)) was a textbook on elementary mathematics by his mathematics teacher Adolf Sickenberger wherein the author preached mathematics as a tool for reasoning. He eschewed excessive rigor in favor of a more intuitive form of presentation.

Einstein performed well at Luitpold (Pyenson 1985, p. 6) yet there is anecdotal evidence that he disliked his years there—its authoritarianism, the teachers and the rote learning (Pais 1982, pp. 37–38). In any case he left the Gymnasium in 1895 without the all-essential final certificate, the *Arbitur*, thereby excluding his chances of a number of "respectable" career opportunities. He became a high-school dropout. In German terms he had left the mainstream of a society that coveted formal education.

Fortunately there lay other possibilities outside Germany. The highly regarded Eidgenössische Technische Hochschule (ETH) in Zurich did not need a German *Arbitur* to admit students, only that they pass an entrance examination. Though only sixteen, two years below the regulation admission age to ETH, "by special dispensation" Einstein was allowed to sit for the entrance examination. He did very well in physics and mathematics but failed in biology and modern languages (Pyenson 1985, p. 8). On the advice of ETH's rector he enrolled in a secondary trade school in Aarau. Passing their school leaving certificate would be the equivalent of passing the ETH entrance examination.

It was an agreeable and fruitful year in Aarau. Much later in life he would recall the school's freedom of instruction and learning (Pyenson 1985, p. 16). There were inspiring teachers in physics, geology and mathematics. He did well in the school leaving certificate examination, his Aarau diploma admitting him to ETH (Pais 1982, p. 521n). By then he was no longer interested in his father's wish that he study electrical engineering. In a brief essay written while still in Aarau he stated that if he gained admission to ETH he would study mathematics and physics with a view to becoming a teacher, but devoting himself to the theoretical parts of physics (Pais 1982, p. 40). He had thus already established for himself, at age sixteen, an interest, indeed something akin to a superneed: to pursue theoretical physics.

Conceptual self-knowledge played a role here. The reason for his decision was his attraction to abstract and mathematical thinking, coupled with an awareness of a lack of practical ability (Pais 1982, p. 40). Moreover, he perceived a "certain independence" in pursuing science, which he found greatly appealing (ibid.).

He had already shown his precocity in physical thinking. In an undated letter to his maternal uncle, a successful financier who lived in Brussels, but probably written in 1894 or 1895 (as recollected by him in 1950), he mentioned his hope of entering ETH. Accompanying the letter was a five-page essay on "The State of Aether in Magnetic Fields" (Clark 1971, p. 22; Pais 1982, pp. 130–131). The paper, he explained to his uncle, dealt with "a very special theme," though he apologized if it seemed "rather naïve and incomplete" as might be expected from someone of his age (Clark 1971, p. 22).

As striking was a question he asked himself while still in Aarau. What would happen if "one runs after a light wave" at the speed of light itself (Pais 1982, p. 131)? Here was a remarkable early manifestation of one of Einstein's principle intellectual tools which he would deploy within a decade with devastating effect: a *thought experiment*, an imagined experiment conducted in the mind but subject to all the constraints and laws attending physical nature. This question was also an early foray into the topsy-turvy world of special relativity he would usher forth in 1905.

Perhaps the young Einstein's most astonishing gesture of independence, defiance and unorthodoxy was his formal rejection of the Fatherland. In January 1896, still a student in the trade school in Aarau, Einstein paid three marks in return for a document issued in his birthplace, Ulm, stating that he was no longer a German national (Pais 1982, p. 41). He was then sixteen. This was his most definitive expression of his anti-Germanism, a feeling that may have resulted from the authoritarianism he had encountered in his Munich schooling. At any rate, for the next five years he would be stateless until, in February 1910, six months after obtaining his diploma from ETH, he became a Swiss citizen, which he remained for the rest of his life (though he also took American citizenship in 1940) (Pais 1982, pp. 45, 529).

In the autumn of 1896 Einstein became a student at ETH. His most distinguished professor there was undoubtedly the mathematician Hermann Minkowski, discoverer of four-dimensional space–time, now a standard aspect of modern physics and even a constituent of the lay consciousness. Einstein admitted that he could have had a solid mathematical education at ETH. Yet he spent most of his time in the physics laboratories, fascinated by the direct contact with physical reality (Einstein 1970, p. 15). He confessed that his interest in natural science, specifically physics, was much stronger than in mathematics.

But there was another reason, and this was that there were several branches of mathematics he could have easily chose as his specialty. But like Buridan's hapless ass (donkey)—though not as fatally—he could not decide which specialty to choose. (In the medieval philosopher Buridan's fable, an ass presented with two equally delectable but separate bundles of hay, could not make up its mind which bundle to eat and as a result died of starvation.) In fact, in the course of his preparatory years, Einstein's relationship to mathematics was strangely contradictory. On one hand, in ETH he took nine courses from Minkowski (Pyenson 1985, p. 21), and according to a friend of the time he demonstrated a consummate mastery of the discipline (ibid.). At the same time he abhorred the "abusive use" of mathematics in physics. And he would insist that mathematics was only a language for expressing the laws of physics. Apparently his experience with Minkowski's courses was instrumental in shaping this view.

At any rate it was clear to Einstein that his mathematical intuition was not sufficiently strong for him to separate the *really* important problems in mathematics from the rest (Einstein 1970, p. 15). More compellingly, he felt that his physical intuition was much stronger: that he could discern the fundamental issues in physics and ignore the rest that otherwise might distract him (p. 17).

I have mentioned that a shared superneed of creative beings is to deviate from the norm, to make history. In Einstein's proactive preparation this took shape as a kind of *meta-goal* to identify and focus on what was *really* the fundamental problems in physics and ignore the rest. Like Sherlock Holmes he had no wish to "clutter up the mind" with inessentials. This demanded, of course, a capacity to *recognize* the fundamentals when one encounters them. In Einstein's case this was rooted in his strong *interest* in physics and his *intuition* about physical phenomena. And how else can we characterize intuition than as unconsciously acquired, experiential, conceptual knowledge about something?

There was still the practical matter of examinations to be passed. This entailed cramming the mind with extraneous things. But this was Switzerland, an enlightened land where students suffered less (than in Germany) from the coercion of examinations. Moreover, Einstein had a classmate, Marcel Grossman (one of his few lifelong friends), who attended all the classes and meticulously took notes that he shared with Einstein. Thus he was afforded freedom in what he chose to pursue, at least until exam time (p. 17).

At age sixty-seven Einstein would meditate upon the place of freedom in education and the pursuit of his curiosity of what truly mattered to him: in the absence of freedom that curiosity could never prevail (ibid.). One is reminded here of Rabindranath Tagore with whom (as mentioned earlier in this chapter) Einstein profoundly agreed on some matters as he disagreed on others. Education was one of their points of agreement. Tagore was also utterly disaffected by the constraints formal education imposed on the creative spirit. As Einstein realized the significance of free and independent inquiry at age twelve so did Tagore discover at the same age the imperative of freedom for the pursuit of intellectual and creative needs (Tagore 2001, p. 216).

So what *were* the fundamentals that the young Einstein came to grasp? For the elderly sage of 1949, peering into his remembered past, it was that in the very beginning, God ("if there was such a thing"), created Newton's laws of motion, and its associated concepts of mass and force. "This is all" (Einstein 1970, p. 19).

This is all! It is as if Einstein was echoing the eighteenth century English poet Alexander Pope's famous couplet: "Nature and nature's laws lay hid in night:/God said, Let Newton be! And all was light."

Motion, mass, force. The science of *mechanics* in other words. But Einstein was setting up a narrative as a straw man to be demolished. In the nineteenth century the power and prestige of mechanics, Einstein wrote, lay not so much in its internal achievements (in advancing and consolidating the science of mechanics itself) but in its ubiquitous presence in domains seemingly unconnected with mechanics—in the theory of light and the theory of gases, for example, and in the theory of heat (Einstein 1970, pp. 19, 21). Even the analysis of electromagnetic phenomena appealed to the laws of mechanics (p. 21). This pulling together of the various strands of physical thought into a mechanical cloth was the signal achievement of the nineteenth century, effecting the great Newtonian synthesis. By the end of the nineteenth century physics was *Newtonian* physics.

But then came the Austrian philosopher and physical theorist Ernst Mach who "shook this dogmatic faith" and whose writings profoundly influenced Einstein (Einstein 1970, p. 21). Unsurprisingly, given his temperament and sensibilities, Einstein greatly admired Mach's skepticism and independence of mind (ibid.).

Einstein then laid out the fundamentals that he came to understand in the form of what we may call metascientific beliefs. First, Newtonian physics was *not* the foundation of physics: this, a fundamental belief for the young Einstein. Second, theory must not contradict empirical facts (ibid.). Third, *a* theory must manifest an "inner perfection" and be logically simple and natural (p. 23). That is, a theory must be aesthetically satisfying. Fourth, mathematical arguments must not substitute for physical reasoning (Pyenson 1985, p. 27).

This concludes our glimpses into Einstein's proactive preparation as his ETH years came to a close. His prepared mind was constituted of some fundamental scientific and metascientific beliefs, along with knowledge of physics and mathematics, all of which entered his personal belief/knowledge space. To these we must add his antipathy toward formal education, the premium he placed on freedom from all kinds of coercion, his anti-Germanism, his anti-authoritarianism and finally his detachment from the "merely personal."

XVII Preparation as the tentative forming of identity

It goes without saying that the nature of the prepared mind is as varied as there are kinds of creative beings. This diversity is part of the complexity (and also the charm) that attends the architecture of creativity. Yet as I have tried to show here, there are some general features amid this diversity that imposes a certain order and enables us to sketch a portrait of the creative being.

One. Proactive preparation originates in some combination of interest and curiosity. Both these, as mentioned earlier, are intentional states. One feels curious *about* something; one feels an interest *in* something. Interest may coalesce into something more objective, a creative interest (in Jonathan Feinstein's (2006) sense): a topic a person wishes to pursue with some intensity.

Two. An outcome of this entwinement of interest and curiosity is the generation of a superneed that pertains to the domain of one's interest. Generically we call this the need to create. In domain-specific terms it manifests as the need to discover (as in science), to invent (as in technology), to design (as in engineering), compose (as in music), to solve (as in mathematics), to dance, to write (as in the literary domain), to understand (as in domains of scholarship) and so on.

Three. Coincident to the need to create is the generation of a second superneed: the need to make history: to be original, to deviate from the norm. This need is a seed for potential creativity. It imposes a kind of constraint on the need to create, otherwise the latter need would be unfettered, thus uncontrolled. This combination of the need to create and the need to be original establishes *a balance between freedom and constraint.*

Four. Proactive preparation entails the formation and accumulation of beliefs and knowledge, guided and controlled by interest/curiosity on the one hand and the twin superneeds to create and make history on the other. The means by which this belief/knowledge cognitive space is formed is a combination of formal learning, self-education and experience. This space is thus a product of one's interaction with her social, cultural and physical environments (her ecological space), by a cognitive process that is partly conscious, partly unconscious.

Five. A special and vital component of the acquired beliefs and knowledge is self-knowledge: about the *I*. Its components concern the environmental, relational and conceptual selves, along the lines Ulrich Neisser (1988) postulated. Their relative importance to the person will depend on other factors such as the domain of interest/curiosity and the nature of the need to create.

Six. In the state of preparation the potential artificer is a consumer of the (abstract and material) artifacts produced by other artificers, past and present, dead or living. To state the obvious, *one must consume before one can create.*

Seven. But one is not *just* a consumer of other artificers' work. She is a consumer who engages in a series of creative encounters with these other artificers. Proactive preparation thus entails forming an identity which is tentative ("soft"), for during subsequent acts of production it may be (indeed should be) altered, enriched, refined, added to, deleted from, to an extent that will consolidate the identity and also modify it in one or more ways. Yet this initial "soft" identity will be "firm" enough for acts of creation to be initiated.

Eight. In general, preparation is an evolutionary process in which the "present" state of affairs along with environmental stimuli gives rise to a new state of mind.

XVIII   Alloying preparation with creation

According to our sixth point above, one must consume before one creates. I think in general this is true but never universally so. A case in point is that of Rabindranath Tagore.

If the American Nobel laureate Herbert Simon was an instance of the polymath in the sciences then Tagore, a much earlier Nobel laureate, was as much an exemplar of the polymath in the "other culture" (in C.P. Snow's (1993) celebrated sense), that is, in the arts, humanities and literature. Much as Simon's 1978 Nobel Prize in economics or his 1975 Turing Award in computer science tell only parts of the story of his creativity so also Tagore's 1913 Nobel Prize in literature reveals only a fragment of the richness of his creative life that spanned poetry, music, fiction, drama, opera, philosophy and painting. (As in the case of Darwin and Einstein, there is a veritable "Tagore industry." The literature on him is vast. For a highly readable, reliable and modern biography, see Dutta and Robinson 1995. Elsewhere (Dasgupta 2007) I have discussed him at some length in the specific context of creativity and the nineteenth century creative movement called the Bengal Renaissance).

It is almost meaningless to speak of Tagore's preparation outside the context of the extraordinary family into which he was born. Both his grandfather and father were preeminent in the making of the Bengal Renaissance (Dasgupta 2007, 2010). Tagore was the youngest of thirteen siblings who were prodigiously gifted, intellectually and creatively, especially as poets, composers, story tellers and translators. Thus from his earliest childhood Tagore was nurtured, indeed embedded in a milieu of art, music, philosophy and literature. His relational self and conceptual self were born in this milieu.

In his case it is difficult to separate proactive preparation from creation. To prepare is to learn, to situate oneself in a cognitive condition in which one can engage in the act of creation. It is a time of intense and sustained consumption. For those people—for instance Herbert Simon, Amrita Sher-Gil and George Rodrigue among my protagonists—who go through a long period of formal education and apprenticeship, it is possible to delineate preparation/consumption from production. But in Tagore's case the blurring between the two is quite pronounced. For one thing (as already mentioned) Tagore was an autodidact in the most immediate sense: he reacted strongly in his early years to formal classroom education (Tagore 2001, p. 40); he eschewed college (and in this he parted ways from Einstein, also a rebel in his school years). Sent by his father at age seventeen to England to study for the Bar, he first entered University College London as a student of English literature, but returned to India after two years with neither a university degree nor legal qualifications. Instead he heard and learnt many British folk and traditional songs that over time he would adapt to his musical needs.

Thus Tagore's preparation was by a more insidious process of osmosis within the milieu of the palatial family mansion in Calcutta (now Kolkata). His personal identity evolved, and was constantly shaped by the identities of his immediate family members including sisters-in-law. Indeed his intellectual and creative environment can be perceived as a small, tightly-bound network (in the jargon of computer science, a "local-area network") of constantly interacting people, passing to one another elements of their respective identities and at the same time creating together a collective identity. Tagore's self-knowledge in childhood, adolescence and young adulthood would have been dominated by his relational selfhood (in Neisser's (1985) sense).

Tagore, in fact, began producing even as he was consuming. Perhaps we might say that his earliest productions were also ingredients of his preparation. He wrote his first verses when he was about eight. And when a relative explained to him the nature of a particular fourteen-syllable meter used in Bengali poetry—Bengali or Bangla, being his native language—poetry-making, he would write later, was no longer a mystery to him (Tagore 2001). There was no holding him back. And when his next older brother, hugely gifted himself, was creating melodies at the piano, the boy Tagore was composing lyrics to go with the tunes.

By the time he was sixteen preparation/consumption and production/creation had melded into one. His first long poem was soon printed in a literary magazine founded by the Tagore siblings and later published in book form. He also embarked on literary experiments, drawing upon poems from an earlier century and imitating their language and form. By the time he left for England at seventeen he was as much the literary producer as consumer. Preparation and creation had alloyed into a single entity.

Note

1 With apologies to Gabriel Garcia Marquez.

7

"THE UNCONSCIOUS MACHINE"

I Being conscious about the unconscious

Historically the unconscious has led a rather fitful life in the study of mind. On the one hand the modern science of psychology began as the study of *consciousness* (Robinson 1995, p. 280). In a manner of speaking the unconscious was legislated out of "academic" psychology virtually at its birth in the mid-nineteenth century. Even now, in a recent textbook on cognition (in its seventh edition) the terms "unconsciousness" or "unconscious" do not appear in the subject index (Matlin 2009). Nor do we find them in a still more recent textbook on cognitive science (Bermúdez 2010). As surprisingly, in his *magnum opus* titled *Unified Theories of Cognition* (1990), based on his William James Lectures at Harvard in 1987, Allen Newell, one of the pioneers of both artificial intelligence and modern cognitive science, deigns to mention anything about the unconscious.

On the other hand the unconscious was much in the mind of certain nineteenth century thinkers who were not academic psychologists. The German philosopher Arthur Schopenhauer (1969) in his influential work *The World as Will and Representation* (first published in 1819) hauntingly anticipating Freud, talked of man being guided by internal, irrational forces of which he is scarcely aware. For Schopenhauer (1969) the will *was* the unconscious. The psychiatrist Pierre Janet invented the word *subconscious* to explain treatment of hysterical patients by raising "fixed ideas" (*idée fixe*) from the subconscious to consciousness (Ellenberger 1970, pp. 102, 147, 149). For the German *savant* Hermann von Helmoltz, visual perception was a process that entailed making "unconscious inferences" (Hernstein and Boring 1965, pp. 151–163). The physician Carl Gustav Carus (1846) began his book *Psyche* with the announcement that to understand one's conscious life one must look into the realm of the unconscious (Ellenburger 1970, p. 207). And in 1868 Eduard von Hartmann wrote his celebrated treatise on *The Philosophy of the Unconscious* (Ellenburger 1970, p. 209).

But it was Sigmund Freud more than anyone else who made the larger world conscious about the unconscious. Psychoanalysis, he would write in *The Ego and the Id*, begins by recognizing that the "psychical" is divided into the conscious and the unconscious (Freud 1989, p. 3). Yet, as psychologist Matthew Erdelyi (1985, pp. 61–65) has noted Freud is also responsible for some of the confusion surrounding the unconscious.

Freud made a distinction between two kinds of unconsciousness. One comprises of processes that are merely "latent" but otherwise do not differ from conscious processes. They are capable of *becoming* conscious and can thus be easily summoned into consciousness. Freud called these processes *preconscious* ("Pcs" for short). For example, in starting out from my house to go the university I may go along a particular route without consciously thinking about it—I may be listening raptly to a program on the car radio—but when necessary I can summon my mental plan of that route into consciousness.

The other kind of the unconscious, termed "dynamic unconscious" by Freud, consists of processes, desires, wishes that are instinctual in origin and are in direct conflict with the civilizing forces that influence the conscious mind. Such mental states are *repressed* and constitute what for Freud was the unconscious "proper" ("Ucs" for short)—which cannot "without more ado" be brought into consciousness (Freud 1989, p. 5). So in the Freudian schema there are three concepts: the conscious (Cs), the preconscious (Pcs) and the (dynamic) unconscious (Ucs) (ibid.).

The Freudian unconscious is both inaccessible "without more ado" and repressed. However, as Matthew Erdelyi (1985, p. 63) asked, are *all* inaccessible mental states the result of repression? Surely not. I follow certain rules of syntax in generating or understanding speech but I am unaware of both the nature of these rules and the fact that I am following them. We construct schemas from our everyday experiences (see Chapter 5) without being aware of it. When waiting to turn at a road intersection I judge the distance and speed of approaching cars from both directions and based on these judgments I make a decision to turn or wait. The judgment may be consciously made but presumably it is based on some kind of mental *computation* the nature of which I am unconscious of.

Fortunately, at least some modern cognitive psychologists have come to unveil something of the nature and extent of unconscious processing that have nothing to do with repression *à la* Freud. Our linguistic skills, our computational skills in judging distances, our construction of schemas constitute examples of what these psychologists call the *cognitive unconscious* (Kihlstrom 1987; Allen and Weber 1999).

A particularly interesting facet of the cognitive unconscious (which may have relevance to creativity) is *implicit memory*: when a person is influenced by some past experience or some piece of knowledge acquired in the past without any awareness of having had that experience or being in possession of that knowledge (Schacter 1996, pp. 161 *et seq*). American psychologist Daniel Schacter, a pioneer in the study of implicit memory, cites the case of the former Beatle George Harrison's song *My Sweet Lord*, a major "hit" of the 1970s. It turned out that the tune was almost exactly identical to another song *He's So Fine* recorded by another band, the

Chiffons in 1962. A lawsuit ensued. Harrison admitted that he had heard the earlier song before writing his own but denied that he had borrowed the tune from the latter. The trial judge ruled that this was a case of copyright infringement by unintentional copying based on something held in Harrison's "subconscious memory" (Schacter 1996, p. 167).

Schacter also speculated that implicit memory may explain the *déjà vu* experience, the feeling a person may have in a situation that he has had this experience before though this is apparently occurring for the first time as far as the person is aware of (p. 172)—the feeling that (to borrow from the Dutch historian of psychology Douwe Draaisma's paraphrase of the Pre-Raphaelite poet Dante Gabriel Rossetti) "this has been thus before" (Draaisma 2004, p. 145). Perhaps, Schacter suggests (p. 173), the current experience triggers an implicit memory of an event that happened before.

II The artificer's sense of mystery

Recall (from Chapter 2) the "divine dispensation" view of creativity Plato first talked about and others such as Milton, William Blake and, more recently, Picasso mused over. In particular the mathematician Henri Poincaré (1985), reflecting on his own mathematical discoveries, related how after worrying incessantly but unsuccessfully over a problem, he would cast it aside and think of other matters. And then a solution would emerge suddenly in the most unexpected of circumstances.

This "out-of-the-blue" character of ideation reported by Poincaré (though not attributed to divinity) is mirrored by the remark made by the poet Stephen Spender of how he would put a line or fragment of a poem aside for days, weeks or even years and then it would surface into consciousness and he would find it to have almost "written itself" (Spender 1985, p. 119). Likewise Lewis Carroll, referring to his nonsense poem "Hunting of the Snark", wrote that its origin lay in a single enigmatic line "For the snark *was* a Boojun you see." This line came to him suddenly in the course of a solitary walk on a summer day (Harding 1942, p. 59).

In the annals of creativity one of the most celebrated solitary walks was one the scientific instrument maker, inventor and engineer James Watt took one Sunday afternoon in a Glasgow park in the spring of 1765. As I will detail in a later chapter, for two years Watt had been thinking and experimenting in an effort to improve the efficiency of Thomas Newcomen's "atmospheric" steam engine of 1812. In practical terms, however, Watt's efforts had been in vain—till that fateful Sunday afternoon. This famous "eureka" moment is known to us from an account Watt gave many years later to an admirer: while on his walk through Glasgow Green, thinking about Newcomen's engine, the crucial idea suddenly came to his mind, and within a very short time, the "whole idea was arranged" in his mind (Hart 1859).

This mystery of where an idea, a poem or a piece of musical composition—an abstract artifact, in other words—comes from is a recurrent theme in autobiographical statements made by poets and artists especially but (as we have just seen) also by scientists, inventors and mathematicians. And it poses a very real problem for those who wish to make sense of creativity, for it forces them to confront what we might call *the dilemma of the unconscious*. For one explanation for such perplexing, eureka-like phenomenon—what Poincaré (1985) Graham Wallas (1926) and Jacques Hadamard (1954) called *illumination*—is that the cognitive process resulting in such *conscious* illumination actually occurs in the cognitive unconscious—processed by what Poincaré called the "unconscious machine." That is, one's conscious awareness of the emergence of an idea or concept is the outcome of a prior *unconscious* process of ideation.

But the plot may be thicker than this.

III Entwinement of the conscious and the unconscious

We know from experience that a person may retrieve knowledge from her knowledge space under conscious awareness. A mathematics student trying to solve an algebra problem may deliberately and consciously search among the rules of algebra either stored in (what psychologists call) her semantic memory or in a textbook (external memory) and select the right rules to apply. When a writer is composing a particular sentence or phrase, or a poet a line, he may select a particular word as the right one from among synonyms by consciously reaching into his mental or external thesaurus. An architect, given the task of designing a new art museum, may consciously retrieve from a stock of "museum schemas" held in his memory or in a book, which he will then draw upon in the course of his project.

But such conscious acts are limited in extent. The poet ruminating consciously upon the choice of the right word may "stumble" upon one she thinks is "just right," but she may be unaware of how the word surfaced in her conscious mind; or for that matter, as in the case of Lewis Carroll, how an entire line appeared in consciousness. The *process* itself was in the unconscious. Thought in general and creative thought in particular seem to demand an *entwining of conscious and unconscious processing*.

IV Germination of the first lines of a poem

Robert Nichols was of the generation of English poets who fought in the First World War and wrote of that experience. They came to be known as the War Poets in the annals of modern English literature, the most well known of which were Wilfred Owen and Rupert Brooke. Unlike Owen and Brooke, Nichols survived the war and in the realm of creativity studies we owe him a debt for an essay titled "The Birth of a Poem" (Nichols 1942) in which he analyzed in detail the process by which he composed a poem called "Sunrise Poem." Here I will use a small fragment of his analysis to get a more concrete handle on the play of the unconscious in the creative process.

In his analysis Nichols recalled how the first line of the poem, "The sun, a serene and ancient poet," originated in his solitary contemplation from a ship's deck of the sun rising on a tranquil sea. This observation filled him with a certain emotion, a core of excitement conjoined with a sense of immense satisfaction (Nichols 1942, p. 110). This emotion in turn prompted the poet to see in the pattern of light reflected on the water an Arabic script of a kind he had seen (he did not remember where or when) in an early sixteenth century holy book.

This recollection has two points of interest. First, the fact that the poet was *reminded* of something he had once seen. The poetic experience necessitates the gift of considerable memory that facilitates not just the storage of knowledge, impressions and experience in the form of schemas but also their *retrieval* by means of the mental operation of *association*. Indeed, for poet Stephen Spender (1985, p. 122) it is this power of storage and associated recall that enables the poet to not only reach back and recollect childhood experience, in often the minutest detail, but also go beyond one's "self-centredness" to recall memories of other people and things: to recall aspects of one's relational self in addition to those of one's conceptual self (see Chapter 6, XII).

The second point of interest is that the poet's power to store in and retrieve from memory is of scant interest if that memory is sparse, content-wise. Poetry-making is a *knowledge-rich* process as all other creative acts are. The poet's personal knowledge space is not restricted to facts, hypotheses, laws and theories—that is declarative or propositional knowledge. It contains autobiographical knowledge (witness Wordsworth's *The Prelude*, first composed in 1798 and rewritten in several versions over some fifty years (Jeffrey 1989)). It encompasses stored impressions of visual scenes, images, sounds and smells. The poet (and the artist) are by no means the sole proprietors of "nonverbal" knowledge: scientists are also known to resort to visual images (Miller 1986, 1989), while engineers dwell more in the realms of drawings and sketches than words (Ferguson 1992) and resort to a form of what art psychologist Rudolf Arnheim (1969) called *visual thinking*. Like artists, engineers engage in *visual talking* which draws upon visual imagery and thinking (Elias 2005).

Of course the poet, like everyone else, is all too human. He may not trust his memory, his ability to recall accurately or at all. Hence the all-important *external* memory: the notebooks and journals, an external record of what one has known, believed, imagined, thought, one's moods, perceptions and impressions. A celebrated and well-studied instance is Wordsworth's great friend and sometime collaborator, Samuel Taylor Coleridge's notebook for the period 1795–1798 in which Coleridge wrote his longest poem "The Rime of the Ancient Mariner" (first published in 1798) and the short, unfinished "Kubla Khan" (completed in 1797 but not published until 1816). We get a sense of the *kinds* of entities that constitute Coleridge's consciousness from the American literary scholar John Livingstone Lowes (whom we encountered in Chapter 5 in discussing Coleridge's prepared mind). In *The Road to Xanadu* (1930), Lowes's quite extraordinary study (itself a highly original enterprise, a brilliant exemplar of the *scholar as a creative being*) Lowes tells us that this notebook is a record of Coleridge's "chaotic" record of the poet's "adventures among books" (Lowes 1930, p. 6).

But poets are not the only ones who externalize their conscious cognitive contents in notebooks and journals. Perhaps as celebrated as Coleridge's notebook are the set of notebooks maintained by Charles Darwin between 1837 and 1839, the seminal years in which he conceived and unfolded his theory of natural selection, and which cognitive scientist Howard Gruber (1981) drew upon in his study of Darwin's creativity.

Robert Nichols did not need recourse to external memory. His self-analysis interests us for the light it sheds on the entwining of the verbal and nonverbal knowledge he retrieved from his own memory and the interleaving of conscious and unconscious cognitive processing in literary composition. The Arabic script he had been reminded of by the sea pattern of reflected light caused him to imagine in the next instance that the script was written on the water by the sun. The sun itself was the poet. No sooner did this notion take shape but he was reminded of a post card he had often bought at the British Museum of a seated poet, possibly Persian, wearing turban, caftan and slippers. Thereupon the line "The sun, a serene and ancient poet" came to him.

The next line is "stoops and writes on the sunrise sea." Consider the first *word* of this line. It originated in Nichols's observation of the sun rising rapidly above the horizon. But in order for the sun to write upon the sea it would have to bend forward and down. The image, combined with the notion of "ancientness" in the first line, led by association to the image of William Blake's painting *The Ancient of Days* (1794) in which the long-bearded old man kneels forward and "sets a compass upon the deep." The poet's recollection of this painting prompts him to think of and select the word "stoop."

Much has taken place in Nichols's mind in composing just the first two lines. The *onset* of this poetry-making was not a matter of chance. Nichols was a poet and poets are driven by the urge—the superneed—to write poetry. A goal to write a poem surfaces with the slightest of stimuli. In his autobiography Rabindranath Tagore recalled an experience akin to the mystical, when he was just twenty-one, when from his house one morning he observed the sun rising through the tops of trees. The world, he wrote, seemed to be "bathed in a wonderful radiance," which engulfed his heart (Tagore 2001, p. 228). The result was a poem that "gushed forth" that very day (ibid.).

Most famously, wherein the poet's superneed found expression in a *dream*, there is Samuel Taylor Coleridge's account of how he came to write "Kubla Khan" (1797): under the effect of "an anodyne" (an euphemism for opium) he fell into a "profound sleep" just when he was reading a passage from a travel book called *Purchase his Pilgrimage* (published 1617) written by one Samuel Purchase. Coleridge tells us, in a "prefatory note" published in 1895 (and reprinted in Ghiselin 1985) that at the moment he fell asleep he was reading the words "Here the Khan Kubla commanded a palace to be built, and a stately garden thereunto. And thus ten miles of fertile ground were enclosed with a wall" (Coleridge 1895, p. 84).

In his sleep he dreamt into composition a few hundred lines of a poem in which the images of things appeared and along with them, their descriptions (Coleridge 1985, p. 85). Upon waking he immediately began to write down the lines (ibid.). In Nichols's case, once he felt an emotion a goal to write a poem in response to this emotion formed in his mind (Nichols 1942, p. 110).

Now if we go by what Nichols has written we might conclude that in arriving at the idea of the sun-as-poet he was more or less thinking continuously about the "problem" at hand. We might think that the poet did not put it aside and attend to other matters before the idea emerged into consciousness. Yet he was not conscious of *all* that happened in the course of composing these lines. The cognitive process that led from his observation of the pattern of sunlight to the concept of the Arabic book (held in his knowledge space); the access to the attributes associated with the book; and the inferences producing the concept "sea-as-book" *all happened below the level of consciousness*. Cognitive psychologists Allan Collins and Elizabeth Loftus (1975) first suggested that such accesses might entail the process called *spread of activation* (see also Thagard 1988, pp. 19–25).

The main idea of spreading activation is that given a network of concepts held in memory connected with one another through links—e.g., a schema system—the activation by way of stimulus of one concept activates in turn the adjacent or associated concepts which then cause the activation of *their* associated concepts, and so on. Thus activation spreads through the network though decreasing over time and "distance" from the original concept. A concept is this activated to the degree it is related to the source of activation.

Of course, activation in Nichols's case may have spread to other regions of the poet's belief/knowledge space. However, the association with book and the pattern of sunlight was evidently sufficiently compelling to dominate other associations; it was this particular connection that surfaced to the level of consciousness.

Nichols then went on to complete the image of "the sun, an ancient, serene poet." By his own account an association was established and strengthened between the sun-as-poet concept and a postcard picture of a seated Persian poet. He tells us he could not utter the first line without "seeing" the postcard picture. This link, however, was unidirectional: from the line to the picture. The reverse link was missing: when he actually sees the picture postcard, he goes on to say, he does not "automatically" recall the line.

The feature of oldness and serenity linked with the Persian poet concept in his belief/knowledge space are, thus, associatively retrieved and conjoined with the sun-as-poet concept to complete the idea of the sun-as-an-ancient-and-serene-poet.

This brief scrutiny of Robert Nichols's poetry-making reveals something about the role of the unconscious in his particular act of production. In his case it participated, among other ways, in *reminding* the poet of certain concepts, ideas and images; in *retrieving* other concepts, images and ideas associatively linked to them by spreading activation; in the *generation* of goals; and in drawing certain *inferences*. It would seem then that Nichols's conscious acts and his unconscious ones were *interleaved* in time.

These cognitive acts *can* occur in the conscious state also. In science, for example, one may deliberately and in full awareness "remind" oneself of ideas, facts, or data through explicit search of an external knowledge base, traditionally the library and now ever increasingly, the World Wide Web and other computer-based data sources. Goals can also be set deliberately; and inferences can be drawn in full awareness.

V The necessity of consciousness: an experiment

As remarked above, all this suggests that in thinking unconscious and conscious processing interleave. Conceptually, it further suggests that the mind consists of two "spaces," one corresponding to the conscious, the other to the unconscious. And thinking—creative thinking in particular—involves wandering freely across the "boundary" between the two spaces. As psychologist and creativity researcher David Perkins (1981) put it, the border between the conscious and the unconscious shifts as and when demanded by the circumstances. In composing a poem a cognitive process is executed, some parts of which the poet is aware of, some he is not.

We have come to this proposition by way of a cognitive–historical analysis of Nichols's experience but a similar conclusion was reached experimentally by psychologist Roy Baumeister and his collaborators (Baumeister, Schmeichel and DeWall 2014). One of their experiments involved a set of graduate music students all specializing in jazz guitar. Given a set of recorded accompaniments (chords) the performers were asked to "jam" along by improvising melodies across these chords. They were not told beforehand what the chords were, so they were hearing them for the first time while they jammed to the accompaniments.

Each musician performed under three different experimental conditions. In the first, the control condition, the musician simply played a solo. In the second, "low cognitive load" condition, each musician was required to count aloud *forward* by one starting with the number fifteen while improvising the solo. In the third, "high cognitive load" condition, the musician played the solo while counting aloud *backward* by six beginning with the number 913.

The solos were all recorded and two "reasonably accomplished" musicians were asked to listen to them and rate them according to a number of criteria. These, then, were the consumers-as-judges. In listening to the solos the judges did not know which of the three experimental conditions prevailed in each case.

The idea embedded in the low-load and high-load conditions was to distract the musicians from their primary task—playing the solos—and making the counting the "foreground" conscious task. Improvising the solos would be done unconsciously. In the high-load condition improvisation would be "forced" even more into the unconscious.

Interpreting the judges' ratings Baumeister et al. concluded that creativity depends on consciousness (p. 190). In particular, the solos improvised under the high-load conditions (counting backward by six) were found by the judges as considerably inferior to the solos produced in the other two conditions (ibid.). The experimenters noted that the "creative quality" was not markedly different between the control and low-load conditions, so the act of counting itself was not the problem but rather the consciousness-loaded task of having to count backward by six.

Yet even in the high cognitive load condition the performance quality did not decline precipitously. A great deal of mental processing still had to be executed in performing the solo and these processes, e.g., keeping beat, staying on key and adopting to sudden key changes, were done well. For Baumeister et al. this was evidence of the remarkable capabilities of the unconscious mind; and yet the judges' evaluations also demonstrated to them that consciousness was as important for creativity to work (ibid.). Based on these and other experiments, including other kinds of tasks performed by other subjects, Baumeister and his collaborators concluded that not only did consciousness play an essential role in creativity but that creativity entails a combination of conscious and unconscious processes (p. 197).

VI   Conscious interludes in streams of unconsciousness

Returning to the example of Robert Nichols, we notice something else: not only does our cognitive–historical analysis suggest that thought freely crosses the boundary between the conscious and the unconscious, it appears to do so in a *fine-grained* fashion. Consider again his experience. According to his account he responded to a goal of wanting to compose a poem in response to a felt emotion at a particular point of time. Yet much happened in the course of this composition process that undoubtedly lay beyond the poet's conscious realm. The scenario, as Nichols described, is reconstructed below augmented with the following conventions: the account is constructed *as if* the poet is thinking aloud as he cogitates. (In experimental psychology the record of such verbalization of one's conscious thinking is called a *protocol* (Newell and Simon 1972, pp. 12–13, 163–166)). This thinking aloud is shown in bold face italics. Cognitive events (access and retrieval, ideation, inferences and other processes) likely to have occurred in the unconscious are presented in regular font.

Some process yields a goal to write a poem in response to a felt emotion:

I need to write a poem

A perceived pattern of reflected sunlight yields the image of an Arabic script in golden letters in a book with wooden covers dated about 1500.

The pattern on the water is rather like Arabic script ... of golden letters in a holy book

Ideation of the sea-as-book and of the text being written in the sea.

The Arabic script is written on the sea

Retrieval by association and spreading activation from the idea of script (text) to the concept of "poem"

> Ideation of the sea-script-as-poem
> Ideation that the sun is a poet

The script has been written on the sea by the sun-poet

According to this scenario much more appears to have happened in the unconscious space than in consciousness. Contrary to William James's famous metaphor of thought being a "stream of consciousness" (James 1950, p. 239), here *there are merely interludes of conscious thought in a stream of unconsciousness.* To paraphrase David Perkins (1981, p. 40) the unconscious is where most of the "action" is.

There is something else of interest in this example. If we look again at the script just outlined we notice that the only entities that are actually presented to consciousness are the *results* of such cognitive processes as the retrieval by association and spreading activation or the acts of ideation. These results are either pieces of knowledge and percepts or goals. Only these appear to enter consciousness, *not the actual cognitive processes giving rise to them.* Thus Nichols became conscious of the *idea* of the sun-as-poet (as he tells us) but not of the *ideation* process itself.

The psychologist (and one of the co-founders of cognitive science) George Miller (1962) noted this phenomenon: one's conscious being provides no hint as to where a thought comes from. (Recall Picasso wondering where his pictures originate.) The process of thinking, Miller wrote, is itself unconscious (p. 56). So also, cognitive neuroscientists Michael Gazzaniga and his co-authors remind us that we are only conscious of the *contents* of our mental life not how these contents came about (Gazzaniga, Levy and Manguin 1998, p. 532). So even protocols, supposedly a record of what one is *thinking*, are really a record of the *result* of thinking not the process of thinking itself. And following their experiments, Roy Baumeister and his co-experimenters came to a very similar conclusion (Baumeister, Schmeichel and DeWall 2014, p. 197).

This does not mean, however, that unconscious mental processes are *never* open to conscious awareness. Freud (1989, p. 5), we recall, referred to the *preconscious* (Pcs) to mean such aspects of the unconscious that can be rendered conscious with relatively little effort. Consider walking on a wet or icy sidewalk: we attend very carefully to the act itself to avoid a slip or a fall. The ordinary unconscious act of walking seems to migrate into the conscious region of the mind. Yet there are limits to what can be "transferred" from the unconscious to the conscious. One may indeed walk deliberately, gingerly, to avoid a fall in the ice but, as David Perkins (1981, p. 39) has pointed out, even in such situations there are uncountable primitive cognitive events induced by a high-level deliberate, goal-driven action that are entirely beyond one's conscious ken. It is still only the intention or goal and the outcomes of innumerable micro-processes that one is conscious of, not the micro-processes themselves.

In essence then, cognitive processing appears to involve an interplay of the conscious and the unconscious. A cognitive process in general is an interleaving of (mostly) unconscious actions and conscious outcomes. Parts of unconscious processes may be brought into consciousness but there will always remain substantial parts that cannot be made conscious (e.g., spreading activation or linguistic procedures that general or parse sentences). These belong to the "cognitive unconscious"; to the "unconscious machine."

VII   The unconscious as a limiting condition

Here then is the dilemma of the unconscious. It *thwarts* our efforts to comprehend and explain the artificer's act of creation, and also the creative encounter as a whole since the consumer's mental process as well the artificer's will comprise of streams of unconsciousness with interludes of the conscious. When Blake, Watt, Carroll, Picasso and Spender (to take my protagonists) admitted to the mysterious character of their own creative experiences, or attribute them to "divine dispensation" as Plato did, to one's muse per Milton, or to the living god-within (*jiban-debata*) as it was with Tagore, we must conclude that from a purely (secular) cognitive perspective, they are the outcomes of (mostly inaccessible) unconscious mental processes.

If this is the case then the unconscious clearly imposes very definite *limits* to our ability to explain creativity. The challenge posed to the creativity researcher, then, is to explore how much he *can* unveil about creativity within the confines imposed by the unconscious. Our discussions in the rest of this chapter and the ones that follow fully accept the presence of the unconscious as a limiting condition. Yet, as we will see, there are ways of circumventing this condition.

But there are several perplexing questions that pertain to the *role of the unconscious* and, indeed, the *role of the conscious* that are worth addressing. The remainder of this chapter identifies and explores these questions.

VIII   Incubation

One of the most widely cited models that explicitly recognizes the place of both the conscious and the unconscious in the creative process entails a line of thinking with a very distinguished pedigree that seemed to have originated in a late nineteenth century lecture by the great scientist Hermann von Helmlotz. However, it was really given proper shape first by mathematician Henri Poincaré (1985), then more thoroughly and systematically by social scientist Graham Wallas (1926), and explored further to account for mathematical invention by another mathematician Jacques Hadamard (1954). Let us then call it, in their collective honor the Poincaré–Wallas–Hadamard model.

We have already encountered the first element of this model (in Chapter 6, I): preparation. For Poincaré and Hadamard this meant reactive preparation that comes into effect once a problem or goal has been identified; for Wallas it meant what I have called proactive preparation, the kind discussed at length in the previous chapter. We will have more to say on reactive preparation later. Our present interest is on another element of the model that Poincaré referred to as "long unconscious work" (Poincaré 1985, p. 27). Wallas (1926, p. 80) gave it the more interesting and evocative name *incubation* and this has been assimilated most favorably into the literature on creative thought. In the Poincaré–Wallas–Hadamard model, incubation follows preparation and immediately precedes the moment when (in Helmoltz's felicitous phrase) the "happy idea" appears "out of the blue" and with little effort. Wallas, following Poincaré, named this *illumination* (ibid.).

Incubation, because it entails the unconscious, has attracted much interest within the realm of experimental psychologists. Based on their experiments with poets and painters as subjects in an experimental setting, some have found it difficult to distinguish incubation as a distinct stage in the act of creation (Patrick 1935, 1937; Eindhoven and Vine 1952). Others could find no evidence that incubation had any impact on the efficacy of creative problem solving (Olton and Johnson 1976). The fact that incubation as a distinct process has resisted attempts to be demonstrated in the psychological laboratory has led at least one psychologist and prominent creativity researcher, Robert Weisberg (1993, p. 49), to doubt its very existence. In contrast another influential creativity researcher, psychologist J.P. Guilford (1979) had no doubt of the genuineness of incubation as a mental phenomenon. That experiments had failed to detect incubation or that they fail to establish any advantage to it may well be due to the contrived conditions in which such experiments were conducted (something Olton and Johnson (1976) conceded in concluding their own study).

David Perkins (2000, pp. 189–190) as a theorist has suggested that incubation might facilitate the act of creation in several different ways. For instance it may allow the artificer to *selectively forget* assumptions and approaches she may have been "trapped within" during conscious thinking; or it allows the unconscious mind to perform "serious extended thinking" on a problem while the conscious mind is focused elsewhere. Perkins was not the first to relate incubation as a kind of forgetting. Jacques Hadamard (1954, pp. 33–37) mentioned and discussed is as the "forgetting hypothesis."

My own view, based on my cognitive–historical studies, is that incubation as a *distinct* unconscious process is neither very meaningful nor useful either in the act of creation or in understanding creativity. In Robert Nichols's giving birth to the first lines of his "Sunrise Poem," for example, where exactly does incubation *as a sustained, uninterrupted* unconscious process fit in? Rather, what is called incubation is simply the unconscious at work. And as I have suggested it is entwined and interleaved with conscious processing and consciously perceived outcomes of unconscious processes.

IX   What is the *point* of interleaving the two processes?

But why does not all mental processing occur in the unconscious? Or why does not all mental processing occur in consciousness? What is the *point* of interleaving unconscious and conscious processing?

An early clue to this issue was offered by William James (1950) when he related consciousness to attention (p. 288). Moreover, he wrote, attention both reinforces and inhibits. The "agency of attention" permits the mind to select one or a few among the many thoughts, the many memories and the innumerable perceptions that crowd upon it and to suppress the rest, at least momentarily. This view of attention-as-consciousness (or consciousness-as-attention) in a more modern setting was addressed by the psychologist Donald Broadbent in a work published in 1958, and considered seminal to the return of the conscious mind to the fold of experimental psychology after languishing for decades (at least in the United States) in the wilderness of behaviorism (Broadbent 1958).

Two points in Broadbent's work are particularly important to our discussion. First, his identification of attention with consciousness; and second, the emphasis he placed on the *serial* nature of attention: *attention (hence consciousness) can only attend to one thing at a time.*

Serial processing and attention are thus two of the manifest features of consciousness. In contrast unconscious processing can proceed without attention. Perhaps then unconscious processing can occur *in parallel* (in the "theater of simultaneous possibilities"). Attention in the conscious state enables deliberative action to be taken and interaction with the environment (including other minds) to be effected. Parallelism within the unconscious enables, as parallel processing should, the execution of many cognitive acts that do not need awareness or attention. *Parallel processing thus offers a possible reason for necessity of the unconscious mind.* Whereas *the demands of serial processing and attention demands the presence of the conscious mind.*

X "The whole idea was arranged in my mind"

Recall (from Section II above) James Watt's Sunday walk in the Glasgow park and the moment when he discovered the solution to his problem "and the whole idea was arranged in my mind." Here is another crucial distinction between the conscious and the unconscious mind: In consciousness a person has fitted, assimilated or reconciled experiences into what psychologist Julian Jaynes (1976) called the "story" of her life—or some part of that life. That is, consciousness comprises of *narratives* that have assimilated new experiences into existing schemas. Watt's remembrance that "the whole idea was arranged" in his mind is telling us that his solution—the idea of the separate condenser as a solution to his problem—forms a coherent story in itself—a "subplot"—that has been assimilated into a larger narrative that tells of the principles of the steam engine.

This idea of narrativization as a feature of consciousness coheres with what cognitive scientist Jerome Bruner has argued: that constructing narratives—story telling—is a powerful way of making meaning out of our experiences (Bruner 1990). Narrating, Bruner wrote, not only organizes how we conceive our lives but also our place in life (Bruner 1994, p. 52).

Bruner was addressing the problem of cognition in general but his thesis is particularly relevant to the roles of the conscious and unconscious minds in the realm of creativity. Consider Watt's illumination; or as famously, Henri Poincaré's experience: he described how he had been struggling to understand a certain class of mathematical functions called Fuchsian functions. Being a man of many intellectual interests, he had gone on a geological excursion that had made him forget his mathematical worries. And it was in the midst of this excursion that the insight about the nature of these functions came to him "out of the blue" (Poincaré 1985, p. 26).

It would seem that what Bruner (and Jaynes) called narrativization and conciliation (or assimilation) are much in evidence in these situations. A sudden "out of the blue" insight—*illumination*, the third facet of the Poincaré–Wallas–Hadamard model—*has already been narrativized*, and it is this narrative that is presented to consciousness, and which is why it makes sense. That is, we can surely infer that when Watt's insight into his technological problem or Poincaré's insight into his mathematical problem surfaced suddenly in the conscious mind something like narrativization and assimilation must have occurred *in the unconscious*. For otherwise their solutions would not have made sense. Meaning-as-narrative is a feature of the conscious mind though the *process* of narrativization is a feature of the unconscious. The telling of the story—"this is the principle of the separate condenser," "this is what the Fuchsian functions are"—is a conscious process, though the making of the story is not.

XI The *I* of consciousness

Ultimately, the element that most fundamentally characterizes consciousness is that, as suggested by William James (1950, pp. 225–226), it is a *first-person* phenomenon. To be in the conscious state is to be one's *self*: the *I* (see Chapter 6, XII). It is *I* who selects (in James's phrase) "from the theatre of possibilities," who is the agent of attention, who narrativizes. It is *I* who is self-aware, and self-knowing, and this self-knowing is the self-knowledge referred to in Chapter 6. And it is the *I* that remains constant, that is the sense of continuity one has in the midst of the continuous flux of experience "across daily cycles of wakefulness and sleep," in the words of psychologist Anand Paranjpe (1998, p. 356), the sense of *identity*. Without the *I* there *is* no consciousness.

But, as we have noted, to be conscious is to be selective. Thus *I* can attend only to one state of affairs at a time. To deploy a computational metaphor, *I is a serial processor*. Yet as we have noted there is much *parallel processing* going on. To deploy another computational metaphor, such parallel processing goes on at different "levels of granularity": "large-grained" parallelism between multiple processes (e.g., our driving a car and listening to the radio simultaneously); "medium-grained" parallelism between actions within a process (e.g., the process of driving a car entails concurrently manipulating the steering wheel, pressing the brake or accelerator pedal, and scanning the road ahead); and "fine-grained" parallelism within a single action (e.g., simultaneous spreading of activation to our perception of direction and linking this with the handling of the steering wheel). Events at these different levels of granularity may also be occurring in parallel, thus producing a *hierarchy* of parallel processes.

But *at any given moment* (in the waking state) *I* is the recipient of a state of affairs of just one of these parallel events, and it is that state which *is in* consciousness. The rest remain in the unconscious. To repeat, *I* is a serial processor. The element that *I* receives may be (and usually is) the outcome of some unconscious process—a piece of information, a belief, a goal, an emotion, an image. a sound. But *I* is not just a passive receiver; *I* can also initiate a process, by way of a need or goal or emotion; and it assimilates and conciliates new experiences and knowledge into existing schemas thus narrativizing such knowledge or experiences.

When *I* is attending to something—the outcome of an unconscious process or a conscious mental action of its own initiation—there may be elements from other unconscious processes demanding *I*'s attention. These belong to one's "fringe" or "peripheral" consciousness (Hadamard 1954, pp. 24–25). But *I* can only attend properly to one thing at a time, what one is truly conscious of. What *I* attends to is what philosopher John Searle (1992, pp. 137–139) called the "center of consciousness."

So conscious states are mere interludes in the individual's "streams of unconsciousness." To say that cognitive processes can be concurrently active in the unconscious is to say that such processes can go on without *I* attending to any one of them. Yet despite the possible plethora of parallel unconscious processes that may be "running" at any time (involving our various senses, our motor activities, speech, reasoning, etc.), despite the general agreement that most of mental processing goes on in the unconscious *one cannot do without the I*.

Why is that? The British sculptor Henry Moore, while conceding the extent of non-logical, intuitive work of the unconscious in artistic activity, believed that the conscious mind is necessary to concentrate the artist's entire personality (Moore 1985, pp. 73–78). It is the *I* that effects this concentration: *I* is needed for control and ordering. When *I* is active—attending to a goal or an emotion or a piece of knowledge or a belief—it is in order to exercise control.

There is resonance between this notion and what cognitive psychologist Alan Allport (1989, p. 648) suggested in the context of visual attention. According to him the selective nature of conscious attention is necessary for controlling action. Furthermore, at any time, there may be many simultaneous tasks demanding attention-for-action and so (Allport tells us) attentional engagement also requires constant monitoring of the priority of tasks as determined by the person's set of intentions, needs, goals and the prevailing environment; thereby selecting for action that which has the highest priority under the given circumstances. In other words, Allport suggested, attention (and prioritization) have an *adaptive* function.

Once more it is tempting to invoke a computational metaphor, this time from the principles in computer systems design called "multiprogramming" and "time-sharing." Whatever be the cause of the *I* to attend to something at a particular moment of time, there may be both a passive and an active mode by which this may happen. The person's attention to one thing—*I*'s attending to one thing—can be interrupted by some outcome of an unconscious process, this being the passive mode. Or *I* can initiate a conscious action or process driven by some intentional state—a need, desire, goal, some sense of dissatisfaction, and emotion, and so on. Both these modes have significance for creativity. The moment of illumination in the Poincaré–Wallas–Hadamard model exemplifies interruption. The process initiated by Robert Nichols's consciously felt desire to write a poem in response to the emotion he felt on witnessing the sunrise seascape exemplifies the active mode.

We might summarize the foregoing as follows:

> Conscious thought (a) is a first-person phenomenon (the presence of the I); (b) is serial; (c) entails attention; (d) is volitional; and (e) is communicable. Unconscious thought (a) is not a first person phenomenon (the absence of the I); thus (b) does not demand attention; (c) afford parallel processing; (d) is not volitional; and (e) is normally and naturally incommunicable.

XII Qualia

The first-person experience is also at the center of what philosophers of mind call *qualia*. For example, philosopher David Chalmers (1996, p. 4) tells us (if I have understood him correctly) that I am conscious in that there is something it is like to be *me*, and you are conscious in that there is something it is like to be *you*. This of course follows the line of philosopher Thomas Nagel's (1974) celebrated essay titled "What is it like to be a bat?". Thus, my consciousness lies in my *my-ness* and your consciousness lies in your *your-ness*. The particular quality of *my* experiences, *my* likes and dislikes, *my* joys and fears, *my* sensation of pain, *my* perception of color and sound collectively constitute *my* consciousness. These qualities of experience are called qualia.

XIII Thinking computationally about the situation

How do conscious and unconscious processes communicate and interact? I have appealed a few times to computational metaphors, and now once more, here is a computational view of this situation.

At any moment of time several cognitive processes can occur concurrently. Such parallel processes *represent* unconscious processes. They constitute what Poincaré called the "unconscious machine." Some of these processes are inherently inaccessible to awareness (though their outcomes may be) and form the cognitive unconscious as, for example, the process of spreading activation or the process by which one applies rules of syntax in framing sentences. Other unconscious processes are of what Freud called the preconscious type (Pcs) and John Searle (1992, p. 162) termed "shallow unconscious"—they may be accessible to awareness under appropriate conditions.

Some of these processes are *always active*; they are initiated by life itself or come into being during a person's ontogenetic development (e.g., vision, memory, speech understanding, color perception or certain kinds of inference processes). These processes end with physical death or because of some serious malfunction of the body/brain. For convenience I will refer to these as "lower-level" unconscious processes and, roughly speaking, these are the processes that are most effectively studied at the neurobiological level.

Other cognitive processes, involved in the kinds of activities we normally associate with creativity—thinking about a particular problem, telling stories, discovering patterns or regularities in nature, inventing theories, painting, composing music, writing poems, designing and so on. I will designate these "higher-level" processes, and these constitute the "streams of the unconscious" with interludes of the conscious. They rely upon and invoke lower-level processes that provide the building blocks, basic capabilities and constraints. (One cannot draw upon a piece of knowledge in making a scientific inference, for example, if one's memory retrieval process is impaired.) To use another computational concept, the elements of a higher-level process are *interpreted* by lower-level processes, rather as the execution of, say, a data base access process is interpreted by a sequence of primitive computer operations (instructions). One can think of these lower- and higher-level processes as constituting two levels of abstraction.

Unlike the lower-level processes the higher-level ones have *limited lives*. They are created by needs and goals, and they may be *suspended* temporarily or *terminated* (when, for instance, the initiating needs or goals are satisfied). Higher-level processes are thus *transient*: they are born, they live for a while and they die. Each time a poet begins work on a poem, each time a designer begins work on a design, each time a mathematician begins to probe a new mathematical problem such new higher-level processes come into existence; if the poet or the designer or the mathematician temporarily abandons his project or puts it aside the process is temporarily suspended; when the poem or the design is completed or the mathematical problem is solved the process dies.

There is one, *innate*, always-active lower-level process of special interest. This represents the *I*, so we will call it the Iprocess. In the waking state a person's Iprocess *selects* at every moment of time some particular subspace of the space of unconscious processes. This subspace may comprise of schemas or subschemas representing elements of beliefs, knowledge, images, scenes; or symbol structures representing goals; or elements of the person's emotion space; or parts or whole of procedures in states of execution. The contents of this *excerpted* subspace constitute that person's *conscious state*. What Iprocess selects is what the person is aware of, what he attends to; what he is *conscious of*.

Iprocess can *switch* from one subspace of the space of unconscious processes to another, thereby changing the contents of one's conscious state. The fact that Iprocess engages with one or another conscious state is what affords the sense of *self*, the sense of continuity. One way this switch may occur is for Iprocess to be interrupted by one of the active, unconscious, parallel processes. Another way is for Iprocess itself to select another subspace of the unconscious process space.

The cognitive unconscious then is where parallel processing occurs. It would seem that such parallelism facilitates multiple combination of ideas that the serial constraint on conscious processing (under control of Iprocess) does not so readily facilitate.

I must emphasize that what has just been described is an instance of *computational thinking*. The idea of computational thinking can be traced back to one of the pioneers of AI Seymour Papert (1980), but the term itself and its further fleshing out is due to computer scientist Jeanette Wing (2006, 2008). Following the lines suggested by Papert and Wing, we may characterize computational thinking as an approach to such activities as problem solving, designing and making sense of intelligent behavior that draws on fundamental concepts of computing (Dasgupta 2016a, p. 121).

For our purposes here, computational thinking thus offers a set of intellectual tools for understanding and a language (more precisely a metalanguage) for describing aspects of creativity in a way no other frameworks allow. The transfer of ideas is from computing to the creative domain and not *vice-versa*. So our computational view of the conscious–unconscious cognitive complex just presented does *not* mean that computational artifacts manifest conscious and unconscious behavior in the human sense of such behavior.

XIV What psychoanalysis says

The psychoanalytic concepts of *primary process thinking* and *secondary process thinking* are also strikingly relevant to the present discussion.

Secondary process thinking is ordinary conscious thinking, largely verbal, and is normally attributed to the mature ego. Primary process thinking, in contrast, is the mode of thought characteristic of very early childhood when the ego is still immature. It is not logical, there are no negatives, no contradictions, opposing thoughts and impulses coexist, there is no sense of linear time, of "before" and "after," of "now" and "then," of past, present and future. It is imagistic rather than verbal, and representations are often by way of analogy. Moreover, several thoughts may be represented by a single thought or image—"condensation," in the language of psychoanalysis—and one idea or image may be represented by another—"substitution" (Brenner 1974, pp. 47–51).

Primary process thinking, then, is thinking associated with dreams and even psychosis, though of itself it is not pathological. In Matthew Erdelyi's (1985, p. 129) phrase it is "idish" thinking, associated with the id. It is symptomatic of ego regression.

The psychoanalyst and art scholar Ernst Kris (1952, p. 29) mentions the "id aspect" of scientific thinking. He wrote that such thinking is never distinctly delineated from the realm of the unconscious, and that analysis of scientists and inventors has suggested a close connection between their creative thinking and unconscious wishes and desires—which may themselves have origins in early childhood. However, for Kris the unconscious in which creative thought occurs is the Freudian preconscious (Pcs) (or, in Searle's term, the shallow conscious) and the shift from the preconscious to the Freudian conscious (Cs) may explain the phenomenon of illumination (*à la* the Poincaré–Wallas–Hadamard model) which results when the solution to a problem is suddenly revealed following what might appear to be a "period of rest" (Kris 1952, p. 313)—incubation in Wallas's language.

Kris further distinguished between "inspirational" and "elaborational" parts of creative thinking in terms of id and ego functions. In the former phase one finds features characteristic of id impulses whereas during elaboration, characteristic ego functions such as reality testing takes over (p. 313). Thus inspirational thinking is primary process thinking corresponding to unconscious incubation in the Poincaré–Wallas–Hadamard model and occurring at the level of unconscious cognitive processes in the computational model described in the last section. Elaboration is secondary process thinking, corresponding to what the Poincaré–Wallas–Hadamard model called *verification*, the stage following illumination.

8

PREPARING FOR ILLUMINATION

I "I myself don't see what I have done"

We have previously reflected on the wonder artificers themselves feel about their own acts of creation. This self-wonderment is no doubt one of the sources of the magical enigma of creativity (Prologue, II). When Picasso asked how someone else can "live" the picture as he had lived it, when "I myself don't see what I have done" (Picasso 1972, p. 12) he was giving voice to that wonderment others like him have expressed in different ways.

The often seemingly astonishing moment when an idea one has been seeking unsuccessfully, sometimes for a very long time, suddenly surfaces in consciousness is normally called *illumination* in the Poincaré–Wallas–Hadamard model mentioned in the last chapter. It is the "climactic" third stage in this four-stage model of the creative process. And its "out of the blue" character suggested to Poincaré that there must be something going on in the mind preceding that moment but in the unconscious. As we have seen this was named incubation (Chapter 7, VIII).

II James Watt's illumination

A particularly celebrated example of this moment of illumination was recorded by the eighteenth century Scottish inventor, engineer, instrument maker and entrepreneur James Watt. And it occurred, as so many illuminations have allegedly occurred, in the course of a walk.

Recall (from Chapter 7, II) Watt's own account. On a fine Sunday afternoon in the spring of 1765, Watt, then in business as a scientific instrument maker but socially engaged with Glasgow's eminent intellectuals, went for a walk in Glasgow Green, the city's most famous park. For two years he had been thinking, experimenting and building apparatus in an unsuccessful effort to improve the efficiency of Thomas Newcomen's "atmospheric steam engine," invented in 1712. That Sunday walk in the park was fateful for it was then that a crucial idea came to him and very soon "the whole idea was arranged in his mind" (Smiles 1904, p. 90).

In describing this moment several authors have emphasized its dramatic quality. For the indefatigable Victorian champion of self-help and British engineering ingenuity Samuel Smiles (1904) it was the moment when "light burst upon" Watt (p. 90). For a late twentieth century economic historian T.S. Ashton (1969) it was the instant when Watt had his "sudden flash of inspiration" (p. 48). Still more recently, according to historian of technology Richard Hills (1989, p. 53), Watt "literally stumbled on the solution."

This was not "just" an interesting moment of illumination. Watt's illumination had enormous consequences, for it became a pivotal event in the development of the steam engine "proper," the workhorse of the Industrial Revolution. The Victorian economic historian Arnold Toynbee (the uncle of the more famous twentieth century historian Arnold J. Toynbee) characterized the invention and development of the steam engine by Watt and his entrepreneurial partner Matthew Boulton as marking the introduction of the factory system (Toynbee 1956, p. 63). And one recent historian of technology, Christine MacLeod (2007, p. 125) has called Watt the "inventor of the Industrial Revolution"—a statement that as a figure of speech makes the point. Technologically, economically and socially Watt's idea, as a key to the development of the steam engine and the Industrial Revolution, propelled him into the realm of C-creativity.

There were scientific consequences also. In addressing the problem to which his illumination was a solution Watt turned the problem of building a *mechanical* device into one of constructing a *heat* engine. As the historian of science Arthur Donovan put it, it constituted a "fundamental intellectual shift" (Donovan 1979, p. 25). It marked the beginning of *thermodynamics*—a new and fundamental branch of physics concerned with the nature and conditions for the transformation of energy (Cardwell 1971). Thus Watt was also scientifically C-creative.

III   Reactive preparation

According to the Poincaré–Wallas–Hadamard model illumination is preceded, first by a preparation stage in which the problem of interest is consciously probed and worried over, and then by incubation wherein the problem disappears into the unconscious. And there it stays until illumination (still, in the model, an unconscious process) occurs. In the fourth and final stage conscious activity resumes in the form of verification that the idea does indeed work.

Such is the "standard" model. But as we have noted in Chapter 7, conscious and unconscious processes interleave over time; that conscious thought *interrupts* some stream of unconscious thinking. A neat separation of one from the other, as the "standard" model has it seems a hopeless idealization. It is not something that happens in *in vivo* creativity. Rather, preparation and incubation (that is conscious and unconscious thinking) blend into a single, amorphous process of interludes of conscious thought in (possibly multiple, parallel) streams of unconscious thought. It is fairer to say that *all* of what precedes illumination, once an artificer has identified a goal to be pursued, is a process of preparation.

This preparation is not the long-term proactive preparation which all creative people seem to undertake through the long, often tortuous, process of formal education, apprenticeship, self-education and experiencing we examined before (Chapter 6). The preparation that now interests us here, the precedent of illumination, is what I designated (in Chapter 6) *reactive* preparation. Reactive preparation will surely draw upon and crucially depend on proactive preparation but it is more compellingly driven by some *immediate* need, goal or desire. Moreover, as we see below, reactive preparation is also a knowledge-producing enterprise—knowledge that may not have been acquired by the artificer before responding to the problem on hand.

IV   What happened before Watt's illumination

James Watt arrived in Glasgow around 1757 after completing an apprenticeship in London (the later part of his proactive preparation) in the trade of scientific instrument making. Through a prior acquaintance with Robert Dick, professor of natural philosophy in the University of Glasgow, Watt obtained rooms within the university precincts wherein he established his workshop and business as an instrument maker.

This situation afforded Watt friendship with some of Glasgow's most eminent academics and intellectuals that a man of his trade (and a man *in* trade) would rarely gain in those times. Visitors to his workshop included, among others, Adam Smith, professor of moral philosophy in the university and, later, author of *An Enquiry into the Nature and Causes of the Wealth of Nations*, generally regarded as the originating text of modern economics; Robert Dick, mentioned earlier; Joseph Black, professor of anatomy and chemistry and the discoverer of an important law in physics (Black's law of specific heat) and the discoverer of the property of latent heat; and John Robison, then a youthful graduate of the university and eventually professor of natural philosophy in Edinburgh. The intellectual and social milieu in which Watt resided was far from what one might expect from an instrument maker and craftsman. It was the milieu of what came to be known as the Scottish Enlightenment (Wood 1992, pp. 275–278).

It was Robison who turned Watt's attention to Thomas Newcomen's atmospheric steam engine. In 1712 Newcomen, an English blacksmith and ironmonger, had invented the first continuously operating self-acting engine powered by a combination of atmospheric force and steam (Dickinson 1939; Rolt 1963). This engine consisted of a large metal cylinder fitted with a piston, the latter connected to one end of a pivoted beam whose other end was attached to a pump gear. (The Newcomen engine was used mostly to pump out water from flooded underground mines.) The cylinder is filled with steam from a boiler beneath, thus equalizing the atmospheric pressure on the cylinder piston. As a result the weight of the pump gear at the other end of the beam causes the piston to rise to the top of the cylinder. When this happens the steam supply from the boiler is cut off, a jet of cold water is sprayed into the cylinder, the steam condenses and a vacuum is created in the cylinder below the piston. Atmospheric pressure then drives the piston down. When it reaches the bottom of the cylinder the spray is cut off, steam supply resumed and the cycle of operation begins anew.

John Robison suggested to Watt that the Newcomen engine—of which by his own admission Watt was "very ignorant" at the time—might be applied to drive the wheels of carriages (Watt 1970b). Despite his self-confessed ignorance of the machine Watt began building a model to explore Robison's idea that the latter had published some time earlier in a magazine (ibid.). Watt was a craftsman and, as a craftsman, *curiosity* was perhaps as much a dominant element of his cognitive identity as was the inventor's superneed, *the need to make things.*

Samuel Smiles tells us that even as a child in Greenock, young James showed mechanical dexterity. Supplied by his father with a few carpenter's tools he soon learnt to use them "with expertness." He would take his toys to pieces and from their parts build new ones. (Here was, surely, *deconstruction* at work centuries before the postmodernists came on the scene.)

He spent much time in drawing, cutting, carving and observing carpenters in his father's shop at work; making small artifacts such as miniature pulleys, pumps and other machines; becoming at home in using tools, in working with metal and wood (Smiles 1904, p. 16).

Watt's *proactive* preparation for a life in invention, craftsmanship and engineering began very early. This preparation was obviously driven by curiosity, interest, inborn skills and a cultural milieu afforded by his father's workshop. But his developing identity was more than that of the traditional craftsman. At Greenock Grammar School, despite his demonstrable acumen in Latin and Greek, his real talent was shown to be in mathematics (Smiles 1904, p. 16). The business he chose to follow was, almost naturally that of a scientific instrument maker (ibid.).

The model of the Newcomen engine Watt built from Robison's description was, Watt discovered, "immoderately" made, thus unsatisfactory. Neither he nor Robison had "… any idea of the true principles of this machine"; and this, coupled with the fact they both had "other avocations" needing more pressing attention caused them to drop the idea (Watt 1970b).

But not entirely. Watt continued to perform "detached experiments" with steam until 1763 (ibid.). He also righted his prior ignorance of the Newcomen engine by reading all that had been written on it. In 1761 he even built a "species of steam engine" that used a "digester" (a pressure cooker in modern terms) developed in 1691 by physicist and inventor Denis Papin. Watt connected Papin's digester to a narrow syringe fitted with a piston. The connection between the syringe and the digester was fitted with a stopcock that would regulate the amount of steam admitted from the digester into the syringe. Another stopcock was attached to the syringe itself, allowing the steam to escape into the air. When the steam passed from the digester to the syringe its pressure forced the piston up. When the latter reached an appropriate height the steam was allowed to escape through the stopcock and the piston would descend.

Watt was apprehensive that the boiler of such a device would burst due to the steam pressure (ibid.). This, along with the difficultly of making the joints airtight and the lack of a vacuum inside the syringe caused him to abandon further investigation of the device.

Clearly though, Watt *had created for himself an initial "steam engine schema"* (the nature of schemas was discussed in Chapter 5) which we may represent as follows:

> **NAME** *Steam Engine*
>
> **STRUCTURE** *A piston-and-cylinder arrangement is connected to a boiler arrangement via a steam-intake control. The piston-and-cylinder arrangement has a steam-outtake control.*
>
> **OPERATION**
> > **REPEAT** *Cycle*
> > > *Activate boiler arrangement;*
> > > *Open steam-intake control;*
> > > *When piston rises to a specified height in cylinder:*
> > > > *Close steam-intake control;*
> > > > *Open steam-outtake control;*
> > **END** *Cycle*

We pause here to note what exactly was going on here. Driven by his inventor's superneed to make things on the one hand and curiosity about the possibility of a steam engine along Robison's lines, Watt embarked on work that was a confluence of both making and learning. *Creation and reactive preparation were entwined.* And along the way he created for himself an abstract artifact, a steam engine schema.

Years passed. We can only wonder whether Watt would have maintained his interest in pursuing Robison's original idea but then, by one of those quirks of chance, he came upon a quasi-real Newcomen engine in the winter of 1763: John Anderson, then professor of natural philosophy in Glasgow, asked Watt to repair a model version of the engine he used for demonstration purpose in his course. The boiler was smaller than a tea kettle and the cylinder was of two inches diameter and had a six inch stroke (Smiles 1904, p. 82).

When Watt had restored the model to working order he discovered that the boiler, though large relative to the cylinder, could not provide enough steam on its own for the model engine to work for more than a few strokes of the piston "unless the fire was violently urged with bellows" (Watt 1970c). The poor performance of the engine needed explanation. Here was a need that became a *goal*:

G0: Explain the poor performance of the model Newcomen engine.

In response Watt began a series of experiments on the model engine. The latter became both an experimental apparatus and an object of investigation.

But what kinds of experiments *could* Watt conduct at this stage. Philosopher of science Karl Popper (1968, pp. 106–107), among others, has insisted that observations in the scientific sense are responses to *prior* expectations or theories: "all observations are theory-laden" as the aphorism goes. But at this stage Watt *had* no theory or expectations about the model Newcomen engine that could suggest appropriate experiments.

But he had a precise *goal* (G0). It was this that prompted him to perform experiments. Thus it is not always that all observations (or experiments) are theory-laden. It is also that observations (or experiments) can be *goal-driven*. In the case of the model Newcomen engine, if his goal was to explain its performance he must at least know something about the engine's current behavior of which he knew very little. So in order to meet goal G0 he generated for himself a *subgoal*:

> **G1:** Acquire knowledge of the working principles of the model Newcomen engine.

Knowledge acquisition in technological and scientific domains can proceed along several lines. To the mechanically or experimentally inclined (as Watt was), one source of knowledge is to directly manipulate the artifact of interest and see what happens. To *tinker* with it in other words. This was what Watt's experiments amounted to at this stage.

The result of these experiments, conducted between 1763 and 1765, was a corpus of empirical *facts* about the model engine that became part of Watt's belief/ knowledge space. Most significant of these was that an "immense Quantity [*sic*] of fuel it [the engine] consumed in proportion to its cylinder" (Watt 1970a, p. 434). Thus the experiments in response to goal G1 had generated another subgoal of G0:

> **G2:** Explain why the steam consumption was so high in the model engine.

We know that G2 was really identified as a goal because of his recollection that he began "Considering the causes of this defect." He then offered a *hypothesis* (Watt 1970b):

> **H0:** The high consumption of fuel and steam is "imputed" to the loss of heat through the wall of the metal cylinder.

This hypothesis in turn generated a new subgoal (Watt 1970a, p. 434):

> **G3:** "… endeavor to improve the engine."

He confabulated with his friend John Robison and from such conversation came the hypothesis that:

> **H1:** If the cylinder was made of wood it would not occasion the loss of so much heat (ibid.).

Furthermore, referring to an idea gleaned from another source, he hypothesized that:

> **H2:** A small boiler and jets of water injected at such times as steam is wanted will reduce heat loss in the cylinder.

Watt then undertook a plethora of experiments to test hypotheses H1 and H2 that were recorded in his "Notebook." As it turned out the experiments refuted both H1 and H2 that were then abandoned. However, in the course of these experiments he arrived at a new hypothesis to explain the high consumption of fuel and steam:

> **H3:** A large proportion of the steam introduced into the cylinder is expended in heating the water (previously condensed) before the excess steam can act upon the cylinder.

In arriving at H3 Watt drew upon items of knowledge concerning the physical properties of steam and relevant geometric attributes of small and large cylinders (Robinson and McKie 1970, p. 417). And he acknowledged that these facts explained one of the puzzles that had originally caught his attention: why the model engine performed so poorly in contrast to the full-scale Newcomen engines that worked in the mines.

There was still more that he came to understand. He alluded to conversations he had had with Joseph Black and John Robison, and to the studies by William Cullen (another eminence of the Scottish Enlightenment, Black's teacher and professor of chemistry and medicine in the University of Edinburgh) on the boiling of ether in vacuum. Based on these studies Watt realized that a vacuum could not be produced in the cylinder unless the latter was cooled by the injected water to a temperature below the boiling point of water, for otherwise the condensed water would boil, producing steam, and prevent the formation of the desired extent of vacuum in the cylinder. From this Watt formulated yet another hypothesis (Robinson and McKie 1970, p. 417):

> **H4:** [Since the injection of cold water condenses the steam and produces a vacuum] the greater the desired "degree of exhaustion" the more must the cylinder be cooled by injection of water, hence the greater the quantity of steam that be condensed before "new" steam is allowed to enter.

Watt's "Notebook" is full of details of various quantitative experiments—on the heating of water, on heat capacities (that is, specific heats) of various materials, the consumption of fuels and the production of steam—experiments pertaining to facts that he needed to ascertain. One experiment produced an effect which "surprised" him so much that he discussed it with Joseph Black and asked him "if it is possible that water under the form of steam could contain more heat than it did when water … was heated to 212" (Watt 1970a, pp. 438–439). Black told him "that had long been a tenet of his & explained to me his thoughts on the subject" (pp. 438–439). The "subject" was the concept of latent heat—the fact that when matter changes state (from solid to liquid, from liquid to gas) it stays at a constant temperature, absorbing heat, until the change of state is complete. Thus Watt had stumbled upon the phenomenon of latent heat that, unknown to him, Black had studied and lectured upon for some time (Fleming 1952, p. 4).

Watt's experiments, in addition to yielding this and other observations, also led him to two seemingly incompatible goals. First, because water boils in a vacuum at a temperature of 100 degrees (F), much less than the boiling point under normal atmospheric pressure, a vacuum could not be induced unless:

G4: The steam in the cylinder is cooled to below 100 degrees F.

Second, since steam is condensed by cold bodies, if it is injected into the cylinder it would be condensed by contact with cold walls and much steam would be lost to condensation before it could begin to accumulate in the cylinder. Hence to avoid condensation at the time steam is injected:

G5: The temperature of the cylinder has to be kept at about 212 degrees F.

These were two *conflicting* goals. Watt had to resolve this conflict in order to improve the performance of the model Newcomen engine (goal G3). *This resolution constituted the illumination* on that Sunday morning walk in May 1765. The product was the principle of the "separate condenser."

Let us summarize what we have learnt about the nature of the long process Watt went through before his famous illumination. In one sense all that preceded the generation of goals G4 and G5 might be seen as Watt's reactive preparation that was triggered by the "top" goal G0. In another sense the whole complex of activities between 1757 to the spring of 1765 (including the moment of illumination) can be interpreted as a single, coherent cognitive process in which reactive *preparation* (knowledge acquisition by way of book learning, experimenting, discussions with close associates) and creative *production* are densely *interleaved*. It all depends on where we draw the line. Much must have happened in the unconscious but much also occurred in the conscious. It seems pointless to claim that some distinct phase of incubation occurred.

V Illumination as event and as process

It is timely at this point to recognize that illumination can interpreted in two ways. In one sense it is an *event*, the sudden emergence of an idea, a concept or a solution the artificer has been seeking. The artificer becomes aware of this "Eureka" moment and so it will surely be (*contra* Poincaré) in her consciousness. But in another sense illumination is a *process* that leads to an outcome. It is the actual act of production itself, possibly fusing with reactive preparation, that ends with an artifact as an output. And as with any cognitive process this too will be an interleaving of the conscious and the unconscious. Henceforth, the meaning will be usually evident from context but, when needed, I will distinguish by speaking of an "illumination moment" or an "illumination process."

Recognizing that illumination may mean a process also suggests that illumination need not always be an eureka-like phenomenon. It makes sense to speak of the illumination process as producing a fruitful and satisfying outcome that meets the artificer's goal but perhaps lacking in the thrilling suddenness of an eureka moment. We will find an example of this in the next chapter.

But let us return to the business of reactive preparation.

VI   The artist building pictorial memoranda

That artists rely on visual memory is well known. Psychologist and music historian Rosamund Harding (1942) had documented many fascinating instances of painters who created "pictorial memoranda" as aids to visual memory. She distinguished between "scientific" and "poetic" painters. The former desires to capture aspects of nature as faithfully as they can, the latter looks to nature as a source of ideas and inspiration for expressing their "poetic dream" (p. 86).

For Harding, Claude Monet was the exemplar par excellence of the scientific painter; one who paints what he *sees* not what he *knows*. Thus Monet painted his "impressions" of a subject as he observed it, as it presented him with "sensations" at any particular instant of time. So he would paint the same subject again and again at different times, capturing the changing impressions of that one subject, of Rouen Cathedral for example. Monet's paintings, Harding noted, were done directly from nature, not second hand, nor from notes, nor from memory (p. 86). Such was the Impressionists' creed. Paul Cézanne wrote to his boyhood friend, the novelist Emile Zola, that no painting done in the studio will ever be as good as those done out of doors (Chipp 1968, p. 16).

In the most extreme case then, the scientific painter does not need pictorial memoranda as aids to visual memory. In contrast the "poetic" painter *à la* Harding paints not so much from nature but from his *visual memory of nature* and to this end he creates pictorial memoranda as an *aide memoire*.

Thus the nineteenth century landscapist Camille Corot kept "copies of my works in my heart and in my eyes." "A landscape painter should be able to paint a country masterpiece without leaving Montmartre" (quoted in Harding 1942, p. 82). So also another nineteenth century landscapist and portraitist of country life, Jean-François Millet, would make sketches outlining the main features of a figure or a landscape, then do the complete painting afterwards in the studio, relying on his memory to capture atmospheric and other effects (p. 82). For the

Post-Impressionist Vincent van Gogh, writing to his art dealer brother Theo, paintings from memory are always "more artistic" to look at than paintings from nature (Chipp 1968, p. 42). The landscapist J.M.W. Turner, who straddled the eighteenth and nineteenth centuries, the quintessential painter of the Romantic Age, would make copious studies from nature but in his final paintings he would change them quite dramatically. Even Turner's great contemporary and compatriot John Constable, though known to be committed to painting landscapes based on "a pure apprehension of natural effect," would make countless oil sketches out of doors but would paint the final versions in his studio (Jansen 1969, p. 469).

The advent of photography brought its own challenges to the naturalist painter: how could his work compete with photographic realism? But the camera also provided a new tool for storing visual memory. Pablo Picasso, for instance, enthusiastically endorsed the, then quite new, technology of photography to build pictorial memoranda. In fact he used the camera as an *experimental research tool* to explore perception, visual illusion, and the "geometrization of nature," effects that would enter into his Cubist paintings as creativity scholar Arthur I. Miller (2001) has so meticulously documented.

VII   George Rodrigue: picture taking for picture painting

My study of the contemporary American artist George Rodrigue (see Chapter 6, IX) yielded rich dividends on building visual memory as a way of reactive preparation in the realm of art. Rodrigue's landscapes and depictions of Cajun life are not naturalistic. The viewer/consumer does not see him capturing the particular nuances of light and shade and form that artists such as Constable or Monet (in their different ways) were concerned with. In Rosamund Harding's parlance Rodrigue was a "poetic" painter in whom visual images, impressions and emotions were transformed into quasi-graphic designs.

He created pictorial memoranda as aids to visual memory by resorting extensively to the camera, especially in his early years. Rodrigue took pictures in order to paint pictures. Building pictorial memoranda was certainly part of his proactive preparation soon after his return to South Louisiana from art school in Los Angeles, but more interesting was how pictorial memoranda worked for him in reactive preparation.

In a sense, taking pictures to paint pictures is the modern artist's equivalent of the scientist's data-gathering activity. But the scientist does not gather data arbitrarily. Usually he observes, measures and gathers data because he has "something in his mind," a theory or hypothesis he wishes to test, confirm or falsify. After all, in even the most specific scientific activity the "data space" is vast; the "observation space" is unbounded in extent, like physical space itself, and so the scientist filters out most of the data space by virtue of some prior hypothesis or theory he wishes to test or some prior expectation he has in mind. Recall Popper's dictum, that all observations or experiments are "theory-laden."

However, as we saw in the case of James Watt, sometimes one may not have anything nearly as well formed as a testable theory to start with or even a reasonably firm expectation. One may have only the vaguest of ideas or the germ of a question. One may not be able to properly articulate the idea or question but it is there, somewhere in one's mind, consciously or unconsciously, and it may be sufficient to serve as a basis for sifting through the data space, to separate (not always correctly) "relevant" from "irrelevant" data. For instance in the case of James Watt, it was the formation of a goal in his mind which drove the series of experiments he carried out. To repeat, "Observations/experiments can be goal-driven."

In Rodrigue's case, his picture taking was very much in the nature of visual experiments driven by specific painterly goals; it was very much a means of his reactive preparation.

Visiting Santa Fe, New Mexico in the late 1980s, Rodrigue met a young Native American woman. He decided to paint her and visited Santa Fe several times thereafter to photograph her. The photographs show her in many different dresses. In fact Rodrigue photographed her in as many as nine different combinations of dresses and poses. These slides (which, in Rodrigue's personal collection, I was allowed to inspect) constituted a whole series of visual and compositional *experiments*. Like experiments in science, they too were bounded by certain parameters that, in Rodrigue's case, were particular design elements: pose, dress design, scarf, color combination in the dress and background. The paintings with this woman as model drew upon these experiments, selected combinations of the design elements and transformed them in the act of painting (Freundlich 1996, pp. 143, 152).

Another series of paintings drew upon a folk song, popular in Rodrigue's Cajun culture, called *Jolie Blonde*. The song, set to a waltz and written in 1928, is a prisoner's lament at the loss of his unfaithful girl. This theme of a prisoner's farewell, of infidelity and of lost love was well entrenched in the repertoire of Cajun music (Ancelet 1989). Rodrigue returned to the *Jolie Blonde* theme repeatedly. Here also, as reactive preparation, he staged various visual experiments and recorded them photographically as pictorial memoranda. He made over thirty photographic slides of the same model (George Rodrigue's personal collection). She had blonde hair and wore the same blue frock with shoulder straps and a wide sash round the waist. In some photographs she wore a wide-brimmed hat, in others she was bareheaded; some showed her sitting in various poses and angles, others had her standing. In some poses she held a stem with a single rose, others showed her holding the hat. A few were close-ups of just her face, some were bust-length and some showed her in full figure. These visual experiments for Rodrigue served as pictorial data. The paintings around the *Jolie Blonde* theme manifested specific design elements that are drawn from the pictorial data.

In 1984 Rodrigue collaborated with a writer in producing a book consisting of a collection of forty paintings by Rodrigue where each painting accompanied a story written by his collaborator (Segura and Rodrigue 1984). Rodrigue had gathered a collection of forty traditional Louisiana tales, essentially in synoptic form, and based on the synopses, he painted the pictures. These in turn served as the bases for the short stories his collaborator then wrote. Thus the paintings came first; the stories expanded the synoptic tales.

One of the paintings called *My Yellow Rolls* is accompanied by a particular ghost story (p. 331). The painting reflects this ghostliness: it shows a read-headed girl in a white dress standing beside and partly in front of a yellow Rolls Royce. She stands between two tombstone slabs. Framing the girl's head and behind the car is an oak tree. Farther beyond is a two-storey house. The red of the hair, the yellow of the car and the black of the tree dominate the picture.

This picture was of great interest because of what it revealed of the artist's reactive preparation in response to a specific goal. As was his custom Rodrigue's preparation involved taking pictures. He prepared at least a score of photographic slides (in his personal collection) before painting the picture. They show various compositional studies of a Rolls Royce car, a red-headed woman in white, tombstones and a tree. Some are studies of the car in relation to the tombstone; the car is placed at various angles relative to the camera's view. Others depict the model in relation to the car and tombstone. In several slides she is wearing a white, ankle-length mink-coat with the collar turned up at various angles and in various positions. One slide shows the car in an almost frontal view with the model standing next to it on the right. She is facing the camera at a slight angle. In another slide the woman in the same dress stands in front of the car partly occluding the radiator grill. In another, the car is in the center, in part profile with the model behind the hood, also in part profile and partly obscured by the car. The cemetery forms the background.

These photographs together constitute Rodrigue's preparation in response to a goal to paint a picture based on a specific theme. They were his experiments. But how did these experiments *participate* in the creation of *My Yellow Rolls?*

One. The fact that all the slides involved permutations and combinations of four elements—tree, woman, car and tombstone—suggests that Rodrigue had already established a *goal* for a composition involving *just* these four elements. The ghost story itself had other elements that he had factored out from the painting.

Two. The fact that the slides varied in the spatial relationships between the four elements or in their individual positions and angles suggest that Rodrigiue was *searching* the "compositional space" for the "right" positioning of the elements and the "right" relationships between them.

Three. In searching the compositional space, Rodrigue took pictures that sometimes included all four elements or three (car/woman/tombstone, car/tree/tombstone) or two (car/woman, car/tombstone) or even just one (car). It is as if his visual experiments involved these as *variables*, some of which he excluded in some experiments and included in others. The word "experiment" in the context of art is thus more than a metaphor borrowed from science. After all, a scientific experiment is an observational situation in which the experimenter controls some selected variables and studies their effects on the phenomenon of interest. This is precisely what Rodrigue was doing. His experiments are to be taken as literally as those conducted by Watt.

Four. One does not find an exact match between *any* of the slides and the actual painting. In the absence of any evidence of draft sketches or other preliminary paintings, we cannot say that the experiments entailed various combinations and permutations of the principal elements from which *one* was selected wholesale for the final picture. Rather (as in the case of the *Jolie Blonde* paintings) we find a process of *partial selection* from various experiments. Rodrigue selected the general posture and the woman's dress from one slide, the general angle of the car from another, and approximated the relative positions of the horizontal tombstone slabs to that of the woman from a third.

VIII   The consumer's preparation

Needless to say, preparation (proactive and reactive) is also demanded of the consumer. When an artifact—a painting, a novel, a film, a scientific theory or model, a philosophical idea, a technological invention or whatever—enters a consumer's consciousness, that artifact must be assimilated into his belief/knowledge space; it must be integrated into his interior schema system. It must enter into the *narrative* that makes up the contents of his consciousness. Otherwise it will remain a mere piece of isolated *information*.

For example, a consumer's encounter with Watt's separate condenser principle will remain just an isolated piece of information in his belief/knowledge space unless it becomes an integral element of some existing schema. But for that to happen the person must already have in place something like a "steam engine schema" along the lines of the schema Watt invented for his own consumption. In the absence of an existing schema the consumer must *build* one in order that Watt's idea can make sense. The possession of a prior schema that can be matched against the encounter with Watt's new idea and the latter's assimilation into that schema means that the consumer has done some prior proactive preparation. The building of a new belief/knowledge subspace or schema entails reactive preparation on the consumer's part. Either or both of these kinds of preparedness are necessary on the consumer's part for a creative encounter to occur between the consumer and the artificer (who, like Watt, may be long dead). Such preparedness is necessary for the consumer to judge the originality of the artifact and the artificer's creativity.

9

THE ACTUAL ACT OF PRODUCTION

I The heart of the affair

As we have seen so far, creativity is a many-faceted affair. But at its very heart is what we have called (in Chapters 3 and 4) the *act of production*. To recapitulate, this refers to the following scenario:

> There is an artificer who in response to a goal state (a need, desire or want) brings into existence an artifact intended to satisfy the goal state. This in turn leads to the artificer experiencing yet another mental state: her response state reflecting her judgment or belief that the artifact has satisfied the goal state. The total process from goal state through artifact creation to response state is the act of production.

It was also suggested that whether the act of production is an *act of creation* will depend on either judgment, on the part of the artificer herself or one or more consumers, that the artificer is original in some sense (Chapter 3) or if a creative encounter occurs between artificer and one or more consumers (Chapter 4).

When people generally ask "what goes on in creativity?" it is the act of production they usually have in mind. When Picasso wondered aloud how far or from where a painting comes to him, he was really asking about this act of production. When the novelist Arthur Koestler (1964)—a man of broad intellectual interests—wrote his remarkable book *The Act of Creation*, the running theme of his richly eclectic study was the nature of the act of production. And this is the subject of this chapter.

The act of production, by this scenario, makes no distinction between incubation and illumination or, sometimes, even between these two and reactive preparation; for, as we saw in the previous chapter, the so-called different "stages" *à la*

Poincaré–Wallas–Hadamard model usually merge into one continuous process and the distinction is often quite blurred. In fact even the fourth "stage" of the model, *verification*—where the result of illumination is allegedly *consciously* verified—is not necessarily a distinct stage nor entirely a conscious process. As we will see, verification can occur at different points in the act of production.

In sum, the *activities* called (reactive) preparation, incubation, illumination and verification, the four stages of the Poincaré–Wallas–Hadamard model, are really *ingredients* in the "stew" that is the act of production. They might be so finely interspersed and interleaved it is meaningless to speak of them as "stages."

The real problem in trying to make sense of the act of production is the incursion of the "unconscious machine" (Chapter 7): the empirical reality of a cognitive process (such as thinking, planning, designing, discovering, inventing, ideating, painting, crafting, composing, etc.) being an entwinement of the conscious and the unconscious, with the latter dominating. So we are severely limited in how specific or precise we can be in uncovering the act of production. In the proper spirit of cognitive history (see Prologue), we must then rely considerably on the archival or historical evidence to circumvent this dilemma.

II   A Darwinian ghost in the discourse

There is, however, a certain ghost that has infiltrated the discourse on creativity in recent decades. This is the ghost of Darwin. Stated briefly (for now) it insists that the act of production is in some real sense a *Darwinian* process: that the act of production entails an essential *blind* (meaning random) component (as Darwinism demands) that generates possible cognitive choices as variations from which a *selection* is made. This suggests that the act of production is a victim of blind happenstance, of randomness, of chance, of contingency. In recent times this issue became a matter of considerable debate and controversy.

A *caveat*: This controversy concerns the place of Darwinism in the realm of *human creativity*. It is unfortunate that the word "creativity" has the same etymological root as "creationism." Our concern with Darwinism has nothing to do whatsoever with creationism or "intelligent design" (as these terms are currently understood and used). As far as we are concerned here, the only kind of intelligence that enters into the creation of artifacts is intelligence of the secular variety, not some transcendental or supernatural agency. And the only kind of creation relevant to us here is that performed by secular agents—usually human beings, but also possibly other animals and even machines.

The Darwinian ghost entered this discourse by way of psychologist Donald Campbell (1960) who advanced an explicitly Darwinian model of "creative thought" and "other knowledge processes." This paper and later writings by Campbell and other like-minded thinkers (including Karl Popper) led the Darwinian model of how new ideas and knowledge are produced to be called "evolutionary epistemology" (Campbell 1987, Radnitzky and Bartley 1987). Perhaps a more appropriate name for this view of the creative process, in parallel with the term "social Darwinism," is *cognitive Darwinism*. Some creativity researchers and historians found this idea irresistible. For example, engineer–historian Walter Vincenti (1992)—though without referring to Campbell—offered a Darwinian model to explain how engineers create new knowledge. A decade before him, historian of technology Brooke Hindle (1981, p. 128) had likened the process of technological invention to Darwinian evolution. Along these same lines economic historian Joel Mokyr (1990, pp. 275 *et seq*) advanced a quite explicitly biological argument to explain how technological change occurs. For Mokyr, the techniques whereby new goods or services are produced "are analogous of species" and the "changes in them have an evolutionary character" (p. 275). In other words, it is these *techniques* (or technological knowledge) that evolve along biological lines (p. 277). And the Darwinian or, more broadly, biological view of creativity has a rich history in the realm of architecture, crafts and the "technical arts" as was brilliantly (but critically) explicated by architectural theorist Philip Steadman (2008).

Arguably the most prolific and passionate advocate of cognitive Darwinism over the past three decades has been psychologist Dean Keith Simonton. Beginning in 1988 with a study of the psychology of scientific discovery (Simonton 1988) he went on, a decade after, to propose a full-blown "Darwinian perspective of creativity" (Simonton 1999), following this with a spate of papers that modified, extended and essentially defended his theory (see, e.g., Simonton 2010a, 2010b). I say "defending" because while there are others who have also advocated cognitive Darwinism (Lumsden 1999, Nickles 2003a, 2010), some (and I am one of them) have vigorously contested cognitive Darwinism as the central process underlying the act of production (see, e.g., Dasgupta 2004, 2010, 2011; Weisberg 2004; Gabora 2007, 2011). There are yet still others who have sought the middle ground between the Darwinian and non-Darwinian perspectives (Runco 2007, 2010; Weisberg and Has 2007).

In cognitive Darwinism we have, then, a genuine scientific controversy—and one of some significance in creativity studies. The bone of contention is not whether the act of production is or is not evolutionary in nature—the opponents of cognitive Darwinism do not question this—but as to the *nature* of this evolutionary process.

III   Varieties of *evolution*

This point is important because in writing on creativity, innovation, change and growth of knowledge, the word *evolution* is used in several different ways.

One. For some, evolution is linked to, and is the source of *diversity*. For example, historian George Basalla (1988) was drawn to the evolutionary idea to *explain* the diversity of technological artifacts by way of an analogy with the diversity of organic species (p. 208). Basalla paid homage to Darwin but his detailed, historically grounded theory of technological evolution did not *demand* a Darwinian process. As he emphasized, there are many ways in which novelty arises among material artifacts, but most of them do not accord a critical place to the Darwinian paradigm (p. 134).

Two. In common usage, something is said to evolve when change is *gradual*, a feature which Joel Mokyr (1990, p. 273) recognized. In the realm of material artifacts a well-known early exponent of this idea was British anthropologist A. Lane Pitt-Rivers who argued that there was an evolutionary relationship among a variety of Australian aboriginal weapons such as shields, clubs and boomerangs (see Steadman 2008, pp. 76–94).

Three. Both diversity and gradualism in the abovementioned senses are characteristics of *macroevolution*—that is, change across significant historical periods. Here we may borrow the biological notion of *phylogeny*. As evolutionary biologist Stephen Jay Gould (1977) defined it, phylogeny is "the evolutionary history of a lineage conventionally … depicted as a sequence of adult stages" (p. 483).

In the context of artifacts (material or abstract) phylogeny would refer to the macroevolutionary *history* of some linked network of artifacts or their forms. Of course biological phylogeny entails spans of millions, even billions, of years whereas artifactual phylogeny involves a time span ranging from tens of thousand years (as in the case of art objects) to as little as a century or so (as in the case of the principles of quantum physics, molecular biology or computer science).

An example from computer science is the evolution of the "Algol family" of programming languages. The time span was from the late 1950s to the early 1970s, and the evolved family of languages included Algol 58 (the oldest), Algol 60, EULER, Algol W, PL/360, Algol 68, Pascal, Concurrent Pascal and Modula (Dasgupta 2014a, pp. 205–216, 2018a, pp. 1–22). A particularly rich case of artifactual phylogeny embraces the artistic style called Cubism that, according to some art historians and critics, had its beginnings in Picasso's *Les Demoiselles d'Avignon* (1907) (Green 2001). Cubism was invented soon after by Picasso and Georges Braque and would be adapted and interpreted by other European painters of the pre-World War I era, such as Juan Gris, Henri Le Fauconnier, Piet Mondrian and Fernand Léger (Cox 2000). In the 1920s it would find its way to an altogether different artistic and cultural tradition in the work of Indian painter Gaganendranath Tagore (Rabindranath Tagore's nephew) (Mitter 2007).

Cubism as a macroevolutionary phenomenon in fact existed at two levels. On one hand the "mature" artifacts that constituted the linked networks of Cubism were *individual* paintings (material artifacts) by Picasso, Braque and others. On the other hand Cubism as a *style* constituted a "mature" abstract artifact and was linked to a variety of other movements and styles in painting, sculpture and architecture, as spectacularly depicted by Alfred H. Barr, the first director of the Museum of Modern Art in New York, in his jacket design for the 1936 exhibition catalogue *Cubism and Abstract Art* (Cox 2000, pp. 390–391).

Four. Evolution suggests a sense of *progress*, the idea that the evolution of some cultural or scientific practice over time results in its "improvement" in some social, economic or intellectual sense. There are Darwinian overtones here since the question, whether biological evolution implies biological progress has long exercised biologists and other commentators on Darwinian evolution including Darwin himself, whose statements on the relationship between evolution and progress reveal a distinct ambivalence (Darwin 1985, pp. 343, 459; Gould 2002, p. 468). This ambivalence is reflected in the thoughts of later authors including Julian Huxley in his influential *Evolution: The Modern Synthesis* (2010) who hedged his bets: while he conceded that "evolutionary progress" was a "biological fact," this progress was of "a particular and limited nature" (pp. 568–569). Another eminent evolutionary biologist Ernst Mayr, in his monumental *Growth of Biological Thought* (1982) alludes to certain biological "innovations" occurring in the course of evolution that "suggest progress." Yet, he adds, the linear inexorability suggested by the word "progressive" is not to be seen in biological evolution (p. 532). All in all, taking into account the paleontological and biological evidence, Mayr concluded "Not all, and perhaps only the smallest amount, of evolution consists of progress" (p. 533).

Thus, in the case of biological evolution there is a great deal of ambivalence about the question of progress. This ambivalence also prevails in the realm of material cultural evolution. For example, economic historian Joel Mokyr (1990, pp. 273–300) is an advocate of the linkage between technological evolution and progress, while the Nobel laureate economist–philosopher Amartya Sen (1993) argues that the "Darwinian view of progress," to the extent it applies to the fitness characteristic of a species, does not entail improvement in the quality of human lives.

We note that in both natural and cultural evolution the association is between progress and *macro*evolution. Elsewhere (Dasgupta 2018a) I have discussed the connection between creativity and progress. But let me end the present discussion by noting that the very *idea* of progress—what we mean by it—has exercised historians, philosophers and social theorists quite independent of evolutionary considerations (Laudan 1977; Bury 1987; Marx and Mazlish 1998).

Five. Evolution carries with it the idea of *growth in complexity*. Here again organic macroevolution enters the picture since biological organisms are considered to have evolved in complexity (Bonner 1988)—though not every biologist shares this view (McShea 1997).

Six. Finally, evolution is viewed as an outcome of the mechanism of *natural selection* and the resulting *adaptation* of organisms to their environments.

Diversity, gradualism, phylogeny, progress, complexity: each has a place in biological evolution. But outside biology, in the realm of the artifactual (the world in which creativity resides), one can easily talk about each of these aspects *without appealing to Darwinism*. None of them are essential to *Darwinian* evolution. It is only the sixth sense, the principle of natural selection and adaptation, that is the *sine qua non* of Darwinism. So it is to natural selection as a possible *core* mechanism in creativity—as a principle of *cognitive Darwinism*—we must turn.

IV Cognitive Darwinism *à la* Donald Campbell

If we take cognitive Darwinism seriously—as a Darwinian model for interpreting the act of production—we must begin with the principle of natural selection. But we must also note that the Darwinian paradigm (in Kuhn's sense of the latter term) has also undergone considerable internal change since its core element, the principle of natural selection was established in the mid-nineteenth century. One major internal change (more precisely, enrichment) was the synthesis, in the 1930s and early 1940s, of "classical" Darwinism (à la *Origin of Species*) with systematics (the science of biological taxonomy and classification) and the then-newly emerged science of genetics into what zoologist Julian Huxley famously called "The Modern Synthesis" (Huxley 2010). This synthesis came to be known as *Neo-Darwinism* (Medawar and Medawar 1983, pp. 196–199).

But matters did not rest there. Stephen Jay Gould (2002), paleontologist, evolutionary theorist and intellectual gadfly, in a series of writings culminating in his opus *The Structure of Evolutionary Theory*, published in the year of his death, told his readers that all was not well with the Neo-Darwinian theory: revisions would have to be made and were being made. Still, Gould insisted that the *core* of "Darwinian logic" still held; the paradigm would not shift (p. 6).

In our discussion of cognitive Darwinism and its possible role in the act of production we will stay within the Neo-Darwinian perimeter, primarily because the Darwinism advanced by Donald Campbell and others in the realm of creativity has been inspired by Neo-Darwinism rather than its more recent perspectives.

In first offering Donald Campbell's original (1960) proposal I will adhere as closely as possible to his language. His argument, thus, was along the following lines.

One. The production of genuine new knowledge—the output of creative thought—demands the *blind* generation of *variations* (of thought products). By "blind" Campbell meant three attributes: (a) the variations are independent of the environment (that is, the problem situation that gave birth to the thought process) in which they arise; (b) specific "correct" variations of thought products are no more likely to occur than specific "incorrect" variations; (c) a variation generated at some stage is never a correction of a previously generated incorrect variation (that is, variation generation is never directed by a prior error).

Two. The variations in thought products are *then* subjected to a *selection* process that weeds out all variations but the one that demonstrates a fit with the environment (the problem situation) at hand. Such a selection demands one or more *criteria* for judging whether the variant thought products have met the problem situation. The variants that fail to meet the criteria adequately are rejected.

Three. There is a mechanism for the *retention* of the selected variant. Only then will a thought product make a permanent contribution to the world of creative thought.

The analogy with Darwinian logic is obvious. Campbell called this process *blind variation and selective retention* (BVSR). Interestingly, in his original paper he did not claim that BVSR was a Darwinian theory or that it was based on an analogy with the Darwinian theory of natural selection. Indeed Darwin was scarcely mentioned. Rather Campbell seemed to claim that BVSR was a *universal process* operating at several *levels*. There were, first, the "lower knowledge processes" active at biological levels (Campbell 1960, pp. 93–94). Here he distinguished between BVSR at the genetic level (Darwinian natural selection) and at the physiological level (e.g., echo-location in fish, porpoise and bats) (pp. 94–95). In contrast the work of BVSR in creative thought is a "knowledge process" operating at the higher cognitive or psychological level (p. 96). So his BVSR theory seems to *subsume* both organic evolution and creativity.

However, while Campbell was reasonably precise about what the variants are at the genetic ("mutant individuals") and physiological (reflected wave pulses in echo location, for example) levels (pp. 93, 94) he is quite elusive in the case of creative thought.

Campbell did not offer any experimental or empirical evidence in support of his theory but rather the theorizing of others who had written before him. He cited the nineteenth century psychologist Alexander Bain who in 1855 (before the publication of *The Origin of Species*) invoked "trial and error" as the process involved (p. 96). Another nineteenth century author, Paul Sourian, wrote in 1881 that "Chance is the first principle of invention," and articulated what was essentially a BVSR schema even using the term "artificial selection" (pp. 97, 98). Campbell also cited the distinguished Austrian physicist and philosopher of science Ernst Mach who delivered an inaugural professorial lecture in the University of Vienna in 1895 on the "part played by accident in invention and discovery" (p. 99).

But Campbell's most extensive citation was from Henri Poincaré's 1913 essay "Mathematical Creation," the work in which he proposed in part the ideas that entered into the Poincaré–Wallas–Hadamard model (Chapter 7). For Poincaré, of course, most of the creative work occurred in the unconscious, the "subliminal self" (Poincaré 1985, p. 28), during incubation.

Poincaré spoke of a *combinational* process. Mathematical discoveries (or inventions), according to him, entailed choosing fruitful combinations of mathematical "ideas" (p. 25). The generation of the combinations and the selection from them the ones that are useful is unconscious work. Poincaré told his reader that a large number of such combinations are first "blindly formed in the subliminal self." Of these only a select few are "harmonious," and thus, both "useful and beautiful," and these are the ones, still formed unconsciously, that are presented to consciousness (p. 29).

There is here a vague anticipation of Campbell's cognitive Darwinism: the combination of mathematical ideas corresponds, rather vaguely, to blind variation; choosing the "interesting" combinations corresponds to selection. This process of selection is effected by the person's "esthetic sensibility" serving as a "delicate sieve." The combinatorial variations are thus blindly formed, and the agent of selection is one's mathematical aesthetic (see Chapter 4, VI on the place of aesthetics in creativity).

Chance, trial and error, blindness. These were the terms Campbell's predecessors used. Collectively they fused into his concept of blind variation.

Over the fifty or so years since Campbell's original paper, the most insistent and vigorous support of his theory has come from the prolific psychologist Dean Keith

Simonton. In two books separated roughly by a decade (Simonton 1988, 1999) and in many papers he extended and shaped BVSR into a detailed theory of the act of production which we may call "Neo-Campbellian" BVSR theory.

In 2010 Simonton wrote an updated review of his Neo-Campbellian position in which he retreated from an explicitly Darwinian perspective. What natural selection and creativity shared, Simonton insisted, was "a mutual dependence on the capacity for generating blind variations, whether those variants constituted organisms of a particular species or ideas in specific domains" (Simonton 2010a, p. 157). Moreover the blind variations in both domains are produced by *combinatorial* means (*à la* Poincaré), though the nature of the combinations may differ.

V   What should a Darwinian act of production look like?

So if we take the Neo-Campbellian version of cognitive Darwinism seriously, here is what the act of production should look like.

One. In the standard Neo-Darwinian account the whole organism—the *phenotype* in biological language (Medawar and Medawar 1983, p. 116)—constitutes the unit of variation on which natural selection works. In creative thinking the variants constitute abstract or material artifacts and their nature will depend on the domain. In natural science they may be theories, laws, observed phenomena or procedures. In mathematics they will be axiom systems, theorems and proofs. In engineering they will be designs, inventions, engineering theories and models, analytical methods or heuristic principles. In painting they will be compositions, representations, styles or techniques. In literary writing the variants will be fragments of or whole poems, short stories, essays, novels, plays, literary styles and genres. And so on. In general, *a unit of variation in the realm of creativity will be a material or abstract artifact that has surfaced in the artificer's conscious mind as a complete, meaningful entity.*

This last point is important if we wish to take cognitive Darwinism seriously. What goes on in the unconscious in forming the variants remains in the unconscious. Only when the *outcomes* enter consciousness does the artificer become cognizant of them. And what enters the conscious state has to be *mature* or *stable* enough to be meaningful, for only they can be tested against the environment.

Two. In the biological realm an organism is the offspring of mature parents. Its *genotype* (the combinations of genes) is inherited from its parents subject to such genetical processes as mutation and recombination. Genes as units of heredity are well-defined, discrete physical entities. In the realm of creativity there is no proper analog to genes. The ingredients that enter into the making of an abstract artifact such as an idea, concept, algorithm, design, literary character or plot can themselves be mature artifacts; or they may be elemental fragments of prior abstract artifacts; or schemas or parts thereof; or they can be bits and pieces of isolated knowledge or beliefs. The ingredients that contribute to the making of a material artifact such as a computer can themselves be other mature material artifacts; or parts thereof.

So all we can say is that the unit of "inheritance" in acts of production is virtually anything contained in the artificer's belief/knowledge space, or suggested by the artificer's cultural environment (including other people's belief/knowledge spaces). The parent–offspring relationship of the organic realm does not hold in the creative realm.

Three. In the biological realm the environment is the physical habitat ("niche") in which an organism has to live and survive. In the creative realm the variant artifact must reside in an environment that is cognitive, cultural, social and/or physical. From the artificer's point of view this environment is *condensed* (I use this word in the psychoanalytic sense) into one or more *needs/goals/desires* the artifact must meet. The *needs/goals thus represent the environmental niche* for which the artifact is created.

Four. In the biological realm the variants are blindly generated. So also the variant artifacts in the creative realm must be *blindly created.* This means (as BVSR theory stipulates) that the production of variant artifacts has no correlation with the needs/goals the artifact must meet. Needs/goals have no influence on the generation of the variant artifacts. Furthermore the variants must not differ "wildly" from one another.

Five. There must be an abundantly large number of variant artifacts for selection to work on. To use the biologists' term the variation process must exhibit *super-fecundity.*

Six. Finally there is the selective retention phase. In the creative realm this means that the variant artifacts must be *tested* to see whether they satisfy the relevant needs or goals—that is, whether the cognitive/cultural/social/physical environment is congenial for the artifact to exist—and to prune out all those variant artifacts found "unfit." The selected artifacts are then "retained" and *communicated* to one or more consumers.

There is no doubt that cognitive Darwinism is an enticing idea: that Darwin resides as much in the artifactual world as in the living world, that he resides in the mind (so to speak) as he does in the body is seductively attractive. After all, science seeks universal, unifying laws and theories and here is one such grand unifying theory that its proponents would claim straddles both the organic and artifactual worlds.

The trouble is that cognitive Darwinism as a *universal* theory of the act of production in the creative realm *does not historically or empirically hold.* The historical evidence refutes cognitive Darwinism as a universal model of the creative act of production. In the rest of this chapter we consider a number of historical case studies from a variety of domains.

VI   The case of the lemon squeezer

Design scholar Nigel Cross (2011) cites the example of the French product designer Phillipe Starck who claimed that the design of a lemon squeezer for the Italian kitchenware manufacturer Alessi and named "Juicy Salif" just came upon him out of the blue (p. 6).

In the late 1980s, Starck was commissioned by Alessi to design a lemon squeezer as one of a series of products designed by internationally renowned designers. Soon after visiting Alessi and discussing the project with their representatives Starck went to dine at a restaurant. The commission was evidently on his mind for he began to make rough sketches of the artifact on a paper placemat. The first sketches were fairly typical forms of lemon squeezers. Thus he was drawing upon a "lemon squeezer schema" stored in his belief/knowledge space. His order of a plate of baby squids arrived at his table. This prompted the designer to sketch forms of the lemon squeezer that had decided squid-like appearances. Several variations were sketched on the placemat, all squid-like with large bodies and long legs, including one that was recognizably similar to the final "Juicy Salif" design (Cross 2011, pp. 16–17, especially Fig. 1.3). To the ordinary consumer or potential buyer the final design would look rather like a three-legged insect with a large elongated body supported on the three legs (Cross 2011, Fig. 1.1).

In this example the environment played a dual role. On the one hand it was the source of the project *goal*: to design a lemon squeezer—an artifact—that would satisfy the function of squeezing lemons and would be original in form as befitting an eminent designer such as Starck was. On the other hand the environment offered a plate of squids that led him to the squid-like form. The variants sketched on the placemat were several and thus *may* be interpreted as fecund. But none of the variants were independent of the environment: they were all shaped by the goal and several were strongly influenced by the plate of squids. The variant generation process was not blind as cognitive Darwinism would have it.

VII The case of the Britannia Bridge

The point is, several variants do often get generated in acts of production though they are hardly ever super-fecund in the Darwinian sense. More importantly, they are not blind variations.

As another example consider a nineteenth century structural engineering project that has excited the attention of engineers, historians and creativity researchers alike, including myself (Rosenberg and Vincenti 1978; Billington 1983; Timoshenko 1983; McNeill 1990; Chrimes 1991; Petroski 1992, 1994; Dasgupta 1994, 1996). This is the Britannia Bridge, designed and built in the 1840s in Wales by the engineer Robert Stephenson and his associates.

The artifact in question was a wrought-iron tubular railway bridge intended to span a 1100-feet wide waterway called the Menai Straits in Wales. The bridge, both in its use of material (wrought iron) and in structure and design (tubular, rather like a long metal tunnel) was H-original. Nothing like it had been built before in the long history of civil engineering, and was hailed as a revolutionary achievement of British engineering. It was also C-original because of the new knowledge about wrought-iron structures that was generated in the course of the project (Rosenberg and Vincenti 1978; Timoshenko 1983). In designing and building the Britannia Bridge, Robert Stephenson was both H-creative and C-creative.

Now, if Stephenson's thought process was Darwinian we would *expect* it to be along the following lines.

Stephenson blindly generated two or more variant designs for the bridge. (So here the variant artifacts would be abstract designs.) By "blind" is meant that the designs were uninfluenced by the goal (a condensation of the physical, geographical and technological environment) mandated for the bridge (by a British parliamentary committee which had commissioned the bridge on behalf of Parliament). The goals were that the bridge must be strong enough to support the passage of trains across the bridge, that it must resist wind forces, that it must not impede shipping navigation along the Menai Strait, and that it be within some specified cost. Moreover, each of the designs was produced by the combination of existing elements in Stephenson's belief/ knowledge space. Finally, Stephenson selected one of the variants that according to his evaluation and judgment best satisfied the goals.

Computer scientists would recognize this scenario as a case of searching through a space of possible designs using a "breadth-first" search strategy: first generate *all* the variant designs, *then* select one from them (Dasgupta 1991, pp. 41–42).

In fact *nothing like this scenario happened*. Stephenson's first step was to select as a candidate a suspension bridge form which had been previously used by the great eighteenth century "father of civil engineering" Thomas Telford to build a road bridge across the Menai Strait. Stephenson's first "variant" was not the product of a combination of elemental engineering ideas or concepts as cognitive Darwinists would have it but a holistic schema (the suspension bridge form) held in Stephenson's knowledge space. Moreover he chose this because, having been already used in a partially similar environment, it seemed a plausible "fit" to the requirements.

But then Stephenson *rejected* this schema because of its insufficient rigidity as a railway bridge. He *then* selected a second schema, a cast-iron arch bridge form that, like the suspension bridge, was a well-established bridge schema in the mid-nineteenth century. Again, this bridge form was not patched together combinatorially from elemental components but was a holistic schema. Nor was it blindly generated. Given the goals it seemed a *plausible* candidate.

The cast-iron bridge form was then also rejected because of the Admiralty's objection that the arches would impede shipping navigation. Thus the schema did not satisfy one of the environmental features. Stephenson then *returned* to the suspension bridge form and considered the possibility of stiffening the deck.

A cognitive Darwinist might claim that there is evidence here of a blind-variation, selective–retention process: that the suspension and the arch bridge forms had roughly equal likelihood of fit but only the former was chosen because of its potential for further development (Simonton 2010a). But this was not what happened. The process was an instance of a "sequential search," not one of breadth-first search: the suspension bridge form was first selected, tested in a preliminary way against the environment and then rejected; *only then* was the arch bridge form chosen; this *then* was also rejected and Stephenson then returned to the suspension bridge form.

VIII The act of production as *purposive* evolution

The complete history of the design of the Britannia Bridge as originally documented in great detail by Stephenson's principle collaborators on the project, Edwin Clarke (his resident engineer) and William Fairbairn, an eminent shipbuilder and structural engineer, tells us that the return to the suspension bridge form was merely the beginning of a long design process (Fairbairn 1849; Clarke 1850). Indeed, the final design of the Britannia Bridge showed only a pentimento of the suspension bridge schema. The choice of the latter was the "seed" from which the eventual design emerged; and this choice was not blind in any reasonable sense of the word, neither in the original Campbellian nor the Neo-Campbellian sense. Rather its selection as a schema simply reflected the fact that at that particular time it represented the most promising schema for long-span bridges.

As it turned out the entire design process was the product of a *purposive, hypotheses-driven, multistage* thought process (Dasgupta 1994, 1996, pp. 78–86). The creative act of production was certainly evolutionary but not in a Darwinian (BVSR) sense. We may call this *purposive evolution*.

IX Darwin in literary minds

Perhaps the realm that most challenges the idea of cognitive Darwinism is the literary one. If we did take cognitive Darwinism seriously then the variations upon which selection will act must be *literary artifacts* that attain sufficient maturity to reach the writer's consciousness as meaningful wholes. Furthermore, following neo-Campbellism, each such literary artifact as a variation will be a combination of some literary "elements."

But what *are* these variants? The analog to the biological phenotype will be complete literary products: novels, short stories, plays, poems, essays, memoirs, biographies and whatever else might count as a "work of literature."

The logical implication is that the variants upon which selection would act are those complete literary products. For example, a novelist *blindly* generates two or more variant novels addressing a particular theme and then *selects* one of them. Or a poet *blindly* produces two or more variant poems on a particular theme then *selects* one of them.

Clearly these are absurd as *general* schemas, though I suppose one can envision such a situation as a rare case.

Perhaps then cognitive Darwinism applies to more *elemental* levels of literary work. Perhaps the literary variations that make Darwinian sense are textual fragments, paragraphs, stanzas, a few lines, sentences, phrases or even single words. Or perhaps the literary variants are abstract artifacts of a non-textual nature: delineation of individual characters in a novel or a play (think of Shylock or Iago or Hamlet in Shakespeare or Jane Austen's Emma), or a literary technique, style or genre (stream of consciousness in Virginia Woolf's *Mrs Dalloway*, magical realism in Salman Rushdie's *Midnight's Children*). These seem more plausible as BVSR candidates.

X   Stephen Spender's "vision of the sea"

The poet and critic Stephen Spender, one of the generation of British poets who came into prominence in the 1930s (and included W.H. Auden, Cecil Day Lewis and Louis McNeice), has recorded his thoughts on how he wrote poetry (Spender 1985).

Spender tells us that his general method was to jot down in his notebooks *ideas*, as many as possible, and then develop some and reject the rest (p. 116). The idea may be a single line or several lines of verse that captures some sort of image or vision.

There seems here a glimmering of BVSR; but the variations here are not related to the composition of a single poem. Rather they represent possible foreshadowings of many different poems. We might think of this as a form of *proactive preparation* (Chapter 6). Writers are commonly known to do this. The scientific equivalent is of a scientist pondering a future project by identifying, perhaps randomly, multiple ideas as potential problems for future investigation. This suggests that *proactive preparation may be prone to a form of cognitive Darwinism.*

Spender then went on to describe what happened in the case of one particular idea or sketch consisting of six lines of verse that encapsulated a "vision of the sea" (p. 117). This vision included the landscape of the top of a cliff overlooking the sea with fields, hedges, horse-drawn carts, barking dogs and so on, while the sea itself is envisioned as a harp, the waves like harp strings capturing the sunlight (recall Robert Nichols's imagining the sunlight reflected on the sea surface as Arabic writings).

Spender tells us that there followed at least twenty versions of the poem elaborating this vision, but we are not told whether these versions were distinct variants elaborating the initial sketch or successive revisions of a single poem (p. 118). However, he picked up a single "phrase" from the initial sketch consisting of "one and a quarter lines" and presented six versions of this phrase before giving us how this vision of the sea appeared in the final version of the poem.

Clearly these seven versions are variations on a single theme—of waves as strings ("wires") of a harp reflecting or glittering in the sunlight. He was seeking the "right" phrase, the right set of lines to capture his initial idea or schema. The representation of this vision of the sea was his goal. Each variant was intended to satisfy this goal. But there was nothing *blind* about the generation of these variants. Each version was *shaped* by the need to satisfy the initial vision. They are not uninfluenced by the goal (a condensation of the environment). Quite the contrary.

XI   How Picasso's mind "crystallized a dream"

In his conversation with art critic and scholar Christian Zervos in 1935, Pablo Picasso spoke of recording photographically the "metamorphosis" of a painting. This would perhaps allow one to see by what path "a mind finds its way towards the crystallization of a dream" (Picasso 1972). Such a record was indeed made of the painting of *Guernica* (1937) in the course of some six weeks in May–June 1937 by Dora Maar, a painter, photographer and Picasso's companion from 1936 to 1945. Picasso also numbered and dated the entire corpus of sketches and compositions that led to the final mural.

A painting, he once remarked, is an "experiment in time." Which is why he numbered and dated them so that, perhaps someday, others may be grateful (Ashton 1972, p. 72). Indeed. The record provided of *Guernica* avails us a rare opportunity to grapple with the act of production and the creation of one of the twentieth century's most significant paintings.

"The artist works by necessity." Picasso's dictum, again from his conversation with Christian Zervos, reminds us of Wordsworth's poet who is "habitually impelled to create" (Wordsworth 1916, p. 14). This is the superneed shared by all creative minds. Picasso's superneed to make art prevailed over a staggering eight decades. But the necessity that gave birth to *Guernica* was of a particular kind for it was rooted in the Spanish Civil War.

According to art historian Herschel Chipp, Picasso was by and large indifferent to public and political events. Yet by his own admission a painting must be "an instrument of war" against some "enemy" (Chipp 1988, pp. 4–6)—a metaphor that was never more appropriate than in the case of *Guernica*.

The beginning and end points of the entire project are clear enough. By January 1937, General Francisco Franco's Nationalistes forces, strongly supported by Nazi Germany and Fascist Italy, had taken control of large areas of Spain, in opposition to the elected Republican government. At that time preparation was also under way in Paris for the 1937 World's Fair. The Spanish ambassador to France, the official representative of the beleaguered Republican government, anxious to let the world know that his government was still in existence, enlisted the help of prominent Spanish artists to create a Spanish pavilion for the exhibition. Picasso was requested by the pavilion's architect to paint a mural of his own choice.

Sympathetic though he was to the Republican cause, Picasso was at first noncommittal. Herschel Chipp (1988) tells us that this was due in part to the artist's reluctance to undertake commissioned work and in part his distaste for polemical painting (p. 17). Thus his first response was to do nothing. But the events that followed would decree otherwise. On April 26, 1937, as part of the Nationalistes campaign to overrun the Basque region of Northern Spain, the German Luftwaffe bombed the Basque town of Guernica. The central part of the town was reduced to rubble; the destruction of human life was massive. Three days after the bombing, after the fires had subsided, Franco's forces entered the town. The news reached Paris on April 27 and on April 30 the first pictures of the devastated town were published in newspapers. On May 1, Picasso began to pencil sketches that eventually became *Guernica*. A goal was established.

Art historians are not entirely sure when exactly the painting was completed since Dora Maar's photographs of the various stages of the canvas are not dated. According to Chipp the painting was probably finished some time between June 4 and June 13, 1937.

At the center of the mural in the finished work is a horse writhing and screaming in agony. Above it is an elliptical sun with an electric bulb at its center. To the right of the horse is a woman leaning out of the window, an outstretched hand holding a lamp. Below her is a fleeing woman and behind, at the extreme right of the mural, is a fallen woman staring up, her hands reaching out high. To the left of the horse is a bull gazing impassively at the viewer, a bird perched on its back. Below the bull, at the very left, a mother carrying a dead child screams, her head thrown back. Below her, sprawling across the bottom of the canvas, is a fallen, stricken man.

The mural occupies a canvas 25 feet 8 inches long and 11 feet 6 inches high. The work is in oil and uses only black, white and various shades of grey. (It presently hangs in the Reina Sofia Museum in Madrid.)

Such is a bald description of *Guernica*. It leaves the viewer in no doubt about the subject matter: suffering, devastation and horror. One does not have to know about the town Guernica to grasp this.

For the creativity scholar, the record of *Guernica*'s development by way of the sketches and compositions and Dora Maar's photographs (all of which are also on display in the Reina Sofia Museum) offers a rare opportunity to explore the act of production; its cognitive history.

XII *Guernica's* cognitive history: I. The primal schema

On May 11, 1937 Dora Maar photographed the first composition of *Guernica* on the full-size canvas. Picasso had done this that same day. She went on to record at least nine other "states" of the canvas. These ten successive photographs taken over a period of some four to five weeks can be regarded as records of successive stages in the ontogeny of *Guernica*. If the first photograph is compared to the last one, one can see that despite considerable differences in detail the first and last stages of the canvas are intimately connected. "State I" is the embryonic schema from which the final form blossomed in full maturity.

But what of state I itself? On May 1, Picasso reached for a pad of blue notepaper and initiated the act of production from which state I emerged ten days later. How did this initial state come into being "from far off?"

Between May 1 and May 11 Picasso drew twenty-two sketches (which have been reproduced by both art psychologist Rudolf Arnheim (1962) and art historian Herschel Chipp (1988) and which are on display at the Reina Sofia Museum). Two of the sketches were in pencil and colored crayon, one in ink, one in pencil and gouache (a kind of pigment), and one in oil. The rest were done in pencil only. Some were full composition studies, some depicted individual figures such as the horse, others examined small groups, especially the bull and the horse, and the mother with dead child. Many sketches were variations on a single theme: variations in the stance and position of the horse, of the bull, of the mother holding the child—crouching in one sketch, on a ladder in another. There are variations on the horse's head depicting many expressions of agony.

The very word *variation* has a Darwinian flavor. In the case of Picasso's preliminary sketches any temptation we may have to appeal to BVSR should be resisted first because of the very idea that the variations were *blind*, and second, that there was any sort of selection process that followed on these particular sketches.

From a cognitive perspective there is a sequence of seven composition studies of the overall picture. They seem to form the backbone of the process as a whole, the main ontogenetic pathway to the first full-size canvas.

Sketch 1 was the first of the composition studies. It shows in very rough fashion a standing bull with a small bird perched on its back, the suggestion of a horse lying on the ground with one leg stretched stiffly up, and a woman leaning out of the window, a lamp held by am outstretched hand. For one who is neither familiar with Picasso's past and who sees this sketch only, the figures of the animal and the human may not even be discernible as horse and woman, but even the novice viewer (or lay consumer) can discern these forms in the first sketch once the later ones are seen. And as the final picture tells these three elements—*bull, horse and woman with lamp*—remain. Once an initial "vision" is formed, Picasso said to Christian Zervos, it does not change though the picture might (Picasso 1972, p. 8). So a picture *evolves*—rather, *unfolds*—around its original "vision," the initial schema. Picasso's comments to Zervos preceded the *Guernica* project by two years, but he may well have been talking about *Guernica*, for this painting unfolded around its initial *primal schema* of bull, horse and woman with lamp.

XIII *Guernica's* cognitive history: II. Remembrance of things past

But why this particular schema? In the case of Picasso the bull and the horse inevitably reminds us of the *corrida*, the Spanish bullfight. Picasso, as is well known, was strongly attracted to, and fascinated by, the drama and the color of the bullring. His drawings and paintings of the *corrida* reached back to his boyhood when he was only eight or nine years old, and some of his early efforts are depicted in the first volume of John Richardson's (1991) monumental biography. Much later, from 1917, he began to concentrate on the struggle between the bull and the horse, the former as aggressor and the latter as target and victim of aggression (Chipp 1988, p. 48). From 1933 the Minotaur, the bull-man of Greek mythology appears, in pen and ink, pencil and, repeatedly, in etchings (Fiero 1983). The Minotaur is depicted in many guises including the purely bestial form in which it assaults a woman in one etching and is put to death by a matador in another (Chipp 1988, p. 55).

There is then ample evidence to support the claim that Picasso's belief/knowledge space contained elements representing a strong association of violence with the bull-and-horse motif. So when the goal of depicting the brutal violence of what happened in Guernica was presented to his consciousness this bull-and-horse motif (a schema in its own right) was retrieved from memory. In Herschel Chipp's words, "the prone bull and the wounded horse provided him with an atavistic symbol powerful enough to express the tragedy of the Spanish town" (Chipp 1988, p. 72). Picasso's own words seem to corroborate this. In an interview with an American admirer Jerome Sickler in

1945, he admitted that in *Guernica* "the bull ... represents brutality, the horse the people" (Ashton 1972, p. 133). Even the form of the supine horse is not new: this posture had appeared in an etching done in April 1936 of a Minotaur pulling a cart in which lay a horse, its legs pointing stiffly up (Chipp 1988, pp. 71–72).

What of the woman leaning out of the window? Here too there is evidence that several variations of this idea were present in Picasso's belief/knowledge space. In 1933 he had completed a sculpture in plastic titled *Woman with a Vase* in which a standing female form stretches out a hand grasping a vase. (This sculpture was also exhibited in the Spanish pavilion at the Paris World's Fair along with *Guernica*.) The motif of the outstretched arm as symbol of patriotic defiance had appeared in a sketch Picasso had done just a few days before May 1 as part of an altogether different project called *The Studio*. There, a sinewy arm is extended upward grasping a hammer and sickle (Chipp 1988, pp. 61, 66).

The general form of the window will remain an unchanging element in all seven composition studies that preceded the first photographic state of the canvas; it prevailed through all the subsequent states. By the time of the sixth sketch (the last of the first day, May 1), the woman's face is recognizable as that of Marie-Therese Walter, his main model, companion and passion from 1927 until Dora Maar entered his life.

Art psychologist Rudolf Arnheim (1962) has noted yet another source of the *Guernica* composition from Picasso's personal artistic past. He pointed out that virtually all the elements of the final canvas were present in the artist's etching *Minotaurmachy* (1935). In that work there is a bull in Minotaur form and a horse visibly in agony, on the back of which lies a female, seminude torero with a Marie-Therese face. A young girl holds up a candle, and in the upper left of the etching is an open window at which two women stand and look down. Arnheim remarked that if the composition of *Minotaurmachy* is laterally inverted (if we make a mirror image of it) the resulting arrangement would strongly resemble the arrangement of the elements in *Guernica*.

Art historians and biographers tell us that *Minotaurmachy* was done at a time when Picasso was undergoing a particularly difficult period in his domestic life—he was not able to get a divorce from his wife Olga Koklova and he had learnt that Marie-Therese was pregnant with their child. The turmoil in his personal life had caused Picasso to virtually stop painting for a period and to turn instead to poetry. Historian Gloria Fiero (1983, p. 26) believed that the basic motif in *Minotaurmachy* was blindness, a metaphor for the failing of artistic powers. And yet this same arrangement was broadly adopted for *Guernica* though the goal of the mural was quite different. Rudolf Arnheim (1962, p. 20) reminds us that a motif—a specific schema—created for one purpose or that bears one meaning may be summoned to serve quite another, possibly contradictory, purpose. This is a case of *affordance* that may not be obvious but which a creative artificer may summon to advantage (see Chapter 4).

But Arnheim's comparison of *Guernica* with *Minotaurmachy* cannot be taken as relevant at the time of the first sketch. All that there is in the latter is the initial vision, the primal schema.

XIV *Guernica's* cognitive history: III. The "spirit of re/search"

Though Picasso never wrote on art he had much to *say*. Thus his spoken views must count as invaluable clues to the working of his artistic mind. Unfortunately we can never be sure as to how much trust we can place on his comments for they often contradict one another. "In art," he said in a 1923 interview, "intentions are not sufficient … what one does is what counts and not what one had intentions of doing" (Ashton 1972, p. 3). But then elsewhere he agrees with his old friend and co-inventor of Cubism Georges Braque that what really matters in painting is the intention: "what counts is what one wants to do not what one does" (Ashton 1972, p. 32). And in the 1923 interview he dismisses the past and the future of a painting. A work of art "must live always in the present," otherwise it does not count as art at all (Ashton 1972, p. 43). Yet in talking to Zervos in 1935 he speaks of preserving photographically the "metamorphosis" of a painting to discover the path followed by the mind in "crystallizing" a dream (Zervos 1985, p. 49).

Again, in 1923: "To search means nothing in painting. To find is the thing." He denied that the "spirit of search" was the main aim in his work. But then yet again a *volte face*: "Paintings are but research and experiment"; all his paintings "are researches." He searched "incessantly," he said, "and there is a logical sequence in all this research"; which is why he numbered his works (Ashton 1972, pp. 3, 72).

The "spirit of re/search" is very much in evidence in the case of *Guernica*. In sketch 2 done on the first day the positions of the bull and horse have changed as has the horse's posture: it is now sitting up. And instead of a bird there is a tiny winged horse, a Pegasus–like beast, sitting on what looks like a saddle on the bull's back.

There are other classical allusions in this sketch. In Greek mythology Pegasus, the winged horse favored by the Muses, helped the warrior Bellerophon kill the fire-breathing monster Chimaera whose body was part lion, part goat, part dragon. There is more: the winged animal reminded Rudolf Arnheim of Psyche, which in Greek means soul. In paintings, Psyche is usually depicted as a maiden with the wings of a butterfly. For Arnheim the Pegasus-like creature is the horse's soul (Arnheim 1962, p. 32).

In sketch 6, the last of the first day, the winged horse appears out of the belly of the screaming horse. We see it no more after that. In the Pegasus-like creature Picasso seemed to be searching for an allegorical representation that he later abandoned.

Sketches 3, 4 and 5, all done on the first day, illustrate still further the extent of Picasso's propensity to search and experiment. New goals that are sufficiently important to the artists create, literally, new conceptual, cognitive *workspaces* (problem spaces) for exploration and solution, and the main workspace, having to do with the overall composition (the main problem space) is put temporarily aside. The horse in particular is explored in a variety of postures, positions and forms—three sketches were done on May 1, three more on May 2, one on May 8, another three on May 10.

XV *Guernica's* cognitive history: IV. Multiprocessing

We also find manifestations of various cognitive processes being spawned both consciously and unconsciously. In one process an association of the horse with the Pegasus-like creature is made; the idea of a winged animal is thus produced and is lodged in the artist's belief/knowledge space. There is a switch back to the "main" process and the winged horse is consciously made a part of the composition. Another process is created for the purpose (or goal) of exploring the figure and posture of the horse. The artist's attention (conscious gaze) switches frequently to this process in the course of the mural's progress. These switches are manifested in the various, isolated, consciously considered sketches of the horse.

The sixth and final sketch of the first day is the first proper compositional successor of the initial sketch (the primal schema). There is a new element here: the figure of a warrior lying supine across the bottom of the sheet grasping a spear. The warrior breaks the thread of continuity immanent in the preceding sketches and its presence is not easy to explain. But Herschel Chipp (1988, pp. 82–83) provides valuable clues. To him it signifies a return to, and completion of, the *corrida* motif. The warrior is the picador who, mounted on the horse, goads the bull into charging. In 1934 Picasso produced a series of etchings called *Femme Torero*. In one of these works, *Femme Torrero III*, the fallen picador lies underneath the figures of the bull and the horse, much in the position of the warrior in sketch 6. Chipp also notes that newspaper photographs of Guernica that first appeared on April 28 included ones of bombed victims lying in similar positions. Again, an intricate but discernible linkage among elements in Picasso's belief/knowledge space can be seen: the supine warrior completes the *corrida* triumvirate and also symbolizes the victim.

An outline of the time sequence of the whole compositional process for *Guernica* might be helpful here.

> *May 1–May 11, 1937.* Picasso drew twenty-two sketches as mentioned before. In this same period we find a sequence of seven compositional studies of the overall picture, the first of which was the "primal schema." These compositional studies form the main ontogenetic pathway to the first full-size canvas.

> *May 11–June 13, 1937.* During this period twenty-four additional sketches were done.

> *May 11–June 13, 1937.* A sequence of the successive stages of the full canvas as photographed by Dora Maar.

What can we say about the nature of Picasso's act of production?

A prominent feature is the *simultaneous presence of several processes* over the period May 1 through June 13, 1937 and the *switching of attention* between these processes. There is a "main process" in which the overall painting unfolds. The sequence of seven compositional studies between May 1 and May 11 are stages in this main process leading to the first state of the canvas photographed by Dora Maar. The subsequent photographed states are further stages of this main process.

This process has its own "workspace" or "problem space" in which the composition unfolds. But the main process also gives birth to several "auxiliary" processes, each of which has its own workspace, each active in parallel, at least for some period of time, to the main process. In the language of computer science what we have here is *multiprocessing*.

One of the auxiliary processes generates variations in the form and posture of the horse figure and we see the intermittent presence of this process from the very first day (May 1) to May 20. Another auxiliary process concerns itself with the woman-and-dead child figure. A third explores variations of the bull figure. A fourth focuses on the fallen warrior.

A fifth auxiliary process which began later (May 24) was preoccupied with variations on the weeping woman theme and this process is in evidence till June 13, by which time *Guernica* had evolved to completion. This process seemed to have become almost independent of the unfolding of the main composition, for later variations of the head of the weeping woman became increasingly fantastic in details yet none of which is in evidence in the development of the main composition. Indeed, we may suppose that this cognitive process continued well beyond the *Guernica* project, for Picasso would later paint his celebrated *Weeping Woman*, a portrait of Dora Maar in October 1937.

The auxiliary and main processes *communicate with one another* at various times. Thus in the compositional study of May 8 the mother-and-dead-child appears. This theme in turn produces its own auxiliary process in which variations of the theme are explored. Several auxiliary processes concerned with the head-of-woman and weeping-woman motifs are also spawned and in all these the postures of the woman's head are inherited from the corresponding posture in the first photographed state, suggesting that these auxiliary processes resulted from the woman's figure in the main composition.

XVI *Guernica's* cognitive history: V. Its principal features

If communicating multiprocesses constitutes *one* prominent characteristic of the act of producing *Guernica*, a *second* is the artist's remembrance of things past: the appeal to his private personal belief/knowledge space containing earlier themes, compositions, paintings, etchings and sculptures he had created as well as themes and impressions stored in what psychologists call "episodic memory." We have noted how art historians have located the woman-leaning-out-of-the-window schema in a number of Picasso's earlier works; and that the bull-and-horse schema is strongly associated with the *corrida* motif that reached back to an early stage of Picasso's artistic past. We have also noted that the basic posture of the woman-with-dead child figure had antecedents in drawings Picasso had done before, showing variations of the rescuer–rescued theme. The inventive process in art is knowledge-rich and in the case of *Guernica* it was rich in the artist's knowledge of his personal past.

The *third* prominent feature of the whole process is the presence of *search*. In the case of *Guernica* search is manifested in two ways. First, there is what cognitive and computer scientist Allen Newell (1990) referred to as *knowledge search*: searching through one's personal belief/knowledge space for ideas, schemas and compositions. Picasso's remembrance of things past was a case of knowledge search.

But there is also what Newell called *problem search*. Each of the constituent multiple processes (main and auxiliary) in the development of the mural is an instance of problem search. Their main common, visible feature is *the generation of variations* on particular themes.

This may raise the question: *Was Picasso's creative act a Darwinian process?* In fact we will be very hard pressed to offer any positive evidence in its favor. For these searches were not random or blind in the BVSR sense. They were, rather, *directed* searches controlled and shaped by immediate goals and the artist's remembrance of past work.

For instance, as noted, the basic posture adopted for the woman–with–dead-child schema had its origins in Picasso's earlier drawings of the rescuer–rescued figures. The posture of the woman's head in the various versions of the head-of-woman and weeping-woman motifs have its antecedents in the woman–with–dead-child figure in the first photographed state. Furthermore, at least one element of the mural, the woman-leaning-out-of-the window, had several antecedents from the artist's prior work.

Furthermore, apropos BVSR theory, even when problem spaces were searched and variations were produced there is no evidence of some straightforward *selection* from among the variations as BVSR would have it. The figure of the horse first appeared in a relatively clear form in the second photographed state of the mural. Picasso sketched several variations of the posture and position of this horse. Yet the form that appeared in the first state of the full canvas is by no means a simple selection from one of these variations *à la* BVSR theory. Rather, it was a complex form that was no doubt *based* on one or more of these earlier sketches.

Moreover, the head of the horse in the second photographed state is inverted. In a slight transformation in the next photographed state it was "righted"; but this was done with only a minimal change to the earlier head (Chipp 1988, p. 119). This does not suggest a case of blind variation followed by selection but rather the *transformation* of an earlier to a later state. In other words, there is no evidence that the ontogeny of *Guernica* followed a Darwinian process. The painting certainly evolved, but not according to Darwinian precepts. It was a case of *purposive* evolution.

XVII   Bisociation and conceptual blending

In his book *The Act of Creation*, Arthur Koestler (1964) proposed a principle as the *sine qua non* of the act of production. He called it *bisociation* by which he meant conceiving an idea "in two self-consistent but *habitually incompatible* frames of reference" (p. 35. My italics).

The surprise that attends the outcome of an act of production stems from this bisociation of two or more possibly unrelated and (more importantly) seemingly incompatible frameworks. In cognitive terms bisociation is the fusion of two or more apparently distinct and unrelated schemas into a new meaningful schema.

Mark Turner, a cognitively influenced literary scholar and investigator of metaphor and other facets of the literary mind, has proposed a theory he called *conceptual* blending which bears similarity to bisociation (though oddly, Turner does not refer to bisociation in his book *The Literary Mind* which first explicated conceptual blending). Like Koestler, Turner sees novel concepts as the result of two or more "input" "conceptual spaces" coming together (blending) (Turner 1996, pp. 59–60). But Turner views blending as the creation of a new "blended space" that manifests its own *emergent* properties absent in the input spaces. Moreover, the blended space can feed back its features into the input spaces so that conceptual blending is not necessarily a unidirectional process (Fauconnier and Turner 2002; also Hogan 2003, pp. 107–114).

XVIII   The janusian effect

Let us hold the ideas of bisociation and conceptual blending for a moment and consider another concept advanced by psychiatrist Albert Rothenberg (1990). He suggested that a fundamental kind of process separating creative people "from the rest of us" is an effect he called the *janusian* process (after Janus, the Roman god of gates who gazed simultaneously in opposite directions). According to Rothenberg the janusian effect is what gives rise to new ideas. In essence it entails the creative artificer conceiving *simultaneously* two or more opposites ("antitheses") to hold, and *consciously* formulating the co-existence of these opposites and integrating them into the production of a new concept (p. 15).

The janusian effect seems to me a stronger case of bisociation. It is not only that the act of production entails the coming together or blending of two or more "habitually incompatible" elements but also, these elements are antithetical.

Whether the janusian effect is a *universal* feature of the act of production is an empirical question. It is certainly evident in many instances of creative thought but one can also find examples of H-creative or C-creative work that does not manifest the janusian effect. Picasso's creation of *Guernica* is a case in point.

Still, the janusian effect (and its weaker generalization, bisociation) begs the question: how do such processes occur? Again, this is an empirical question that we can explore, perhaps through cognitive–historical inquiries into actual acts of production. In the following sections we consider two such situations.

XIX   James Watt's janusian conundrum

Consider once more James Watt's eureka moment on that Sunday morning walk in a Glasgow park in 1765 (Chapter 8, II–IV). His conundrum and its resolution is

a remarkable example of the janusian effect. For, he was posed with two antithe
goals both of which had to be satisfied:

> **G4:** Condense the steam in the cylinder to below 100 degrees F so as to
> produce a "good" vacuum in the cylinder.

> **G5:** Maintain the temperature of the cylinder at about 212 degrees F to avoid
> steam condensation (when new steam is injected).

As we recall (from Chapter 8) Watt was still confined to his Newcomen steam
engine schema. Replacing one schema by another—a *schema shift*—is certainly a
hallmark of the highest form of creativity when it entails the invention of the new
schema. Watt's eureka-style "Scottish enlightenment" entailed precisely such a
schema shift. The point is that there was no algorithm or guaranteed-to-succeed
procedure one could summon to resolve goals that are mutually *interfering*. However,
AI researchers have identified several *heuristic strategies* that are relevant for resolving
such interference. For example, computer scientist Jack Mostow (1985) suggested
the following as especially relevant to designing artifacts:

a   They may be serialized so that first one goal is satisfied and then the problem
    is transformed so as to satisfy the other.
b   Order the goals so that the most critical decisions are made first and then other
    decisions are built around them.
c   The least commitment strategy: goals are ordered so that the earlier decisions
    impose fewest restrictions on later decisions.
d   Budget a solution: decompose goals into subgoals.

It seems that Watt's reasoning entailed some combination of heuristics (b), (c) and
(d). The most critical point in G4 is to produce a "good" vacuum in the cylinder.
Condensing the steam to below 100 degrees F was conceived as a means to do this.
Yet G5 must also be satisfied.

But a vacuum can be achieved by *expelling* the steam from the cylinder. So a
subgoal to achieve a vacuum would be:

> **G6:** Remove the steam from the cylinder and condense it outside.

Now Watt knew the following facts: (a) Any elastic fluid in a closed vessel when
connected to an evacuated chamber will expand into that chamber; (b) Steam is an
elastic fluid. So G6 could be achieved by way of two *serialized* subgoals:

> **G7.1:** Transfer the steam from the cylinder to an evacuated vessel outside.

> **G7.2:** Condense the steam in the outside vessel.

Achieving these two goals would satisfy the parent goal G4 and at the same time G5 is achieved. Watt's janusian conundrum could thus be resolved. This gave birth to his "separate condenser" principle and a new steam engine schema was invented displacing the old. Watt's personal "Scottish Enlightenment" took the form of a *technological schema shift* producing the following schema.

NAME *Separate condenser steam engine*

STRUCTURE *A piston-and-cylinder arrangement is connected to a boiler arrangement via a steam-intake control. The piston-and-cylinder arrangement is also connected via a steam outtake control to an evacuable–condenser arrangement.*

OPERATION
    REPEAT CYCLE
        Activate boiler arrangement;
        Open steam-intake control;
        When piston rises to a specified height in cylinder
            Close steam-intake control;
            Open steam-outtake control and expel steam into evacuable–condenser arrangement

---

XX   Schema shift

My use of the term "schema shift" is obviously inspired by Thomas Kuhn's (2012) famous term "paradigm shift." According to Kuhn, at any given time, a paradigm defines the relevant *science*. A paradigm shift, the displacement of one paradigm by another, the redefinition of the science, is a *revolutionary* event.

A schema shift in contrast pertains to an *individual's* personal belief/knowledge space. Accordingly I take a schema shift to be an individual's *cognitive* experience. A schema shift may *lead* to a paradigm shift if and when a new schema invented by an individual artificer and communicated to others is socially accepted and displaces the dominant components of the prevailing paradigm. Or it may lead to the creation of a new paradigm where none previously existed. James Watt's schema shift from the atmospheric engine to the separate condenser was one of the instrumental factors in the construction of a new techno-scientific paradigm concerning steam power and thermodynamics (Hills 1989; Cardwell 1989) as well as a major contributor the social–economic–technological transformation we call the Industrial Revolution (Ashton 1969; Musson and Robinson 1969; Hardy 2006).

On the other hand, an artificer's personal schema shift or his invention of a new schema might give rise to that artificer's particularly idiosyncratic *cognitive style* (mentioned briefly in Chapter 5, on which more later in this book) without necessarily influencing others or having any *major* consequence for the field in question. The artist George Rodrigue, desiring to dedicate his art to the landscape and cultural of his birthplace, South Louisiana (see Chapter 6) rejected existing painterly styles (schemas) and instead invented new schemas (see below). But, as of this writing, one cannot claim that he effected a *movement* in art (the equivalent of a paradigm in science).

XXI   Rodrigue: inventing a schema by bisociation and evolution

George Rodrigue is one of my recurring protagonists in this book. Recall (from Chapter 5) that his proactive preparation led him to such modern American movements as Abstract Expressionism and Pop Art. But his superneed to be original, to make history, prompted him to declare, after his formal studies were over, that he would find his own painterly voice.

His originality like those of all who wished to make history in the creative realm did not begin with a *tabula rasa*. His proactive preparation was certainly one source of ideas. His personal experience of being born and bred in South Louisiana, immersed in its landscape and geography, its history and culture, was another source. His personal belief/knowledge space was populated not only with all he had learnt during proactive preparation as an artist but also with the history and folklore and myths, the cultural traditions and practices of his people, the Cajuns, and with the images of the South Louisiana landscape. He wanted to paint Louisiana "but in a different way."[1]

The art that emerged manifested bisociation. On the one hand, "From Abstract Expressionism training I was very conscious of shapes," and from Pop Art there were the techniques of "repetitive imagery" and the use of a "hard edge'. On the other hand there was South Louisiana, its culture, history and geography. Two quite distinct frames of reference *à la* Koestler.

To the outsider, Louisiana evokes a stereotypical picture: a land of swamps and Spanish moss and lazy waterways called bayous. Many painters before Rodrigue had painted this landscape; indeed, Louisiana had a long tradition of landscape painters and photographers reaching back to the nineteenth century (Weisendanger and Weisendanger 1971). Their naturalistic landscapes depict bayous, live oaks, swamps, marshlands and lakeside cabins. Most of these painters however were not native to the region, some being trained in Europe, like the nineteenth century artist Richard Clague who had studied at the prestigious École des Beaux Arts in Paris. Their works left Rodrigue dissatisfied because they missed "the basic traits of South Louisiana" (Rodrigue 1976, p. ix). One "basic trait" was a certain *feeling* the landscape evoked in him, a feeling that had as much to do with his intimacy with the history of the Cajuns as with his sensibility to the landscape itself. He wished to see the landscape with his Cajun eyes. At the same time he wished to see it with the mind and eye of an artist who sought to be original.

How did he achieve these twin goals? The solution did not emerge immediately. At first:

> I painted landscapes with a lot of stuff in it ... but dissatisfied ... then I photographed for a week ... I photographed what interested me ... back in the studio I looked through all these pictures ... I realized after looking at all the photographs that the one thing in all of them was the tree ... the oak tree was the security, protection, shade, coolness ... the tree became the thing ... just the tree.

Other Louisiana artists had also painted the oak tree. However,

> I was looking at a lot of Louisiana paintings in New Orleans ... the tree was there but at the bottom of the paintings ... no one had painted the tree as a focus ... so I would paint the whole tree.
> ... so I painted the whole tree ... the first symbol—my painting of the tree became darker and darker, it became an abstract thing—it can be anywhere in a square ... an abstract shape—my tree was moodier, evoking something, a mystery going on ... when I started cutting the top of the tree I realized the important thing was the shape and the sky that was left ... then juxtapose the darkest part of the tree and the lightest part of the sky....

In fact Rodrigue had *invented a landscape schema*. Its basic features were a dark tree with sharp, staccato-edged lines, a light, framed sky, and a dark foreground. These became the "three major positive shapes" or "graphic elements" (as he called them) in his work of that period.

In creating this schema Rodrigue appears to have performed a bisociation where the unrelated frames of reference (*à la* Koestler) were (a) the hard-edged graphic images he had learnt during his proactive preparation, and (b) his intimate awareness of the landscape itself. But this bisociation did not occur suddenly. It was *not* an eureka experience. Rodrigue's earliest landscapes, painted in 1969, indicate that the schema *evolved* into being. When viewed collectively they reveal a *purposive development* in which each step is an experiment and what the painter learnt from one experiment was carried over to the next.

By 1970 the oak tree was not only the central element in the schema, it also assumed a harder, more graphic, more abstract form with the moss becoming an inseparable extension of the branches and the shape of the foliage delineated by way of sharp, staccato lines (as seen in Anon 2003, pp. 20, 23, 67, 72).

The invention of the landscape schema was the first of Rodrigue's H-creative acts of production. Once it was in place he returned to it again and again, but each time with a different painterly eye. Each painting was an *instantiation* of the landscape schema. Each instantiation varied some aspect of the oak tree/sky/ foreground schema in color or form or positioning, sometimes with additions such as a bridge. At the same time the schema was *enriched* by each new painterly experience. The different instantiations became new "optional" elements of the landscape schema: subschemas. They entered into Rodrigue's belief/knowledge space as new images, new forms to be accessed and retrieved when appropriate.

We may think of Rodrigue's creativity in this stage of his artistic career as a twofold affair. The invention of his landscape schema was his *primary act of production* wherein he brought into being an abstract artifact. The instantiations of this schema in the form of actual paintings—material artifacts—were his *secondary acts of production*. Each of his landscape pictures was, no doubt H-original; that they induced creative encounters with consumers is evidenced by their purchase by devoted collectors from the very beginning of his painterly career. But it was their abstraction, the landscape schema that was his greater H-creative invention.

XXII   Schema instantiation as verification

But we must not denigrate schema instantiation for it also has a twofold role in creativity. First, instantiating an original schema is a form of *testing* or, better still, *verifying* the efficacy of the schema—verification is, of course, the fourth stage of the Poincaré–Wallas–Hadamard model.

When George Rodrigue, having invented his landscape schema, sought to instantiate it in the form of actual paintings he was demonstrating the viability of the schema—that they actually satisfied his need to be original and his desire to paint Louisiana in a way that captured his feelings about his environment; and that the schema (an abstract artifact) was rich and flexible enough in its potential for producing actual paintings (material artifacts) which met both his aesthetic needs and those of consumers of his art. Each of his landscape paintings would, of course, have to stand on its own. Its production began with its own specific goals and the "success" of the painting would depend on whether the goals were satisfied. Rodrigue's creativity in producing a particular painting would depend on its *own* originality as well as whether the artist could engage in creative encounters by way of the work with viewers and collectors.

In fact, at the level of individual paintings, *the schema would not matter*. The schema was like a scaffolding that had done its job but could be dispensed with as far as the lay consumer was concerned. The latter, looking at a particular landscape painting, may be quite ignorant of the presence of an underlying schema. The effect the picture has on his aesthetic sensibility and his cognitive identity is what matters.

On the other hand, a collector of Rodrigue's works who already possesses some of his paintings may respond quite differently. He may well be (perhaps unconsciously) aware of Rodrigue's landscape schema though he may call it his *style*. The collector collects "Rodrigues" because he has engaged with the artist in creative encounters, not so much by way of individual paintings but *via* the landscape schema itself. Here too, the individual paintings serve as verifications of the schema's potential *as a generator of paintings*.

XXIII   Implementation as schema instantiation

Implementation of a technological or scientific schema serves a similar purpose. James Watt, for instance, invented a new abstract schema for the steam engine but of course matters did not end there. The invention was followed by a lengthy and often frustrating stage of verification and this entailed implementing (building) an actual steam engine based on the separate condenser idea. Thus implementation is also a case of schema instantiation though this instantiation may have progressed to a detailed *design* of the artifact before a physical artifact can be built.

As historian of technology Richard Hills (1989) has recorded, the first implementation of a steam engine based on the separate condenser principle involved much experimentation, construction, observation, measurement and modification (of the schema itself) over a period of about four years until a British patent was awarded to Watt in early 1769 for "a method of lessening the consumption of steam and fuel in fire engines" (pp. 54–57).

In fact, to an engineer, Watt's act of production could not end until an implementation was successfully executed. The schema itself, though H-original, would not suffice. To the engineer it is the material artifact (a physical separate-condenser-based steam engine that performs at a satisfactory level) that is the created product, not the abstract artifact that is the schema. Yet, from a historical perspective it is the separate condenser principle that has survived the test of time not the first physical steam engine, as in Rodrigue's situation the invention of the abstract schema was the primary act of production and the design and implementation of the first steam engine based on, and instantiating, this schema was a secondary act of production. Watt's patent was granted for the schema ("a method") but that schema's *validity* depended on the implementation that took him several years to complete.

XXIV   Schema instantiation as a primary act of production

Let us consider a historical example of a schema instantiation that was H-creative and C-creative in its own right, and thus much more than a secondary act of production. This was the design and implementation of the world's first fully operational stored program electronic computer.

In 1945, John von Neumann, mathematician, co-inventor of game theory and computer theorist wrote a paper titled "First Draft of a Report on the EDVAC" (von Neumann 1945). This report was a proposal for the design of an electronic digital computer to be called EDVAC. And it was one of the two documents that laid the foundation for a paradigm that would define the future discipline of computer science (Dasgupta 2014a, Chapter 8).

This "von Neumann report" (as it came to be known) made two fundamental contributions to the creation of the *computational paradigm*. One was its emphasis on the *logical* design and principles of computers and their separation from the *physical* design and implementation. The former later came to be called a computer's "architecture" and would give rise to the branch of computer science called "computer architecture" (see Dasgupta 2016a, Chapter 5 for a brief description of this discipline). The other original contribution was concerned with the nature and function of a computer's internal memory: it would hold not only the data on which computations would be performed but also the computer program that would perform the computation. This principle came to be called the *stored program computer* principle.

These two concepts constituted the core elements of the computational paradigm that took gradual shape in the late 1940s and through the 1950s. Taken together they formed what we may call the *stored program computing schema*. For convenience I will call this the SPC schema, and it characterized what almost all future computers to this day would instantiate and implement.

A schema was thus invented. It was an abstract artifact and it became the blueprint for a number of projects initiated on both sides of the Atlantic to build physical machines. In effect the common goal of these projects was to instantiate the SPC schema and build practical computers.

Here I will describe the very first two such projects to be completed, one conducted at Cambridge University, the other at Manchester University. The former led to a machine called EDSAC, the latter to the Manchester Mark I.

The main protagonists in these two research projects were Maurice Wilkes in Cambridge and Frederick Williams in Manchester—both of whom, incidentally, would be eventually knighted. (I am simplifying the picture somewhat because both Wilkes and Williams led teams of collaborators in their respective projects (Dasgupta 2014a, Chapter 8)). Each of these protagonists had assimilated and internalized the principles laid out in the von Neumann report but each *instantiated* the SPC schema differently, the outcomes being two different subschemas, each embodying two distinct sets of design and implementation principles.

The design and implementation of the EDSAC and the Mark I constituted *experiments* that demonstrated the viability of the principles laid out in the von Neumann report; they were instances of verification *á la* the Poincaré–Wallas–Hadamard model. But they were no humdrum experiments for they brought into the world a new kind of material artifact never known before in history. EDSAC's and the Mark I's originality lay above and beyond the originality of the von Neumann SPC schema for they entailed translations of an original abstract artifact into fully operational material artifacts that performed automatic computation in ways never before performed by any other previous automata.

Thus their originality lay in the *engineering* realm rather than the logical (or architectural) realm. In addition, as fully operational computers, they incorporated significant features that were not present in the SPC schema. *Implementation/instantiation necessitated invention.*

For example, the Mark I contained a memory concept later known as the "index register" which greatly facilitated programming (Dasgupta 2014a, p. 125). Frederick Williams and his student/collaborator Tom Kilburn also invented and patented a cathode ray tube-based memory device that came to be called the Williams tube (Williams and Kilburn 1949; see also Dasgupta 2014a, p. 124). As for the EDSAC the very goal of creating a practical operational computer led the EDSAC team to invent, among other things, new principles and methods of programming—new artifacts—the likes of which had never existed before (Wheeler 1951; Wilkes and Renwick 1950; Wilkes, Wheeler and Gill 1951. See also Dasgupta 2014a, pp. 142–145).

In conceiving, designing and building the EDSAC and the Mark I, Wilkes (and his team) and Williams (and his collaborators) were not only H-creative, they were also C-creative since the respective designs (abstract artifacts in their own rights) included features that were adopted and copied by computer designers thereafter. These were instances of implementations that were unequivocally primary acts of production.

XXV   The oldest surviving traces of the creative tradition

I will end this chapter by considering what appears to be the oldest surviving evidence of the creative tradition and of the creative act of production. I am referring to the invention of the first stone tools.

Around 2.5 million years before the present (BP), the first species of the genus *Homo* emerged: *Homo habilis*. They would become extinct around 1.6 million BP, by which time *Homo erectus* had appeared (around 1.8) BP. *H. erectus* is believed to have existed from 1.8 million BP to about 300,000 BP. "Archaic" *Homo sapiens* emerged a little less than half a million years ago and "modern" *Homo sapiens* (*H. sapiens sapiens*)—human beings "like us"—about 100,000 BP.

These periods are by no means exact nor is there complete agreement among anthropologists and prehistorians about the time spans (compare, for example, Schick and Toth 1993, pp. 81 *et seq*; Leakey 1994, Chapter 1; Mithen 1996, pp. 24–25; Benton 2008, pp. 163–164). But for our present purposes these approximations suffice.

What interests us in particular is that along with *H. habilis* appeared the first stone tools—crude choppers and flakes. With *H. erectus* there emerged the more sophisticated hand axe. Collectively, choppers, flakes and hand axes constitute what anthropologist Nicholas Toth (1987) called the "first technology"; they are the oldest *surviving* traces of the creative tradition. (Prehistorians have pointed out that there may well have been earlier tools of less robust material such as wood that have not survived.)

In what is called the Middle Paleolithic period (about 60,000–40,000 BP) the hand axe, characterized by relatively sharp point at one end and a cutting edge along one or more sides, was something of a general purpose tool: anthropologists have shown that it can be used as much to dig up edible roots, chip small animal bones and prepare pit traps as to cut meat. Later developments led to chisel-like artifacts called burins and scrapers. With the emergence of modern *H. sapiens* there appeared a more distinctive kind of technology that relied on finely made stone blades. Blade technology flourished around 40,000 years ago.

What sort of *knowledge* did our hominid ancestors, early *Homo*, acquire or possess that they could build such stone tools? What was the nature of their acts of production? One of the ways by which paleo-anthropologists (that is, anthropological specialists on the Stone or Paleolithic ages) have gained insight into these questions is by making artifacts of earlier times under physical conditions that are believed to have then existed. This is one of the rare opportunities wherein creativity researchers might *simulate* the past: perform *in vitro* experiments as it were, that reproduce long past creative phenomena. Thus, using the same kind of material as did early *Homo*, investigators have studied the kind of techniques that *may* have been employed in order to create such stone tools.

In the 1930s one of the *doyens* of paleo-anthropology Louis Leakey conducted such experiments (Leakey 1960). Some fifty years later Nicholas Toth and Kathy Schick conducted a study of making stone tools of the kind excavated at a collection of sites in Koobi Fora in Northern Kenya. More precisely they created "experimental sites" composed of "replicated stone tools and animal bones" that reproduced aspects of the excavated sites, and performed experiments on how the stone tools found in Koobi Fora "could have been made" (Schick and Toth 1993, p. 110; also Toth 1987).

The remains of the excavated sites were dated between 1.9 and 1.4 million BP and thus corresponded to the Lower and Middle Paleolithic periods when the genus *Autralopithecus*, the earliest known hominides, coexisted with early *Homo*. Toth (1987) argued, however, that the evidence spoke against the australopithecines being toolmakers since there was no evidence of tools when *Australopithecus* lived prior to the emergence of *Homo*. These tools must have been the work of *Homo*. (See also Schick and Toth 1993, p. 46.)

Using the same kind of rocks that existed in Paleolithic times in the Koobi Fora region, Toth conducted experiments on different types of tool making all of which had been long established as part of early lithic (that is, stone) technology. These included (a) what Louis Leakey (1960) had named the "hammerstone" technique, in which holding a pebble in one hand and using it as a hammer (an instance of affordance, see Chapter 4, XIV) caused flakes to be removed from another stone (called the "core") so as to shape the latter into a rough form; (b) the "anvil" technique wherein the core is struck on a stationary stone (the anvil); and (c) the "bipolar" method, a hybrid in which the core is struck with the hammerstone while the former is rested on the anvil.

Comparing the patterns of fracture on both the cores and the flakes produced with the patterns seen in the archeological remains at Koobi Fora, Toth concluded that the tools found in the sites were made predominantly using the hammerstone method. This technique, Leakey had found, was far from easy—for the worker had to *learn* the correct angle at which the blow must be struck so as to detach a flake at the desired point in the desired direction. Furthermore, the point at which the blow had to be struck must be near the edge of the stone.

Toth's experiments yielded further insight. He found that three conditions had to be met in order to remove flakes from the core: (i) the latter must have an edge with an acute (less than 90 degrees) angle; (ii) the core had to be hit a glancing blow at a point about a centimeter from the acute edge; and (iii) the blow "should be directed through an edge of high mass such as a ridge or a bulge" (Toth 1987).

Both Leakey's and Toth's experiments show how the past *might* be simulated to yield glimpses of the *kind* of knowledge early *Homo* must have acquired in order to make their tools. This sort of knowledge goes by various names: "know-how" is perhaps the commonest. The first technologists acquired knowledge of *how* to make their tools. Indeed, they invented this knowledge.

Know-how is one type of a category of what AI researchers call *procedural knowledge* in contrast to "know-that" or *propositional* knowledge (see, e.g., Rosenbloom 2013, p. 224). The chemist–philosopher Michael Polanyi (1962, p. 176) also referred to such knowledge as *operational principles*. In the case of the hammerstone technique, Leakey's insight can be expressed as a rule of the form:

> If the goal is to remove a flake from a stone in "X" direction [*demonstrate direction*] and at "Y" point [*show point*].
> Then target the hammer blow at region near the edge of the "Y" point in "Z" direction [*demonstrate direction*].

Nicholas Toth's principle may need to be expressed more elaborately in the form of a procedure:

1   Select core with edge of "W" shape or angle [*demonstrate shape or angle*];
2   Select a point at distance "X" from the edge [*demonstrate distance*];
3   Strike the core at point "X" using blow "Y" [*demonstrate the glancing blow*] in direction "Z" [*demonstrate direction*].

In describing his experiments Toth remarked that the makers of the Koobi Fora tools must have possessed considerable cognitive and motor skills in order to shape these tools. Such skills would likely necessitate that the toolmakers acquire operational principles of the abovementioned kind.

But how would such operational principles come into being? In addition to his own experiments, Toth also had others, having no prior experience or training attempt to produce stone tools. Though their first attempts were not successful, within a few hours they had mastered the basic technique and were soon able to produce a broad range of tools.

Obviously we must not conclude that early *Homo* was successful as quickly as the modern day experimenters. Not only were there substantial differences in *brain capacities* between early *Homo* and modern *H. sapiens*—an average of 800cc for *H habilis* (Leakey 1994, p. 27) and from 750–1250cc for *H. erectus* (Mithen 1996, p. 25), and between 1200cc and 1700cc for modern *H. sapiens* (ibid.)—but modern human's belief/knowledge and operational spaces are incomparably richer than those of early *Homo*. Furthermore, both Toth and his novices would have known what was expected of them; they would have identified the appropriate goal, whereas the first inventors of stone tools had to *acquire* such expectations. (This is why one can never conduct experiments that can truly reproduce past creative phenomena.)

Nevertheless, Leakey's and Toth's experiments do shed light on the act of creation of the first technologists: it was an act of *evolutionary learning*, involving a long process of many cycles of trial and error—cycles involving the formation of a procedure, testing it, observing the outcome and then, based on the observations, altering the procedure.

There is a caveat to this scenario. We do not know over what period of time the learning process ensued before a satisfactory operational principle emerged. Nor can we presume that the whole learning process occurred in the mind of a single individual. A more plausible scenario is that the outcome of a particular cyclic sequence of trial and error entailed the participation of—their observations and transmission between—many individuals.

A further point is noteworthy. From *our* point of view, *our* position in historical time, choppers and hand axes may seem unbearably crude as products of the creative tradition. But to take such a view is precisely to adopt the crassest of Whiggish position (Chapter 3, XII), the position in which one passes judgment on past events and actions in the light of present achievements.

In the case of the first stone tools, if we pause to consider the act of invention itself, quite a different picture emerges. These inventions necessitated the production of knowledge *in the absence of any prior knowledge to build upon*. There was virtually nothing the first technologists could draw upon except for observations of sharp rocks and stones in nature—that is, drawing upon their natural space (Chapter 1, IV). The making of hand axes (material artifacts) demanded the invention of operational principles (abstract artifacts).

If it was the case that the first technologists had to invent operational principles for which there were no antecedents at all, and that the use of these principles led to artifacts of a kind that had not existed before, then we can surely claim that the invention of lithic technology not only marked the beginning of the creative tradition, it also heralded a *revolution*. In other words we can say that the birth of the creative tradition did not begin with a whimper but with a bang: a kind of "big bang" of technological culture.

Note

1 The quoted remarks, unless stated otherwise, are from two audiotaped interviews of George Rodrigue carried out by the author on September 30, 2002 and December 13, 2002 in the artist's home/studio in Lafayette, Louisiana.

10

INVENTING COGNITIVE STYLE

I The biographical engagement

Recall the idea of the creative encounter between an artificer and a consumer *via* the produced artifact (Chapter 4). Such encounters relate to singular acts of creation, for example W.B. Yeats's creative encounter (as a peer consumer) with Rabindranath Tagore as artificer by way of the poems *Gitanjali*, or my creative encounter (as a lay consumer) with Beethoven while listening to his Sixth Symphony.

Now consider a consumer's engagement with an artificer across significant spans of the latter's life, even his entire working life. Cognitive scientist Howard Gruber (1981) engaged with the life of Charles Darwin over a twenty-year period of his life, from 1837 to 1859. I engaged with the Indian science pioneer Jagadis Chandra Bose across the part of his life history spanning 1894–1937 (Dasgupta 2009) and with polymath scientist Herbert Simon across much of his adult life, from the late 1930s to 2000 (Dasgupta 2003a, 2003b). Historian and philosopher of science Arthur Miller (2001) engaged with Picasso for the duration of the latter's life from the turn of the twentieth century till up to about 1910. Historian of science Frederick Holmes (1985) engaged with the eighteenth century French chemist Antoine Lavoisier through the *savant's* entire creative life and that of Nobel laureate biochemist Hans Krebs (Holmes 1989, 1996).

Extended engagements of these sorts between artificer and consumer are usually prompted by the consumer's need or desire to probe into the nature of the artificer's creative *life*. The consumer in such situations is likely to be a creativity researcher who is seeking not so much to judge the artificer's creativity on a singular act of production but to elicit the character of a creative life over a significant span of time.

It may well be that such probings do indeed pertain to a single act of production that happens to span a large part of the artificer's life as in the case of Gruber's study of Darwin. But it may also relate to the fact that over the artificer's life (or a seminal portion of it) she may be engaged in *multiple* acts of production. Such was the case in my studies of the polymath Herbert Simon and Jagadis Chandra Bose, and in Frederick Holmes's inquiries into the lives of Lavoisier and Hans Krebs.

I term such relationships between artificer and consumer *biographical engagements*. Here, the consumer becomes a cognitive biographer and the artificer is her subject.

II Cognitive style

But a consumer-as-biographer has a specific mandate in engaging with the artificer. Her goal is to tease out what I have elsewhere called an artificer's *cognitive style* (Dasgupta 2003a, 2005)—by which I mean:

> A compendium of one or more identifiable patterns or regularities under-pinning an artificer's cognitive acts of production in the course of his or her creative life.

So a person's cognitive style refers to certain features of her ways of thinking, reasoning and doing that are idiosyncratic to her and thus establish her *identity* as a creative being. We normally associate cognitive style with artists, composers and writers (Gombrich 1969, pp. 3–32; Wollheim 1987, pp. 25–84; Gaiger 2002); cognitive scientist Margaret Boden (2010) has called this trait the artist's "personal signature" and indeed that is an apt descriptor. But cognitive style is also manifested, though less visibly, by scientists, designers and engineers (Holmes 1989; Davidson 1999; Dasgupta 2003a).

The cognitive historian's reason for eliciting an artificer's cognitive style is twofold. First, it is a way of circumventing the dilemma of the unconscious (Chapter 7). As we recall, much of the cognitive process underlying acts of production occur in the unconscious, thus frustrating the creativity researcher's task. Luckily various aspects of an artificer's cognitive process becomes visible in the form of certain patterns of regularities. It is these that I am calling one's cognitive style. Indeed, an artificer's cognitive style is an *abstraction* of actual cognitive processes. More interestingly, an artificer's cognitive style can be viewed as the *schema underlying his many acts of production* across a period of the artificer's life (see Chapter 5). And just as an artificer may invent a schema and then instantiate it in different ways in singular acts of creation (as we saw in the case of George Rodrigue (Chapter 9)) so also he may (perhaps unconsciously) *invent* a cognitive style and instantiate it in many ways across his creative life. So here lies the second reason why the creativity researcher desires to excavate an artificer's cognitive style: as a means of delineating the general character of the artificer's creative life, her creative *identity*.

Literary theorist Norman Holland (1988), who was also trained in psycho-analysis, wrote of a person's "identity theme": this seems very similar to what I am calling cognitive style. For Holland, an identity theme is "the sameness, consistency or style of a person" (p. 20). The artificer's acts of production are then "variations played on that identity theme" (p. 38). Writing on American poet Robert Frost, Holland wrote that it was the poet's identity theme that endowed him with a "certain Frost-ness in the way the poet wrote and read and lived" (p. 20).

III   The cognitive historian as biographer

Of course, not all biographers concern themselves with what we are calling here "cognitive style." Yet we can find a niche for it in the biographer's art. Hermione Lee (2009), a preeminent literary biographer of our time as well as an acute student of biographical writing, presents and then critiques ten possible "rules of biography" (pp. 6–18). Her aim was to identify commonly held views of what a biography "should be," and then contest them by pointing to their violations by way of actual biographical examples. (Her tenth rule is that "There are no rules of biography" (p. 18)). But one of these contested rules is that "Biography is an investigation of identity" (pp. 14–16)—meaning that a biography should reveal or explicate the subject's identity or "self." Lee notes that there are however many "rival" ways by which disciplines other than biography attempt to understand identity: the human sciences such as psychoanalysis, sociology, ethnography and history; creative writing itself (poetry and fiction); and philosophy (p. 15). To these "rival" disciplines we may add cognitive history, with the caveat that the cognitive historian is a biographer of a special kind: in seeking to elicit an artificer's cognitive style her sole concern is to identify the artificer's *creative* identity.

IV   A writer's cognitive style

As I have noted, cognitive style is most visible in the realm of the arts—visual, performing, cinematic and literary. But even in these realms much effort must be expended by the cognitive historian-as-consumer in probing into the artificer's life. The former must enter into a biographical engagement with the latter. This was precisely what my former student, cognitive scientist and literary scholar Carmen Comeaux (2006), did with American writer Flannery O'Connor. Much as Norman Holland explored Robert Frost's cognitive style, his "Frost-ness" so also Comeaux unveiled aspects of O'Connor's "O'Connor-ness."

O'Connor died of lupus disease in 1964 at age thirty-nine. Her literary *oeuvre* comprised of thirty-one short stories, two novels, speeches, letters and reviews (Comeaux 2006, p. 5). As such she is most identified with the short story *genre*. She is also regarded as a "Southern writer": she was born in Savannah, Georgia and though she spent parts of her life in the American Midwest and the North East she lived most of her short life in Georgia.

Her creativity and her place in the American literary canon have been well recognized. In her lifetime she received numerous literary awards including, thrice, the prestigious O'Henry Prize for short story writing (p. 5). She has been the subject of at least five biographies; she was listed in the *Dictionary of Literary Biography*; and her stories have been anthologized in school and college English textbooks (p. 6). According to literary critics—peer consumers—her creativity lay in her influence on the evolution of the American short story, (Ousby 1988, p. 727), her "gem-like prose" (Karl 1988), her "chilling" vision of the American rural South and her mastery of the "Southern Gothic" (Hobson 1988, p. 474). So as a short story writer we can claim with some confidence that she would be judged C-creative. But if we are to get to the nitty-gritty of her creativity we must visit her cognitive style for, ultimately, as with many other artists, her creativity lay in her invention of a cognitive style all of her own.

Carmen Comeaux's biographical engagement with Flannery O'Connor entailed delving into her short stories (O'Connor 1989), her letters (Fitzgerald 1979), interviews with her (Magee 1987) and biographical and critical writings on O'Connor (Baumgarter 1978; Getz 1980). As Comeaux discovered, O'Connor's cognitive style consisted primarily of a compendium of dichotomies and their relationships and resolutions. The most prominent of these were the following.

Universalism/Regionalism. Her stories were Southern stories but she told them to unveil aspects of the universal human condition (Comeaux 2006, p. 255). As a Southerner, the reality she portrayed would have a Southern "accent," but her aim was to go beyond, to a larger "essence" (Magee 1987, p. 48).

Youth/Old Age. O'Connor never married and never had children of her own. But she was acutely aware of the formative influence of childhood experience on the shaping of people's adult lives (Comeaux 2006, p. 256). Most strikingly almost all her stories had the presence of at least two generations and usually they were in some sort of oppositional relationships, often because of differing generational world views (pp. 256–257). But she did not take sides. Rather, she used her stories to show how these generational conflicts, sometimes within the same family, resolve themselves.

North/South. Perhaps the Southern writer can hardly ever elude this dichotomy just as the African-American writer cannot entirely avoid the racial dichotomy or a postcolonial writer cannot elude the colonizer/colonized binary.

O'Connor lived in both North and South within the United States. Up to age twenty-one she lived in Savannah (her birthplace) and Midgeville, Georgia. Graduating from Georgia State Women's College she went to graduate school at the University of Iowa Writers Workshop. After earning her master's degree she spent some time in an artists' colony in Yaddo, New York and then with her friend Sally Fitzgerald (the editor of her letters) in Connecticut where she was diagnosed with lupus. She then returned to Georgia where she lived with her mother the rest of her short life (Comeaux 2006, p. 258).

As might be expected, O'Connor's Southernness and her Georgian life informed most forcefully her fiction. But a result of her North/South experiences was that she constructed, according to Comeaux, definite *schemas* about Northern and Southern living. The South was characterized by a sense of its own history and certain tradition-bound, formal codes of behavior; the North manifested innovation and change, an indifference to the past, and an absence of the codes of behavior inherent to the South (p. 259).

Many of her short stories explored the interaction of these schemas and their resolutions (p. 260).

Urban/Rural. Though O'Connor spent a substantial portion of her formative years in Savannah and visited other large cities in the course of her life, she also spent considerable time in her mother's farm Andalusia in Midgeville, Georgia. Comeaux tells us about the schemas O'Connor constructed about the urban and rural ways of life and her depiction in her stories of the effect of displacement from one to the other, an effect that worked both ways. In one of her best-known stories the main characters go from their rural home to "big city" Atlanta and find themselves unable to cope with this alien environment. Other stories tell of the urban dweller moving to the country and having a similar experience.

Catholicism/Protestantism. O'Connor herself lived a dichotomous life as a devout Catholic in a predominantly Protestant part of the South. Her Catholicism informed the very nature of her writing: "I write the way I do because I am a Catholic" (Getz 1980, p. 108. Quoted by Comeaux 2006, p. 263). While she peopled her stories mostly with Protestant characters in Protestant *milieux* the God in the stories was a Catholic God and the stories were Catholic in their emphasis on the redeeming merits of God's grace and its transforming power (Comeaux 2006, p. 263).

This latter theme—"the healing power of God's grace"—was itself an element of O'Connor's cognitive style (p. 256). It was a kind of superneed that drove her creative enterprise and that left its imprint, as Comeaux records (p. 265), in each of her stories.

Comeaux identified a schema in O'Connor's stories around this superneed. Many of these stories followed a pattern involving main characters who are initially secure and unquestioning in their Protestant faith and in their place in the world. Some kind of crisis follows, and the central character, humbled, chastened, is faced with the choice of accepting God's grace or rejecting it. If the former, they are granted mercy, if the latter, they are driven into a state of humiliation (p. 263).

Actual Life/Contemplative Life. O'Connor's lupus inevitably limited her physical activity in her later years. In Andalusia, the family farm where she returned to live with her mother after being diagnosed with the disease, she was forced into a far more contemplative life than she may have desired (p. 263). This polarity of the active and the contemplative life found its way into her writing. The "intellectuals" in some of her stories do not lead very meaningful lives. Comeaux finds that in many of O'Connor's stories reading and learning are not necessarily conducive to contentment or even independence (p. 266). But then the least educated and most physically active characters are not better off either. There has to come about a balance between the active and the contemplative to have a complete life (p. 267).

Black/White. O'Connor lived at a time when segregation and Jim Crow laws ruled the Deep South. A Southern writer of her era could scarcely evade the issue of racism.

As Carmen Comeaux saw it O'Connor's views of race were complicated. She was certainly not "color blind" (p. 164). In one letter she curses both "houses" in the matter of the "race business" (Fitzgerald 1979, p. 537. Quoted in Comeaux 2006, p. 166). Yet she writes that just as humans are "are harder to handle" than animals, so also are white people compared to Black folks (Magee 1987, p. 58; Comeaux 2006, p. 267). The implication is clear enough: there is a hierarchy from lesser to greater thinking capacity with animals the lowest, Blacks in the middle and Whites at the top. Her use of the word "nigger" in her letters also tells us that her attitude to Black people was consonant to the Southern White view. Comeaux noted that African-Americans in O'Connor's stories were "not given much iden- tity" in contrast to Whites. The latter were "fully fleshed out" and "given real personalities" (p. 166). In one letter she refers to "my colored idiots" (Fitzgerald 1979, p. 547. Quoted in Comeaux 2006, p. 166). She admitted that she did not understand Blacks in the way she understood Whites (Magee 1987, p. 58; Comeaux 2006, p. 161).

These dichotomies, then, constituted elements of O'Connor's cognitive style which, Comeaux argued, the writer resolved in her stories by a kind of dialectic synthesis rather than having them negate each other (Comeaux 2006, p. 268). To which let me add: in the case of Flannery O'Connor, if her fiction was her first order creation, her cognitive style was the second, higher-order invention.

V   A natural scientist's cognitive style

In the annals of the history of modern science in India no one looms larger than Jagadis Chandra Bose. He was India's first scientist to gain international recogni- tion. Working as a physicist in the 1890s in almost complete isolation in Calcutta (now Kolkata), then capital of the *Raj* (British India), he was the first to produce millimeter-length radio waves and study their properties. Then, at the height of his success as India's first internationally acknowledged physicist, Bose changed course and through a curious set of circumstances (which I have recounted in some detail elsewhere (Dasgupta 2009)) transformed himself into a plant physiologist and bio- physicist. Here too, he was India's first. In both fields Bose proved to be a brilliant inventor of scientific instruments. And yet the Western reception of Bose's science in his own time and after was deeply ambivalent. As a pioneer of microwave physics his reputation in his time was impeccable and won him the fellowship of the Royal Society (FRS) and a British knighthood. In plant physiology and biophysics the instruments he designed (which I had the privilege of seeing in working condition in Kolkata) and the delicate and ingenious experiments on plant responsiveness he performed with these instruments elicited almost universal admiration in the West. However, his theoretical interpretations of his experimental work in the realm of plants evoked both warm admiration and intense antagonism, even ridicule and wrath among his Western peers. The controversy over his plant biophysics remains to this day, as the Australian plant physiologist Virginia Shepherd (2009) has recounted.

Thus Bose was something of an enigma, manifesting many striking polarities and paradoxes in the course of his scientific life. Having obtained a degree in the natural sciences tripos in Cambridge at a time when Lord Rayleigh was the Cavendish professor of physics and the Cavendish Laboratory was entering its most glittering phase as an international epicenter of experimental physics (Crowther 1974), Bose returned to India to conduct science in an essentially science-deprived environment. His was an Eastern mind dwelling in the realms of Western science. He was an interdisciplinary thinker in an ethos in which confinement within a discipline was already the norm in professional science. As we have noted, in midstream he abandoned the comfort of solid achievements in mainstream physics to begin anew in plant science. In his scientific writings he did not hesitate to combine the languages of literature and science. He pursued the most abstract of ideals with the most delicately constructed physical instruments. He was an establishment man in some ways and a marginal man, an outsider in others, And though in his scientific methodology he cohered within the Western scientific tradition, his larger and ultimate aspirations went beyond what Western science could deliver. Bose's science was imbued with a heavy dose of quixotry which science, even in his time as an active scientist, from the mid-1890s to his death in 1937, does not normally admit into its inner sanctum. All of this constituted significant aspects of Bose's creative identity.

Thus the very nature of this identity and Bose's place in establishing a serious scientific *milieu* in India compel attention. It certainly compelled mine and led me to an extended biographical engagement with Bose's scientific life and a critical study of his science and his complex, wayward and what I called his "flawed" genius (Dasgupta 2009).

Our interest here lies in what we can glean of his cognitive style as the shaper of his striking creative identity.

Analogical reasoning

Arguably the most prominent feature of Bose's cognitive style was a predilection for analogical reasoning. It pervaded his scientific thinking from his earliest work in physics right to his construction of a controversial thesis concerning the relationship of living and nonliving matter.

Returning to Calcutta from a successful European lecture trip in 1897 and further pursuing his research goal of determining the "optical" properties of radio waves (then called "electric waves") he proposed that the plane of polarization of such waves could be rotated. (In the case of a wave such as that of visible light the vibrations constituting the wave occurs in all planes perpendicular to the direction of wave transmission. In polarization the vibrations are confined to one plane only.) Here he drew an analogy between light waves and radio waves. This suggested an experiment: Bose had previously shown that jute fibers had polarization properties, so he decided to use jut fibers as the polarization agent in his experiment.

Analogical thinking went further in this piece of research. It was known that certain organic compounds rotated the plane of polarization in certain directions. It was also known that certain crystalline forms of such compounds rotate the plane of polarization in one direction while other "mirror image" crystalline forms (called "isomers") rotated them in another direction. Bose knew these facts; he wanted to "imitate" such rotations as, for instance, was obtained by saccharine solutions. He drew an analogy between the mirror image forms of isomers such as sugars and oppositely twisted jute fibers. His experiments on rotating the polarization plane thus used jute fibers twisted in two opposite directions (Bose 1898).

Analogical thinking is also evident in Bose's design of the apparatus he invented to carry out his researches on the properties of radio waves. He employed hollow tubes as wave guides and mounted a "lens of sulphur or glass" at the end of the tube to obtain a parallel beam of radio waves (Bose 1896a). Here the analogy drew on the parallelization of light waves to hypothesize that a similar arrangement would work for radio waves. Likewise, to prevent reflection of the radio waves on the inner surface of the wave guide he drew on the analogical notion that lampblack was an effective absorbent of light waves, so he hypothesized that lampblack would also absorb radio waves (Bose 1897).

Thus Bose used analogy as a *heuristic device* to generate goals and subgoals and to *search* through his belief/knowledge space. Like many heuristics, the analogy worked on some occasions (as in the case of the twisted jut fibers and in his use of wave guides and lenses) while on other occasions it failed (as in the instance of the lampblack).

Numerous other instances of his propensity to analogize populate his writings. He drew an analogy between radio wave receivers ("coherers" as they were then called) and the eye and this prompted him to advance his ideas on vision and the development of an "artificial retina" (which would be awarded a U.S. patent (Bose 1904)). He found an analogy between certain properties of his coherer and photographic plates and from that he advanced an (incorrect) theory about photographic action (Bose 1901). He justified his theory of "coherer action"—why a certain kind of radio wave receiver worked the way it did—using various arguments including an analogy with certain effects (called "allotropoic change") of visible light on certain kinds of matter (Bose 1900).

But the analogy of largest consequence to Bose's scientific life, precipitating his morphing from physicist to plant physiologist/biophysicist, was the one he drew between the inorganic coherer and living muscle in their respective responsiveness to stimuli (Bose 1902). This led to what I termed elsewhere the "Boseian thesis" (Dasgupta 2009, Chapters 4 and 5), namely: *There is no discontinuity between the living and nonliving with respect to their responsiveness to stimuli.*

Inventing scientific instruments

Analogical reasoning was certainly the dominant feature of Bose's cognitive style but there were others. One was his propensity for making his own scientific instruments. Of course building experimental apparatus and designing experiments are the *sine qua non* of experimental science, but Bose's propensity to make ingenious, delicate, quite unique experimental artifacts was so distinctive that we can justifiably label it as an aspect of his particular cognitive style.

This propensity was evident in the very first apparatus he made for both generating and receiving radio waves which he carried with him to demonstrate his lectures in England and the Continent in his lecture tour of 1896–1897, as for instance at the annual 1896 meeting of the British Association for the Advancement of Science (Bose 1896b) and in his presentation at the famed Friday Evening Discourses (instituted by Michael Faraday) at the Royal Institution of Great Britain in 1897 (Bose 1897). But this propensity became particularly visible in his "post-physics" life, from 1900 onward. He became remarkably prolific in designing and making instruments of different *varieties* that he then deployed for detecting and measuring plant response and other properties. And as his whim dictated he coined Sanskrit names for several of them (Dasgupta 2009, p. 201).

Communicating original science through books

A curious element of Bose's cognitive style as a plant scientist was that with the publication of his first book in 1902 (advocating the Boseian thesis) Bose virtually abandoned communicating his original scientific research as papers in the standard scientific periodicals (such as *Proceedings of the Royal Society* that had contained most of his communications on radio waves). Between 1902 and 1927 Bose published five, quite massive, books. He did return to publishing papers after 1917 (when he formed his own research institute, the Bose Research Institute) but these papers were almost entirely published in his own house journal, *Transactions of the Bose Research Institute*.

In presenting original science in books Bose digressed to a style of scientific communication that had more or less died out by the beginning of the twentieth century. Scientists did, of course, write books and some of them became classics, but they were either integrative works of synthesis and interpretation of a chosen topic—for example, physicist Ernest Rutherford's *Radioactive Substances and Their Radiations* and physiologist Charles Sherrington's *The Integrative Action of the Nervous System*, two Nobel laureates who were Bose's contemporaries—or of historical or philosophical import, such as Henri Poincaré's *Science and Hypothesis*. Bose's books were neither. Especially idiosyncratic (and even eccentric) was the virtual absence of citations of other scientists' works. His books were tomes dedicated entirely to the propagation of his own work. His plant science was a solipsistic world.

VI A painter's cognitive style

We have previously encountered the painter Amrita Sher-Gil (see Chapter 6, X). You will recall that Sher-Gil, having trained in Paris for five years, decided to return to India at the end of 1934 because she believed India was where her destiny lay (Sher-Gil 2002, p. 355).

It must have been difficult for a gifted, emerging artist to abandon what was still the world's epicenter of *avant garde* Western art and move to a place that for her was *terra incognita* as far as modern art was concerned. Yet in a sense we understand

Sher-Gil's decision to return to India. Departing or deviating from the past is every creative being's superneed as we have noted before. The ambitious painter, like the ambitious scientist and the ambitious writer or musician, wants to make history. For Amrita Sher-Gil making history meant creating a painterly style all her own (Sher-Gil to Victor Egan, 1935, month unknown. Quoted in Dalmia 2006, p. 53). For a brash, gifted, confident, sexually as well as cognitively charged, twenty-one-year-old, solidly grounded in the techniques, forms and content of contemporary European painting, India was not only unknown territory painting-wise, it was probably a *tabula rasa*, a vast empty canvas at her disposal to be filled as she desired.

In fact, the opening decades of the twentieth century had given birth to an Indian modernism in art. At the time Sher-Gil returned to India there was a flourishing school of painting, the so-called "Bengal School" (Mitter 2007, pp. 27ff.). But the only modernists Sher-Gil valued were Rabindranath Tagore who famously took up painting in 1928 at age sixty-seven (and produced more than 2500 paintings and drawings in the last thirteen years of his life (Anon 2004, p. vii)), and the painter Jamini Roy. She was scathingly critical of the rest (Sher-Gil 2002, p. 355).

In any case, when Sher-Gil returned she did not know much know about Indian art. The gaps in her knowledge would fill after she met in Bombay (now Mumbai), in November 1936, Karl Khandalavala, a noted art connoisseur and collector who became her admirer and champion and through whom she discovered Rajput, Pahari, Mughal and Bahsoliu paintings of the eighteenth century (Sunderam, n.d.). She visited and was captivated by the frescoes in the Ajanta Caves and the cave sculptures in Ellora (Sunderam, n.d.).

These tours might be thought of as the continuation of her proactive preparation. But by then Sher-Gil had already begun inventing a cognitive style for herself, what I will call here "Sher-Gil Modern." In 1935, in her first year back from Paris, she did four paintings, *Three Girls, Nude Group, Hill Men,* and *Hill Women* (Anon 2007, plates 46–49). These, her first "Indian paintings" remind the consumer–viewer of Gaughin but in a very different way. The subjects, for one, were Indian. "Sher-Gil Modern" is an Indian modern but at a vast distance from how her Indian predecessors and even contemporaries defined "Indianness."

Sher-Gil's modernism lay in brutal, primitive concreteness. She has been described as a "primitivist," a direct link to Gaughin (Mitter 2007, p. 55). Her subjects lay in the Indian rural, the poor, the silent majority, the *subaltern* (Chapter 3, V for the meaning of this word in this context). Hers was the imagining of village India, a *milieu* of "luminous, yellow-grey land," of "incredibly thin," dark-skinned, silent, melancholic, resigned men and women (Sher-Gil 2002, p. 355). She had found her material. The subaltern became her subjects but never sentimentally so. She perceived the poor with the objective mind of the disciplined painter, not with the heart of a Gandhian reformer.

Sher-Gil's paintings of 1935 established a schema for her modernist cognitive style: (1) her subjects were of subaltern India; (2) the figures were elongated; (3) the colors were somber—even the lighter colors; (4) figure and ground were virtually on the same plane, more flat than solid; (5) the figural forms were simplified.

But like all good schemas her schema was plastic, with room for refinement, expansion and change. Within the basic schematic framework her cognitive style evolved over the seven remaining years of her life. Influenced by the art critic Clive Bell she progressively deviated from naturalism to search for what Bell famously called "significant form" (Sher-Gil 2002, p. 354). And so we see the schema concerned more and more with color rather than form; it was as if she used color to represent significant form. The skins of her people became darker, dark red ochre or chocolate brown, the features barely discernible (as in *Two Women* (*c.*1936), *Fruit Vendor* (1937), *Red Verandah* (1938) and *Haldi Grinder* (*c.*1940); Anon 2007, plates 54, 55, 56, 87).

Sher-Gil's cognitive style was the "miraculous marriage of Indian and Western," in the words of art critic Charles Fabri, a close friend of hers (quoted in Dalmia 2006, p. 100). On the one hand there was the realism of the Post-Impressionists, and primitivism, and the search for significant form, all products of the West. On the other hand there were the influences of the Ajanta frescoes (as, e.g., in *Bride's Toilet* (1937) and *Brahmacharis* (1937)), both painted after her return from the tour of Ajanta and Ellora (Anon 2007, plates 56, 59). And there were the Rajput/Basohli/ Mughjal miniature tradition Karl Khandalavala had introduced her to, as evident in *Siesta* (1937) and *Women Resting on a Charpoy* (1940) (Anon 2007, plates 62, 99).

VII   The cognitive style of a scientific polymath

We have previously encountered the phenomenal eclecticism of Herbert Simon (Chapter 6, IV). His was a case of multidisciplinary creativity (Dasgupta 2003a). In a working life spanning over sixty years Simon made seminal contributions to administrative theory, axiomatic foundations of physics, economics, sociology, econometrics, cognitive psychology and the methodology of science. He was a co-creator of two new sciences artificial intelligence (AI) and cognitive science. Above all he made us conscious in a way no one had done before of the sciences of the artificial, of which AI and (in his view) cognitive science were instances. Here was surely a creative encounter of the first order between Simon and his readers by way of his classic book *The Sciences of the Artificial* (1996) whereby many of his readers' identities (including mine) were reshaped. Simon was profoundly H-creative and C-creative.

What does his creative life reveal about his cognitive style? Indeed what does his cognitive style tell us about the mind of a polymath, a Renaissance mind? Almost a year before his death Simon wrote to me that:

> [T]he "Renaissance mind" is not broader than other intelligent minds but happens to cover a narrow swathe across the multidimensional space of knowledge that happens to cut across many disciplines which have divided up the space in many other ways. My own narrow swathe happens to be the process of human problem solving and decision making, and almost everything I have done lies in that quite narrow band.
>
> *(Personal communication, February 21, 2000)*

Here we have a glimmer of an important insight: a polymathic mind is not fragmented into multiple insulated chambers. Rather to make sense of such a mind we have to understand that it achieves *integration* and *unification* of its different enterprises. The manner in which this is achieved characterizes that person's cognitive style. So it may well be in the case of Herbert Simon, who is one of the rarest of breeds in the twentieth century, a scientific polymath whose range spanned the social sciences, the behavioral sciences, computer science and philosophy of science. So what were the components of his cognitive style?

A commitment to realism

Throughout Simon's long creative life we observe an unmistakable commitment to *realism*. This commitment was a central element of his belief/knowledge space. And while he clearly understood the distinction between the empirical natures of the social and the natural sciences (Simon 1976, p. 251), ontologically he also believed that as in the natural realm so also in the human–social there is a reality demanding to be described and understood. Reflecting on this near the end of his life he wrote to me:

> I consistently maintained that science is concerned with describing and explaining how the world is (including the world of human behavior). "How the world is" includes what preferences inhabitants of the world hold and apply to their choices … [T]his description and explanation does not include the preferences or values of the observer … doing this science.
>
> *(Personal communication, May 26, 2000)*

Simon admitted that the observer "must hold certain values in order to do effective science," but "[h]ow the world is—how its really is"—is independent of the observer's values (ibid.).

Between 1937 (when he was twenty-one) and about 1960 Simon produced (first by himself, then with his longtime collaborator Allen Newell) three *models of the human thinker* of progressively greater generality, the second evolving from the first, the third from the second and each an outcome of his commitment to realism. These three models, in increasing levels of generality (or abstraction), I have named elsewhere the "administrative decision maker" (ADM), the "universal decision maker" (UDM) and the "symbolic problem solver" (SPS) respectively (Dasgupta 2003b).

For example, by the early 1950s Simon's commitment to realism had extended from the administrative–organizational realm to the economic realm. His first model (ADM) described in his first book, *Administrative Behavior* (first published in 1947) evolved into a richer, more detailed model that unified the administrative and economic decision maker, and even automata into UDM, his second model (Dasgupta 2003b).

The essence of UDM were four propositions about how humans *really* make decisions: (i) The *principle of bounded rationality*: that the human mind is limited or bounded in its capacity for formulating and solving complex problems in a fully rational manner. (ii) The *principle of satisficing*: the decision maker establishes aspiration levels (acceptable or "satisficing," not necessarily optimal, goals) and seeks means to achieve such aspirations or meet such goals. (iii) The *principle of heuristic search*: the decision maker seeks a satisfying decision by searching the space of possible choices and selecting the one that meets the satisficing goal. (iv) The *principle of adaptive behavior*: organisms and organizations alike cope with the uncertainty of the future and their inability to accurately predict the future by way of locally adaptive behavior—that is, continually adjusting actions or behaviors to changing environment according to information received from the environment.

From the early 1950s till the very end of his life Simon railed against the anti-realism of mainstream (that is, neoclassical) economics. There the economic actor was a maximizer of satisfaction, a perfectly rational, omniscient being who was wholly at odds with Simon's vision of the real, boundedly rational decision maker. Mainstream economics, he wrote in his final book, "has spent too much time spinning gossamer webs of mathematical theory that are attached to the world by hypothetical "facts" having little or no basis in observation" (Simon 1999, p. xi).

A commitment to empiricism

By "empiricism" I mean that the realism of human–social phenomena must be understood using the methods of the empirical natural sciences. We might think of this as a *methodological* rather than ontological issue although realism and empiricism clearly go hand in hand.

Simon's commitment to empiricism in the social sciences extended to the idea of performing social experiments. In *Administrative Behavior* he deliberated on "administrative experiments" wherein the investigator would study one specific organizational phenomenon of interest by isolating it from all other aspects of the organization (Simon 1976, pp. 42–43) much as is done in experiments in the natural sciences. In 1976 Simon and Allen Newell, collaborators in the creation of AI, spoke of computer science as an empirical discipline (Newell and Simon 1976). They were not suggesting that computer science is a natural science but rather, as in the natural sciences, one gains knowledge by way of experiments. Computer scientists build computational artifacts as ways of conducting experiments since only by building such artifacts and putting them into action can one discover new phenomena or comprehend better-known phenomena. Almost two decades later Simon (1995) returned to this point in the context of AI in an article that must be seen as his *summa* about a field he had helped create. Almost all we have come to know about artificial intelligence, he wrote, is by way of building AI programs, running them, observing their behavior, changing them, re-running them and so on. Empiricism here means a variety of purposive evolution (Chapter 8).

Models as schemas

Simon's successive models of the human thinker (ADM, UDM and SPS) were not only produced by his commitment to realism. They also became schemas that were instantiated and elaborated in other acts of production in a variety of fields. To put this another way, his models of the human thinker served as common representations *onto which he mapped problem situations from different disciplines.* Here was another prominent element of his cognitive style and one that was especially significant for his multidisciplinary creativity.

The idea of mapping from different problem domains into a common representation was not, of course, unique to Simon. Mathematical modeling is the classic exemplar: representing problem situations in mathematical language is especially common in physics, engineering mechanics, and economics. But Simon differed in two important ways.

First, while economists, physicists and engineers are usually adept in mapping from just *one* problem domain (their respective fields of specialization) into mathematical representation, Simon mapped from *multiple* disciplinary domains onto his schematic models of the human thinker. Second, in the process of mapping from different domains onto his schemas Simon *evolved* his schemas. Thus, when he recalled that his "narrow swathe across the space of knowledge across many disciplines … happen to be the process of human problem solving and decision making," the *evolution* of this schema was a core element of this "swathe." The construction of ADM, its expansion into UDM and the latter's evolution into SPS were themselves key constituents of his cognitive style.

We find many instances of the ways in which Simon's models of the human thinker served as schemas in different domains and because of the centrality of this element of his cognitive style in interpreting his creative identity, it is worth considering these instances in some detail.

a   *Group behavior.* Here, he appealed to the work of sociologist George Homans (1950) who postulated several hypotheses about the behavior of small groups. Simon wished to model group behavior that would not only lend more "precision and clarity" to Homan's propositions but also help produce additional testable propositions (Simon 1952). He did this by drawing on a number of different concepts from his richly interconnected belief/knowledge space and by making the principle of adaptive behavior (one of the four elements of his UDM model) the centerpoint of his model. The universal decision maker was used as a schema that was instantiated to explain small-group behavior, though (it must be noted) the instantiation was far from trivial.

b   *Learning.* In a similar vein Simon recognized that learning (as this concept was then understood by psychologists) was an instance of adaptive behavior. Accordingly, he deployed it to model the learning individual as one engaged in activity which became "progressively easier" to do the more it was done (Simon 1954a, p. 402).

c   *Unifying the social and the individual.* The two examples above highlight yet
    another facet of Simon's cognitive style by envisioning both individual and
    group behavior as instances of adaptive behavior. Simon moved seamlessly
    between the social and the individual. In fact, he recorded that the model of
    the individual learner itself originated in a group behavioral problem encoun-
    tered in a situation involving communication between accountants and shop
    floor operators (Simon 1954a, p. 405). This was a social problem that prompted
    him to construct a model of individual behavior that was then retranslated into
    the social domain.

d   *The symbol problem solver (SPS) model.* This was the most evolved and most
    general of Simon's model of the human thinker, and a product of his 20-year
    collaboration with Allen Newell. And while it is very difficult to distinguish
    between their respective creativity in the formulation and evolution of the SPS
    model we can certainly say that in Simon's context it represented a fusion of
    his thinking on social phenomena, individual cognitive phenomena, and auto-
    matic information processing (as performed by the computer).

The seminal works outlining the SPS model were two papers published in the
second half of the 1950s (Newell and Simon 1956; Newell, Shaw and Simon 1958).
The SPS model then became a schema that was richly exploited by Simon (and his
collaborators, especially Allen Newell) in several ways in the realm of AI, cognitive
psychology, design theory,and the logic of scientific discovery. Here I give just one
example from the realm of *creativity studies*.

On April 30, 1957 Simon confided to psychologist (and one of the founders of
cognitive science in the late 1960s) George Miller (Herbert Simon Papers, Carnegie
Mellon University Archives) that creativity was not nearly as mysterious as it was
made out to be; it was after all, he wrote, just another instance of those mental processes whose "mystery" had been "pretty well stripped away."

Simon's brash confidence lay in his situating creative thought within the realm
of the SPS model. The latter was the schema and understanding creative thinking
an instantiation of this schema. To back this claim, in 1962, Simon, Newell and
their collaborator Cliff Shaw addressed in some detail the "processes of creative
thinking" (Newell, Shaw and Simon 1962). They reiterated what Simon had
written to Miller: creative thinking was just a special kind of problem solving
behavior: creative processes are just special instances of the kind of processes SPS
describes. A theory of creative thinking, they wrote, should consist of a computer
program that specifies the behavior of mechanisms or organisms such that given
"appropriate" starting conditions it would "think creatively." That is, the program's behavior would exhibit the kind of behavior one normally associates with
creative thinking. Furthermore, they claimed, by abstracting from the program its
most general features one could obtain a general theory of creative processes. These
general features, they claimed, were nothing but the SPS model of the human
thinker.

A commitment to operationalism

In 1947, the year in which the first edition of Simon's first book *Administrative Behavior* (Simon 1976) appeared he published a paper on the foundations of classical (Newtonian) mechanics (Simon 1947).

Despite the huge intellectual distance between these two disciplines, one administrative theory (or management decision making), the other classical physics, Simon's approaches to the two had in common a commitment to *operationalism*. This is a principle that prescribes that any proposition, theory or model concerning a natural or artifactual system *must rest on one or more operations, rules or procedures that one can carry out to corroborate or falsify the proposition.*

Simon's operationalism appears to have originated in the late 1930s under the influence of the philosophical doctrine of logical positivism. In part this came by way of his encounter with philosopher Rudolf Carnap, then a professor at the University of Chicago, whose course Simon took as a graduate student. (Letter from Simon to Carnap, August 2, 1937. Herbert Simon Papers, CMU Archives); but more powerfully by way of his familiarity with another philosopher, A.J. Ayer's (1971) influential book *Language, Truth and Logic* first published in 1936. Simon acknowledged Ayer's considerable influence in *Administrative Behavior*. Five decades later he would recall "My later reading of Ayer was, in fact, … important in solidifying my ideas …" (personal communication, email, December 1, 1999).

The core idea of logical positivism was the "verification theory of meaning." This asserted that a proposition about something in the real world is meaningful if and only if the proposition is empirically verifiable. In other words, a proposition is only meaningful if one knows *how* to verify its truth.

The verification theory of meaning is one guise in which operationalism can be expressed and it played a very concrete role in Simon's thinking about administrative decision making. His affinity for operationalism was the basis of his severe criticism of the administrative theory prevalent in the late 1930s (Simon 1976, pp. 20–44). Every science, he wrote, must begin with concepts and current administrative theory had its fair share. But concepts must be *useful* for the task at hand and the concepts of current theory were *not* useful because they were not operationally defined—meaning that they did not specify how decisions can be made. An administrative theory must specify rules and procedures for decision making. Simon's own theory of administrative decision making was precisely such an operational theory. At its core was the model of the administrative decision maker (ADM) who is constrained and guided by the principle of bounded rationality (mentioned earlier, this chapter). The statements of his theory were rules in an *if–then* form, following two general schemas:

IF a goal is to be achieved THEN take such and such action.

IF such and such action is taken THEN such and such consequence will follow.

But how does his theory of administrative decision making relate to his publication on the foundations of classical mechanics, published the same year (1947) as was *Administrative Behavior*? The connection lay in that the latter also manifested a commitment to the same operationalism that shaped the former.

He "took on" none other than the highly influential nineteenth century scientist and philosopher Ernst Mach. Simon's criticism of Mach's axioms governing classical mechanics was that they were non-operational. And in response he offered a new model involving operational definitions of such physical entities as "unit of length," "simultaneity of events," and so on (Simon 1947). Several years later he compared his own work on the axiomatization of classical mechanics with that published by another group of authors and noted that while they desired mathematical rigor his aim was not only to achieve such rigor but also to present the subject in an "*operationally significant way*" (Simon 1954b. His italics).

With the emergence of the digital computer Simon's operationalism took the shape of *computational models*, whether expressed as algorithms, flowcharts, if–then rules or complete working programs. Programs, of course, are the most uncompromising expressions of operationalism, and the entire corpus of Simon's collaborative work with his collaborators in cognitive psychology and AI from the 1960s onwards were fundamentally computational in nature (Simon 1979, 1989). His psychology of scientific discovery (Langley, Simon, Bradshaw and Zytkow 1987; Kulkarni and Simon 1988; Klahr and Simon 1999) was both an instantiation of his SPS schema and an explicitly operational psychology built around the principle of heuristic search (mentioned earlier, this chapter).

Analogical reasoning

Simon resorted to analogical thinking in creating his model of the administrative decision maker (ADM): he drew an analogy between game playing and administrative decision making. He argued that making a decision entailed exploring alternatives, pursuing their consequences over "future" time, and selecting an end based on a comparison of alternate pathways. The decision maker must, therefore, mentally *simulate* possible futures. Simon called such mentally constructed alternative scenarios "strategies" (Simon 1976, pp. 66–67)—a concept influenced by his reading of John von Neumann and Oscar Morgernstern's pioneering classic *The Theory of Games and Economic Behavior* (1947), the book which ushered in game theory. (Simon noted (p. *67n*) that while his basic ideas had been "worked out" in 1941, the book had shaped the "reformulation" of his theory.) Comparing his concept of "strategy" with the relevant discussion by von Neumann and Morgernstern (1947, p. 79) it seems that Simon drew an analogy between administrative decision making and game playing after reading their book and accordingly "reformulated" his concept of strategy.

One of Simon's most remarkable analogies was between models of *economic behavior* and *physical reality* (Simon 1959). Both physics and economics are concerned with the empirical universe, the "real world"—in the former case the physical, in the latter case the economic/social. Both physics and economics have advanced by constructing axiomatic systems to model their respective realities: that is, (a) by way of fundamental definitions and postulates (axioms) that are assumed to be true and that purportedly reflect their respective empirical realities; and (b) exploring the consequences of these axioms and definitions using mathematical reasoning and empirical testing. (This method originated with Isaac Newton's great work *Philosophae Naturalis Principia Mathematica* (1687), the so-called "Newtonian method" or "Newtonian style" (Cohen 1995)).

In an axiomatic system that describes some empirical world there must be (among other things) "primitive terms" that correspond to "observable entities" and these must be distinguished from "definable terms." Simon's concern was with this distinction and how to make it. In particular he wished to challenge Polish logician Alfred Tarski's (1956) definition of "definability." (Here we find a feeling of *dissatisfaction* originating a creative act of production just as Simon's dissatisfaction with administrative theory had stimulated his work on administrative behavior.)

Fundamental to Simon's (1959) argument was his proposal of a concept he termed "defined almost everywhere." Its relevance lay in that in arriving at his definition of "defined almost everywhere" Simon drew an analogy between the problem of definability in physics and a problem in econometrics (a discipline straddling economics and statistics concerned with economic measurements) called the "identification problem." Simon's writings suggest that he discovered an analogy between the two problems and drew upon this analogy to derive his concept of "defined almost everywhere."

Simon's friend, the mathematical economist Tjalling Koopmans, was among those who had studied the identification problem. In an earlier work on classical mechanics Simon (1954b) had referred to Koopmans and had remarked on the analogy with the definability problem in physics. In 1959 he returned to this connection: the definability problems in the axiomatization of empirical theories, he declared, was the same as the identification problem in econometrics.

Communicating, concurrent cognitive processes

This is the final, clearly discernible element of Simon's cognitive style.

If we take 1937–1958 as the first period in Simon's creative life we find that in these twenty years Simon was engaged in acts of creation in *at least four different domains*: administrative theory, economics, foundations of physics and cognitive psychology. And he had initiated a *fifth* field, artificial intelligence. Interspersed with these five major concerns were also contributions to sociology, econometrics, and statistics (Simon 1947, 1954a, 1954b, 1955, 1957, 1959, 1976, 1977; Newell and Simon 1956; Newell, Shaw and Simon 1958).

But it was not the case that Simon would work in one domain for a period, then abandon it and move to another. Nor were they mutually independent. Rather, the picture before us is that of *a network of communicating cognitive processes* some of which might be temporarily suspended then resumed, but any one time two or more processes were concurrently active.

For example, his 1937 dissertation outline indicated an interest in both the logic of administrative decision making and the logic of classical physics with the former being influenced by the latter (Simon 1937). There was an interaction, beginning in the mid-1950s between Simon's thinking about administrative decision making and his work on boundedly rational *Homo economicus*. Between 1952 and 1956 he published his seminal papers on economic rationality, work that led to his model of the universal decision maker (UDM)—and a Nobel Prize twenty years later (see in particular Simon 1955).

By 1950 he was pondering the implications of his work on decision making on the theory of organizations (Simon 1950). Cognitive processes concerning decision making and problem solving merged into one. His ruminations on mathematical economics and econometrics (as we have noted above) strongly influenced his ideations in the foundations of classical mechanics.

To repeat, over this twenty period alone Simon's creative life was composed of a network of communicating, concurrent, cognitive processes, a manifestation of Howard Gruber's (1989) idea of a network of purposive enterprises. This was yet another dimension of Simon's cognitive style, underpinning his polymathic, Renaissance mind.

VIII   A filmmaker's cognitive style

In world cinema certain filmmakers are known as supreme representatives of their respective country's cinematic art. For India such was (and still is twenty-five years after his death in 1992) Satyajit Ray who, as a native of Bengal in Eastern India made all but one of his twenty-seven feature films in Bangla (the Bengali language). In addition he made over half-a-dozen documentaries and short films. Ray's creativity as a filmmaker was unequivocally established with his very first film *Pather Panchali* ("Song of the Little Road," 1955). Its originality and cinematic quality were recognized both in India and the West, and it garnered a host of awards including the "Best Human Document" award at the Cannes Film Festival (1956) and the Selznick Golden Laurel at the Berlin Film Festival (1957). Over the years it has consistently appeared as one of the "top 50 films of all time" polled by the prestigious British film periodical *Sight and Sound*.

Ray's second film *Aparajito* ("The Unvanquished," 1956) won the Golden Lion of St. Mark at the Venice Film Festival (1957). *Charulata* ("The Lonely Wife," 1964), his twelfth film was awarded the Silver Bear for Best Director at Berlin (1965) as did *Mahanagar* ("The Big City," 1963) in 1964. Indeed, the majority of Ray's feature films received prizes of one sort or another within and outside India.

At a personal level Ray's honors were numerous, most prominently an honorary doctorate from Oxford University (1978), only the second film personality (after Charles Chaplin) to be so recognized by this university; the Légion d'Honneur (1987) from the President of France; an Honorary Oscar for Lifetime Achievement (1992) from the American Academy of Motion Picture Arts and Sciences; and the Bharat Ratna, the Government of India's highest civilian recognition (1992). In that same year, the year of his passing, *Sight and Sound*'s "Critics' Top Ten Poll" ranked Ray as the seventh in its "top 10 directors" of all time.

Ray was more than a supreme film director, the ultimate *auteur*. If Herbert Simon was a twentieth century Renaissance person of science, Satyajit Ray was a twentieth century Renaissance person of the arts. Trained as an artist in Rabindranath Tagore's famed university in Santiniketan in Bengal, he was a consummate graphic artist and illustrator. He invented a print type font; and was an immensely popular writer of children's stories and the creator of a detective character much beloved by his young readers. Beginning with his ninth film *Kanchenjungha* (1962), Ray composed and scored the music (and wrote the lyrics of some of the songs) for all his subsequent films.

But here I will consider only the most prominent elements of Ray's cognitive style as a filmmaker.

Experimentalism

In the context of Indian cinema Ray's *Pather Panchali* was an experiment writ large. Years later he would claim that his goal had been to break "all manner of conventions" (Ray 2005, p. 17), by which he meant that his film would use actual locations, under natural conditions, with non-professional actors, and be almost documentary in its grittiness and realism. These features, along with its depiction of mainly subaltern lives, were the characteristics of Italian Neo-Realism (Sobcheck and Sobcheck 1987, p. 218). Vittorio De Sica's *The Bicycle Thief* (1948) was perhaps the archetype of this genre: the French critic André Bazin (1971, p. 50) asserted that *The Bicycle Thief* affirmed "the entire aesthetic" of the Neo-Realist. Ray first viewed this film in London in 1950 and the effect on him, he wrote, was electrifying. He emerged from the cinema theater his mind made up (Ray 2005, p. 15): he would make a film of the Bangla novel *Pather Panchali* (by the writer Bibhuti Bhusan Banerjee), a project that had been on his mind for some time, along De Sicaresque lines. Neo-Realism would be his chosen schema. Here was a creative encounter, with De Sica as artificer, *The Bicycle Thief* as the artifact, and Ray as consumer.

Even before the film was completed, with some 9000 feet of "rough cut," it was clear to Ray that *Pather Panchali* had no precedence in Indian cinema nor, for that matter in world cinema (Ray 1994, p. 73). But in making his film Ray instantiated the Neo-Realism schema in a way that emphasized his experimentalism: the film was quintessentially Indian; he had invented an *Indian* Neo-Realism. The film itself and the style were both C-creative in the history of cinema.

Experimentalism need not always be writ large. It can be present in bits and bobs, as we find in several of Ray's films: in the opening seven minutes of *Charulata* (1964) and in the freeze shot with which the film ends, and in several death scenes (in *Pather Panchali*, *Aparajioto*, and *Pratidwandi* ("The Adversary," 1970). We see experimentalism in a dream sequence in *Devi* ("The Goddess," 1960) in which three eyes set against a pitch black background and thus suggestive of the Hindu goddess Kali's eyes are metamorphosed into a girl's two eyes and a *tilak* mark on her forehead.

We see a shared experimental technique in *Kanchenjungha* (1962) and *Aranyer Din Ratre* ("Days and Nights in the Forest," 1969). In both Ray explored the idea of the ensemble plot in that there is no central character with others as supporting characters nor single core story, but rather a constellation of characters playing out their relationships through multiple interwoven stories.

A machine aesthetic

In Western modernist thought the machine has an ambivalent place, and no one thinker has realized more acutely this ambivalence than historian and social theorist Lewis Mumford. In a series of classic works beginning with *Technics and Civilization*, Mumford has both celebrated and excoriated the machine (Mumford 1962). For all his dismay with technology he could not reject it out of hand. He desired to "subdue" the machine and adapt it to human purposes; and in art Mumford found a countervailing force against a technology that had historically dehumanized, against a humanity that had become mechanized (Mumford 1952). Through art Mumford dreamt of integrating the human spirit with the mechanical ethos.

The possibility of harnessing the machine to artistic ends has been explored by a variety of artists and architects of the last and present centuries. They created for themselves a *machine aesthetic* in which the "spirit of the machine" was absorbed and utilized to shape a new aesthetic (Banham 1981; Wright 1979). Recently, Margaret Boden (2010) has given us an extended meditation on a machine aesthetic built around the computer—the ultimate machine, one might say—as an agent.

Since cinema is an art that was founded on, and relies heavily on, technology, the filmmaker as an artist is perpetually posed, and must come to terms, with this ambivalence. So the fact that Ray, like other filmmakers, should cultivate a machine aesthetic should not surprise. What does interest us is its specific nature and the way it took shape as an element of his cognitive style.

To understand Ray's machine aesthetic we must recognize that the words "machine," "mechanical" and "mechanistic" do not only refer to physical machines; they also signify procedures, operations, algorithms, programs and so on: abstract artifacts that are of a mechanistic nature, intended to solve specific problems.

There is a much admired scene in *Pather Panchali* in which the principal characters, the little boy Apu and his older sister Durga, wander somewhat afar from their village and Apu momentarily loses sight of his sister. He walks through the tall *khaas* flower clumps, stopping, searching for Durga, then walking a bit more, eventually spotting her.

As Ray described it, the first take of this scene was a disaster. He had instructed the little boy playing Apu what he should do in this scene: walk, then stop, turn his head one way then another, look for his sister, then resume his walk (Ray 1994, p. 73). The result in the first take was a "stiff, zombie-like walk" quite unlike what Ray had envisioned. His solution was entirely mechanistic. He placed three members of his crew behind clumps of *khaas* in various places and stances from one another, and instructed them to call out the boy's name at certain points of time.

The boy was to respond by turning his head in the direction of the calls without stopping his walk. In addition Ray put twigs in the boy's path at irregular intervals for him to step over (Ray 1994, p. 42; Blue 2007, p. 21).

Ray's solution to the problem of Apu's walk was to invent an "operational principle" (Polanyi 1962, p. 16; see also Chapter 8, XIV)—that is, any rule or procedure that facilitates action for solving some practical problem. The essence of a technological mentality is the ability to invent and deploy operational principles; indeed, perhaps the most fundamental kind of technological knowledge learnt and stored in one's belief/knowledge space is knowledge of operational principles (Dasgupta 1996, p. 167).

Another of Ray's invented operational principles was deployed in the making of his fourth film *Jalsaghar* ("The Music Room," 1958). In one scene the protagonist, an aged, widowed, aristocratic and once imperious *zaminder* (a feudal style landowner with large land holdings) called Biswambar Roy, living out his last years alone save for a few devoted servants, is seen one evening slumped on an easy chair on the roof terrace of his mansion. Strains of some music drift in from a neighbor's house. The music lover that he is, he listens engrossed. In his right hand he is grasping a cane and as the music reaches a certain rhythmic climax we see his right index finger rise in anticipation and fall back on the cane in synchrony with the rhythm.

Biswambar Roy's passion for music is one of the central themes of the film. Unfortunately, while shooting, Satyajit Ray learns, belatedly, that the actor who played Bswambar Roy (a leading patrician of the mainstream Bengali cinema of the time) had no musical sense whatsoever: he could not keep rhythm.

Ray's solution was to invent an operational principle: he shot the scene without any music but instructed the actor to raise his right index finger whenever he wished and strike the cane gently, just once. The actor complied. Later, when sound was added to the film the relevant piece of music was synchronized *with* the movement of the finger (Ray 2005, p. 203).

We see yet another expression of Ray's machine aesthetic in his use of that icon of the nineteenth century machine, the steam locomotive, as an emblem of the spirit of the machine in Ray's imagination. Before the advent of the airplane the steam locomotive/train served as a symbolic condensation (in the Freudian sense) of a complex of images, percepts, values and emotions.

In Ray's belief/knowledge space, as we detect it, the train/locomotive was not just a machine. It was a schema representing the mysterious but accessible geographic region "out there" (in *Pather Panchali*), a psychological condensation of urban life and the passage from the rural to the urban, from the traditional to the modern, a symbol of promise and hope in *Aparajito* ("The Unvanquished"); and as the grim, tawdry, intrusive face of modernism in *Apur Sansar* ("The World of Apu," 1959)—the three films forming the "Apu trilogy."

In an interview given in 1970 Ray commented briefly on the presence and significance of the train in the Apu trilogy. The train, he said, served as a motif symbolizing a journey. It also symbolized the nexus of rural and metropolitan India (Isaakson 2007, p. 43).

A feminist consciousness

Throughout his filmmaking life Ray resisted being labeled one thing or another. And just as his Left sympathies were evident yet he never actually called himself a Marxist, so also his feminist consciousness was manifestly transparent though he may well have balked at being labeled a feminist.

Cognitively speaking, "to be" a feminist is to own a schema that connects and relates several elements. The schema will include consciously held knowledge of the minority and unequal status of women throughout history; a belief in the wrongness and unjustness of this status; and knowledge of various strategies to right this wrong—to make women equal to men in significant respects and empower women so that they may take control of their own lives.

In such characters as Doya in *Devi* ("The Goddess," 1960), Labanya and Monisha in *Kanchenjungha* (1962), Arati in *Mahanagar* ("The Big City," 1963), Karuna in *Kapurush* ("The Coward," 1965), Charu in *Charulata* and Aparna in *Aranyer Din Ratri* ("Days and Nights in the Forest," 1969) we see attributes that collectively suggest a schema held in Ray's mind of a feminist consciousness. In this schema we find a consciousness of the plight and powerlessness of women under male domination as in the case of Labanya in *Kanchenjungha* and Doya in *Devi*; and an awareness that for some such as Doya the only liberty from such domination is to escape from reality itself. We find in the case of Arati in *Mahanagar* a representation of women's desire for self-improvement and self-empowerment; in Monisha in *Kanchenjungha* a desire for psychological independence. We find in Arati's case an awareness of women's need for economic and social freedom and an awareness that such freedom brings with it a liberation from the claustrophobia of the home and the family as the alpha and omega of a woman's existence.

Ultimately, this schema capturing Ray's feminist consciousness rests on the idea of freedom. The freedom that Charlotte Perkins Gilman's (1892) hapless protagonist in the story "The Yellow Wallpaper" craved for but was denied and which Lily Briscoe in Virginia Woolf's (1927) novel *To the Lighthouse* possessed and cherished, comes in various forms. For Gilman's narrator it was to be liberated from her powerlessness, her husband's control over her body, her health and even whether she should be allowed to write. For Lily Briscoe it was to live the life she wanted, to paint, to eschew the burden of the married state.

Gilman's protagonist could only find this freedom in escape from reality and into a psychotic state just as Doya did in *Devi*. And much as Lily Briscoe's freedom gave her an identity whereby she was equal to men—women *can* paint, women *can* write—so also Charu in *Charulata*: her literary gifts distanced her from other women, especially of her Bengali upper class, and placed her in the same site as men, including her husband's literarily aspiring cousin with whom she fell in love. And just as Lily Briscoe's work as a painter gave her an identity so also Arati's work as a salesperson in *Mahanagar* gave her an identity she never previously had and came to value.

The French writer Simone de Beauvoir found her freedom at age twenty by living on her own in lodgings in Paris (de Beauvoir 1965). She wrote this three decades after Virginia Woolf's polemical essay *A Room of One's Own* was published in which Woolf spoke passionately of how for a woman to write, to be creative, she must have money and a room of her own. The space coveted by Woolf and de Beauvoir was as much metaphorical as literal. It was the space the elderly Labanya in *Kanchen-jungha* was deprived of her entire married life and which she was determined her daughter would possess. It was the space that enabled women to gain control of their lives, their own destinies.

When we hear Ray say that he was interested in a certain "type" of women, one who could cope with certain situations (Gupta 2007), or that he had no interest in "subservient" women (as he stated in a BBC television documentary by Andrew Robinson in 1984), we are reminded on Karuna in *Kapurush* ("The Coward," 1965). The coward here is a man but this relatively short feature film is really about a woman's courage of a certain kind.

The story is told partly in flashback in which we learn that the eponymous coward, Amitava, then Karuna's boyfriend, would not commit himself to marrying Karuna when she desperately needed that commitment because of family pressures. So they parted ways. Some years later they meet in unexpected circumstances. Karuna is now married to a garrulous, bluff, boorish, alcoholic but not unkind nor abusive tea planter. Amitava, still single, confesses to her his unhappiness all the years since they parted. He pleads with her to forget the past, leave her husband and come away with him. Only at the very end of the film, where he is waiting at a railway station to leave does he (and the viewer) learn of Karuna's decision. She chooses not to go with him. Her rejection of him is the act of courage that counterpoints Amitava's former cowardice.

For much of the film Karuna is silent, and her silence leaves Amitava (and the viewer) in the dark about her true feelings toward her husband (who is blissfully unaware that his wife and Amitrava have a history) as well as how she feels about her former lover. But what is *not* ambiguous is that *she* is in control of her self. It is *her* choice whether to stay with her husband or rejoin her former boyfriend. It is *her* choice to find the kind of happiness, contentment or discontentment she sees fit. She does not even need to verbalize her choices—indeed, it is her choice to remain silent. And in her silence, as much as in Amitava's maudlin utterances, we are left in no doubt of Satyajit Ray's respect for this woman's strength and his contempt for that man's weakness.

The room of one's own Virginia Woolf wrote of is necessary for the woman writer; as is economic independence. But space and money are not enough (Woolf 1979, pp. 57–67). As the woman in a room of her own begins to write she is confronted with an enemy who Woolf called "the Angel in the House," a phantom lady, sympathetic, charming, unselfish, pure, an ideal in domestic matters who, as the writer is about to review of some (male) author's work whispers in her ear words of caution: "the author is a man, so be aware," the Angel whispers, "be sympathetic, be tender, flatter, deceive, use your feminine guile; you must not let on that you have a mind of your own."

We find such a phantom inside the mind of another of Ray's woman characters, Aparna in *Aranyer Din Ratri* ("Days and Nights in the Forest"). In this film four male friends have gone out of Calcutta (the "big city" of *Mahanagar*) for a holiday in a forested part of Bengal peopled largely by tribals. There they meet and befriend a small, well-off, evidently sophisticated family, also holidaying, comprising of an elderly man, his unmarried daughter Aparna and a widowed daughter-in-law.

A tentative relationship develops between Aparna and one of the male quartet, Asim, an urbane corporate executive. In one scene we observe the four men and the two women sitting outdoors playing a memory game: someone begins by saying the name of a "famous" person, the next player repeats the name and adds another, the next player repeats the two names and adds a third, and so on. The list of names becomes progressively longer and thus harder to accurately recall. Anyone who makes an error (omits a name in the list or mangles the order) is eliminated. Ultimately the one who remains after all the others have dropped away is the winner.

The game reached a point at which only Aparna and Asim remain. It is Aparna's turn. Thus far we, the viewers, have seen that she has been the most fluent, the most effortless in her ability to recall. But now Aparna hesitates. She looks in Asim's direction, then turns away and says, looking elsewhere that "I don't think I'll be able to go on." She then looks at Asim with a hint of a smile and says "Asim wins."

The viewer is left in no doubt. Aparna *allowed* Asim to win. Like Karuna in *Kapurush* she was in control of the situation. "I could have beaten you," she seemed to say, "but it doesn't matter to me, whereas for you it's important that you don't lose to a woman in front of your friends, you don't want to be humiliated. I'll let you save face."

Later, confronted by Asim, Aparna admits that she deliberately lost. He asked why she chose to lose. He must surely understand, she replies. Would he have felt good if she had won? Shamefaced but disarmingly he admits the point. The phantom Angel in Aparna's head had intervened. She must not let on that not only did she have a mind of her own but in some respects it was superior to a man's.

There is yet another phantom the woman writer must contend with, Virginia Woolf (1979) asserted: male values, expectations, opinions about what a woman—even a writer—should or should not say. This phantom forbids the woman from pursuing and writing of things she must not speak of.

Arati in *Mahanagar* is neither a writer nor an intellectual. But her newly gained space as a woman in the workplace has revealed new, hitherto unknown, possibilities. And like Woolf's writer she too faces a phantom. She must conform to the male values and expectations of the *bhadrolok* (the Bengali upper-caste, middle-class gentry) about what a woman can or cannot do. She cannot outshine her husband; she cannot explore a more expansive space than the one her husband, her family and her in-laws inhabit. And so the phantom within Arati insists that she resigns her job and that she retreats from her newly won space.

IX The creation of a creative *life*

I began this chapter by suggesting that we may regard a person's cognitive style as an abstraction, a schema characterizing her creative life. I also suggested that a cognitive style is itself an invention: an abstract artifact that the artificer creates. This implies that the invention of a cognitive style by an artificer is itself a creative act of production: the creation of a creative *life*.

So a biographical engagement between a consumer–biographer and an artificer–subject works two ways, has two purposes. First, the biographer excavates the artificer's cognitive style by examining the latter's creative life. This was the purpose of the case studies in this chapter of my various subjects. Second, the consumer–biographer can discover how the artificer created a personal creative life. In the first the biographical study is the means, the elucidation of a cognitive style the end. This is the goal we have pursued in this chapter so far. In the second, articulating the cognitive style is the means and elucidating how a creative life is created is the end. Let us pursue this second perspective further.

The picture that emerges is that in the case of the individual artificer creativity is a three-tiered affair. There is, first, the "primary" artifact that the artificer produces. In the case of Flannery O'Connor these were her short stories and novels; in the case of Jagadis Chandra Bose they were his discoveries of the optical properties of millimeter-length radio waves, the Boseian thesis, his plant physiological discoveries, and his instruments; for Amrita Sher-Gil they were her individual paintings; for Herbert Simon they were his theories and models of the human thinker; for Satyajit Ray these were his feature films, documentaries and shorts. Let us call these *first order* acts of creation.

For some artificers there are *second order* acts of creation entailing the invention of schemas (Chapter 9, XX–XXIV). These are especially visible in the realm of the arts but they can also be seen in the sciences (natural and artificial) and in engineering. We have seen, for example, Amrita Sher-Gil's schema for her Indian paintings and George Rodrigue's Cajun landscape schema. Robert Stephenson's tubular bridge form was a structural engineering schema while the stored program computing (SPC) principle invented by John von Neumann and his associates was a computational schema (Chapter 9, XXIV). Indeed, Donald Campbell's blind variation, selection retention (BVSR) model of the creative process (discussed in Chapter 9, IV) was a cognitive schema for theorizing about creative processes.

Schemas when especially powerful and universal in scope may become the epicenter of a paradigm. Darwin's natural selection schema as the core element of the Darwinian paradigm is an obvious example from the natural sciences. The SPC schema formed the core element of the computational paradigm (Dasgupta 2014a, pp. 108–133).

Finally we have a *third order* of individual creativity: the invention of cognitive style. This is what we have witnessed in this chapter. A cognitive style imbues the artificer with a uniqueness, a personal creative identity. It characterizes the artificer's creative life. Schemas may be essential components of cognitive styles but they are not all there are. For our protagonists in this chapter—O'Connor, Bose, Simon and Ray—it is not so much schemas that attract attention but entire compendia of cognitive features that comprise their respective styles.

11

THE PSYCHOHISTORIAN'S CONTRIBUTION

I Freud decoding Leonardo

In 1910 Sigmund Freud published his famous and controversial essay on Leonardo da Vinci (Freud 2001). While this was not the first application of psychoanalysis to historical figures (pp. 2–3) it was the earliest that would profoundly influence later writers, both those who were sympathetic to the psychoanalytical approach and those who were antipathetic to it. This study is often regarded as launching the twin activities of *psychohistory* and *psychobiography*.

Freud was not really interested in Leonardo for what his creative powers produced or in how they were produced (as a cognitive historian would); nor was he concerned with the specific form in which Leonardo's art developed (as an art historian would be). He accepted Leonardo's genius and the fact that the artist–engineer–scientist was a brilliant exemplar of the "Renaissance man." Rather, Freud's interest lay in Leonardo's *underachievement*, especially as an artist. Why was it, Freud asked, that Leonardo left so much of what he began incomplete? What was the reason for this "flaw of instability" in him? (p. 11).

Freud alluded to the explanations offered by Leonardo's later admirers: that it was a general characteristic of major artists; and that whether a work of art was unfinished or not depended in essence on whether the artist believed or declared it to be the case. Such excuses did not satisfy Freud. Valid though they may be, they did not tell the whole story. There were indeed other artists, Freud noted, who also struggled with a project, fled from it, and became indifferent to it. But this trait was manifested in the extreme in Leonardo (p. 11). And it demanded explanation.

Freud cited accounts left behind by Leonardo's contemporaries about the artist's legendary slowness: he took so long in painting *La Gioconda* ("Mona Lisa") that he could not bring it to completion soon enough to deliver it to Francesco del Giocondo who had commissioned it (p. 12). And yet there were the innumerable sketches and studies Leonardo left behind of almost "every *motif*" that appeared in his paintings (p. 13).

Leonardo was also a bundle of other contradictions. On the one hand the artist was noted for his "peaceableness," his tendency to avoid antagonism and controversy—he did not eat meat; he abhorred war and bloodshed—and yet he would witness the passage of criminals to their executions so that he could sketch their fear-induced, distorted features. And, of course, he earned his living as a military engineer, devising machineries of war for his various patrons and employers (p. 14).

There was also, Freud noted, Leonardo's "cool repudiation of sexuality" (p. 15). He was known to have lacked relationships with women. Indeed, Freud even doubted whether Leonardo's propensity to surround himself with boys and youth—including Francesco Melzi, his companion to the time of his death and trustee of his celebrated notebooks—extended to sexual activity (p. 19).

Thus, Freud revealed his real interest in Leonardo: to connect the particular nature of the latter's emotional and sexual life with his life as an artist and scientist (p. 19). And for Freud the crux of the connection lay in a statement Leonardo was said to have made: "One has no right to love or hate anything if one has not acquired a thorough knowledge of its nature" (quoted, p. 20). And so, Freud believed, this acquisition of knowledge became a substitute for loving itself (p. 22).

It is this connection between Leonardo's *thirst for knowledge* and his "flaw of instability" that Freud undertook to establish. In fact, he associated causally Leonardo's thirst for knowledge with his inability to complete his paintings.

There is nothing intrinsically *psychoanalytical* in this causal account. If anything, it is a hypothesis that would be of interest to the cognitive historian. She would want to test it in cognitive terms. She would begin with the thirst for knowledge as a given superneed—the "need to know"—as a root goal in order to understand any of Leonardo's works, be it a painting, a study of nature, or the design of a machine. She would strive to determine if the archival data was available to support or refute this hypothesis. The cognitive historian would want to trace the patterns of knowledge accessed in the course of such an endeavor. She may even strive to explain the larger pattern of Leonardo's multi-chambered studies of art, nature and artifact beginning with the superneed to know as the originating goal. Unveiling a trace of the connections between Leonardo's artistic, scientific and engineering works in terms of goals, knowledge and reasoning is exactly what the cognitive historian *would* be interested in. (Our investigation of a modern "Renaissance man," Herbert Simon, was precisely this kind of inquiry (Dasgupta 2003a), as discussed in earlier chapters of this book).

Freud, however, was *not* interested in this sort of inquiry. His hypothesis—that Leonardo's inability to complete his projects was causally connect to his thirst for knowledge—did *not* interest him. Rather, the question that drew his attention was: What was the source of his thirst for knowledge which manifested itself in this extreme tendency toward tardiness? The explanation must lie in some particular "disposition" (p. 24).

What disposition did Freud hope to find? The clue lay in the findings of his psychoanalytical studies that provided, in its theoretical formulations, certain expectations Freud sought to confirm in his study of Leonardo (p. 24). First, Freud expected that the source of this craving for knowledge lay in Leonardo's earliest childhood; and second, that it was reinforced by (sexual) instinctual forces. Here then was the *psychoanalytical* problem Freud posed for himself: to trace Leonardo's excessively intense instinct to investigate—a *neurosis*—to his childhood and earliest sexual instincts. To pursue this objective Freud must then bring his psychoanalytical methodology to Leonardo's case. The artist became his "patient."

II   The psychohistorian's craft

We will not pursue Freud's analysis any further since my aim is to illustrate the psychoanalytical strategy just to the level of detail that unveils the essence of the psychohistorian's (or more saliently, the psychobiographer's) craft. And, more importantly, to address the question:

> What light can psychohistory shed on creative phenomena—especially creative lives—that cognitive history cannot (or does not)?

According to psychoanalyst Erik Erikson (1959) the essence of the psychohistorical approach is to bring to bear what he called the *psychotherapeutic encounter* to the historical situation. As Erikson described it, such an encounter entails a "therapeutic" contract between the patient and a professional therapist. There is a complaint—a dysfunction or disturbance that the patient communicates verbally to the therapist and there are certain symptoms whereby the disturbance is manifested. The therapist attempts to construct the oetiology of the disturbance, a process called "anamnesis." She brings to bear various kinds of theoretical knowledge and procedures to this process. But in diagnosing the cause of the dysfunction the therapist also casts her net wider and brings the art of *interpretation* to the situation. In so doing she makes the patient a participant in the treatment process.

Complaint, anamnesis and interpretation, Erikson noted, form the very basis of the psychotherapeutic encounter. But, he pointed out, interpretation entails a substantial element of subjectivity. While a variety of methods are deployed to make the psychotherapeutic encounter objective, Erikson emphasized that the therapist has to incorporate a very definite sense of self-awareness, thus a basic element of subjectivity into the encounter (p. 76).

This scenario contains a strong historical element: the therapist both builds up a "case history" in the course of successive therapy sessions and reaches back to the patient's past, to his personal history—Erikson quotes R.G. Collingwood (1956): the past survives in the present. And with the caveat that the historian does not—cannot—correct events as he goes about recording them; the psychotherapeutic encounter is a historical one.

Just as the historicity of creative phenomena led to the idea of cognitive history (see Prologue), so also historicity in psychotherapy led to the psychohistorical approach, and other writers—historians, philosophers and psychoanalysts—have reiterated this point, some more forcefully than Erikson. Thus, to the philosopher Hans Meyerhoff (1987) the psychotherapeutic encounter is essentially a historical process in which, much like the historian who must interpret historical evidence and reconstruct the past as it survives in the present (Collingwood again), the therapist must draw upon his own emotional as well as intellectual, imaginative, moral and ideological, in addition to logical, resources to resolve the patient's distress (p. 21).

So what exactly does *psychohistory* entail? For one historian–psychoanalyst, Peter Loewenberg (1983) there are several essentials to the psychohistorical approach (pp. 15–16):

One. It appeals to the unconscious as revealed by such phenomena and symptoms as sublimation, slips and errors, accidents, dreams, neuroses, psychoses, and inhibitions. (The unconscious appealed to here is what Freud called the "dynamic unconscious," Ucs—and more commonly called the "subconscious"—not the "cognitive unconscious" of the cognitive scientist (see Chapter 7).)

Two. It stresses origins, reaching back to childhood, even infancy. It seeks always to connect the "present" reality of a given historical person to an earlier or earliest past.

Three. The theoretical basis of psychohistory is psychoanalysis, not just the body of ideas propounded by Freud and his immediate disciples but those of the many post-Freudians (as, e.g., described by Mitchell and Black 1995). As yet another writer, Saul Friedlander (1978, p. 11) comments, while the psychohistorian may legitimately seek other branches of science for explanation—psychology, neuroscience and genetics for instance—at the end of the day it is only psychoanalysis that affords the most appropriate theoretical framework for the psychohistorian. As such, psychohistory necessarily pays attention to such psychoanalytical concerns as aggression, fantasy and sexuality. The historian will need to pay attention to the typical symptoms of internal conflict such as bouts of depression, suicidal tendencies, visions and phobias; signs that, as Cushing Strout (1968) has pointed out, have prompted psychoanalytical inquiries into such figures as Martin Luther, Charles Darwin, John Stuart Mill, Wolfgang Goethe, William James and, indeed, Freud himself. In particular, the psychohistorian must reject the "myth of asexuality and innocence" in his subject.

It is important to note at this point that psychohistory has been subject to a great deal of criticism—by historians primarily—as the (psychoanalytically trained) intellectual historian Peter Gay (1985) pointed out, because of their belief that one cannot psychoanalyze the dead (p. 3). There were other auxiliary reasons, for example, the argument that for centuries commonsense reasoning, experience and honest-to-goodness scholarship had sufficed for historians; and even if one seeks psychological explanations then why not appeal to other psychologies than psycho-analysis? (p. 4). Gay's book *Freud for Historians* was a systematic and eloquent argu-ment against such charges, but informed by the caveat that psychoanalysis provided but one source of insights the historian should rely on.

Indeed, psychohistory as it has been practiced extended its scrutiny beyond the strictly psychological. Erik Erikson, among the most influential of late twentieth century psychoanalysts who turned his gaze to history and biography, cautioned his reader that in every stage of an individual's life cycle the latter's perspective of his infantile past is conditioned and influenced by social and institutional forces (Erikson 1958, p. 20). Erikson's celebrated studies of Martin Luther and Mahatma Gandhi treated both subjects within an integrated *psychohistorical–social* framework.

In the case of Gandhi Erikson sought to explain the origin and maturation of Gandhi's principle of militant nonviolence, *Satyagraha*. Here was, in fact, a problem of the birth of an idea, a problem in intellectual history but one a cognitive historian would also be much interested in. However Erikson's actual event of interest was a strike of cotton textile workers in 1918 in the Western Indian city of Ahmedabad, an event in which Gandhi employed to the full the technique of *Satyagraha* (includ-ing the deployment of the fast) that he had developed some years earlier in South Africa (Erikson 1969). Erikson was drawn to this event because he felt that it repres-ented what came to be called a "mid-life crisis" in Gandhi's life (he was in 1918 forty-eight years old) and marked the transition point between Gandhi the (already) historical figure and *a* "mahatma" ("great soul") and the Gandhi who became *the* India-wide Mahatma (p. 47).

My intent in referring to Erikson's *Gandhi's Truth* here is only to shed some further light (albeit inadequate because of brevity) on the method of psychohistory so that we can later contrast it to the method of cognitive history. In a long essay titled "On Psycho-Historical Evidence," Erikson discussed in some detail the meth-odological aspects and concerns of his study of Gandhi, and here I draw on this essay (Erikson 1975).

For his evidence, Erikson appealed to a variety of sources as any historian would, including biographies, memoirs, Gandhi's own writings and newspaper articles. Two key sources were surviving witnesses to the event (including the mill owner, a prominent industrialist, and his sister; they were on opposite sides of the conflict) and Gandhi's autobiography, published in 1927.

An Autobiography (Gandhi 1993) is of obvious importance in Erikson's work. He desired to study an event that took place when Gandhi was forty-eight, well into middle age. To this end he wished to determine the extent to which Gandhi's leadership quality that would manifest in the particular way it did was traceable to his earlier existence, and to chart the course of the development of the Mahatma's leadership. Erikson likened *An Autobiography* to the great "confessions" of St. Augustine and Jean-Jacques Rousseau—two books that inevitably appear in any discussion of autobiography (see, e.g., Anderson 2001). It was to play the role, at least in part, of the patient's verbal revelations in the psychotherapeutic encounter.

But a patient enters knowingly into the therapeutic situation, and all that he reveals is grist to the therapist's analytical–interpretative mill. By what frame of reference should an event or moment in an autobiography (granted that it may well have been written in a revelatory spirit) be regarded as psycho-historically valid? According to Erikson, a psychohistorically interesting item can emerge only after taking into account both that immediate moment and the overall trend, the person's life cycle as well as the communal dynamic (Erikson 1975, p. 137).

But in psychoanalysis the record does not stand on its objective own. There is also the psychoanalyst, the reviewer of the record along with his subjectivity. So also does the psychohistorian participate in the review of an autobiographical record. The psychohistorian, Peter Loewenberg (1983) notes, is as vulnerable to transference and counter-transference, anxiety and defense mechanisms as any other being. These may well influence her interpretation (p. 5). Yet, he states, the historian should turn these facets to his advantage and so too for Erikson. In inter-preting the historical subject the psychohistorian must take into account the stage *of his own life cycle* in which the autobiographical record is reviewed, his *own* life history, his own contemporaneous culture and the history of that culture (Erikson 1975, p. 142).

This self-awareness of the psychohistorian is not unique to the psychohistori-cal situation. Erikson pointed out that a psychohistorian's choice is very often rooted in the latter's own identity (p. 148). But this may be the case in the writing of history, historical biography or intellectual biography in general. Historian E.H. Carr (1964) in *What is History?*—his celebrated meditation on the nature of history—advised his reader to study as much the historian as the facts (p. 23). (I have elsewhere recorded my own identifications that prompted me to embark on my biographical study of the Indian science pioneer Sir Jagadis Chandra Bose (Dasgupta 2009, pp. 5–6)). And James Moore (1996, pp. 272–275) has reflected on his own predilections that led to his co-authorship of Darwin's biography.) However, in the "non-psychohistorical" situation the historian/biographer—and this includes the cognitive historian—*consciously attempts to factor out her anxieties and motivations.* If we are to believe Erik Erikson this can never be the case in psychohistory.

III   When is psychohistory justified?

The individual/social, subjective/objective tensions and complementarities dis-cussed above are thus relevant to all modes of historical inquiry. What motives a historical subject is driven by are all grist to the historian's mill. Nor are the historian's ideals and ideologies entirely invisible in historiography. One does not have to seek psychoanalytical explanations in all such cases (Strout 1968, p. 28). (Indeed, as I have noted above, historians skeptical of psychohistory would argue that psychoanalysis is not necessary in any case of historical writing.) Leaving aside the skeptics, the question is: *when* is one justified in seeking psychoanalytical explanation for an historical event and when is one not? *When is psychohistory justified?* In particular, in the realm of creative phenomena this question seems particularly relevant. For the psychohistorian any explanation that posits a rational account for how an artifact comes into being or how it evolves over time—the kind of explanation cognitive history endeavors to provide—is, to paraphrase Gerald Izenberg (1975), a shroud for some other thing (p. 140). What justification is there, Izenberg asks, for the psychohistorian to make this assertion, to wave aside the intellectual processes whereby historical subjects may have arrived at their ideas (or, in our language in this book, their artifacts) and postulate instead "unconscious impulses, phantasies, defenses or conflicts" to account for such phenomena (p. 140)? In partially answering this question Cushing Strout suggested that the historian may be so justified if the evidence reveals specific paradoxes produced by contradictory desires or unexpected or unwarranted affects, or when a person's self-image is out of joint with what he wishes his image to be (Strout 1968, p. 294).

The historian Gerald Izenberg (1975) has explored this matter more fully in the context of the history of ideas and though he does not contrast the psychoanalytical with the *cognitive* approach, much of what he says is of value to our issue, namely, the connection and contrast between cognitive history and psychohistory.

Izenberg pointed out that there are two kinds of criteria we use to suspect that a particular event, behavior or action demands psychoanalytical explanation. The first is when we discern a discordance between a subject's stated purpose and the means adopted to achieve this purpose—in other words, a discordance between ends and means. For AI researchers and some cognitive scientists, matching means to ends is a manifestation of rationality (see, e.g., Newell 1982, p. 98) and if we see no evidence of rationality (as thus interpreted) we may want to know why in terms of psychological probings. It is possible, of course (indeed, *very* possible) that because of limits to one's cognitive capacity or incomplete knowledge—*bounded rationality* (see Chapter 1, IV)—a person's choice of means was mistaken. Izenberg recognized this caveat: he did not use the term "bounded rationality" but it was clear that this concept was in his mind when he talked of insufficient information deployed in one's reasoning (Izenberg 1975, p. 142). But in the event the person's intellectual capacity is beyond doubt or when there is a *pattern* of contradictory mismatches between means and ends we may well suspect motives and beliefs other than what the subject may explicitly acknowledge.

This criterion is related to what the subject states to be her goals or purpose. For convenience let us call this the *local* criterion. The second criterion pertains to the person's action or behavior in a larger context. We may suspect something untoward in a person's behavior or action if it is found to deviate markedly from the relevant social or cultural norms. In this case, psychoanalytical explanations of such behavior or actions may be invoked because the behavior's inconsistency with what is normatively *expected* (p. 143)—assuming, that is, that the norms are internally consistent. We may term this the *global* criterion.

In sum, according to Izenberg's thesis, the crucial distinction that selects or rejects the psychohistorical approach is the distinction between rational and irrational behavior either in the local or global contexts.

This is not always an easy judgment to make, especially in the realm of creativity. For instance, as remarked, bounded rationality may make an action or behavior *seem* irrational whereas it may just be the best that can be achieved under the circumstances. Or the psychohistorian may jump into the fray too hastily just because an artificer deviated from the social/cultural norms. After all it is a fundamental characteristic of creative beings to *seek* to deviate from the norm (Gruber 1989), what I have referred to as the superneed to make history (Chapter 1, IV). So a particular creative act may both violate the order, coherence and internal consistency of the norms of the time *and yet* be explicable in non-psychoanalytical terms; for example, by exploring the needs/goals, reasoning, knowledge and style deployed by the artificer—the way of the cognitive historian, in other words.

On the other hand, if the origins of a creative act of production appears to deviate startlingly from the norms or the prevailing paradigm then explanations of how the goal/problem, the very root of the creative act may have arisen in the artificer's mind may well demand psychoanalytical probings. The strictly cognitive approach may be inadequate or even inappropriate.

The art historian E.H. Gombrich (1971), reflecting on the place of psychoanalysis in the history of art, discussed the "significance" of Picasso's poster *The Peace Dove* (1950). Every work of art, of course, has a private and a public meaning: there is what the viewer/consumer sees in it, and there is its personal meaning to the artificer. The public meaning of the dove as a symbol of peace is fairly obvious, but what of its meaning to Picasso? Here, the language of psychoanalysis may prove to be useful. Indeed, Gombrich appealed to it as he related the meaning of Picasso's painting the dove in relation to his father. Here, the cognitive–historical approach had nothing useful to contribute.

In the same essay Gombrich pointed to a far subtler problem in the history of art which psychoanalytical theory may serve to illuminate. This is the role of the consumer/viewer in the development of the artist's skill—what elsewhere he referred to as the "beholder's share" (Gombrich 1969, part 3). Gombrich described the development of the artist's representation of the female form from Botticelli's *The Birth of Venus* (c.1845) through Raphael's *Triumph of Galatea* (c.1514) to Titian's *The Rape of Europa* (1561), a period spanning some eighty years in which, he pointed out, there was a significant growth, not only in the artist's representational skill but also in the *beholder's capacity to make sense of the representation*. The development of an artistic style, according to Gombrich, is as much a function of the consumer/beholder's desire to participate in the work of art as in the artist's creative urge (p. 35). And he attributed this insight into the interplay of artist and beholder to the psychoanalyst Ernst Kris. For Kris (1952), the beholder's response to a work of art is multistage: there is, first, a recognition stage where the subject is familiarized. In the second stage the beholder identifies with the subject. Finally, the beholder identifies with the artist. The beholder creates or rather *re*-creates the work of art in her mind. The artist and the beholder become "co-creators" (Kris 1952, p. 56). (The concept of the *creative encounter* between artificer and consumer described in Chapter 3 was influenced by Kris's model.)

For Gombrich this insight of the psychoanalyst was invaluable, for without it certain aspects and developments in the history of art would be inexplicable. For instance, he compared the contemporaneous Venice of Titian's time with Shake-spearean London. It would not have been that the mind of the Londoner, of Shake-speare's audience was less sophisticated than that of Titian's Venetian public. Gombrich ascribed the contrast between Titian's "miracles" and the "stuffed dummies" that were Elizabethan portraits to the absence of the artist–beholder interplay in Shakespeare's London (Gombrich 1971, p. 36).

IV Complementary approaches?

A creative *life* (or for that matter a creative *movement*) in general entails many *individual* creative projects. Cognitive history is concerned with the origins and devel-opment of such projects—the birth and growth (ontogeny) of individual ideas within a creative movement as they may have occurred in individual minds. The cognitive approach is grounded in the intendedly (but boundedly) rational thought and purposeful work of the individual artificers. Cognitive explanations and under-standing are composite pictures built within the cognitive–historical framework (Chapter 1).

This may suffice to illuminate a particular creative act of production. Elsewhere, we have explored the computer pioneer Maurice Wilkes's invention in 1951 of the principle of microprogramming for designing the computer's control unit (Dasgupta 1994). For Wilkes, this was a *private* problem that no other computer designer of the time had "seen." (Admittedly, there were not many such designers in those halcyon days of early computing.) As I explained (pp. 69–71), Wilkes's "seeing" this problem lay in his personal philosophy of design, compounded of a desire for regularity and simplicity of form with the practical need for reliability of computer components. In this instance the origins of the project had clear empirical roots—in computer technology itself. One need not appeal to psychohistory.

On the other hand if a creative phenomenon is grounded in the artificer's emo-tional *conflicts* one may indeed need to examine that individual's internal conflicts, identity struggles, identifications and other aspects of the psyche (Izenberg 1975, p. 150). And the more idiosyncratic the conditions under which an idea takes shape or a problem is solved the greater the justification for the psychohistorical approach. Here then, is a scenario in which cognitive history and psychohistory are *com-plementary* to each other: they do not compete, they are not alternative modes of history writing; each has its own appropriate place for application.

We may go further. Insofar as such concepts as *identity* and *identification* derive from psychoanalysis, it is entirely possible to *assimilate* these concepts—and to that extent, psychoanalytical theory—*into* cognitive history (see Chapter 4). In my study of the nineteenth century intellectual and creative movement in India called the

"Bengal Renaissance," I suggested that the individual creative encounters of a remarkable group of Indian Bengalis contributed collectively, over the course of the century, to a new shared *cognitive identity*, and that this identity effected a cognitive *revolution* in nineteenth century India (Dasgupta 2007, Chapter 1 and Epilogue). This new identity and the revolution it engendered would carry over to the twentieth century. Here I "appropriated" the psychoanalytical concept of identity and assimilated it into the framework of cognitive history.

A particular creative life may be characterized by a certain theme that threads its way through many creative acts of production through the course of that artificer's life. The cognitive historian may undertake explanations of the individual acts of production with that theme as an initial given: a root goal, a superneed. But an explanation of *why* this theme plays such a fundamental role in that artificer's life may demand psychoanalytical inquiry.

My study of the scientist Jagadis Chandra Bose serves to illustrate several aspects of the complementarity of cognitive history and psychohistory. A fundamental theoretical idea that I called the "Boseian thesis" underpinned a great part of Bose's scientific work. The thesis is that "there is no fundamental demarcation between living and nonliving matter." Our account traced the particular *logic* that led to his formulation of this (extremely controversial) thesis in cognitive historical terms (Dasgupta 2009, Chapter 4). The Boseian thesis *as a given* also served to explain, in our account, why Bose turned from the physics of radio waves to plant physiology and biophysics, and why he pursued relentlessly one series of experiments after another in the realm of plant responsiveness for the last thirty years of his life (Dasgupta 2009, Chapter 5). I even connected the Boseian thesis to a form of pan-vitalism and to the monistic theme in Hindu philosophy. But in fact this thesis, an *idée fixe*, demands a further explanation which cognitive history alone cannot provide. Were there deeper motivational, emotional reasons for Bose to cling to a doctrine that, in strictly scientific terms, was at profound odds with the way physicists and biologists of the time thought about life and non-life?

Bose himself provided some hints on this in his various writings. In one of his books written in 1927 when he was nearly seventy, he recapitulated his researches on the relationship between the living and nonliving, and then confessed how he came to understand the message of his remote ancestors—that only those who perceive a unity in the manifold phenomena of the universe can attain "eternal Truth" (Bose 1927b, p. 64). Perhaps—and here is a conjecture—his *idée fixe*, the Boseian thesis, was a vindication of the ancient glory of the Motherland, a glory that had been forgotten. The matter begs for a psychohistorical inquiry.

The complementarity between the cognitive and psychoanalytical approaches to Bose is well illustrated by contrasting my study of Bose's scientific life, an exercise in cognitive history with the psychologist and social critic Ashis Nandy's (1995) analysis of Bose. In my work we deal in considerable detail with the origins and development of Bose's physics, the ontogeny of the Boseian thesis, his metamorphosis from physicist to plant biophysicist and the evolution of his plant researches (Dasgupta 2009).

We make mention several times of the motivational, emotional and (non-cognitive) psychological aspects that appeared in the course of Bose's science. An example was his emotional dependence on the poet–philosopher and (later) Nobel laureate Rabindranath Tagore, especially between 1900 and 1902 when the Boseian thesis was being formulated. Other instances were his nationalism and his ambivalence toward the British who were both his masters (politically) and his peers (scientifically), on whom he depended for both logistical and financial support and intellectual sustenance.

There was also a curious episode that Bose would relate to Tagore. On the very eve of a crucial lecture he was to deliver in May 1901 at the Royal Institution in London, a time when he was very tense and apprehensive, he had a dream in which an emaciated, wretched figure in the Hindu widow's garb appeared before him. She had come to receive and welcome him, she said, and then the image dissolved. The effect was immediate, Bose wrote to Tagore: all his uncertainty and apprehension disappeared. The next day he spoke at the Royal Institution before a large audience at the famed Friday Evening Discourse as if he was an altogether changed man (Dasgupta 2009, p. 145).

My study of Bose alludes to this dream-woman briefly as a possible representation of the Motherland that so haunted Bose. But clearly more is demanded of an interpretation of this dream. In particular Ashis Nandy has explored in some detail the character of Bose's mother and his relationship with her. Nandy referred to the clash between the two when she refused to let the young Bose cross the seas to go to England for advanced studies (though she later relented). She was also reported to exhibit symptoms of obsession–compulsion, and give vent to outbursts of rage whenever her particular standards of ritualistic finickiness were not met. Nandy posited a definite ambivalence in Bose's relationship to the mother who was widowed in 1892 and dies in 1894 (Nandy 1995, pp. 27–28). Nandy did not write of Bose's dream of 1901 but it would be of interest to see what he would have made of this dream in the light of the mother–son relationship on which he wrote. But then, whatever the interpretation of that dream, it seems to have no bearing on any of the cognitive–historical aspect of Bose's scientific life.

Nandy's analysis of what he called Bose's "alternative science" is, in fact, very much a psychohistorical study. He alludes to such issues as the "ego–ideal" (p. 28), obsessive–compulsive traits and "aggressive ritualism" (p. 27), inferiority complex (p. 24), the image of a "rejecting mother," "aggression" (p. 27), identification with the father (p. 30), of anxiety induced by "role confusion," preoccupation with violence, "aggressive fantasies" (p. 31), the teacher as father-figure (p. 36), identity-formation and self-definition, "sublimation" and "ego-defences" (p. 37), compulsive behavior (p. 42), "oral aggressiveness" (p. 51), guilt complex, and "unconscious destruction fantasies" (p. 71). We are clearly reading the language of psychoanalysis. "Object relations" in the psychoanalytical sense (Brenner 1974, pp. 97 *et seq*; Mitchell and Black 1995, pp. 192 *et seq*)—an individual's attitude toward "objects" (persons or things)—dominate.

Our respective studies of Bose offer an example par excellence of the complementarity of cognitive history and psychohistory. Nandy's analysis offers insight into Jagadis Bose's *cultural identity* in the broad Eriksonian sense, an identity that was apparently shaped by the Bengali–Indian cultural geography Bose was nurtured in, and the historical context of living under colonial rule in a time of ever-increasing Indian nationalism. According to Nandy it was this identity that Bose *brought to his science*. For Nandy, Bose's creativity *began* with an already formed identity; the nature of that creativity as a cognitive enterprise held no interest for him. On the other hand my study delineated the development of Bose's *scientific identity*. It was an exercise in cognitive history in which the "object relations" Nandy wrote about were irrelevant. Bose's science was almost entirely explicable within the confines of the cognitive–historical space, with almost no need to appeal to the psychohistorical space Nandy explored.

But, as we have discussed elsewhere (Dasgupta 2014b), Nandy's psychohistorical study also demonstrates the pitfalls of this approach in creativity studies, especially in the realms of scientific and technological creativity. Bose's psychohistory (or psychobiography) *à la* Nandy ignores Bose's science entirely. It is difficult to imagine how a serious examination of *any* creative phenomenon can ignore the very *stuff* of that phenomenon.

12

OF CREATIVE MOVEMENTS

I   Inventing a mentality

It seems fitting to devote this final chapter to our third kind of creative phenomena (see Prologue). Whereas the act of creation focuses on the single artifact (and its associated artificer and consumer), and the creative life engages with the single artificer, the *creative movement* embraces multiple artificer–artifact–consumer three-somes, sometimes active synchronically, sometimes diachronically. This *multiplicity* of artificer–artifact–consumer complexes is one of the necessary features of a crea-tive movement.

Temporally, a creative movement may be active over a relatively short period of time, as brief as a year, or it may span an extended period, perhaps decades or longer, perhaps even longer than that of its artificers' or consumers' individual life spans. So the time *duration* is not a stipulative parameter in the creative movement.

What makes something a movement is not always easy to discern. Sometimes its participants may be aware that they are part of an ongoing, evolving, historically significant movement, other times this awareness may only be realized after the movement has reached a certain zenith, or even after it has tapered off.

But the second *and most fundamental* feature of the creative movement is this: each artificer may well be engaged in the production of a distinct kind of artifact that attracts a distinct group of consumers. And collectively the artificers *invent a mentality* that is at the very least H-original but may well turn out to be C-original. *This shared mentality is the supreme product of a creative movement.* It is an abstract arti-fact that enters as a cultural element into one or more communities.

Now, historians are quite familiar with the idea of mentality. In particular, since the 1930s a school of influential French historians called the *Annales* School have emphasized the significance of *l'histoire des mentalités*, embracing what is conceived intellectually and what is felt emotionally, in the practice of their craft (Brett 2002, pp. 124–125). Mentality as historians broadly understand it has to do with *commonality of mind*: a sharing of emotions, beliefs and ideas by a community (Ray 2003, p. 36).

II Shared mentality = shared cognitive style

Of course, a mentality does not *have* to be shared. We can certainly imagine an individual with a highly idiosyncratic mentality that seemingly sets him or her apart from all others. But such an individualistic mentality of itself does not produce a *movement*. For that to happen at the very least an original mentality originating in an individual must be transmitted or disseminated to others within a community. So our interest in the context of creative movements must lie in the nature of *shared* mentalities.

Actually, we have already encountered the notion of individualistic idiosyncrasy in our discussion of *cognitive style* (Chapter 10). Recall that cognitive style refers to a pattern or regularity underpinning an artificer's acts of production in the course of her creative life. Thus, cognitive style refers to certain features of an artificer's way of thinking, reasoning and doing that are idiosyncratic to her and thus establish her identity as a creative being. As I noted (in Chapter 10), an artificer's cognitive style is itself a *schema* that abstracts the common features from her multiple acts of production.

Let us postulate that a shared mentality *is a shared cognitive style* characterizing the creative lives of a community of artificers. To recognize and understand a creative movement is to recognize and understand a shared (H- and/or C-original) cognitive style. The question is: How does an original cognitive style come to be shared in the making of creative movements?

We consider here three historical case studies, taken from very different cultural domains of the creative tradition: one from the realm of computer science, the second from the realm of religion—the former set in the late twentieth century in Europe and America, the latter in nineteenth century India—and the third from the domain of craft making as practiced in a part of Louisiana in the late twentieth century.

III The structured programming movement

This is a story that involves the interaction between three kinds of abstract artifacts: computer *programs*, programming *languages* and programming *methodology*. For those less initiated in the vocabulary and ways of computing, here are brief but (I hope) adequate working definitions of these classes of artifacts.

> Computer program: The precise and unambiguous specification of a procedure designed to solve a particular problem such that the execution of this procedure by an agent (a human being or a computer) effects the solution to the problem.

> Programming language: A system of notation that obeys rules of syntax (grammar) and semantics (meaning) in which programs can be specified such that an agent (human or computer) having knowledge of these rules can carry out the execution of programs written in the language.

> Programming methodology: The logic and theory of the methods by which computer programs can be systematically designed.

So a program in a particular language is a piece of *text* that is, so to speak, a call for action. And an agent knowing the language can execute or *interpret* the program. The result is a computational *process* that converts the textual call for action into an actual piece of action. Again, the interpreting agent may be a human being or a computer. Finally, the design of a program is a non-trivial *cognitive* process. The study of such design processes is called "programming methodology", and since a particular design method is itself a human invention, program design methods are also abstract artifacts: they do not obey the laws of physical nature.

The *structured programming (SP) movement* entailed the participation of these three classes of computational artifacts.

IV   Origins of the SP movement

The story properly begins in 1965. That year a Dutch mathematician-turned-computer scientist named Edsger Dijkstra posed a certain problem: *How can one acquire confidence that a computer program produces the result the programmer intended it to produce?* (Dijkstra 1979a).

Dijkstra's dilemma lay in two conflicting propositions: (a) That humans have limited cognitive capacity (p. 5); and (b) that programs can be extremely complex entities. And so, how can we, with our limited cognitive capabilities cope with such complexity and ensure that our programs are correct?

There was nothing startling or original about this question. By the mid-1960s extremely large and complex industrial-grade programs had been designed and implemented and were being used. But the conventional wisdom for demonstrating that such programs did what they were supposed to do was by empirically *testing* them. That is, by executing a program with prepared "test data" as its inputs and predicted outputs, and checking that the program's execution produced results that matched the predicted outputs.

But Dijkstra was dissatisfied with conventional wisdom. He offered a simple but realistic *thought experiment*. Suppose a programmer, believing his (tested) program to be correct, "runs it" on a certain input. Suppose further that the programmer has no independent and computationally efficient way of checking the output. What reason then does he have in believing that the program's execution on this particular input was correct?

For example, consider a program that generates all the prime numbers less than some "input" number x. The programmer then selects a number, say 100, mentally calculates all the prime numbers less than 100, and tests the program with $x = 100$ as input. Suppose the program's outputs are identical to his calculated outputs. He then believes the program to be correct. He then "runs" the program with a very large number as x, say 10,000. He has no independent (and efficient) way of determining whether the numbers generated as output are indeed all the prime numbers less than 10,000. So how would he conclude that the program's output is indeed correct?

This is, in fact, a special instance of what philosophers of science call the "problem of induction": that no matter how many confirmations are obtained for an empirical theory there is no guarantee that the theory is true, for there may be some instance "out there" that violates the theory that we do not know (and may never know). It was this problem of induction that led philosopher of science Karl Popper (1965, 1968) to famously conclude that induction can never prove a theory in science, since no amount of confirming instances can ever *prove* the truth of a theory (though a single *disconfirming* evidence suffices to *falsify* it).

Dijkstra drew an analogy between the programmer's situation and that of the mathematician who desires to prove the truth of a theorem. And while freely acknowledging that a mathematical proof may itself be faulty—*its* correctness may demand a further proof, and so on, *ad infinitum*—Dijkstra argued that despite its deficiencies, mathematical reasoning offers an exemplary model of how the cognitively limited mind/brain can cope with complex structures (p. 5).

Dijkstra's specific analogy lay in the realm of what he would later call the "intellectual management of complexity." The mathematician manages complexity by resorting to a time-honored technique: *Divide et impera* (Divide and rule) (p. 5). The mathematician has at her disposal a body of axioms and previously proven theorems. Her goal is to prove a theorem, and she manages this problem by dividing the proof into parts. First, propose and prove smaller, relatively simpler propositions (called "lemmas") which are then used to prove more complex propositions and then, eventually, the goal theorem.

The programmer's situation is similar, Dijkstra suggested. The programmer begins his task with the primitive statements of a programming language and a library of previously constructed programs (called "subroutines"). His goal is to construct a program and demonstrate that it is correct. Here, Dijkstra departs from the ways of the mathematician: rather than prove that a given theorem is correct, he proposed that the principle of divide and rule is applied to the *construction* of the program in a stepwise fashion that guarantees *by construction* that it does what it is supposed to do. Thus, Dijkstra proposed the following steps:

1   Subdivide the overall computational task into a set of parts.
2   Develop complete functional specifications of the individual parts.
3   Demonstrate that the goal problem is solved provided that the parts of the program satisfy their respective specifications.
4   Construct the individual parts to meet the specifications.

Now, the individual parts may themselves be still rather complex, in which case each may have to be *refined* or *decomposed* into subparts. This would mean that step [4] would itself be implemented *recursively* as steps [1]–[3]. And this recursive decomposition would continue till the subparts are sufficiently primitive to be expressed directly in terms of the primitive statements of the programming language and/or the library components. No further decomposition is then necessary.

Collectively, the procedure Dijkstra offered combined the principles of *abstraction, refinement* and *hierarchy*. Abstraction lay in that steps [1] and [2] would identify parts and reveal only those features of the parts needed to carry out step [3]. Refinement lay in the process stipulated in step [4]: details abstracted away in step [3] are revealed during refinement. And the overall iterative conduct of the four steps led to the hierarchical progression of the program from a more abstract to a more concrete form—what would also be called "top-down" development.

Dijkstra's creativity lay in that he *invented an analogy* between the mathematician's task and the programmer's task. By this I mean that based on a schema in his belief/knowledge space for what we may call "mathematical reasoning" he constructed *a new schema* for program design that was structurally similar to the former. But the reader familiar with the ways of mathematics will also realize that Dijkstra extracted only one element of the mathematical reasoning schema: the principle of divide-and-conquer as the source of his analogy. (After all, there is much more to mathematical reasoning than this principle.)

Precisely what pattern of reasoning went into this invention we cannot say. But we have a clue in his remark that, in his view, this technique (that is, the four-step procedure outlined above) constituted a fundamental pattern for human reasoning and understanding; thus a technique that might be promising for the problem of concern to programmers (p. 6). So it might seem that the divide-and-conquer principle was *extracted* from his mathematical reasoning schema, *generalized* into a "basic pattern" of reasoning and then *instantiated* into a program design schema. (Scientists, of course, do this as a matter of course: from a particular observation they hypothesize a general principle, then predict a particular consequence which then becomes an object of observation.)

Now Dijkstra, like all other well-trained programmers of that time (the mid-1960s), possessed a much more elaborate *programming schema system* as part of his cognitive–historical space. Chunks of this would be publicly shared with other programmers—as parts of a shared (Kuhnian) programming paradigm. His new schema for program design would then be *linked* to his own larger programming schema system (and become a new constituent of this system within his belief/knowledge space), and perhaps enter as a constituent of the belief/knowledge spaces of the more perceptive of the readers of his 1965 paper.

But Dijkstra had more to say in this same paper. His concern for coping with complexity also entailed the problem of increasing the *clarity* of program structures—what we would now call "greater transparency." Toward this concern a necessary feature of the parts identified and specified in steps 1–3 of his procedure is what he called the "principle of non-interference" (p. 6). For instance, in conducting step 3 the assumption is that the correct functioning of the whole program can be demonstrated in terms of the functional specifications of the parts only (step 2) and not their internal workings. And in step 4 this same principle of non-interference may reappear, for the assumption is that the construction and refinement of each part does not depend on the construction/refinement of the other parts (ibid.). In other words, the parts should be *modules* that fit together by way of their respective external behaviors and should not interfere with one another.

Thus, it was important, according to Dijkstra, that the programming language in which the program would finally be expressed should support the principle of non-interference; that is, the language should explicitly *constrain* the programmer to using the language in a disciplined manner so as to support the principle of non-interference.

Unfortunately, Dijkstra stated, there was one common statement type in most programming languages of the time that worked against this principle and, concomitantly, against the desire for program clarity. This was the **goto** statement, a language feature that allowed one program part to "interfere" with the inner workings of another program part in an undisciplined fashion. Thus, he suggested, rather tentatively, that language designers should "try to do away with the goto statement" (p. 8).

It took Dijkstra three more years to make this into a *diktat*. In a letter to the editor of a major computing journal published in 1968, he proposed that the **goto** statement should be eliminated from programming practice; that it should be banished from all programming languages (Dijkstra 1968).

His argument in support of this proposition appealed once more to his theme of the brain's cognitive limitations in coping with complexity. He now located one of the sources of program complexity: our intellectual powers, he noted, are adapted to the mastery of static structures and are less adapted to the comprehension of dynamic processes. A program is a static piece of *text*, written and read as any other text, in linear fashion as it unfolds in space. The computation it evokes is a dynamic process that unfolds in time, and what we desire is that the *temporal ordering of the dynamic process preserves the spatial ordering of the text*. The problem with the **goto** statement is that its uncontrolled use violently disrupts this static–dynamic, space–time, text–process correspondence.

From a historical perspective it would soon become clear that Dijkstra's 1965 paper augmented with his 1968 letter to the editor put forth the fundamentals of what came to be called structured programming. Dijkstra (1979b) also coined the term as the title of a paper presented in a NATO-sponsored conference and then, most influentially as the lead monograph titled "Notes on Structured Programming" in a book titled *Structured Programming* (1972) co-authored by Dijkstra, an Englishman, C.A.R. Hoare and a Norwegian, O-J. Dahl (1972). The impact of "Notes" was such that it was this, rather than his 1965 paper, that we must recognize as the founding document of the SP movement.

Curiously, the term "structured programming" never appeared anywhere in the text of "Notes." So what exactly *did* Dijkstra mean by the term? In fact, it referred to two things: as applied to *programs*, and as applied to *program development*. Structured programming as a method of program development was, in fact, laid out in the form of the four-step procedure proposed in his 1965 paper. In "Notes" Dijkstra elaborated greatly on this procedure with examples. As for programs, Dijkstra argued that a *well-structured program* was one that was composed out of a limited set of statement types that preserved the correspondence between text, occupying space and process spread over time. The **goto** statement has no presence amid this set of statements.

V   How SP became a shared cognitive style

For an event, an idea or an action to generate a movement it must influence others; it must become consequential. Dijkstra had invented a cognitive style: a way of thinking about the craft of programming. One of its components, the idea of "**goto**-less programming" was influenced, by his own account (Dijkstra 1968, p. 148), by others before him. Still, overall, the *idea* of structured programming as Dijkstra elaborated in great detail in "Notes" must be deemed as H-original, if we are to go by the opinions of his contemporaries. For example, the American Donald Knuth (1974), arguably one of the most influential computer scientists of the time, would remark that anyone who read Dijkstra's monograph, "Notes on Structured Programming," published in 1974 would experience a kind of epiphany (p. 261).

Knuth's comment suggests a creative encounter (Chapter 4) between Dijkstra as artificer and Knuth as consumer. But Knuth's 1974 paper (on which more later) was part of a phenomenon that we may call a case of *cooperative creative encounters* in which a small number of computer scientists *participated as both artificers and consumers*. It was by way of these multiple, cooperative creative encounters that SP became a creative movement.

This came about because in his concern with the management of complexity Dijkstra was not alone. There were others of a like-minded disposition with whom he was in extremely close professional contact. For, in the late 1960s Dijkstra was a member of a "working group" on programming languages (named WG2.1) under the auspices of the International Federation for Information Processing (IFIP), a world-wide "United-Nations-like" organization. WG2.1 had been charged with the design and development of a new "universal" programming language as a successor to Algol 60 developed at beginning of the decade. The history of this new language, named Algol 68, has been recounted elsewhere (Dasgupta 2018a, Chapter 1). Of relevance to our present story is that among the members of WG2.1, along with Dijkstra, there were at least two other computer scientists who dissented strongly with the line of thinking the rest of the working group were espousing. The shared concern of these dissenters was the matter of the complexity of the new proposed language Algol 68.

The second of the dissenters was Niklaus Wirth; the third was C.A.R. Hoare. There were others (as we will note) who belong to this story, though not as members of WG2.1. And our understanding of how SP emerged as a movement rests on appreciating the *interactions* among these scientists in what we can only describe as a constellation of mutually cooperative creative encounters.

By the end of the 1960s Niklaus Wirth had resigned from WG2.1 and was pursuing his own quest for a successor to Algol 60. He was in search, as he would write later, of a language that would include just those features he deemed essential and would exclude all features that might prove difficult to implement (Wirth 1985). Like Dijkstra he was in search of simplicity. But while Dijkstra's search led *primarily* to a contribution to programming methodology—though he was profoundly language-conscious, he was not in the business of systematic language design—Wirth's quest was *primarily* in the domain of programming language design and implementation. Wirth's place in the annals of computer science lay as an enormously influential designer of programming languages.

Wirth's search entailed a succession of languages, some designed with collaborators (Wirth and Hoare 1966; Wirth and Weber 1966a, 1966b) others designed by himself (Wirth 1968), arriving, in 1971, in the design and implementation of the language he named Pascal (Wirth 1971a, 1971b).

And if Dijkstra the programming methodologist was language-conscious, Wirth the language designer was as profoundly methodology-conscious. In 1971, the same year he announced Pascal, he published a paper on developing programs using a technique he called *stepwise refinement* in which he used Pascal notation without mentioning the name of the language (Wirth 1971c). Wirth's "stepwise refinement" was in fact Dijkstra's "structured programming." This was not an instance of simultaneous "parallel" invention or discovery as sometimes happens in the annals of science and technology. Wirth's paper both refers to Dijkstra's (1969) original unpublished version of "Notes on Structured Programming" and acknowledges the benefit of his discussions with Dijkstra (p. 227). Interestingly, however, Dijktsra's published "Notes" (1972) acknowledges several computer scientists but not Wirth. It seems reasonable to assume that here was a case of a creative encounter with Dijkstra the artificer, SP the (abstract) artifact, and Wirth the consumer; but in his persona as language designer, Wirth was the artificer and Pascal was the artifact. In his exposition of the method of stepwise refinement Wirth (1971c) seemed to have *assimilated* SP into his belief/knowledge space and had combined it with Pascal: this paper was an exposition of the same cognitive style as Dijkstra's but couched in "Pascalese." Dijkstra and Wirth were sharing a cognitive style, enriched now with a language that was a tool for structured programming.

C.A.R. Hoare was another of the WG2.1 members who had sharply dissented over Algol 68. Like Dijkstra and Wirth, Hoare's concern about the programming craft spanned both language and methodological issues, but his most original contribution within these domains lay in his espousal of an explicitly mathematical view of programming: in 1969 he published what would become a seminal paper on the axiomatic foundations of programming that was as at least as consequential as Dijkstra's "Notes" (Hoare 1969). Hoare began this paper with the bald announcement that programming was a *mathematical* science. And just as a mathematical discipline begins with a set of axioms and definitions from which further propositions (theorems) are logically deduced, so also a programming language is characterized in terms of definitions, axioms and rules of deductions—collectively forming the mathematical "laws" of programming—using which the behavior of a program (what it does in execution) can be logically deduced. The logic of programming as laid out by Hoare came to be known as "Hoare logic."

So while Dijkstra had drawn an analogy with the mathematical approach in constructing his method of structured programming, Hoare conceived of programming as a mathematical craft. Most strikingly, the concern Dijkstra had expressed with matching static program text with dynamic program execution, was manifested also in Hoare's thinking though in a slightly different way: all that was required to deduce a program's dynamic behavior during execution was captured by the program text itself along with the mathematical laws governing the language in which the program was expressed.

Hoare had previously collaborated in 1966 with Wirth in the development of a successor to Algol 60 that they called "Algol X" (Wirth and Hoare 1966)—a language that eventually led to Wirth's Pascal. In his methodological paper on "stepwise refinement" Wirth (1971c) had acknowledged Hoare's contribution to his line of thinking. Clearly there was a close exchange of ideas between them as there was between Wirth and Dijkstra. We now find evidence of a creative encounter between Hoare the artificer, his mathematical laws of programming as artifact and Wirth as consumer in the publication by Wirth (1973) of a slim but elegant book titled *Systematic Programming: An Introduction* in which Wirth laid out the principles of abstraction, hierarchy and refinement—the SP approach, in other words—as would apply in composing Pascal programs. Along with SP Wirth showed how Hoare logic could be used in deducing the behavior of Pascal programs. That same year Hoare and Wirth (1973) published a lengthy paper that presented the mathematical laws governing almost the entirety of the Pascal language.

It seems fair to claim that by 1973 structured programming as a cognitive style had firmly emerged, situated primarily in the work by Dijkstra, Hoare and Wirth. Each had produced C-original artifacts. Each was a C-creative artificer. We have also seen evidence of a creative encounter between Dijkstra as artificer and Wirth as consumer; and between Hoare as artificer and Wirth as consumer. Wirth in turn was more than a "mere" consumer of the others' works: he was, of course, a profoundly influential language designer/artificer in his own right—in addition to Pascal he would later design another important language called Modula (Wirth 1977). In *Systematic Programming* (1973) he had demonstrated how the principles of abstraction, hierarchy and refinement and Hoare logic could be integrated into a unified approach to programming in Pascal. Indeed, *Systematic Programming* was the first elementary *textbook* embodying the principles of SP as conceived by Dijkstra, Hoare and Wirth. It was the first exposition of this shared cognitive style.

There were at least two other creative encounters with Dijkstra as artificer we must note. The book *Structured Programming* co-authored by Dahl, Dijkstra and Hoare began with Dijkstra's "Notes on Structured Programming." The second and third chapters were by Hoare (1972) and Dahl and Hoare (1972) respectively.

Hoare's monograph was titled "Notes on Data Structuring" and the Dahl–Hoare chapter was on "Hierarchical Program Structures." Both monographs built on the principles of abstraction, hierarchy and refinement Dijkstra had espoused and articulated in great detail in "Notes." Hoare's chapter focused on how these same principles had implications in the design of *data structures*—the technical term in computer science for the ways in which complex data objects could be represented in programming languages. The Dahl–Hoare chapter explored the principles of hierarchy and abstraction in the context of a well-known language for computer simulation applications called SIMULA designed by Dahl and his collaborators (Dahl, Myrhaug and Nygaard 1968). The imprint of Dijkstra's "Notes" on these monographs is explicitly acknowledged by Hoare in the preface to this book. He records that his chapter on data structuring describes how Dijkstra's principles can be applied to data structure design; and that the monographs by (mainly) Dahl and Hoare provides a synthesis of the principles of the two earlier chapters.

VI   Characterizing SP as a shared cognitive style

As remarked in Chapter 10, an artificer's cognitive style is some discernible pattern of thinking and behavior across her creative life. A *shared* cognitive style is an expression of a mentality common to a community of artificers. In the case of SP we can describe it along the following lines.

Structured programming was a cognitive style that emerged between circa 1965 and circa 1973 primarily in the minds of Edsger Dijkstra, Nicklaus Wirth and C.A.R. Hoare.

(I)   Its domain was the craft of programming.

(II)   Its goal was to manage and control the complexity of both program structure and program development so as to preserve a close correspondence at each stage of program design, between the (static) program text and the (dynamic) computational process resulting from the program's execution: a correspondence between "program in space" and "process in time."

(III)   The methodological means to achieve this goal is to develop a program (and its associated data structures) in a fundamentally top-down, recursively unfolding, hierarchical manner involving (a) the twin principles of abstraction and hierarchy; such that (b) in any stage of this process each distinct program part satisfies the single-entry, single-exit (SNSX) property.

(IV)   A necessary corollary to this goal and this methodological means is the enlisting and deployment of a programming language that actively supports the means.

(V)   As a desideratum in support of (IV), the programming language should enable the programmer (artificer) and/or program reader (consumer) to use the methods of mathematical reasoning to demonstrate the program text-generating process correspondence.

VII   How SP became a movement

Structured programming emerged from the preoccupations of a tiny set of academic computer scientists into the wider realm of computing as other computer scientists from both academia and industry pondered its nature and implications. SP became an abstract artifact that drew the attention of other consumers who assimilated it into their belief/knowledge spaces and who, in turn, were stimulated by it to become artificers in their own right. The December 1973 issue of a widely read and respected "trade" periodical called *Datamation* (now extinct) carried a series of short articles by authors from the industrial sector (Baker and Mills 1973; Donaldson 1973; McCracken 1973; Miller and Lindamood 1973). The same year, Richard Conway and David Gries published an elegant textbook showing how the SP style could be used to write programs in a version of PL/1, a widely-used commercial programming language invented in IBM (Conway and Gries 1973). This was an exercise in *mutual adaptation* between two abstract artifacts—methodology and language—that had not been originally "made for each other."

In fact, there were signs of the making of a movement even as Dahl, Dijkstra, Hoare and Wirth were evolving SP. In particular, Dijkstra's *diktat* of banishing the **goto** statement provoked an enormous amount of interest. Some supported him (Hopkins 1972), some contested him (Wulf 1972). Some explored the design of programming languages that excluded the **goto** from its features (Wulff, Russell and Haberman 1971).

There were also the more theoretically inclined computer scientists who concerned themselves with the mathematics of structured programming *à la* Hoare. Some desired to show that one could mechanically and systematically transform "**goto**-present" programs into "**goto**-less" programs (Ashcroft and Manna 1971). Others explored in more detail the mathematical principles or laws governing the structured programming style (Mills 1972).

Arguably (and characteristically) the most sustained and thorough inquiry into the role of the **goto** in structured programming was by Donald Knuth, among the most influential and creative computer scientists in what I have elsewhere called the second age of computer science (Dasgupta 2018a)—from *c.*1970 to *c.*1990. First, in 1971, in collaboration with his Stanford colleague Robert Floyd he argued the case for avoiding the **goto** (Knuth and Floyd 1971). Three years later, in response to the book *Structured Programming* by Dahl, Dijkstra and Hoare (1972) Knuth published a lengthy monograph in the journal *Computing Surveys*, provocatively titled "Structured Programming *with* **goto** Statements." Here was a clear case of a creative encounter between Dijkstra as artificer and Knuth as consumer: Knuth, by his own admission was profoundly affected by it. Yet the book transformed this consumer into a *critical* and *contesting* artificer: Knuth argued the case for how and when one might effectively deploy the **goto** yet retain the spirit of the structured programming style (Knuth 1974). And he would conclude that SP had nothing to do with eliminating the **goto** statement. Rather, in broad argument with C.A.R. Hoare

(1972) he believed that the deployment of the abstraction/refinement principle was the "essence" of this cognitive style.

If this was indeed the case then computer scientist David Parnas's (1972) work must also be considered a contribution to the making of the SP movement. Parnas explored the problem of how to partition a program into parts (modules) so as to satisfy a principle of abstraction he named "information-hiding." Parnas's concern was not the stepwise development of programs à la Dijkstra, Wirth and Hoare, but rather the problem of deciding how a software *system* should be initially partitioned into modules (or parts) *before* program development began—step (I) of the Dijkstra-vian procedure. Parnas's paper was published the same year that *Structured Programming* appeared so it is unsurprising that this book was not cited. But Dijkstra's unpublished version of "Notes on Structured Programming" was so widely known it is inconceivable that Parnas was unaware of it. Yet there is no mention of it or any related publications, including Wirth's 1971 paper, in Parnas's bibliography. So we cannot *claim* that Parnas's reading of Dijkstra (or Wirth) influenced his thinking. At the very least, we *can* claim that Parnas's "information-hiding" principle constituted another, possibly independently generated, contribution to SP as a shared cognitive style.

These, then, were the various prominent episodes that effected the making of SP into a creative movement centered on a common cognitive style. It is also worth noting that it was also a movement in a geographic sense: what had originated primarily in the European milieu migrated to North America.

VIII   The making of a monotheistic movement

As a sharp cultural contrast to the making of a late twentieth century, Western, techno-scientific movement (as SP was), let us consider the invention of an early nineteenth century Eastern religious movement. I am referring to the creation of a non-idolatrous, monotheistic, reformed Hindu faith called *Brahmoism* whose institutional base was called the *Brahmo Samaj* ("Brahmo" = Supreme Being, "Samaj" = Society).

Brahmoism was largely the invention of one person, a remarkable intellectual called Rammohun Roy (1772–1833), whom we would now call an "activist"—in the realms of education, women's rights and emancipation, and cultural and religious practices; but he was also a theologian, a scholar of Persian, Arabic and Sanskrit, a composer of songs, a rational thinker; and a man of business who, born into wealth, made more wealth for himself by lending money to the British officials of the East India Company, and as a *zamindar* (feudal style owner of landed estates).

Elsewhere I have called him "warrior-raja" (Dasgupta 2010, p. 100): he was given the princely title of "Raja" by Akbar II, the Mughal king of Delhi but, above all, he was a lifelong warrior who fought major and consequential social, cultural and intellectual battles. Here, we will dwell on just one aspect of this colorful man's work, a person whom scholars have called "The Father of Modern India" (Chakravarti 1935; Robertson 1995) and the harbinger of a "New Learning" in India (Dasgupta 1988).

In fact, we have already encountered Brahmoism in this book. In discussing knowledge schemas, I presented as examples schemas representing Hinduism and Brahmoism to illustrate how one schema might be modified to produce another (Chapter 4). What interests us now is how did this transformation of Hinduism to Brahmoism happen and in what sense did the Brahmo Samaj become a creative movement.

The story is long and complicated and its cognitive history has been discussed in some detail elsewhere (Dasgupta 2007, 2010). Here I will give a compressed account of this creative phenomenon as a creative movement.

IX The preparation of a disputatious mind

Among all the protagonists who have peopled this inquiry none perhaps meets more Wordsworth's precept of the child being the father of the man than Rammohun Roy. It was not only that his youth and early adulthood bore the clear imprint of what would follow in his more mature years; it was also that his intellectual precocity—I am reminded of Herbert Simon—was such that his proactive intellectual preparation was virtually indistinguishable from what we might call his creative life.

Roy lived in a time when there were no universities (in the modern sense of the term) in India. (The first universities, in Calcutta (now Kolkata), Bombay (Mumbai) and Madras (Chennai), were all founded in 1857, a quarter century after Roy's death.) Thus, higher education for someone with the desire and the means to pursue it meant private education and self-learning. So it was that in his early teens, obedient to his father's wishes, Roy went to the city of Patna to study Persian and Arabic, read the poetry and philosophy of the Sufis, study the Koran, and Euclid and Aristotle in Arabic (Collett 1988, p. 4; Sastri 1933, p. 9). He also studied Sanskrit and the "theological works written in it" (Roy 1935, p. 23).

By age sixteen, back in Calcutta, filial devotion had expired. He engaged in theological disputes with his father, opposing the latter's Hindu orthodoxy (Collett 1988, p. 6). He began writing a text questioning the practice of idolatry by Hindus. Several commentators have argued that these early questionings may have been influenced by his Persian, Arabic and Islamic studies (Sastri 1933, p. 9; Das 1974, p. 18; Collett 1988, p. 4; Raychaudhuri 1999, pp. 99–100).

At any rate, partly to remove himself from his father and other orthodox relatives, he left Calcutta. He traveled to Tibet and learnt Buddhism, apparently regularly disputing with the disciples of the living Dalai Lama (Home 1933, pp. 29–30). His preparation was that of a disputatious mind.

In 1799 he went to the city of Benares (now Varanasi), a leading center of Hindu *punditry* and, perhaps, furthered his knowledge of the *Vedanta*, one of the major texts on Hindu philosophy. By 1804, back in Calcutta, and following his father's death the year before (and thus free of the burden of filial conformance) he published his first work, a treatise in Persian with an Arabic introduction titled *Tuhfat-ul-Muwahhdin* ("A Gift to the Monotheists") in which he rejected blind faith in religious authority and propound the use of reason as a protection against religious dogmatism, against idolatry, and in support of monotheism.

One scholar who has closely studied Roy's theological works found *Tuhfat* to be inconsequential to his later theological writings (Robertson 1995, p. 29). Elsewhere, from a cognitive perspective, I have argued otherwise (Dasgupta 2007, p. 58). *Tuhfat* surely represented a crucial aspect of Roy's belief/knowledge space at the time—his emerging cognitive identity. We cannot claim that he was by then a committed monotheist, and certainly not a religious reformer; but, in the light of his later writings *Tuhfat* must surely serve as an early representation of his preparation for a life as an intellectual and a disputatious writer on matters theological.

It would actually take almost another quarter century before preparation would lead to the invention of Brahmoism and the birth of a creative movement. But along the way we witness the gradual consolidation of certain *ideas* that would become the theoretical and intellectual underpinnings of the new belief system.

Between 1804 and 1815, Roy, already a man of wealth—as a moneylender and landowner—would consolidate his wealth. He also strengthened connections with the British and other Europeans of the city. An important aspect of this was that he gained employment as an assistant to one John Digby, an East India Company official. He established a residence where he entertained friends both Indian and British (Biswas and Ganguli 1988). With Digby's help he began a serious study of the English language and European thought, literature and culture (Biswas 1992, pp. 21–23). This too would count as another significant element of Roy's proactive preparation.

X   Preparation flowing into production

In 1815, now aged about forty-two or forty-three, the intellectual floodgates opened. Over the next five years Roy wrote some fourteen Bangla (the language of the Bengalis) and ten English works on various aspects of the Hindu scriptures and what they had to say about idolatry, polytheism and *sati* (Home 1933). Some were translations from Sanskrit to Bangla, others were translations into English. His principle sources were the *Vedanta* and the *Upanishads*, philosophical texts that complemented the *Vedas*, the earliest sources on Hinduism that reached back to about 1500 BCE. His *goal* in translating these texts, he stated, was to persuade his fellow Bengalis to a more rational and truthful understanding of their own scriptures, and to offer evidence to his "European friends" that the "pure spirit" of Hinduism represented in the ancient texts were entirely at odds with the actual superstitious practices of the Hindu religion (Roy 1935, p. 4).

Concurrently, he became a social activist by launching a campaign against *sati*—and here he may have been influenced by the distinguished English Indologist Henry Thomas Colebrooke's studies on the *Vedas* whereby Colebrooke concluded that the Hindu widow did not *have* to commit *sati*.

If all this was not enough, attracted to Christ's teachings but rejecting the doctrine of the Trinity and the divinity of Christ, he espoused Unitarianism (Biswas

1992, pp. 19–20) and was soon engaged in arguments with the orthodox Christians of the city (Collett 1988, p. 140; Biswas 1992, pp. 88–89, 147). The overall outcome was that Roy both antagonized the Bengali Hindus of Calcutta and enraged the Christians.

Should all these activities count as a continuation of his proactive preparation? Or should we think of them as constituting the beginning of a creative act of production? Perhaps they were both, for sometimes—as I have remarked before apropos Rabindranath Tagore (see Chapter 6, XVII)—preparation flows into production.

XI The birth of Brahmoism

At any rate, the idea of translating his beliefs about the "true" nature of Hinduism into a more concrete form may have occurred to Roy in 1815 when with some like-minded people he founded a small society called the *Atmiya Sabha* (Society of Friends). They met weekly to recite from the scriptures and sing hymns composed by Roy and other members of the *Sabha*—hymns speaking to monotheistic beliefs. This gathering eventually came to nought but in 1823 Roy, an Englishman named William Adam, a former Baptist minister who had converted to Unitarianism, and one of the regular attendees at the meetings of the *Atmiya Sabha*, Dwarakanath Tagore (grandfather of Rabindranath Tagore) established the Calcutta Unitarian Committee and the Unitarian Press (Kopf 1979, pp. xxi, 12).

A link was thus forged in Roy's mind between Hindu monotheism and Christian Unitarianism. And if Roy was making public his ideas about the "true" nature of Hinduism according to his reading of the scriptures, then one of the first consumers of his ideas was Dwarakanath Tagore, a wealthy businessman but also an intellectual and a man of culture, twenty-two years Roy's junior, and a far more orthodox Hindu than Roy (Kripalani 1981, pp. 33–36). Here was the germ of a creative encounter between Roy the artificer, Tagore the consumer, and Roy's idea of a monotheistic Hinduism as the artifact.

But the artifact itself was still work-in-progress. It took fuller shape in 1828 when Roy established the Brahmo Samaj, the goal of which, according to its trust deed, was to establish a church and a community dedicated to the worship of the "Eternal and Immutable Being" (Ghose 1885, pp. 489–495). Furthermore, the church would not refer to any *particular* being, nor would it admit idolatry into the church.

Thus, the Brahmo Samaj were established, and Brahmoism, dedicated to anti-idolatry, monotheism and the worship of *Brahman*, the Supreme Being, was born. As an act of production Brahmoism began with the basic pattern of Hinduism from which were weeded out undesirable or unwanted aspects (idolatry, multiple gods, many Hindu customs and rituals) and were replaced with new principles (e.g., the Christianized Brahmo marriage service, a communal place of worship, and Christian-like communal worship and hymn singing). The schemas depicted in Chapter 4 (VIII) show the broad relationship between Brahmoism and its parent Hinduism.

As an abstract (theological) artifact the originality of Brahmoism is worth noting. The schema did not obliterate all features of Hinduism, indeed, that was not Roy's goal. Rather, some major components of the Hinduism schema, especially pertaining to polytheism and idolatry, were removed and a new "subschema" grafted in their place. The outcome deviated from the parent Hinduism schema in fundamental ways. It is thus that the originality of Brahmoism (and the Brahmo Samaj) as an invented schema, as Roy conceived it in the period 1828–1830, is manifested, in comparison to the principles, precepts and practices of orthodox Hinduism.

It is also worth considering the nature of Roy's *reasoning* that gave rise to Brahmoism (Dasgupta 2007, pp. 44–45). Roy's sources of ideas were the *Vedas* and the *Vedanta*. For him, these texts not only proclaimed that there is only one God, one Supreme Being, but also that the Supreme Being is *formless*. As evidence he cited the *Vedas* (Roy 1885, p. 7). The Supreme Being can only be known by observing the wondrous, manifold universe, and the creation, preservation and destruction of its elements; for only by way of such observations can one conclude of the presence of the Supreme Being (ibid.).

Here Roy was appealing to a form of reasoning called *abduction*. This has the following pattern:

Observation: Some phenomenon P needs to explained.

Premiss: P would be explained if hypothesis H were true.

Conclusion: Therefore there is reason to believe that H is true.

In Roy's case P is the observation of the manifold universe; the premiss is that P can be explained by the hypothesis H: "Assume that there is a Supreme Being or Creator"; hence the conclusion that "It is the case that there is a Supreme Being."

Roy's basis for the premiss was an instance of *analogical reasoning*. He drew an analogy from the commonplace world of material artifacts—much as "from the sight of a pot we conclude the existence of its artificer" (Roy 1885, p. 8) so also from observing the manifold and wondrous universe we infer the existence of an artificer, the Supreme Being. His analogy is hauntingly similar to the "argument from design" the advocates of *natural theology* of the eighteenth and nineteenth centuries put forth. We are particularly reminded of the English clergyman and Cambridge don William Paley's highly influential book *Natural Theology; or the Evidence of the Existence and Attributes of the Deity* (originally published 1802) in which Paley famously argued that if we stumble upon a watch and observe its intricate workings we infer that there must have been a maker of that watch (Paley 1998, p. 3). So also, Paley argued, when we examine the intricacies of a work of nature (such as the eye) we must deduce a maker of that work: an "intelligent Creator." Paley summoned extensive evidence from the natural world, both organic and inorganic, in support of his doctrine arriving at the conclusion of the existence of God (Paley 1998, p. 441).

Was Rammohun Roy's analogy influenced by his reading of Paley? There is no documentary evidence for this but it seems quite probable that Roy had come across *Natural Theology*, a book much discussed in early nineteenth century England and which could well have drawn the attention of the intelligentsia of Kolkata, especially someone so deeply engaged in comparative religion as Roy was. Indeed, Roy summoned the "argument from design" in several of his writings.

XII   And so a movement takes shape

Dwarakanath Tagore was one of the executors of the Samaj's Trust Deed of 1830, the year that saw the opening of a physical space as the Samaj's church. As historian David Kopf (1979) would trace in superb detail, the subsequent history of the Brahmo Samaj was never a smooth one. Roy passed away in 1833 (in England where he was buried, adopted by the English Unitarians as one of their own), and stewardship of the Samaj would go to other converts—consumers in creative encounters with Roy's spirit so to speak. It went through much internal strife and controversies in the course of the nineteenth century. Splinter factions would be formed. Yet as a religious belief system, its basic tenets, captured in the schema, would be preserved. At the institutional level by 1872, despite the different factions, over a hundred Brahmo Samaj organizations were established in different regions of India and even Burma (Kopf 1979, pp. 325–327). On the other hand, it would remain a "minority faith" in terms of its practitioners. In its appeal to monotheism, its rejection of idolatry and the Christian influences upon it, it was a religion of the intellectual elite; it never drew a mass following (Raychaudhuri 1999, p. 100). The consumers of Brahmoism were elite rather than subaltern (Chapter 2, V and VII).

But precisely therein lay the most *consequential* effect of the invention of Brahmoism. David Kopf (1979) titled his book *The Brahmo Samaj and the Shaping of the Modern Indian Mind*. Rammohun Roy in his various writings and activism was the root figure of the much larger century-wide movement called the *Bengal Renaissance* on which much has been, and continues to be written (see, e.g., Kopf 1969; Dasgupta 1970, 2007, 2010; Sarkar 1971; Raychaudhuri 2002). What Kopf called the "modern Indian mind" and I called a "cross-cultural mentality" (Dasgupta 2007, Chapter 4) and the "Indo-Western mind" (Dasgupta 2010) were the great consequences of the Bengal Renaissance. The metaphysical and social features of Brahmoism (see the schema in Chapter 4)—if not its strictly religious aspects—were surely among the ingredients of this "modern Indian" or "Indo-Western" mind. Herein lay the most significantly consequential element of Brahmoism as a creative movement.

XIII   The craft-men of South Louisiana

To be creative is to make history. Such history, as we have seen, can be personal or what I have called world–historical, encompassing time and space beyond the limits of the individual's life span. In the particular instance of creative movements, I have suggested that such movements are characterized by two essential features: (a) there are manifest a multiplicity of the artificer–artifact–consumer triads, some active synchronically, some diachronically; and (b) these artifacts give rise to the invention of a historically original (H- and/or C-) shared mentality among the artificers.

The primary artifacts characterizing our two case studies above—a reformed religion and a programming style, respectively—were both abstract and what I have called "intellectual" artifacts (Chapter 2, IX). They engage with the mind primarily as ideas (which however have utilitarian consequences). But the vast history of the creative tradition also manifest creative movements wherein the primary artifacts that fuel the movement are uncompromisingly material in form and are severely utilitarian in purpose.

As a final example, we consider a creative movement from the recent past wherein the primary artifacts of interest are precisely of this material and utilitarian nature. It also offers an interesting contrast, in its nature, its place in historical time and geographical space, and in cultural *milieu*, which is as far removed from the relatively esoteric worlds of mid-twentieth century computer programming and mid-nineteenth century religious reformation as one can imagine.

We enter the milieu of what folklorist John Laudun (2016) called "aquaculture," and it is to his studies and writings we turn for an explication of this quite distinctive creative movement.

Laudun's focus was a small constellation of about a dozen artificers from a particular region of South Louisiana. One of the principal products for which this region is particularly known is crawfish, which are farmed in flooded rice fields or shallow ponds; and the people who were his subjects were the artificers who collectively invented an amphibian craft that could traverse both land and water, so that the crawfish farmer could both navigate the fields or ponds in which crawfish is harvested, and also cross levees and "drive" across land to move from one field or pond to another. These crafts are called *crawfish boats*.

We are, thus, in the realm of material artifacts of a specialized nature. The consumers of the crawfish boat are farmers, and the artificers themselves—the conceivers, creators and builders of the crawfish boat—were deeply embedded in the culture of this crawfish farming community, many indeed being born into the community, many starting out in crawfishing. Some of these artificers were self-taught in boat-craft, some learnt by watching and doing in the tradition of apprenticeship, some had university engineering degrees.

The story John Laudun tells us offers a remarkable exemplar of a creative movement in which thinking and making were inextricably entwined; whose outcome was the coming into being of a particular H-original and C-original artifactual *schema* generically called the crawfish boat, with the caveat that the H- and C-originality was restricted to a particular geographic region; and entailed an intricate network of creative encounters between artificers, and between artificers and the farmer–consumers. This, in fact, engendered a form of *distributed* cognition that drew upon the exchange of cognitive elements (beliefs, knowledge, goals and needs, etc.) between the respective cognitive–historical spaces of both artificers and consumers. We are in the presence of artificers who were in part inventors, part maintenance and repair technicians, part metal technologists, part designers, part tinkerers, part experimenters whose workplaces were (work)shops rather than factories. Most worked on their own or at most with a partner, often a sibling. We are in the presence of artificers whose ecological space (Chapter 1, IV) comprised of the same physical, technological and socio-cultural environment that had served as the root of artist George Rodrigue's creative work (Chapter 6, IX): broadly speaking, the "Cajun country" of South Louisiana.

Generically, a crawfish boat is a wide-hulled, flat-bottomed craft for harvesting crawfish with appropriate paraphernalia for trapping and collecting crawfish as the craft moves through water. Its most distinguishing features are two, relatively small wheels at the front, and an engine–pump–hydraulic motor complex which drives a large wheel hanging off the back of the boat. The crawfish boat is an amphibian craft that can move along the bottom of a flooded rice field and also be driven along roads.

The generic form of the crawfish boat can thus be characterized by a schema (see Chapter 5). Particular, individual boats are instantiations of this schema, and reflect the cognitive styles of individual boat makers. John Laudun tells us that this craft, which looked like no other boat one has seen, completely altered the mode of crawfish farming in this part of South Louisiana (p. xii). It was thus, both H-original and, because of its influence on the nature of crawfish farming, C-original. Yet the invention of this craft—the development of its generic form—was not the work of any one person.

There is a further aspect of the short history of the crawfish boat—spreading over roughly thirty years—that is of particular interest to us. To understand this, let us refer to the design scholar Christopher Jones's (1980) characterization of the *craft tradition* in terms of a number of features, the most striking of which are the following:

1   Craftsmen do not (usually) externalize their works in terms of symbolic descriptions (external representations such as drawings, equations, specifications, etc.).
2   The form of an artifact evolves by a process of trial and error, and will involve many failures and successes of the evolving artifact.
3   The form of an artifact is changed only to correct errors or in order to meet new requirements.
4   The accumulated knowledge concerning the evolution of form is stored in the artifact itself and *in the minds of the craftsmen*. Such knowledge is transmitted by craftsmen and learnt by their successors through a process of doing and watching during apprenticeship.

In a very similar vein architectural theorist Christopher Alexander (1964)—though speaking of builders of buildings—wrote of the *unselfconscious* process wherein:

1   The maker of the artifact is also its user.
2   Failure and repair are closely intertwined.
3   There is little *explicit* thought about what rules to apply. Rather, the rules for creating or modifying an artifact are embodied in the action itself.
4   There are no external or written means for communicating ideas.
5   There is practically no division of labor, and thus specialization is rare.

In the case of the crawfish boat the consumers were farmers who were not only living and working in the same location as the artificers and, thus, of the same cultural *milieu*; some were also themselves artificers. And, as Laudun points out, there were few drawings or other external representations of the work that was performed by these boat makers in their shops. Designs, as such, were encapsulated in the boats themselves (p. 33), much along the lines Jones has stated.

If we add to these the fact that crawfish boats are made in small numbers in a handful of workshops all located in South Louisiana, that these artificers who brought the crawfish boat into being were emotionally engaged with their work (p. 9), and that none of the parts of the crawfish boat nor the boat as a whole was ever patented (p. 25), then there is a distinct and unmistakable sense that the invention and fabrication of crawfish boats conformed to the culture of the craft tradition. As a creative movement, it falls within the creative tradition of craftsmanship. Perhaps their one feature, which neither Christopher Jones nor Christopher Alexander considered, was the distributed nature of this particular craft movement, spread across fabricator–artificers and their farmer–consumers.

So how does one elicit this knowledge embedded in the craft-based artificer's mind? As an anthropologically-trained folklorist, John Laudun went to the source itself: he spent several years observing the boat makers at work, talking to them, listening to them as they talked with their fellow artificers and with the farmer–consumers of their products. And from his observations and understanding we can elicit a cognitive–historical picture of the overall creative phenomenon.

XIV   The making of a distributed creative movement

Drawing on ideas from computer science (Dasgupta 2016a, p. 84), a *distributed* system can be characterized as a constellation of actors distributed across a region of geographical space, each performing his or her own task, but communicating with one another and exchanging information as and when required. There is no hierarchy in such a system: no one controller of the system as a whole. A distributed system is, in this sense, an egalitarian one.

We have seen some semblance of a distributed system in the case of the structured programming movement (this Chapter, IV–VII). But the invention of the crawfish boat exemplifies this phenomenon much more starkly. In particular, while Dijkstra can be clearly identified as the originator of the SP movement, there is no one artificer who can be so identified in the case of the crawfish boat movement.

In our present story, the actors are primarily the fabricator–artificers; but there are also the farmer–consumers. And in some cases (as previously remarked) they are the one and the same. Information exchange and communication between them is not by the written word but by way of observation and conversation. This was how creative encounters occurred between artificer and artificer, between artificers and consumers, even between consumer and consumer.

Laudun's examples include a pair of brothers who ran a machine shop and who might be engaged in building a tool or a machine that a farmer sees while visiting the shop. He would want such a machine, and the artificers would build one for him. Another farmer sees this machine at work in another farm, and he too would want this machine; the artificers would then build one for him. Or sometimes, the artificers, observing faults with a machine or tool of their own making would modify it (Laudun 2016, p. 35).

Laudun gives another example in which a crawfish farmer was using an older mode of fishing using a traditional boat called the pirogue (a characteristic Louisiana craft reaching back to the early twentieth century), which he would haul as he waded through the water and used for both carrying the bait and the harvested crawfish. Tiring of this mode of operation he mentioned to a friend that it would be nice if he could in some fashion mechanize his crawfish farming (p. 83). His friend obliged producing an early mechanized boat powered by an engine.

The identity of each artificer and consumer was, of course, defined by his personal cognitive–historical space. (In this story the protagonists are indeed all men.) But a distributed system is also embedded in a common socio-cultural ecological space that they draw upon for ideas and knowledge. The fundamental form of the crawfish boat was developed from about the mid-1970s to the mid-1980s, a time in which the main cities of South Louisiana collectively became a center for oil exploration in the Gulf of Mexico. And so men acquired skills in metal working, skills such as welding and shaping metal structures that they brought back to their community; knowledge perhaps embedded in their minds and hands (p. 84).

Like most creative phenomena, the crawfish boat movement began in the farmers' *dissatisfaction* with the traditional method of crawfishing, a slow, laborious process as exemplified by the use of pirogues mentioned above. Laudun writes of one of his protagonists, who began crawfish farming in which he pulled a boat through flooded rice fields, employing traps located along the edges of the fields. Dissatisfaction with this modus operandi led to a goal: to build a boat that would pull *him* around and also allow him to fish in the middle of the rice fields (Laudun 2016, p. 113). For other farmers, dissatisfaction with the way they deployed boats to collect crawfish from traps was compounded with unhappiness with the way crawfish was collected in the traps. Inventing improved methods of crawfish farming thus entailed improvement in both boat and trap. As one farmer put it to Laudun, the two evolved together (p. 94).

The movement seemed to have begun in the late 1970s with what Laudun calls "proto-boats" (p. 95): crafts driven by small engines at the back of the boat—a feature that would remain a constant in later developments. Laudun characterizes this stage as a preliminary period of experimentation (ibid.)—though, of course the entire movement (as we will see) can be seen as one long, continuous *distributed* experiment. At any rate, from this proto-boat phase emerged, in the late 1970s, a craft called the "tiller-foot" boat. This comprised of a commercially available boat hull to which was added an assemblage comprising of a part of a garden rotary tiller driven by a low-horsepower engine, the two separated by a long boom (ibid.). Its inventor had a university degree in industrial technology, but before going to college he had many years experience welding and operating machinery and his ecological space embedded a familial culture of making and building, of *know-how* or *operational* knowledge (p. 118). He was also intimately familiar with crawfish farming. Starting with the tiller-foot boat, through the course of the 1980s and the 1990s, this man operated his own business making, experimenting with, innovating and continually improving his boats (p. 120). His main innovation was in evolving from tillers to chain-drives to a hydraulic-drive system that would allow navigation of the boat at the proper speed in flooded rice fields and ponds with sticky mud at the bottom. Here, again, the inventor drew upon a personal knowledge space that had been enriched by his tinkering with race cars; as told to Laudun by another participant of this story, this inventor was probably the first to deploy a power-steering mechanism on a crawfish boat (p. 121). In the language of automotive engineering, chain-drive boats had "rear-wheel drives" while hydraulic-drive boots offered "front-wheel drives." In the language of crawfish boat culture, front-wheel drives were called "pull boats" and real-wheel ones were "push-boats." This particular artificer built both types but eventually, because of its advantages, switched entirely to hydraulic boats which, by appropriate design of the hull could actually serve as both as a pull-boat when collecting traps, and as a push-boat when crossing levees (p. 123).

But the farmers also innovated to keep up with the development of the mechanized boat: the traditional "pillow" trap (so-called because it resembled a large pillow) that caught crawfish slowed down the boat, so they modified it to a form they called the "trash can trap" (that looked like trash cans) to, eventually, the "pyramid trap" which became the standard design (p. 97).

Contemporaneously, in other parts of South Louisiana were other artificers who, independently and sometimes unbeknownst to one another, were developing their own forms of the crawfish boat. According to Laudun, the invention of the modern crawfish boat is largely attributed to one of these artificers (p. 102) who, like so many others, was nurtured in a natural and cultural ecology that included both technology and machinery on the one hand and aquaculture on the other. He also possessed a university engineering degree and had followed this with several years of industrial education, especially in hydraulic technology (p. 104) so that by the time he began thinking seriously about improving the technology of crawfishing, his was very much a proactively prepared mind (Chapter 6) both technologically and aquaculturally.

So the picture that emerges from Laudun's account is one in which several boat makers were working concurrently, some aware of others, some not, to develop the shape of the crawfish boat. Some possessed university engineering degrees augmented by industrial experience in some particular technology; some were farmers/crawfish fishermen-turned-boat makers. The technology manifest in their ecological spaces was the directing factor: in their cultural and technological *milieu* hydraulics was increasingly the preferred means for power distribution in machinery (p. 117). The signature feature of the evolved crawfish boat, *c.*1983 was a massive steel wheel, hanging out of the stern of the boat into the water by means of the arm of a plow—the latter an instance of *affordance* (Chapter 2, XI). The wheel had cleats or treads that provided it with the necessary traction as it rolled along the bottom of the shallow, flooded rice fields.

But in Laudun's account, the invention that made the crawfish boat into a genuinely *amphibian* craft—and consolidated its world–historical originality—was due to one particular boat maker, a consummate machinist (p. 129) who lived and worked, in partnership with his brother, in yet another part of South Louisiana, operating an agricultural machinery repair shop founded by his father. In the mid-1980s, this artificer, in response to farmers' complaints that the bottoms of their boats were wearing out because the farmers took their crafts into the roads (mostly dirt lanes, some graveled) to go from one rice field, reasoned that since these crafts were going onto roads it made sense to put in small front wheels. Thus, on land the boat became a vehicle that moved on two front wheels and the large cleated rear wheel.

This was the crucial change in the evolution of the crawfish boat to its archetypal form; it had attained its mature form as an amphibious vehicle that could drive through a rice fields to retrieve crawfish, then climb up onto a road and drive along it to the next field and so on (p. 132).

As a creative movement this story, as Laudun tells it, does not end here. Some of the pioneering artificers would retire or move onto other endeavors. Some continued on in their businesses. New, younger boat makers entered the scene, and they in turn would make new innovations. New technologies like computer-aided design (CAD) and computer-aided manufacturing (CAM) would be introduced. Yet the essential *craft* nature of the enterprise prevailed: later artificers continued to work largely on their own, possibly with familial partners as their predecessors had done. Others combined their boat making with other kinds of fabrications (pp. 125–126). And repair work was an integral part of these enterprises.

XV The shape of a distributed creative movement

So what can we say about the nature and shape of this creative movement as a whole? First, the *multiplicity* of the artificer–artifact–consumer triplets is very much in evidence. Each artificer, functioning in his own ecological space, possessed of his own belief/knowledge space resulting from his own training, education and experience, responding to his farmer–consumers' needs and goals, working on his own, with at best a partner. Sometimes, as in the evolution of the traps, the farmers were also artificers in response to their needs as consumers.

Second, the artificers and consumers formed a *distributed system of creative encounters*—communicating and interaction with, and learning from, one another by way of observing and conversing. Farmers identified with boat makers, one boat maker identified with another, and so on.

Third, as an essential feature of a distributed system, no one artificer could be said to have been the begetter of this movement. In John Laudun's account certain boat makers are identified and named as especially prominent. But, unlike, say, Rammohun Roy in the case of the Brahmo movement or Edsger Dijkstra in the case of structured programming, all these protagonists in the case of the crawfish boat story contributed importantly to the emergence of the crawfish boat.

Fourth, the shared *goal* for all the artificers was to improve the state of the art of crawfish farming. The artifacts—the crawfish boat and the associated traps—resulting from the ensuing cognitive–historical process (as far as Laudun's study indicates) could not have been anticipated or predicted. The originality of the resulting boat lies as much in the *surprisingness* of its form and its amphibian functionality, neither of which was predictable at the onset.

Finally, perhaps most significantly, this same shared goal for an improved, mechanized crawfish farming system conjoined with the shared ecological space—physical, social and cultural—along with the preservation of a craft (rather than a factory-based manufacturing) tradition collectively constituted the *shared mentality* that characterizes a creative tradition.

Notice that this distributed system is both synchronic and diachronic: we see artificers who are active concurrently, drawing upon one another's ideas and work, but we also see artificers who draw upon the work of their predecessors. Laudun mentions later boat makers whose creative work began where the pioneers had left off. The core of the crawfish boat schema remained intact: an observer would have no difficulty in recognizing a later artificer's craft as a crawfish boat (p. 144). What changed were the specifics, perhaps a change in materials, tools and mode of making, in the off-the-shelf technology available. Such diachronic processes modified the crawfish boat making schema by adding subschemas.

The exchange of information and knowledge in this distributed movement occurred between artificers and artificers, artificers and consumers (the farmers), and between consumers and consumers. But *artifacts are also repositories of knowledge.* A crawfish farmer observing another farmer's boat in operation in a field gleaned knowledge from it that he then incorporated into his own boat, his own farming operation.

As for creative encounters, we see its manifestation in a farmer's observation of a boat made by a boat maker leading to the former to identify with the latter, to realize that what the artificer intended for his boat was also what he, the consumer desired.

EPILOGUE

I Premises and consequences summarized

The basic premises underlying this book are twofold.

One is that creative phenomena manifest *historicity* in a number of ways, most notably in that: (a) Creative beings (artificers) make history and thus are makers of the creative tradition. (b) "Real world" creative phenomena are events that have already happened: they belong to the past. (c) Judgment of particular acts of creation demand historical analysis pertaining to the artifacts produced; that is, demand investigations of the *antecedent* and *consequential* histories of the relevant artifacts. (d) Understanding how individual artificers create original artifacts necessitates the study of the artificers *personal* histories. (e) Long-term creative movements are, by their very nature, movements *in* history as are social, cultural and political movements. And finally (f) As a consequence of (a)–(e), explaining a creative phenomenon may be most appropriately one using the *narrative* mode; that is, telling a historically and empirically grounded story of how the phenomenon "came to be."

The other premise is that creative phenomena, while shaped by, and shaping social, cultural and natural worlds, lie ultimately in the workings of the *mind*—the minds of both artificers and consumers, working in solitude or cooperatively. Thus to make sense of such creative phenomena one must enter into the realm of human *cognition*.

These two premises leads us to *cognitive history*, an "inter-discipline"—originating largely in the pioneering work of Howard Gruber (1981) and given a name by Nancy Nersessian (1995)—at the juncture of historical and cognitive modes of inquiry, a symbiosis of historiography and cognitive science. Along with the many other ways in which the past is understood—politically, socially, culturally, intellectually, economically and psychoanalytically—we add the cognitive way. In particular, if we wish to understand the mentality of the *creative tradition*, a tradition reaching back to *Homo habilis* of the practice of bringing into being of new and valuable artifacts, then it seems that cognitive history offers a mode of investigation and narration uniquely suited to this task. A history of the creative tradition must be a *cognitive* history of the creative tradition.

The aim of this book was to demonstrate the ingredients and principles of cognitive history as an "inter-discipline" and show how it can effectively illuminate how minds make history and thereby contribute to the creative tradition. Toward this end, we undertook case studies of three kinds of creative *phenomena*—the invention of particular artifacts, the shaping of artificers' cognitive styles and the development of creative movements.

II   Cognitive history and intellectual history

Other than psychohistory (discussed at length in the context of creativity in Chapter 11), cognitive history's closest sibling discipline is perhaps *intellectual history*. This raises a question: what is the relation, if any, between cognitive history and intellectual history?

Intellectual history was formerly called the *history of ideas*, a term that is fairly self-explanatory. In a sense the long history of philosophy is itself a history of ideas and insofar as ideas are thoughts, the history of ideas is also the history of thought. Going still further, when philosopher R.G. Collingwood (1946) famously stated that "All history is history of thought" (p. 215), it would seem that all of history is intellectual history. Collingwood's influential book is titled *The Idea of History* and when he began by asking about the process by which modern European history came into being (p. 14), he was asking precisely the kinds of questions asked by a historian of ideas.

But the twentieth century *locus classicus* of history of ideas as a discipline is Arthur O. Lovejoy's *The Great Chain of Being*, originally delivered as the William James Lectures at Harvard University in 1933. Here, Lovejoy argued that any complex system of thought is really composed of a combination of a small number of basic components which he called "unit-ideas" (Lovejoy 1964, pp. 3, 4). He drew on an analogy with the method of analytical chemistry: just as the many variety of chemical compounds are the outcome of different arrangements of a relatively small number of chemical elements so also "unit-ideas" are the elements from which systems of thought are composed. And having isolated a particular unit-idea the historian's task—the task of the history of ideas—is to track the manifold pathways this unit-idea traversed, whether in philosophy or science or literature or art and so on (p. 15). So the history of an unit-idea may thread its way through multiple domains of thought. One such unit-idea may be that of "progress."

Lovejoy also linked his vision for history of ideas with creativity when he stated that one of the tasks of history of ideas must be to uncover the origins of new ideas and beliefs; yet another, how ideas are dislodged from people's minds or are replaced by others (p. 20).

Having introduced the nature of what history of ideas as a discipline should look like, the bulk of *The Great Chain of Being* is devoted to history of one particular idea called "the chain of being"—the idea that the universe comprises of a vast, hierarchical structure connecting the humblest, lowliest beings to the most elevated species (the human being) and beyond to the "Absolute Being" (p. 59).

What Lovejoy conceived as history of ideas is now better known as intellectual history. Its concern still remains *ideas* though Lovejoy's concept of "unit-ideas" has been largely rejected. Paraphrasing the words of a modern intellectual historian, Richard Whatmore (2016), intellectual history is concerned with ideas and how they are transmitted, translated and received (p. 14).

Since ideas are both abstract and human inventions, they belong to the realm of abstract artifacts. So an intellectual historian may well be a creativity researcher. Therein lies one kind of kinship between the disciplines of intellectual history and cognitive history.

Yet they are *not* identical. In the interpretation of Annabel Brett (2002), intellectual history as now practiced has removed the thinker (and her mind) from its realm and now focuses on the ideas themselves (p. 114). If Brett is correct, it is the ideas-as-artifacts that matter rather their artificers; the thought rather than the thinking.

Most significantly, as intellectual history is presently practiced, it is entirely a *textual* practice.

Consider, for example, the question with which Robert Nisbet (1994) began his magisterial *History of the Idea of Progress*: Was the idea of progress present in classical thought? (p. 10). Nisbet believes it was, and by way of justification, he appeals to the *writings* of antiquity—Homer, Protagoras, Hesiod, Aeschylus, Thucydides, Plato, Aristotle, etc.—ascertaining whether and how their writings reveal discussions of the idea of progress.

Likewise, in asking about the origins of the idea of scientific revolution, David Wootton (2015, Chapter 2) sought his answers in large part in the words of the Renaissance and post-Renaissance thinkers, and by unravelling the senses of such keywords as "science," "scientific," "revolution," "nature," "natural philosophy," and so on as manifest in the texts of the times. Wootton also discussed how explorers and scientists of the fifteenth–seventeenth centuries found it awkward to describe their findings (of new lands and new features of the heavens) in the absence of the concept of, and the word, "discovery" (pp. 57–62). So also, Richard Whatmore talks of the problem of understanding the eighteenth century philosopher Jean-Jacques Rousseau's political ideas. This demands, Whatmore proposes, reading not only his major book, *The Social Contract* but also his other writings relating to this work, including his letters, as well as the writings of his predecessors and his contemporaries (Whatmore 2016, p. 17).

In other words, intellectual history resides in *linguistic–textual* space. Indeed, because of the influence of such historians as Hayden White (1978) and Dominick LaCapra (1983), modern intellectual history has taken a decidedly "linguistic turn." As Brett (2002, p. 115) notes, the way in which one thinks about the history of human ideas is quite substantially by way of uncovering how language was used in the past (p. 117), a view with which Wootton (2015) concurs (p. 63). Along these lines LaCapra (1983) asserts that intellectual history is properly speaking a history of texts (p. 35).

So *words and texts matter* to the intellectual historian in an essential sort of way, as Whatmore (2016) reiterates; for it is words, whether carved in stone or calligraphed in parchment or printed on paper, that represent and communicate ideas, and it is the meaning and evolution of such ideas, including the evolution of the meaning of the words expressing ideas, that is the intellectual historian's meat and pudding.

Intellectual history, then, is devoted to linguistic–textual space. It seeks to elicit the meaning of texts and the ideas texts refer to. This means that the artifact that truly matters in intellectual history is the text; and the artificer that matters is the author of that text.

To a historian of computer science, for example, the question of who "invented the computer" would demand an intellectual–historical analysis if by "computer" is meant the *idea* of the computer: the computer as an abstract artifact. The historian would go to key texts such as Alan Turing's seminal paper of 1936 in which Turing laid out the principles of an abstract device that he termed a "computing machine" (Dasgupta 2014a, pp. 49–56). He might then ask whether Turing's idea had any influence on John von Neumann and his colleagues when they developed the idea of the "stored program computer" a decade later (p. 113). If any text authored by von Neumann (or any of his collaborators) on the idea of the stored program computer cited Turing's 1936 paper, here would be evidence of that influence.

But supposing von Neumann's discussion contained no reference to Turing at all (as was the case). The historian might have to resort to a cognitive–historical mode of thinking: he might need to investigate and ascertain through other sources whether it was conceivable that von Neumann's belief/knowledge space contained a representation of Turing's work; and/or whether the cultural space in which von Neumann and his colleagues resided *circa* 1945 had representations of Turing's work; and/or whether there is any evidence that Turing was part of von Neumann's social space. Any evidence of Turing's presence in von Neumann's ecological space, would suggest the presence of the former's work in the latter's belief/knowledge space, in which case a plausible argument can be made that von Neumann's development of the idea of the stored program computer was influenced by Turing (Dasgupta 2014a, p. 113).

Intellectual history, as the discipline is currently understood, is limited in another significant sense. There is no place in intellectual history for all the other kinds of artificers who have appeared in this book: artists, musicians, filmmakers, engineers, inventors, craftspeople and scientists have no place in intellectual history unless the artifacts created by such artificers, whether abstract or material, are cast in ideational (thus, textual) form. The boat makers of South Louisiana, the artists Picasso, Amrita Sher-Gill and George Rodrigue, the engineers James Watt, Robert Stephenson and Robert Maillart, the computer scientists Edsgar Dijkstra, Niklaus Wirth, C.A.R. Hoare and Donald Knuth, the scientist Jagadis Bose, the filmmaker Satyajit

Ray were not in the business of creating textual artifacts, though we may appeal to their writings and what they said as sources of understanding. The artifacts they produced were emphatically non-textual.

Thus, intellectual history fails when we wish to understand the overall pattern of Satyajit Ray's filmmaking mind or the overall pattern of Herbert Simon's poly-mathic inventive mind (Chapter 10, VII, VIII). We are interested in eliciting the nature and evolution of their respective *cognitive* styles. Here the cognitive–historical space beckons.

Here is another point of contrast: as we have noted, the intellectual historian is concerned with ideas by way of exacting the meanings of texts. But recall Jerome Bruner's (1990) proposition that cognition is also a meaning-making enterprise (Chapter 1, II). The significant difference lies in that cognition is the means by which we make sense of *all* our experiences in the world, not just texts. The scope of cognitive history is the entire creative tradition; it operates in cognitive space, asking questions, posing problems pertaining to cognition "in the large." Intellec-tual history operates in textual–linguistic space, asking questions, posing problems in the realm of verbalized thoughts alone.

This of course does not mean that the practitioners of cognitive history and of intellectual history cannot borrow from each other. Indeed, one may be both. One may often profitably wander across the "boundary" between the two if it is appro-priate to do so. Recently I argued that in writing *The Second Age of Computer Science* (2018a) I was engaged in the practice of both intellectual history and cognitive history (p. xxii). As an example of the former, I tried to show, through the *writings* of some computer scientists, how the *idea* of universality in computer programming languages was met in one particular language (pp. 8–12). Certainly cognition entered this narrative insofar as the computer scientists' *goals* or *intentions* had to be taken into account in this explanation, but no more. This would count as a sliver of the intellectual history of computer science.

On the other hand, elsewhere in the book, I write about certain computer sci-entists' creativity. I am *judging* these scientists' creativity (why such and such sci-entist must be deemed C-creative or H-creative) and in so doing I am in cognitive–historical space. I needed to bring to the conversation such issues as the knowledge embedded in a particular computational artifact which then entered the ecological space shared with other computer scientists, and thereby entered their individual belief/knowledge spaces (Dasgupta 2018a, pp. 117–118, 197–198). In writing these segments of the book I am engaging in slivers of the cognitive history of computer science.

III On the (*very* brief) history of cognitive history

Cognitive historiography—writing cognitive history—is then a different kind of history writing from other modes of historiographical modes. It is also a very new kind of history writing. We find no mention of it in even relatively recent texts and ruminations on historiography such as David Cannadine's (2002) edited volume

What is History Now?, Peter Burke's (2008) *What is Cultural History?* or Richard Whatmore's (2016) *What is Intellectual History?*—the titles of which were all inspired by E.H. Carr's (1964) classic *What is History?* Nor does the idea or the term appear in Judith Brown's (2009) lectures on life histories, *Windows into the Past* where, given its topic, one might have expected some mention of cognition as a conceptual tool in life–historical writing.

A relevant work, however, is Rajat Kanta Ray's *Exploring Emotional History* (2001). By "emotional history," Ray meant the *history of emotions* and how social structures and contexts shape and reshape people's emotions and feelings (Ray 2001, pp. vii–viii). Ray's social context was situated in nineteenth century India and, especially the movement I have mentioned earlier as the Bengal Renaissance (see Chapter 12, XII).

Toward his purpose, Rajat Ray draws extensively on the psychoanalytic literature and to the psychohistory I have referred to earlier in this book (Chapter 11). He also takes cognition as the basis of intellectual history and affect as the basis of emotional history (p. 17). This separation of affect and cognition is along the lines of a more traditional psychology as was mentioned earlier (Chapter 1, IV), whereas, as we have noted, other psychologists such as Jerome Bruner (1990) have argued persuasively that affects shape cognition, a view reflected in the cognitive–historical space presented in Chapter 1.

A prominent concern in Ray's discussion of emotional history is the notion of mentality. Ray's characterization of this notion is consistent with the notion of mentality presented in this book (Prologue, I) and so, his concept of emotional history has a connection to the cognitive–historical approach as interpreted in the present work. But there are limits to this connection. There seems little doubt that Ray's main psychological stimulus came from psychoanalysis and psychohistory (p. 313). Cognitive science, or its subspecialty cognitive psychology, has very little to offer to Ray's history of emotions. We find extensive citations of "id," "ego," "drive," "libido," "psychoanalysis," "psychohistory," "superego"—standard psychoanalytical terms—and to Freud, Erik Erikson and Girindrasekhar Bose (a pioneer of Indian psychoanalysis) in the index. "Cognition" does not appear at all, nor "cognitive psychology" nor, it goes without saying, "cognitive science."

As we have noted cognitive history owes its name to Nancy Nersessian's (1995) paper pertaining to the history of science (see Prologue, VI). Well before Nersessian coined the name Howard Gruber (1981) had pioneered cognitive history as an investigative method in his study of Charles Darwin—which Nersessian acknowledged in her paper (footnote 18, p. 203). The collection of essays titled *Creative People at Work* edited by Doris Wallace and Howard Gruber (1989) is also a compendium of cognitive–historical studies of artificers in the natural sciences, psychology, fiction writing, poetry and art. So also, the volume titled *Inventive Minds* (1992) edited by Robert Weber and David Perkins (1992) consisted of cognitive–historical analyses of technological inventions. My own books *Creativity in Invention and Design* (1994) and *Technology and Creativity* (1996) were cognitive–historical studies of invention and design in the realm of technology. In none of these works, however, did the term "cognitive history" appear.

Yet in all these writings the *spirit* of cognitive history was in evidence. They were all concerned with how minds make history (see Prologue, I). They were all historical studies of a variety of creative endeavors—in art, technology, science and literature. And what they shared was a desire to make sense of past creative phenomena in terms of how artificers' minds worked; the cognitive basis, in other words, of selected aspects of the creative tradition. Of course, as we have noted, creativity studies entails a variety of approaches, and the cognitive–historical approach is just one.

A particularly interesting appeal to cognitive history is found in an article by philosopher of science Larry Laudan (1990). Writing on the relationship between the disciplines and practices of history of science and philosophy of science, Laudan chastises the (post-) modern trend in history of science to ignore the theories of scientific change as propounded by philosophers—theories that speak to the scientists' *beliefs* about the nature of the world (p. 50). Laudan remarks that almost all theories of scientific change rest on the philosophers' preoccupation with the cognitive bases of such change; yet such cognitive concerns are entirely outside the current fashions in history of science. Laudan actually uses the term "cognitive history" in his essay.

Laudan is a rare exception. As of this writing the term "cognitive history" is still barely known. A few years ago I gave a lecture at one of the University of California campuses on the topic to an interdisciplinary department comprising of scholars and students in the various disciplines constituting cognitive science, including psychology, linguistics, anthropology and computer science. Several members of the audience told me that they had never heard of cognitive history before. If one googles the term the returns are extremely sparse; more often than not, the term returns items on the history of cognitive science.

But there are a few encouraging signs. We find a "cognitive–historical case study" of art historian E.H. Gombrich's ideas on creativity in the *Creativity Research Journal* (Kozbelt 2008). Another instance is the collection of papers titled *Past Minds: Studies in Cognitive Historiography* (2011), edited by Luther Martin and Jesper Sørensen (2011), two religious studies scholars. Most of the contributors to this volume were specialists in theology and the history of religion. Only one, Christophe Heintz (2011) was a cognitive scientist who discussed the relationship of cognitive history and what he has termed "cultural epidemiology." His chapter was also the only one in which "cognitive history" appeared in the title. The "past minds" of interest to these authors were mostly those pertaining to the history of religious movements and ideas—along the lines of my own contribution to the cognitive study of Brahmoism in nineteenth century India (Chapter 12, VIII–XII; also Dasgupta 2007). Luther Martin's (2011) introductory paper tells us that, in fact, the idea of a "proto-cognitive" approach to historical studies reaches back to the early twentieth century when one classical scholar proposed understanding religion in terms of behavioral features (p. 3). Elsewhere, the present writer has traced a connection between Herbert Simon's (1996) seminal work *The Sciences of the Artificial* and the emergence of cognitive history (Dasgupta 2016c).

The time seems ripe to introduce cognitive history to the larger public, both lay and academic in a principled way. I hope this book makes a contribution to the realization of this ambition by its demonstration of the method of cognitive history and how it can shed light on the mentality of the creative tradition.

BIBLIOGRAPHY

Aitchison, L. (1960). *A History of Metals*. New York: Interscience Publishers.

Alba, J.W. and Hasher, L. (1983). "Is Memory Schematic?" *Psychological Bulletin*, 93, pp. 2013–2031.

Alexander, C. (1964). *Notes on the Synthesis of Form*. Cambridge, MA: Harvard University Press.

Allen, A.R. and Weber, A. (1999). "Unconscious Intelligence." In: W. Bechtel and G. Graham (ed.). *A Companion to Cognitive Science*. (1st ed.). Oxford: Blackwell, pp. 314–323.

Allport, A. (1989). "Visual Attention." In: M. Posner (ed.). *Foundations of Cognitive Science*. (1st ed.). Cambridge, MA: MIT Press, pp. 631–672.

Ananth, D. (2007). "An Unfinished Project." In: Anon (ed.). *Amrita Sher-Gil: An Indian Artist's Family of the Twentieth Century*. (1st ed.). Munich: Shirmer/Mosel, pp. 13–32.

Ancelet, B. (1989). *Cajun Music: Its Origin and Development*. Lafayette, LA: Center for Louisiana Studies, University of Louisiana at Lafayette.

Anderson, L. (2001). *Autobiography*. London: Routledge.

Anon (2003). *The Art of George Rodrigue*. New York: Harry N. Abrams.

Anon (2004). *The Art of Tagore*. New Delhi: Rupa & Co.

Anon (2007). *Amrita Sher-Gil: An Indian Artist's Family of the Twentieth Century*. Munich: Schirmer/Mosel.

Appel, K. (1984). "The Use of the Computer in the Proof of the Four Color Problem," *Proceedings of the American Philosophical Society*, 128, 1, pp. 35–39.

Arbib, M.A. and Hesse, M.B. (1986). *The Construction of Reality*. Cambridge: Cambridge University Press.

Armstrong, K. (1993). *A History of God*. New York: Ballantine Books.

Arnheim, R. (1962). *Guernica: The Genesis of a Painting*. Los Angeles, CA: University of California Press.

Arnheim, R. (1969). *Visual Thinking*. Berkeley, CA: University of California Press.

Arnold, M. (1970). "Culture and Anarchy." In: P.J. Keating (ed.). *Selected Prose*. (1st ed. 1869). Harmondsworth: Penguin Books, pp. 202–300.

Ashcroft, E.A. and Manna, Z. (1971). "Translation of 'goto' Programs to 'while' Programs," *Proceedings 1981 IFIP Congress, Volume 1*. Amsterdam: North-Holland, pp. 250–255.

Ashton, D. (ed.). (1972). *Picasso on Art*. New York: De Capo Press.

Ashton, T.S. (1969). *The Industrial Revolution 1760–1830*. Oxford: Oxford University Press.

Ayer, A.J. (1971). *Language, Truth and Logic*. (1st ed. 1936). Harmondsworth: Penguin Books.

Bailey, S. (2001). *Essential History of American Art*. Bath: Paragon.

Baker, F.T. and Mills, H.D. (1973). "Chief Programmer Teams," *Datamation*, 19, 12, pp. 58–61.

Bambrough, R. (ed.). *The Philosophy of Aristotle* (J.L. Creed and A.E. Wardman, tr.) New York: Mentor Book.

Banham, R. (1981). *Theory and Design in the First Machine Age*. Cambridge, MA: MIT Press.

Barbot, B., Tan, M. and Grigorenko, E.L. (2013). "The Genetics of Creativity: The Generative and Receptive Sides of the Creativity Equation." In: O.V. Vartanian, A.S. Bristol and J.C. Kaufman (ed.). *Neuroscience of Creativity*. 1st ed. Cambridge, MA: MIT Press, pp. 71–94.

Barnett, L. (2005). *The Universe and Dr. Einstein*. (1st ed. 1957). New York: Dover.

Barsalou, L.W. (2010). "Editor's Introduction: 30th Anniversary Perspective on Cognitive Science: Past, Present and Future," *Topics in Cognitive Science* (TOPICS), 2, 3, pp. 322–327.

Bartlett, F.C. (1932). *Remembering*. Cambridge: Cambridge University Press.

Basalla, G. (1988). *The Evolution of Technology*. Cambridge: Cambridge University Press.

Baumeister, R.F., Schmeichel, B.J. and DeWall, C.N. (2014). "Creativity and Consciousness: Evidence from Psychology Experiments." In: E.S. Paul and S.B. Kaufman (ed.). *The Philosophy of Creativity*. New York: Oxford, pp. 185–198.

Baumgarter, J. (1978). *Flannery O'Connor: A Proper Scaring*. Wheaton, IL: H. Shaw Publishers.

Bazin, A. (1971). "Bicycle Thief." In: *What is Cinema? Volume II*. (H. Gray, tr.). Berkeley, CA: University of California Press, pp. 47–60.

Beardley, M.C. (1966). *Aesthetics from Classical Greece to the Present*. New York: The Macmillan Company.

Bensande-Vincent, B. and Newman, W.R. (2007). "Introduction: The Artificial and the Natural: State of the Problem". In B. Bensande-Vincent and W.R. Newman (ed.). *The Artificial and the Natural*. Cambridge, MA: MIT Press, pp. 1–20.

Benton, M.J. (2008). *The History of Life: A Very Short Introduction*. Oxford: Oxford University Press.

Berenson, B. (1968). *Italian Painters of the Renaissance. 2. Florentine and Central Italian Schools*. (1st ed. 1952). London: Phaidon Press.

Bermúdez, J.L. (2010). *Cognitive Science*. Cambridge: Cambridge University Press.

Biagioli, M. (1993). *Galileo Courtier*. Chicago: University of Chicago Press.

Billington, D.P. (1979). *Robert Maillart's Bridges: The Art of Engineering*. Princeton, NJ: Princeton University Press.

Billington, D.P. (1983). *The Tower and the Bridge: The New Art of Structural Engineering*. New York: Basic Books.

Biswas, D.K. (ed.). (1992). *The Correspondence of Raja Rammohun Roy, Volume 1*. Calcutta: Sarswat Library.

Biswas, D.K. and Ganguli, P.C. (1988). "Supplementary Notes II" to Chapter II. In: S.D. Collett. *The Life and Letters of Raja Rammohun Roy*. (4th ed, 1st ed. 1900). Calcutta: Sadharan Brahmo Samaj, pp. 45–50.

Blue, J. (2007). "Interview with Satyajit Ray" (1968). In: B Cardullo (ed.). *Satyajit Ray Interviews*. Jackson, MS: University Press of Mississippi, pp. 14–33.

Boden, M.A. (1991). *The Creative Mind*. New York: Basic Books.

Boden, M.A. (2006). *Mind as Machine: A History of Cognitive Science* (Volumes 1 and 2). Oxford: Clarendon Press.

Boden, M.A. (2010a). "Personal Signatures in Art," In: M.A. Boden. *Creativity and Art*. Oxford: Oxford University Press, pp. 91–124.

Boden, M.A. (2010b). *Creativity and Art*. Oxford: Oxford University Press.

Boden, M.A. (2014). "Creativity and Artificial Intelligence: A Contradiction in Terms?" In: E.S. Paul and S.B. Kaufman (ed.). *The Philosophy of Creativity*. New York: Oxford University Press.

Bohm, D. (2004). *On Creativity*. (1st ed. 1996). London: Routledge.

Bondyopadhyay, P. (1998). "Sir J.C. Bose's Diode Detector Received Marconi's First Transatlantic Wireless Signal of December 1910," *Proceedings of the IEEE*, 86, 1, pp. 259–285.

Bonner, J.T. (1988). *The Evolution of Complexity by Natural Selection*. Princeton, NJ: Princeton University Press.

Bose, J.C. (1896a). "On the Polarization of Electric Rays by Doubly Refracting Crystals," *Journal of the Asiatic Society of Bengal*, 64, pp. 291–296.

Bose, J.C. (1896b). "On a Complete Apparatus for the Study of the Properties of Electric Waves." *Report of the 66th Meeting of the British Association, Liverpool, September 1896*. London: John Murray, p. 725.

Bose, J.C. (1897). "Electro-Magnetic Radiation and the Polarization of the Electric Ray". Friday Evening Discourse, The Royal Institution. In: J.C. Bose (1927). *Collected Physical Papers*. London: Longmans, Green & Co., pp.177–201.

Bose, J.C. (1898). "On the Rotation of the Plane of Polarization of Electric Waves by a Twisted Structure," *Proceedings of the Royal Society*, A63, pp. 146–152.

Bose, J.C. (1900). "On Electric *Touch* and the Molecular Changes Produced in Matter by Electric Waves," *The Electrician*, 44, pp. 626–628, 649–652.

Bose, J.C. (1901). "On the Strain Theory of Photographic Action," *Proceedings of the Royal Society*, A70, pp. 185–197.

Bose, J.C. (1902). *Response in the Living and Nonliving*. London: Longmans, Green & Co.

Bose, J.C. (1904). U.S. Patent No. 755,840. March 29.

Bose, J.C. (1927b). "Electro-Magnetic Radiation and the Polarization of the Electric Ray." (1st ed. 1897). In: J.C. Bose. *Collected Physical Papers*. London: Longmans, Green & Co.

Bowers, M.A. (2004). *Magic(al) Realism*. London: Routledge.

Braudel, F. (1980). *On History* (S. Matthew, tr.). Chicago: University of Chicago Press.

Brenner, C. (1974). *An Elementary Textbook of Psychoanalysis*. (2nd ed.). New York: Basic Books.

Brett, A. (2002). "What is Intellectual History Now?" In: D. Cannadine (ed.). *What is History Now?* Basingstoke: Palgrave Macmillan, pp. 113–131.

Brinch Hansen, P. (1975). "The Programming Language Concurrent Pascal", *IEEE Transactions on Software Engineering*, 1, 2, pp. 195–202.

Brinch Hansen, P. (1996). *The Search for Simplicity: Essays in Parallel Programming*. Los Alamitos, CA: IEEE Computer Society Press.

Broadbent, D.E. (1958). *Perception and Communication*. London: Pergamon Press.

Brown, J.M. (2009). *Windows into the Past*. Notre Dame, IN: Notre Dame University Press.

Bruner, J.L. (1979). "The Conditions of Creativity." In: *On Knowing*. Cambridge, MA: Harvard University Press, pp. 17–30.

Bruner, J.L. (1990). *Acts of Meaning*. Cambridge, MA: Harvard University Press.

Bruner, J.L. (1994). "The Remembered Self." In: U. Neisser and R. Fivish (ed.). *The Remembered Self.* Cambridge: Cambridge University Press, pp. 41–54.

Burke, P. (2008). *What is Cultural History?* (2nd ed.). Cambridge: Polity.

Bury, J.B. (1987). *The Idea of Progress.* (Originally published in 1932). New York: Dover.

Butterfield, H. (1973). *The Whig Interpretation of History.* (1st ed. 1931). Harmondsworth: Penguin.

Campbell, D.T. (1960). "Blind Variation and Selective Retention in Creative Thought as in other Knowledge Processes," *Psychological Review*, 67, pp. 380–400.

Campbell, D.T. (1987). "Evolutionary Epistemology." In: G. Radnitzky and W.W. Bartley, III. (ed.). *Evolutionary Epistemology, Rationality and the Sociology of Knowledge.* La Salle, IL: Open Court, pp. 47–90.

Cannadine, D. (ed.). (2002). *What is History Now?* Basingstoke: Palgrave Macmillan.

Cantor, N. (1981). *Inventing the Middle Ages.* New York: Quill/William Morrow.

Cardwell, D.S.L. (1989). *From Watt to Clausius: The Rise of Thermodynamics in the Early Industrial Age.* (2nd ed.). Ames, IA: Iowa State University Press.

Carlson, S. (1979). "The Prize for Economic Science in Memory of Alfred Nobel, Les Prix Nobel 1978." Stockholm: The Nobel Foundation.

Carney, J.D. (1991). "Individual Style," *Journal of Aesthetics and Art Criticism*, 49, 1, pp. 15–22.

Carr, E.H. (1964). *What is History?* Harmondsworth: Penguin Books.

Carroll, N. (2014). "The Creative Audience: Some Ways in which Readers, Viewers, and/or Listeners Use Their Imagination to Engage Fictional Artworks." In: E.S. Paul and S.B. Kauffman (ed.). *The Philosophy of Creativity.* New York: Oxford University Press, pp. 62–81.

Chalmers, D.J. (1996). *The Conscious Mind.* New York: Oxford University Press.

Chakravarty, S. (ed.). (1935). *The Father of Modern India: Commemoration Volume of the Rammohun Roy Centenary Celebration 1933.* Calcutta: Rammohun You Centenary Committee.

Chandrasekhar, S. (1987). *Truth and Beauty: Aesthetics and Motivation in Science.* Chicago: University of Chicago Press.

Chaudhuri, N.C. (2001). *The Autobiography of an Unknown Indian.* (1st ed. 1951). New York: New York Review Books.

Chauvet, J-M., Deschamps, E.B. and Hilaire, C. (1986). *Dawn of Art: The Chauvet Caves.* New York: Harry N. Abrams.

Chipp, H.B. (1968). *Theories of Modern Art.* Berkeley, CA: University of California Press.

Chipp, H.B. (1988). *Picasso's Guernica.* Berkeley, CA: University of California Press.

Chrimes, M. (1991). *Civil Engineering 1839-1889.* London: Thomas Telford/Shroud: Alan Sutton.

Clark, R.W. (1971). *Einstein: The Life and Times.* New York: World Publishing.

Clarke, E. (1850). *The Britannia and Conway Tubular Bridges (Volumes I and II).* London: Day & Sons.

Clayton, S. and Opotow, S. (2003). "Identity and the Natural Environment." In: S. Clayton and S. Opotow (ed.). *Identity and the Natural Environment.* Cambridge, MA: MIT Press, pp. 1–24.

Cohen, I.B. (1995). "Newton's Method and Newton's Style." In: I.B. Cohen and R.S. Westfall (ed.). *Newton.* New York: W.W. Norton, pp. 126–143.

Coleridge, S.T. (1985). "Prefatory Note to Kubla Khan." (Originally published in 1895.) In: B. Ghiselin. *The Creative Process.* Berkeley, CA: University of California Press, pp. 83–84.

Collett, S.D. (1988). *The Life and Letters of Raja Rammohun Roy* (D.K. Biswas and P.C. Ganguli, ed., 4th ed.) Calcutta: Sadharan Brahmo Samaj.

Collingwood, R.G. (1956). *The Idea of History*. (Originally published 1946.). Oxford: Oxford University Press.

Collins, A.M. and Loftus, E.F. (1975). "A Spreading Activation Theory of Semantic Processing," *Psychological Review*, 82, pp. 407–428.

Comeaux, C. (2006). "The Literary Mind: A Cognitive Case Study of Flannery O'Connor." PhD Dissertation. Lafayette, LA: University of Louisiana at Lafayette.

Conan Doyle, A. (1984). *The Penguin Complete Sherlock Holmes*. Harmondsworth: Penguin Books.

Conway, R.W. and Gries, D.G. (1973). *Introduction to Programming: A Structured Approach Using PL/1 and Pl/C*. Cambridge, MA: Winthrop Publishers.

Cox, N. (2000). *Cubism*. London: Phaidon Press.

Craik, K.H.C. (1943). *The Nature of Explanation*. Cambridge: Cambridge University Press.

Cross, N. (2011). *Design Thinking*. Oxford: Berg.

Crowther, J.G. (1974). *The Cavendish Laboratory 1874–1974*. New York: Science History Publications.

Csikzentmihalyi, M. (1988). "A Systems View of Creativity." In R.J. Sternberg (ed.). *The Nature of Creativity*. Cambridge: Cambridge University Press, pp. 325–339.

Csikzentmihalyi, M. (1996). *Creativity*. New York: HarperCollins..

Dahl, O-J., Dijkstra, E.W. and Hoare, C.A.R. (1972). *Structured Programming*. New York: Academic Press.

Dahl, O-J. and Hoare, C.A.R (1972). "Hierarchical Program Structures." In: O-J. Dahl, E.W. Dijkstra and C.A.R. Hoare. *Structured Programming*. New York: Academic Press, pp. 175–220.

Dahl, O-J., Myrhaug, B. and Nygaard, K. (1968). "The SIMULA 67 Common Base Language." Norwegian Computing Center, Oslo.

Dalmia, Y. (2006). *Amrita Sher-Gil: A Life*. New Delhi: Penguin/Viking.

Damasio, A.R. (1994). *Descartes' Error: Emotion, Reason and the Human Brain*. New York: Grosset/Putnam.

D'Andrade, R. (1995). *The Development of Cognitive Anthropology*. Cambridge: Cambridge University Press.

Darwin, C. (1985). *The Origin of Species by Means of Natural Selection*. (1st ed. 1859). Harmondsworth: Penguin Books.

Das, S.K. (1974). *The Shadow of the Cross: Christianity and Hinduism in a Colonial Situation*. New Delhi: Munshiram Manoharlal Publishers.

Das, S.K. (ed.). (1996). *The English Writings of Rabindranath Tagore, Volume 3. A Miscellany*. New Delhi: Sahitya Akademi.

Dasgupta, R.K. (1970). "The Nineteenth Century Indian Renaissance: Fact or Fiction." Unpublished Manuscript. Simla: Indian Institute of Advanced Study.

Dasgupta, R.K. (1988). "Rammohun Roy and the New Learning." In: B.P. Barua (ed.). *Rammohun Roy and the New Learning*. Calcutta: Orient Longman, pp. 24–42.

Dasgupta, S. (1991). *Design Theory and Computer Science*. Cambridge: Cambridge University Press.

Dasgupta, S. (1994a). *Creativity in Invention and Design*. New York: Cambridge University Press.

Dasgupta, S. (1994b). "Testing the Hypothesis Law of Design," *Research in Engineering Design*, 6, 1, pp. 38–57.

Dasgupta, S. (1996). *Technology and Creativity*. New York: Oxford University Press.

Dasgupta, S. (2003a). "Multidisciplinary Creativity: The Case of Herbert A. Simon," *Cognitive Science*, 27, pp. 683–707.

Dasgupta, S. (2003b). "Innovation in the Social Sciences: Herbert Simon and the Birth of a Research Tradition." In: L.V. Shavinina (ed.). *International Handbook on Innovation.* Kidlington: Elsevier, pp. 458–470.

Dasgupta, S. (2004). "Is the Creative Process Darwinian?" *Creativity Research Journal,* 16, pp. 403–413.

Dasgupta, S. (2005). "Cognitive Style in Creative Work: The Case of the Painter George Rodrigue," *PsyArt: An Online Journal for the Psychological Study of Art,* www.clas.ufl.edu/ipsa/journal/2005_dasgupta01.shtml.

Dasgupta, S. (2007). *The Bengal Renaissance: Identity and Creativity from Rammohun Roy to Rabindranath Tagore.* New Delhi: Permanent Black.

Dasgupta, S. (2009). *Jagadis Chandra Bose and the Indian Response to Western Science.* (1st ed. 1999). New Delhi: Permanent Black.

Dasgupta, S. (2010). *Awakening: The Story of the Bengal Renaissance.* Noida: Random House India.

Dasgupta, S. (2011). Contesting (Simonton's) Blind-Variation, Selective-Retention Theory of Creativity," *Creativity Research Journal,* 23, 2, pp. 166–182.

Dasgupta, S. (2013). "Epistemic Complexity and the Sciences of the Artificial." In: H. Anderson, D. Dieks, W.J. Gonzalez, T. Uebel and G. Wheeler (ed.). *New Challenges to Philosophy of Science.* Dordecht: Springer, pp. 313–324.

Dasgupta, S. (2014a). *It Began with Babbage: The Genesis of Computer Science.* New York: Oxford University Press.

Dasgupta, S. (2014b). "Science Studies *sans* Science: Two Cautionary Postcolonial Tales," *Social Scientist,* 42, 5–6, pp. 43–61.

Dasgupta, S. (2016a). *Computer Science: A Very Short Introduction.* Oxford: Oxford University Press.

Dasgupta, S. (2016b). "Disentangling Data, Information and Knowledge," *Big Data and Information Analytics,* 1, 4, pp. 377–389.

Dasgupta, S. (2016c). "From *The Sciences of the Artificial* to Cognitive History." In: R. Franz and L. Marsh (ed.). *Mind, Models and Milieux: Commemorating the Centennial of the Birth of Herbert Simon.* Basingstoke: Palgrave Macmillan, pp. 60–70.

Dasgupta, S. (2018a). *The Second Age of Computer Science.* New York: Oxford University Press.

Dasgupta, S. (2018b). "Judging Creativity: The Case of the Early Jagadis Bose," *Indian Journal of the History of Science,* 53, 4, pp. 60–67.

Davidson, A.L. (1999). "Styles of Reasoning, Conceptual History and the Emergence of Psychiatry." In: M. Biagoli (ed.). *The Science Studies Reader.* London: Routledge, pp. 124–136.

Davis, P.J. and Hersch, R. (1981). *The Mathematical Experience.* Boston, MA: Houghton-Mifflin.

Dawkins, R. (1976). *The Selfish Gene.* Oxford: Oxford University Press.

de Beauvoir, S. (1965). *The Prime of Life* (P. Green, tr.). Harmondsworth: Penguin.

Desmond, A. and Moore, J. (1992). *Darwin.* London: Penguin.

Dickinson, H.W. (1939). *A Short History of the Steam Engine.* Cambridge: Cambridge University Press.

Dijkstra, E.W. (1968). "Goto Statement Considered Harmful," *Communications of the ACM,* 11, pp. 147–148.

Dijkstra, E.W. (1969). "Notes on Structured Programming," EWD 249. Technical University of Eindhoven, Eindhoven.

Dijkstra, E.W. (1972). "Notes on Structured Programming." In: O-J. Dahl, E.W. Dijkstra and C.A.R. Hoare. *Structured Programming.* New York: Academic Press, pp. 1–82.

Dijkstra, E.W. (1979a). "Programming Considered as a Human Activity." (Originally published in 1965.) In: E. Yourdon (ed.). *Classics in Software Engineering*. New York: Yourdon Press, pp. 3–9.

Dijkstra, E.W. (1979b). "Structured Programming." (Originally published in 1969.) In: E. Yourdon (ed.). *Classics in Software Engineering*. New York: Yourdon Press, pp. 43–50.

Dijkstra, E.W. (1980). "Some Beautiful Arguments using Mathematical Induction," *Act Informatica*, 13, 1, pp. 1–8.

Donaldson, J.R. (1973). "Structured Programming," *Datamation*, 19, 12, pp. 52–54.

Donaldson, M. (1992). *Human Minds: An Exploration*. London: Allen Lane.

Donovan, A.L. (1979). "Toward a Social History of Technology: Joseph Black, James Watt and the Separate Condenser." In: G. Bugliarello and D.B. Boner (ed.). *History and Philosophy of Technology*. Urbana, IL: University of Illinois Press, pp. 12–30.

Draaisma, D. (2004). *Why Life Speeds Up As You Get Older*. Cambridge: Cambridge University Press.

Dutta, K. and Robinson, A. (1995). *Rabindranath Tagore: The Myriad-Minded Man*. New York: St. Martin's Press.

Eakin, J.P. (1988). "Relational Selves, Relational Lives." In: G.T. Houser and J. Fichtelberg (ed.). *True Relations: Essays in Autobiography and the Postmodern*. Westport, CT: Greenwood Press, pp. 63–82.

Eakin, J.P. (1999). *How Our Lives Become Stories*. Ithaca, NY: Cornell University Press.

Eindhoven, J.E. and Vine, W.E. (1952). "Creative Processes in Painting," *Journal of General Psychology*, 47, pp. 139–164.

Einstein, A. (1970). "Autobiographical Notes" (P.A. Shilpp, tr.). In: P.A. Schilpp (ed.). *Albert Einstein Philosopher-Scientist*. (3rd ed.). La Salle, IL: Open Court, pp. 1–95.

Eliade, M. (1978). *The Forge and the Crucible*. (2nd ed.) (S. Corrin, tr.). Chicago: University of Chicago Press.

Elias, J. (2005). "The Engineering Design Mind: A Cognitive Model and a Case Study." PhD Dissertation, University of Louisiana at Lafayette, Lafayette, LA.

Eliot, T.S. (1962). *Notes Towards the Definition of Culture*. London: Faber & Faber.

Ellenberger, H.E. (1970). *The Discovery of the Unconscious*. New York: Basic Books.

Ellman, R. (1982). *James Joyce* (New and revised ed.) Oxford: Oxford University Press.

Erdelyi, M.H. (1985). *Psychoanalysis: Freud's Cognitive Psychology*. New York: W.H. Freeman & Co.

Erikson, E.H. (1958). *Young Man Luther*. New York: W.W. Norton.

Erikson, E.H. (1959). "The Nature of Clinical Evidence." In D. Lerner (ed.). *Evidence and Inference*. Glencoe, IL: The Free Press, pp. 73–96.

Erikson, E.H. (1969). *Gandhi's Truth*. New York: W.W. Norton.

Erikson, E.H. (1975). "On the Nature of 'Psycho-Historical' Evidence." In: *Life History and the Historical Moment*. New York: W.W. Norton, pp. 113–168.

Evans, R.J. (2000). *In Defence of History*. London: Granta.

Fairbairn, W. (1849). *An Account of the Construction of the Britannia and Conway Tubular Bridges*. London: John Weale / Longman, Brown, Greene & Longmans.

Fauconnier, G. and Turner, M. (2002). *The Way We Think: Conceptual Blending and the Mind's Hidden Complexity*. New York: Basic Books.

Feinstein, J. (2006). *The Nature of Creative Development*. Stanford, CA: Stanford University Press.

Ferguson, E. (1992). *Engineering and the Mind's Eye*. Cambridge, MA: MIT Press.

Feyerabend, P. (1978). *Against Method*. London: Verso.

Fiero, G. (1983). "Picasso's Minotaur," *Art International*, 26, November, pp. 23–30.

Fillimore, C.J. (1975). "An Alternative to Checklist Theories of Meaning," *Proceedings of the 1st Annual Meeting of the Berkeley Linguistic Society*, 1, pp. 123–131.

Fitzgerald, S. (ed.). (1979). *The Habit of Being: Letters of Flannery O'Connor.* New York: Farrar, Strauss and Giroux.

Fleming, D. (1952). "Latent Heat and the Invention of the Steam Engine," *ISIS,* 43, pp. 3–5.

Forbes, R.J. (1964). *Studies in Ancient Technology, Volume VIII.* Leiden: E.J. Brill.

Fotopoulo, A. and Tsakiris, M. (2017). "Mentalizing Homeostasis: The Social Origins of Interoceptive Inference," *Neuropsychoanalysis,* 19, 1, pp. 3–28.

Frank, P. (1965). *Einstein: His Life and Times.* New York: Alfred A. Knopf.

Freundlich, L. (1996). *George Rodriguez: A Cajun Artist.* New York: Viking Penguin.

Freud, S. (1989). *The Ego and the Id.* (Originally published 1920). New York: W.W. Norton.

Freud, S. (2001). *Leonardo da Vinci: A Memoir of His Childhood* (A. Dyson, tr.). (Originally published 1910). London: Routledge.

Friedlander, S. (1978). *History and Psychoanalysis* (S. Suleiman, tr.). New York: Holmes & Meier Publishers.

Gabora, L. (2007). "Why the Creative Process is Not Darwinian," *Creativity Research Journal,* 19, pp. 361–365.

Gabora, L. (2011). "An Analysis of the Blind Variation and Selective Retention Theory of Creativity," *Creativity Research Journal,* 23, 2, pp. 155–165.

Gaiger, J. (2002). "The Analysis of Pictorial Style," *British Journal of Aesthetics,* 42, 1, pp. 20–36.

Gandhi, M.K. (1993). *An Autobiography, or The Story of My Experiments with Truth* (M. Desai, tr.). (Originally published 1927). Boston, MA: Beacon Press.

Gardner, H. (1985). *The Mind's New Science.* New York: Basic Books.

Gardner, H. (1997). *Extraordinary Minds.* New York: Vintage Books.

Gardner, J. (1991). *The Art of Fiction.* (1st ed. 1984). New York: Vintage Books.

Gay, P. (1985). *Freud for Historians.* New York: Oxford University Press.

Gazzaniga, M., Levy, R.B. and Manguin, G.R. (1998). *Cognitive Neuroscience: Biology of the Mind.* New York: W.W. Norton.

Geertz, C. (1973). *The Interpretation of Cultures.* New York: Basic Books.

Getz, L. (1980). *Flannery O'Connor: Her Life, Library and Book Reviews.* New York: The Edward Mellen Press.

Ghiselin, B. (1985). *The Creative Process.* Berkeley, CA: University of California Press.

Ghose, J.C. (ed.). (1885). *The English Works of Raja Rammohun Roy, Volume 1.* Calcutta: Oriental Press.

Gibson, J.J. (1966). *The Senses Considered as Perceptual Systems.* Boston, MA: Houghton-Mifflin.

Gill, S. and Wu, D. (ed.). (1994). *William Wordsworth: A Selection of His Finest Poems.* Oxford: Oxford University Press.

Golding, J. (2000). *Paths to the Absolute.* Princeton, NJ: Princeton University Press.

Golding, J. (2001). "*Les Demoiselles d'Avignon* and the Exhibition of 1988." In: J. Green (ed.). *Picasso's* Demoiselles d'Avignon. Cambridge: Cambridge University Press, pp. 15–30.

Gombrich, E.H. (1969). *Art and Illusion.* (2nd ed.). Princeton, NJ: Princeton University Press.

Gombrich, E.H. (1971). "Psychoanalysis and the History of Art." In: *Meditations on a Hobby Horse.* London: Phaidon Press, pp. 30–44.

Gombrich, E.H. (1993). *A Lifelong Interest: Conversations on Art and Science.* London: Thames and Hudson.

Gould, S.J. (1977). *Ontogeny and Phylogeny.* Cambridge, MA: Belknap Press of Harvard University Press.

Gould, S.J. (2002). *The Structure of Evolutionary Theory*. Cambridge, MA: Belknap Press of Harvard University Press.

Gould, S.J. (2006). *The Richness of Life*, D. McGarr and S. Rose (ed.). London: Vintage Books.

Grandy, R.E. (2007). "Artifacts: Parts and Principles." In E. Margolis and S. Laurence (ed.). *Creations of the Mind*. Oxford: Oxford University Press, pp. 18–32.

Green, J. (2001). "An Introduction to *Les Demoiselles d'Avignon*." In: J. Green (ed.). *Picasso's Demoiselles d'Avignon*. Cambridge: Cambridge University Press, pp. 1–14.

Gregory, R.L. (1987). "Cognition". In : R.L. Gregory (ed.). *The Oxford Companion to Mind*. Oxford: Oxford University Press, p. 149.

Gruber, H.E. (1981). *Darwin on Man: A Psychological Study of Scientific Creativity*. (2nd ed.). Chicago: University of Chicago Press.

Gruber, H.E. (1989). "The Evolving Systems Approach to Creative Work." In: D.B. Wallace and H.E. Gruber (ed.). *Creative People at Work*. New York: Oxford University Press, pp. 3–24.

Guilford, J.P. (1979). "Some Incubated Thoughts on Incubation," *Journal of Creative Behavior*, 13, 1, pp. 1–8.

Gupta, U. (2007). "The Politics of Humanism: An Interview with Satyajit Ray" (1982). In: B. Cardullo (ed.). *Satyajit Ray Interviews*. Jackson, MS: University Press of Mississippi, pp. 122–132.

Hadamard, J. (1954). *The Psychology of Invention in the Mathematical Field*. (Originally published 1949). New York: Dover.

Haken, W., Appel, K. and J. Koch, J. (1977). "Every Planar Map is Four Colorable," *Illinois Journal of Mathematics*, 21, 84, pp. 429–567.

Haraway, D. (1991). "A Cyborg Manifesto." In: *Simians, Cyborgs and Women: The Reinvention of Nature*. New York: Routledge, pp. 291–324.

Harding, R.E.M. (1942). *An Anatomy of Inspiration*. (2nd ed.). Cambridge: W. Heffer & Sons.

Hardy, G.H. (1969). *A Mathematician's Apology*. (2nd ed, Originally published 1940) Cambridge: Cambridge University Press.

Hardy, W. (2014). *The Origin of the Idea of the Industrial Revolution*. Sheperton: The Aidan Press.

Harré, R. (1981). *Great Scientific Experiments*. Oxford: Phaidon Press.

Harrington, E. (1987). "Whigs, Prigs and Historians of Science," *Nature*, 329, September 17, pp. 233–234.

Hart, R. (1859). "Reminiscences of James Watt". *Transactions of Glasgow Archeological Society*. Quoted in S. Smiles (1904). *Lives of the Engineers: Boulton and Watt*. London: John Murray, p. 90.

Hayes Tucker, P. (1998). "Making Sense of Eduard Manet's *Le Dejeuner sur l'Herbe*." In: P. Hayes Tucker (ed.). *Manet's* Le Dejeuner sur l'Herbe. Cambridge: Cambridge University Press, pp. 1–37.

Heintz, C. (2011). "Cognitive History and Cultural Epidemiology." In: L.H. Martin and J. Sørensen (ed.). *Past Minds: Studies in Cognitive Historiography*. London: Equinox, pp. 11–28.

Hernstein, R.J. and E.G. Boring, E.G. (ed.). (1965). *A Source Book in the History of Psychology*. Cambridge, MA: Harvard University Press.

Hills, R.L. (1989). *Power from Steam: A History of the Stationary Steam Engine*. Cambridge: Cambridge University Press.

Hindle, B. (1983). *Emulation and Invention*. New York: W.W. Norton.

Hoare, C.A.R. (1969). "An Axiomatic Basis of Computer Programming," *Communications of the ACM*, 12, 10, pp. 576–580, 583.

Hoare, C.A.R. (1972). "Notes on Data Structuring." In: O-J. Dahl, E.W. Dijkstra and C.A.R. Hoare. *Structured Programming.* New York: Academic Press, pp. 83–174.

Hoare, C.A.R. and Wirth, N. (1973). "An Axiomatic Definition of the Programming Language PASCAL," *Acta Informatica,* 2, pp. 335–355.

Hobsbawm, E. (1983). "Inventing Tradition." In: E. Hobsbawm and T. Ranger (ed.). *The Invention of Tradition.* Cambridge: Cambridge University Press, pp. 1–14.

Hobson, F. (1988). "Casting a Long Shadow: Faulkner and Southern Literature." In: B. Ford (ed.). *The Pelican Guide to English Literature, 9: American Literature.* London: Penguin, pp. 461–477.

Hodges, A. (1983). *Alan Turing: The Enigma.* New York: Simon & Schuster.

Hogan, P.C. (2003). *Cognitive Science, Literature and the Arts.* New York: Routledge.

Holland, J.H., Holyoak, K.J., Nisbett, R.A. and Thagard, P.R. (1986). *Induction.* Cambridge, MA: MIT Press.

Holland, N. (1988). *The Brain of Robert Frost.* New York: Routledge.

Holmes, F.L. (1985). *Antoine Lavoisier and the Chemistry of Life.* Madison, WI: University of Wisconsin Press.

Holmes, F.L. (1989). "Antoine Lavoisier and Hans Krebs: Two Styles of Scientific Creativity." In: D.B. Wallace and H.E. Gruber (ed.). *Creative People at Work.* New York: Oxford University Press, pp. 44–68.

Holmes, F.L. (1996). *Hans Krebs: The Formation of a Scientific Life 1900–1933.* New York: Oxford University Press.

Homans, G. (1950). *The Human Group.* New York: Harcourt, Brace & Co.

Home, A. (1933). "A List of the Principal Publications and Other Writings of Raja Rammohun Roy." In: A. Home (ed.). *Rammohun Roy: The Man and His Work.* Calcutta: Centenary Publicity Booklet, pp. 133–147.

Hopkins, M.E. (1972). "A Case for the GOTO," *Proceedings of the 25th National ACM Conference,* pp. 787–790.

Huxley, J.S. (2010). *Evolution: The Modern Synthesis.* (2nd ed.). Cambridge, MA: MIT Press.

Isaakson, F. (2007). "Conversations with Satyajit Ray." In: B. Cardullo (ed.). *Satyajit Ray Interviews.* Jackson, MS: University Press of Mississippi, pp. 34–52.

Izenberg, G. (1975). "Psychohistory and Intellectual History," *History and Theory,* 14, pp. 139–155.

Jack, I. (2001). "Introduction." In: N.C. Chaudhuri. *Autobiography of An Unknown Indian.* (2nd ed.). New York: New York Review of Books, pp. ix–xv.

James, W. (1950). *Principles of Psychology, Volume 1.* (1890 ed.). New York: Dover.

Jammer, M. (1999). *Einstein on Religion.* Princeton, NJ: Princeton University Press.

Jansen, H.W. (1969). *History of Art.* Englewood-Cliffs, NJ: Prentice-Hall.

Jaynes, J. (1976). *The Origins of Consciousness and the Breakdown of the Bicameral Mind.* Toronto: University of Toronto Press.

Jeffrey, L. (1989). "Writing and Rewriting Poetry: William Wordsworth." In: D.B. Wallace and H.E. Gruber (ed.). *Creative People at Work.* New York: Oxford University Press, pp. 69–90.

Jenkins, K. (2003). *Re-thinking History.* London: Routledge.

Johnson-Laird, P.N. (1988). *The Computer and the Mind.* Cambridge, MA: Harvard University Press.

Jones, J.C. (1980). *Design Methods: Seeds of Human Future.* New York: John Wiley.

Karl, F.R. (1988). "Black Writers—Jewish Writers—Women Writers." In: B. Ford (ed.). *The Pelican Guide to English Literature, 9: American Literature.* London: Penguin, pp. 566–582.

Keswani, G.H. (1980). *Raman and His Effect*. New Delhi: National Book Trust.

Kihlstrom, J.F. (1987). "The Cognitive Unconscious," *Science*, 237, September 17, pp. 1445–1452.

Klahr, D. and Simon, H.A. (1999). "Studies of Scientific Discovery: Complementary Approaches and Convergent Thinking," *Psychological Bulletin*, 125, 3, pp. 524–543.

Knuth, D.E. (1974). "Structured Programming *with* goto Statements," *Computing Surveys*, 6, 12, pp. 261–301.

Knuth, D.E. (1986). *Computers and Typesetting* (Volumes A–D). Reading, MA: Addison-Wesley.

Knuth, D.E. (1992a). "Computer Programming as an Art." In: *Literate Programming*. Stanford, CA: Center for the Study of Language and Information, pp. 1–16.

Knuth, D.E. (1992b). "Literate Programming." In: *Literate Programming*. Stanford, CA: Center for the Study of Language and Information, pp. 99–136.

Knuth, D.E. and Floyd, R.W. (1971). "Notes on Avoiding go to Statement," *Information Processing Letters*, 1, pp. 23–31.

Koestler, A. (1964). *The Act of Creation*. London: Hutchinson.

Kopf, D. (1969). *British Orientalism and the Bengal Renaissance*. Berkeley, CA: University of California Press.

Kopf, D. (1979). *The Brahmo Samaj and the Shaping of the Modern Indian Mind*. Princeton, NJ: Princeton University Press.

Kovac, J. and Weisberg, M. (ed.). (2012). *Roald Hoffmann on the Philosophy, Art and Science of Chemistry*. New York: Oxford University Press.

Kozbelt, A. (2008). "E.H. Gombrich on Creativity: A Cognitive-Historical Case Study," *Creativity Research Journal*, 20, 1, pp. 93–104.

Kripalani, K. (1981). *Dwarakanath Tagore. A Forgotten Pioneer: A Life*. New Delhi: National Book Trust.

Kris, E. (1952). *Psychoanalytic Explorations of Art*. Madison, WI: International University Press.

Kubler, G. (1962). *The Shape of Time*. New Haven, CT: Yale University Press.

Kuhn, T.S. (1970). "Reflections on My Critics." In: I. Lakatos and G. Musgrave (ed.). *Criticism and the Growth of Knowledge*. Cambridge: Cambridge University Press, pp. 231–278.

Kuhn, T.S. (1977). "Second Thoughts on Paradigms." In: *The Essential Tension*. Chicago: University of Chicago Press, pp. 293–319.

Kuhn, T.S. (2012). *The Structure of Scientific Revolutions*. (4th ed.). Chicago: University of Chicago Press.

Kulkarni, D. and Simon, H.A. (1988). "The Processes of Scientific Discovery: The Strategy of Experimentation," *Cognitive Science*, 12, pp. 139–176.

LaCapra, D. (1983). *Rethinking Intellectual History*. Ithaca, NY: Cornell University Press.

Lakatos, I. (1978). *The Methodology of Scientific Research Programmes*. Cambridge: Cambridge University Press.

Lakatos, I. and Musgrave, G. (ed.). (1970). *Criticism and the Growth of Knowledge*. Cambridge: Cambridge University Press.

Langley, P. Simon, H.A., Bradshaw, G.L. and Zytkow, J. (1987). *Scientific Discovery*. Cambridge, MA: MIT Press.

Laudan, L. (1977). *Progress and Its Problems*. Berkeley, CA: University of California Press.

Laudan, L. (1990). "The History of Science and the Philosophy of Science," in R.C. Colby, G.N. Cantor, J.R.R. Christie and M.J.S. Hodge (ed.). *Companion to the History of Science*. London: Routledge, pp. 47–59.

Laudun, J. (2016). *The Amazing Crawfish Boat*. Jackson, MS: University Press of Mississippi.

Leakey, L.S.B. (1960). *Adam's Ancestors: The Evolution of Man and His Culture.* (Originally published 1934). New York: Harper & Row.

Leakey, R. (1994). *The Origin of Humankind.* New York: Basic Books.

Lee, H. (2009). *Biography: A Very Short Introduction.* Oxford: Oxford University Press.

Lewis, M.T. (2000). *Cézanne.* London: Phaidon Press.

Lovejoy, A.O. (1964). *The Great Chain of Being.* (Originally published 1936). Cambridge, MA: Harvard University Press.

Loewenberg, P. (1983). *Decoding the Past: The Psychohistorical Approach.* New York: Alfred A. Knopf.

Lowes, J.L. (1930). *The Road to Xanadu: A Study in the Ways of the Imagination.* Boston, MA: Houghton Mifflin.

Ludden, D. (2002). "Introduction: A Brief History of Subalternity." In: D. Ludden (ed.). *Reading Subaltern Studies.* New Delhi: Permanent Black, pp. 1–42.

Lumsden, C.J. (1999). "Evolving Creative Minds: Stories and Mechanisms". In: R.J. Sternberg (ed.). *Handbook of Creativity.* Cambridge: Cambridge University Press, pp. 153–168.

MacLeod, C. (2007). *Heroes of Invention: Technology, Liberalism and British Identity 1750–1914.* Cambridge: Cambridge University Press.

Magee, R. ed. (1987). *Conversations with Flannery O'Connor.* Jackson, MS: University of Mississippi Press.

Mandler, G. (1985). *Cognitive Psychology.* Hillsdale, NJ: Lawrence Erlbaum Associates.

Martin, L.H. (2011). "Evolution, Cognition, and History." In: L.H. Martin and J. Sørensen (ed.). *Past Minds: Studies in Cognitive Historiography.* London: Equinox, pp. 1–10.

Martin, L.H. and Sørensen, J. (ed.). (2011). *Past Minds: Studies in Cognitive Historiography.* London: Equinox.

Marx, L. and Mazlish, B. (ed.). (1988). *Progress: Fact or Illusion?* Ann Arbor, MI: University of Michigan Press.

Mason, M.G. (1980). "The Other Voice: Autobiographies of Women Writers." In: J. Olney (ed.). *Autobiography: Essays Theoretical and Critical.* Princeton, NJ: Princeton University Press, pp. 207–235.

Masterman, M. (1970). "The Nature of a Paradigm." In: I. Lakatos and G. Musgrave (ed.). *Criticism and the Growth of Knowledge.* Cambridge: Cambridge University Press, pp. 59–90.

Matlin, M.W. (2009). *Cognition* (7th ed.). New York: John Wiley.

May, R. (1994). *The Courage to Create.* New York: W.W. Norton.

Mayr, E. (1982). *The Growth of Biological Thought.* Belknap Press of Harvard University Press.

McCauley, A. (1988). "Sex and the Salon: Defining Art and Immorality in 1863." In: P. Hayes Tucker (ed.). *Manet's le Dejeuner sur l'Herbe.* Cambridge: Cambridge University Press, pp. 38–74.

McCracken, D.D. (1973). "Revolution in Programming: An Overview," *Datamation,* 19, 12, pp. 50–52.

McCulloch, W.S. and Pitts, W.S. (1943). "A Logical Calculus of the Ideas Immanent in Nervous Activity," *Bulletin of Mathematical Biophysics,* 5, pp. 115–133.

McShea, D.W. (1997). "Complexity in Evolution: A Skeptical Assessment," *Philosophica,* 59, 1, pp. 79–112.

McNeill, I. (1990). "Roads, Bridges and Vehicles." In: I. McNeill (ed.). *Encyclopedia of the History of Technology.* New York: Routledge.

Medawar, P.B. (1974). *The Hope of Progress.* London: Wildwood.

Medawar, P.B. (1990). "Creativity—Especially in Science." In: *The Threat and the Glory: Reflections on Science and Scientists.* Oxford: Oxford University Press, pp. 83–90.

Medawar, P.B. and Medawar, J. (1983). *Aristotle to Zoos: A Philosophical Dictionary*. Cambridge, MA: Harvard University Press.

Meyerhoff, H. (1987). "On Psychoanalysis as History." In: G. Cocks and J.L. Cosby (ed.). *Psychohistory*. New Haven, CT: Yale University Press, pp. 17–29.

Miller, A.I. (1986). *Imagery in Scientific Thought: Creating 20th Century Physics*. Cambridge, MA: MIT Press.

Miller, A.I. (1989). "Imagery and Intuition in Creative Scientific Thinking: Albert Einstein's Invention of the Special Theory of Relativity." In: D.B. Wallace and H.E. Gruber (ed.). *Creative People at Work*. New York: Oxford University Press, pp. 171–188.

Miller, A.I. (2001). *Einstein, Picasso*. New York: Basic Books.

Miller, E.F. and Lindamood, G.A. (1973). "Structured Programming: A Top-Down Approach," *Datamation*, 19, 12, pp. 55–57.

Miller, G.A. (1962). *Psychology: The Science of Mental Life*. New York: Harper & Row.

Mills, H.D. (1972). "Mathematical Foundations of Structured Programming." IBM Corp. Report FSC-72–6012. Gaithesberg, MD: IBM Corporation.

Minsky, M.L. (1975). "A Framework for Representing Knowledge." In: P.H. Winston (ed.). *The Psychology of Computer Vision*. New York: McGraw-Hill, pp. 211–277.

Mitchell, S.A. and Black, M.J. (1995). *Freud and Beyond*. New York: Basic Books.

Mithen, S. (1996). *The Prehistory of the Mind*. London: Thames & Hudson.

Mitter, P. (2007). *The Triumph of Modernism*. London: Reaktion Books.

Mokyr, J. (1990). *Lever of Riches*. New York: Oxford University Press.

Moore, H. (1985). "Notes on Sculpture." In: B. Ghiselin. *The Creative Process*. Berkeley, CA: University of California Press, pp. 73–78.

Moore, J. (1996). "Metabiographical Reflections on Charles Darwin." In: M. Shortland and R. Yeo (ed.). *Telling Lives in Science*. Cambridge: Cambridge University Press, pp. 267–282.

Morris, F.L. and Jones, C.B. (1984). "An Early Program Proof by Alan Turing," *Annals of the History of Computing*, 6, 2, pp. 139–143.

Mostow, J. (1985). "Toward Better Models of Design Processes," *AI Magazine*, Spring, pp. 44–57.

Mumford, L. (1952). *Art and Technics*. New York: Columbia University Press.

Mumford, L. (1962). *Technics and Civilization*. (Originally published 1934). New York: Harcourt, Brace & World.

Musson, A.E. and Robinson, E. (1969). *Science and Technology in the Industrial Revolution*. Toronto: University of Toronto Press.

Nagel, T. (1974). "What Is It Like to Be a Bat?" *Philosophical Review*, 83, pp. 435–460.

Naipaul, V.S. (1984). *The Overcrowded Barracoon*. New York: Vintage Books, p. 59.

Nandy, A. (1995). *Alternative Science: Creativity and Authenticity in Two Indian Scientists*. (2nd ed.). New Delhi: Oxford University Press.

Neisser, U. (1988). "Five Kinds of Self Knowledge," *Philosophical Psychology*, 1, pp. 35–59.

Nersessian, N. (1995). "Opening the Black Box: Cognitive Science and History of Science," *Osiris* (Second Series), 10, pp. 194–211.

Nervi, P.L. (1966). *Aesthetics and Technology in Building*. Cambridge, MA: Harvard University Press.

Newell, A. (1982). "The Knowledge Level," *Artificial Intelligence*, 18, pp. 87–127.

Newell, A. (1990). *Unified Theories of Cognition*. Cambridge, MA: Harvard University Press.

Newell, A., Shaw, C.J. and Simon, H.A. (1958). "Elements of a Theory of Human Problem Solving," *Psychological Review*, 65, 3, pp. 151–166.

Newell, A., Shaw, C.J. and Simon, H.A. (1962). "The Processes of Creative Thinking." In: H.E. Gruber, G. Terrell and M. Wertheimer (ed.). *Contemporary Approaches in Creative Thinking*. New York: Lieber-Atherton, pp. 63–119.

Newell, A. and Simon, H.A. (1956). "The Logic Theory Machine," *IRE Transactions on Information Theory*, IT-2, 3, pp. 61–79.

Newell, A. and Simon, H.A. (1972). *Human Problem Solving*. Englewood-Cliffs, NJ: Prentice-Hall.

Newell, A., and Simon, H.A. (1976). "Computer Science as Empirical Inquiry," *Communications of the ACM*, 19, pp. 113–126.

Nichols, R.B.M. (1942). "The Birth of a Poem." In: R.E.M. Harding. *Anatomy of Inspiration*. (2nd ed.). Cambridge: Heffer, pp. 104–126.

Nickles, T. (2003a). "Evolutionary Problems of Innovation and the Meno Problem." In: L.V. Shavinina (ed.). *International Handbook on Innovation*. Kidlington: Elsevier, pp. 54–78.

Nickles, T. (ed.). (2003b). *Thomas Kuhn*. Cambridge: Cambridge University Press.

Nickles, T. (2013). "Creativity, Nonlinearity and the Sustainability of Scientific Progress." In: W. Gonzalez (ed.). *Creativity, Innovation and Complexity in Science*. La Coruña: Netbiblio, pp. 143–172.

Nisbet, R. (1994). *History of the Idea of Progress*. New Brunswick, NJ: Transactions Publishers.

Norman, D.A. (1989). *The Design of Everyday Things*. New York: Doubleday.

Nozick, R. (1989). *The Examined Life*. New York: Simon and Schuster.

Oatley, K. (1992). *Best Laid Schemes: The Psychology of Emotions*. Cambridge: Cambridge University Press.

O'Connor, F. (1989). *The Complete Stories*. New York: Farrar, Strauss & Giroux.

Olby, R. (1974). *The Path to the Double Helix*. London: Macmillan.

Olney, J. (1998). *Memory and Narrative: The Weave of Life Writing*. Chicago: University of Chicago Press.

Olton, R.M. and Johnson, D.M. (1976). "Mechanisms of Incubation in Creative Problem Solving," *American Journal of Psychology*, 89, pp. 617–630.

Ousby, I. (ed.). (1988). *The Cambridge Guide to Literature in English*. Cambridge: Cambridge University Press.

Pais, A. (1982). '*Subtle is the Lord…*': *The Science and Life of Albert Einstein*. New York: Oxford University Press.

Paley, W. (1998). *Natural Theology* (12th ed.). Ann Arbor, MI: University of Michigan Humanities Text Initiative, www.hti.umich.edu/cgi. Retrieved September 30, 2014.

Papert, S. (1978). "The Mathematical Unconscious." In: J. Weschler (ed.). *On Aesthetics in Science*. Cambridge, MA: MIT Press, pp. 105–120.

Papert, S. (1980). *Mindstorms*. New York: Basic Books.

Paranjpe, A.C. (1998). *Self and Identity in Modern Psychology and Indian Thought*. New York: Plenum Press.

Parnas, D.L. (1972). "On the Criteria to be Used in Decomposing Systems into Modules," *Communications of the ACM*, 15, 12, pp. 1053–1058.

Patrick, C. (1937). "Creative Thought in Artistic Activity," *Journal of Psychology*, 4, pp. 35–73.

Perkins, D.N. (1981). *The Mind's Best Work*. Cambridge, MA: Harvard University Press.

Perkins, D.N. (2000). *Archimedes' Bathtub*. New York: W.W. Norton.

Petroski, H. (1992). "The Britannia Tubular Bridge," *American Scientist*, May–June, pp. 220–224.

Petroski, H. (1994). *Design Paradigms: Case Histories of Error and Judgement in Engineering.* Cambridge: Cambridge University Press.

Pfeiffer, J. (1982). *The Creative Explosion.* New York: Harper & Row.

Piaget, J. (1976). *The Child and Reality.* Harmondsworth: Penguin.

Picasso, P. (1972). "Conversations with Christian Zervos" (Originally published 1935). In: D. Ashton (ed.). *Picasso on Art.* New York: DeCapo Press, pp. 7–13.

Plotkin, H. (2003). *The Imagined World Made Real: Toward a Natural Science of Culture.* New Brunswick, NJ: Rutgers University Press.

Poincaré, H. (1985). "Mathematical Creation" (G.B. Halstead, tr.) (Originally published 1913). In: B. Ghiselin. *The Creative Process.* Berkeley, CA: University of California Press, pp. 22–31.

Polanyi, M. (1962). *Personal Knowledge.* Chicago: University of Chicago Press.

Popper, K.R. (1965). *Conjectures and Refutations: The Growth of Scientific Knowledge.* New York: Harper & Row.

Popper, K.R. (1968). *The Logic of Scientific Discovery.* New York: Harper & Row.

Popper, K.R. (1972). *Objective Knowledge.* Oxford: Clarendon Press.

Pye, D. (1978). *The Nature and Aesthetics of Design.* London: Herbert Press.

Pyenson, L. (1985). *The Young Einstein.* Bristol: Adam Hilger.

Pylyshyn, Z. (1984). *Computation and Cognition: Toward a Foundation for Cognitive Science.* Cambridge, MA: MIT Press.

Radhakrishnan, S. and Moore, C.A. (ed.). (1957). *A Source Book on Indian Philosophy.* Princeton, NJ: Princeton University Press.

Radnitzky, G. and Bartley, III, W.W. (ed.). (1987). *Evolutionary Epistemology, Rationality and the Sociology of Knowledge.* La Salle, IL: Open Court.

Raman, C.V. and Krishnan, K.S. (1928). "A New Type of Secondary Radiation," *Nature,* 121, p. 501.

Ray, R.K. (2001). *Exploring Emotional History.* New Delhi: Oxford University Press.

Ray, R.K. (2003). *The Felt Community.* New Delhi: Oxford University Press.

Ray, S. (1994). *My Years with Apu.* New Delhi: Viking.

Ray, S. (2005). *Speaking of Films* (G. Majumdar, tr.). New Delhi: Penguin Books India.

Raychaudhuri, T. (1999). *Perceptions, Emotions, Sensibilities: Essays in India's Colonial and Postcolonial Experiences.* New Delhi: Oxford University Press.

Raychaudhuri, T. (2002). *Europe Reconsidered.* (2nd ed.). New York: Oxford University Press.

Richards, R.J. and Daston, L. (ed.). (2016). *Kuhn's* Structure of Scientific Revolutions *at Fifty.* Chicago: University of Chicago Press.

Richardson, J. (1991). *A Life of Picasso, Volume I.* New York: Random House.

Robertson, B.C. (1995). *Raja Rammohan Roy: The Father of Modern India.* New Delhi: Oxford University Press.

Robinson, A. (1984). *The Cinema of Satyajit Ray.* A Documentary. London: BBC.

Robinson, D.N. (1995). *An Intellectual History of Psychology.* (3rd ed.). Madison, WI: University of Wisconsin Press.

Robinson, E. and McKie, D. (ed.). (1970). *Partners in Science: James Watt and Joseph Black.* Cambridge, MA: Harvard Univeristy Press.

Robinson, J.M. (1981). "Style and Significance in Art History and Art Criticism," *Journal of Aesthetics and Art Criticism,* 40, 1, pp. 5–14.

Rodrigue, G. (1976). *The Cajuns of George Rodrigue* (G. and J. Planel, tr.). Birmingham, AL: Oxmoor House.

Rodrigue, G. (2003). *The Art of George Rodrigue.* New York: Harry N. Abrams.

Roe, N. (2005). "Introduction." In: N. Roe (ed.). *Romanticism*. Oxford: Oxford University Press, pp. 1–12.

Rolt, L.T.C. (1963). *Thomas Newcomen*. London: David & Charles/Dawlish MacDonald.

Rosenbloom, P.S. (2013). *On Computing*. Cambridge, MA: MIT Press.

Rothenberg, A. (1990). *Creativity and Madness*. Baltimore, MD: Johns Hopkins University Press.

Rosenberg, N. and Vincenti, W.G. (1978). *The Britannia Bridge*. Cambridge, MA: MIT Press.

Rouse, W.H.D. (tr.), (1984). "Ion." In: *Great Dialogues of Plato*. New York: Mentor, pp. 28–68.

Roy, R. (1885). "Translation of an Abridgement of the Vedant or the Resolution of All the Veds". (Originally published in 1816). In: J.C. Ghose (ed.), 1885. *The English Works of Raja Rammohun Roy, Volume 1*. Calcutta: Oriental Press, pp. 1–20.

Roy, R. (1935). "Autobiographical Sketch." (Originally written 1833). In: M. Carpenter. *The Last Days in England of Rajah Rammohun Roy*. (3rd ed.). Kolkata: The Rammohun Library and free Reading Room, pp. 22–26.

Rubin, D.C. (1995). *Memory in Oral Traditions: The Cognitive Psychology of Epic, Ballads, and Counting-Out Rhythms*. Oxford: Oxford University Press.

Rubin, W., Seckel, H. and Cousins, J. (1994). *Les Demoiselles d'Avignon*. New York: Museum of Modern Art.

Rumelhart, D. (1989). "The Architecture of Mind: A Connectionist Approach." In: M. Posner (ed.). *Foundations of Cognitive Science*. Cambridge, MA: MIT Press, pp. 133–160.

Rumelhart, D., Smolensky, P., McClelland, J.L. and Hinton, G.E. (1986). "Schemas and Thought Processes in PDP Models." In: J.L. McClelland and D.E. Rumelhart and the PDP Research Group. *Parallel Distributed Processing: Explorations in the Microstructure of Cognition, Volume 2*. Cambridge, MA: MIT Press, pp. 7–57.

Runco, M.A. (2007). "Chance and Intentionality in Creative Performance," *Creativity Research Journal*, 19, pp. 345–360.

Runco, M.A. (2010). "Creative thinking May Be Simultaneous as Well as Blind: Comment on 'Creative Thought as Blind-Variation and Selective Retention: Combinatorial Models of Exceptional Creativity' by Dean Keith Simonton," *Physics of Life Reviews*, 7 (2), pp. 184–185.

Runyon, W.M. (1982). *Life Histories and Psychobiography*. New York: Oxford University Press.

Ruse, M. (1973). *The Philosophy of Biology*. London: Hutchinson.

Ruse, M. (1993). *The Darwinian Paradigm*. London: Routledge.

Rushdie, S. (1997). "Introduction". In S. Rushdie and E. West (ed.). *Mirrorwork: 50 Years of Indian Writing 1947–1997*. New York: Henry Holt, pp. vii–xx.

Said, E.W. (1994). *Culture and Imperialism*. New York: Vintage Books.

Sarkar, S. (1971). *On the Bengal Renaissance*. Kolkata: Papyrus.

Sastri, S. (1933). "Rammohun Roy: The Story of His Life." (Originally written 1911). In: A. Home. *Rammohun Roy: The Man and his Work*. Calcutta: Centenary Publicity Booklet, pp. 7–27.

Schacter, D.C. (1996). *Searching for Memory*. New York: Basic Books.

Schick, K. and Toth, N. (1993). *Making Silent Stones Speak: Human Evolution and the Dawn of Technology*. New York: Simon & Schuster.

Schneider, D.E. (1962). *The Psychoanalyst and the Artist*. New York: Mentor/New American Library.

Schopenhauer, A. (1969). *The World as Will and Representation* (Originally published 1819). New York: Dover.

Searle, J. (1984). *Minds, Brains and Science.* Cambridge, MA: Harvard University Press.

Searle, J. (1992). *The Rediscovery of the Mind.* Cambridge, MA: MIT Press.

Seckel, H. (1994). "Anthology of Early Commentary on Les Demoiselles d'Avignon." In: W. Rubin, H. Seckel and J. Cousins. *Les Demoiselles d'Avignon.* New York: Museum of Modern Art, pp. 213–256.

Segura, C. and Rodrigue, G. (1984). *Bayou.* Baton Rouge, LA: Inkwell Publications.

Sen, A.K. (1993). "On the Darwinian View of Progress," *Population and Developmental Studies,* 19, pp. 123–137.

Sen, K.M. (1961). *Hinduism.* London: Penguin.

Sengoopta, C. (2003). *Imprint of the Raj.* London: Pan Macmillan.

Shannon, C.E. and Weaver, W. (1949). *The Mathematical Theory of Communication.* Urbana, IL: University of Illinois Press.

Shepherd, V.A. (2009). "From Semiconductors to the Neurobiology of Plants: The Biophysical Researches of J.C. Bose," *Physics News* (Bulletin of the Indian Physics Association), 39, 4, pp. 39–56.

Sher-Gil, A. (1936). "Modern Indian Art—Imitating the Forms of the Past," *The Hindu,* November 1.

Sher-Gil, A. (2002). "Evolution of My Art." (Originally written 1942.) In E. de Souza and L. Periera (ed.). *Women's Voices.* New Delhi: Oxford University Press, pp. 354–356.

Simon, H.A. (1937). "The Logical Structure of a Science of Administration." Unpublished memorandum, July 28. Pittsburg, PA: Herbert A. Simon Papers, Carnegie-Mellon University.

Simon, H.A. (1947). "The Axioms of Newtonian Mechanics," *Philosophical Magazine,* Ser. 7, 38, pp. 889–905.

Simon, H.A. (1950). "Modern Organization Theories," *Advances in Management,* October, pp. 2–4.

Simon, H.A. (1952). "A Formal Theory of Interaction in Small Groups," *American Sociological Review,* 17, pp. 202–211.

Simon, H.A. (1954a). "Some Strategic Considerations in the Construction of Social Science Models." In: P. Lazarsfierld (ed.). *Mathematical Thinking in the Social Sciences.* Glencoe, IL: The Free Press, pp. 388–415.

Simon, H.A. (1954b). "Discussion: The Axiomatization of Classical Mechanics," *Philosophy of Science,* 21, pp. 340–343.

Simon, H.A. (1955). "A Behavioral Model of Rational Choice," *Quarterly Journal of Economics,* 60, pp. 99–118.

Simon, H.A. (1957). *Models of Man.* New York: John Wiley.

Simon, H.A. (1959). "Definable Terms and Primitives in Axiom Systems." In: D. Henkin, P. Suppes and A. Tarski (ed.). *The Axiomatic Method.* Amsterdam: North-Holland, pp. 443–453.

Simon, H.A. (1976). *Administrative Behavior.* (3rd ed.). New York: The Free Press.

Simon, H.A. (1977). *Models of Discovery.* Dordecht: Reidel.

Simon, H.A. (1979). *Models of Thought.* New Haven, CT: Yale University Press.

Simon, H.A. (1989). *Models of Thought, Volume 2.* New Haven, CT: Yale University Press.

Simon, H.A. (1991). *Models of My Life.* New York: Basic Books.

Simon, H.A. (1995). "Artificial Intelligence: An Empirical Science," *Artificial Intelligence,* 77, pp. 95–127.

Simon, H.A. (1996). *The Sciences of the Artificial* (3rd ed.). Cambridge, MA: MIT Press.

Simon, H.A. (1999). *Models of Bounded Rationality, Volume 3.* Cambridge, MA: MIT Press.

Simonton, D.K. (1988). *Scientific Genius.* Cambridge: Cambridge University Press.

Simonton, D.K. (1999). *Origins of Genius: Darwinian Perspectives on Creativity*. New York: Oxford University Press.

Simonton, D.K. (2010a). "Creative Thought as Blind-Variation and Selective Retention: Combinatorial Models of Exceptional Creativity," *Physics of Life Reviews*, 7, pp. 156–179.

Simonton, D.K. (2010b). "Reply to Comment. Creative Thought as Blind-Variation and Selective Retention: Combinatorial Models of Exceptional Creativity," *Physics of Life Reviews*, 7, pp. 190–194.

Smiles, S. (1904). *Lives of the Engineers. The Steam Engine: Boulton and Watt*. London: John Murray.

Snow, C.P. (1993). *The Two Cultures* (Canto ed. Originally published 1959). Cambridge: Cambridge University Press.

Sobcheck, T.C. and Sobcheck, V.C. (1987). *An Introduction to Film*. Glenview, IL: Scott, Foresman & Co.

Sørensen, J. (2011). "Past Minds: Present Historiography and Cognitive Science." In: L.H. Martin and J. Sørensen (ed.). *Past Minds: Studies in Cognitive Historiography*. London: Equinox, pp. 179–196.

Spender, S. (1985). "The Making of a Poem" (Originally published 1936). In: B. Ghiselin. *The Creative Process*. Berkeley, CA: University of California Press, pp. 113–126.

Sperber, D. (1996). *Explaining Culture: A Naturalistic Approach*. Oxford: Blackwell.

St. Fleur, N. (2018). "Oldest Known Drawing is Found in South Africa," *New York Times* (International Edition), September 17, 2018.

Steadman, J.P. (2008). *The Evolution of Designs*. (2nd ed.). Cambridge: Cambridge University Press.

Stipp, D. (2017). *A Most Elegant Solution*. New York: Basic Books.

Storr, A. (1972). *Dynamics of Creation*. London: Martin Secker and Warburg.

Strout, C. (1968). "Ego Psychology and the Historian," *History and Theory*, VII, 3, pp. 281–297.

Sunderam, V. (n.d.) "Amrita Sher-Gil—Life and Work." www.sikh-heritage.co.uk/arts/amritashergil.html. Retrieved May 12, 2011.

Sunderam, V. (ed.). (2010). *Amrita Sher-Gil: A Self-Portrait in Letters and Writings*. New Delhi: Tulika Books.

Tagore, R. (1912). *Gitanjali (Song-Offerings)*. London: The India Society.

Tagore, R. (1972). Letter to William Rothenstein, April 20, 1927. In: M. Lago (ed.). *Imperfect Encounters: Letters of William Rothenstein and Rabindranath Tagore, 1911–1941*. Cambridge, MA: Harvard University Press, p. 321.

Tagore, R. (2001). *Reminiscences* (S. Tagore, ed.) (Originally published 1917.). New Delhi: Macmillan India.

Tarski, A. (1956). *Logic, Semantics, Metamathematics*. Oxford: Clarendon Press.

Taylor, C.W. (1988). "Various Approaches to and Definitions of Creativity." In: R.J. Sternberg (ed.). *The Nature of Creativity*. Cambridge: Cambridge University Press, pp. 99–124.1988.

Thagard, P.R. (1988). *Computational Philosophy of Science*. Cambridge, MA: MIT Press.

Thagard, P.R. (1992). *Conceptual Revolutions*. Princeton, NJ: Princeton University Press.

Thomasow, M. (1995). *Ecological Identity*. Cambridge, MA: MIT Press.

Thomasson, A. (2007). "Artifacts and Human Concepts." In: E. Margolis and S. Laurence (ed.). *Creations of the Mind*. New York: Oxford University Press, pp. 52–73.

Timoshenko, S. (1983). *History of Strength of Materials*. New York: Dover Publications.

Tomasello, M. (1999). *The Cultural Origins of Human Cognition*. Cambridge, MA: Harvard University Press.

Tooby, J. and Cosmides, L. (1992). "The Psychological Foundations of Culture." In: J. Barkow, L. Cosmides and J. Tooby (ed.). *The Adapted Mind*. New York: Oxford University Press, pp. 19–136.

Toth, N. (1987). "The First Technology," *Scientific American*, 256, 4, pp. 112–121.

Toynbee, A. (1956). *The Industrial Revolution* (Originally published 1884). Boston, MA: The Beacon Press.

Tribble, E. and Sutton, J. (2011). "Cognitive Ecology as a Framework for Shakespearean Studies," *Shakespearean Studies*, 39, pp. 94–103.

Turing, A.M. (1949). "Checking a Large Routine." *Report on the Conference on High Speed Automatic Calculating Machines*. Cambridge: University Mathematical Laboratory, pp. 67–68.

Turing, A.M. (1950). "Computing Machinery and Intelligence," *Mind*, LIX, pp. 433–460.

Turner, M. (1996). *The Literary Mind*. New York: Oxford University Press.

Venkataraman, G. (1988). *Journey into Light: The Life and Science of C.V. Raman*. Bangalore: Indian Science Academy.

Vincenti, W.G. (1992). *What Engineers Know and How They Know It*. Baltimore, MD: Johns Hopkins University Press.

von Eckardt, B. (1993). *What is Cognitive Science?* Cambridge, MA: MIT Press.

von Neumann, J. (1945). "First Draft of a Report on the EDVAC." Unpublished memorandum. Philadelphia, PA: Moore School of Electrical Engineering.

von Neumann, J. (1951). "The General and Logical Theory of Automata." In L.A. Jeffress (ed.). *Cerebral Mechanisms in Behavior: The Hixon Symposium*. New York: John Wiley, pp 1–41.

von Neumann, J. (1958). *The Computer and the Brain*. New Haven, CT: Yale University Press.

von Neumann, J. and Morgernstern, O. (1947). *The Theory of Games and Economic Behavior*. Princeton, NJ: Princeton University Press.

von Staden, H. (2007). "Physis and Technē in Greek Medicine." In B. Bensande-Vincent and W. Newman (ed.). *The Artificial and the Natural*. Cambridge, MA: MIT Press, pp. 21–50.

Wallace, D.B. (1989). "Studying the Individual: The Case Study Method and Other Genres." In: D.B. Wallace and H.E. Gruber (ed.). *Creative People at Work*. New York: Oxford University Press, pp. 25–43.

Wallace, D.B. and Gruber, H.E. (ed.). (1989). *Creative People at Work*. New York: Oxford University Press.

Wallas, G. (1926). *The Art of Creativity*. New York: Harcourt, Brace, Jovanovich.

Watson, G.F. (1991). "Masaru Ibuka," *IEEE Spectrum*, December, pp. 22–28.

Watson, J.D. (1968). *The Double Helix*. New York: Athenium.

Watt, J. (1970a). "Notebook" (1765). In: E.A. Robinson and D. McKie (ed.). *Partners in Science: Letters of James Watt and Joseph Black*. Cambridge, MA: Harvard University Press, pp. 431–479.

Watt, J. (1970b). 1805. "James Watt's Recollection of His Friend Dr. J. Robison, April 9, 1805." In: E.A. Robinson and D. McKie (ed.). *Partners in Science: Letters of James Watt and Joseph Black*. Cambridge, MA: Harvard University Press, pp. 410–413.

Watt, J. (1970c). 1809. "Letter to J. Playfair, Jan. 4, 1809." In: E.A. Robinson and D. McKie (ed.). *Partners in Science: Letters of James Watt and Joseph Black*. Cambridge, MA: Harvard University Press, pp. 416–419.

Weber, R. and Perkins, D.L. (ed.). (1992). *Inventive Minds*. New York: Oxford University Press.

Weingart, A.J. (1977). *Self, Interaction and the Natural Environment*. Albany, NY: State University of New York Press.

Weisberg, R.M. (1993). *Creativity: The Myth of Genius.* New York: W.H. Freeman.

Weisberg, R.M. (2004). "On Structure in the Creative Process: A Quantitative Case Study of the Creation of Picasso's *Guernica,*" *Creativity Research Journal*, 22, pp. 23–54.

Weisberg, R.M. and Hass, R. (2007). "We Are All Partly Right: Comment on 'The Creative Process in Picasso's *Guernica* Sketches: Monotonic Improvement versus Nonmonotonic Variants,' *Creativity Research Journal*, 19, pp. 345–360.

Weisendanger, M. and Weisendanger, M. (1971). *The 19th Century Louisiana Painters and Paintings.* New Orleans, LA: W.E. Grove Gallery.

Whatmore, R. (2016). *What is Intellectual History?* Cambridge: Polity Press.

Wheeler, D.J. (1951). "Automatic Computing with the EDSAC." PhD Dissertation, University of Cambridge.

White, H. (1978). *Tropics of Discourse.* Baltimore, MD: Johns Hopkins University Press.

White, R. (1992). "Beyond Art: Toward an Understanding of the Origins of Material Representation in Europe." In B. Siegerl, A. Beals and S.A. Tyler (ed.). *Annual Review of Anthropology*, 21. Palo Alto, CA: Annual Reviews, pp. 537–564.

White, R. (2003). *Prehistoric Art: The Symbolic Journey of Humankind.* New York: Harry N. Abrams.

Wilkes, M.V. (1951). "The Best Way to Design an Automatic Calculating Machine." Manchester University Computer Inaugural Conference, Manchester.

Wilkes, M.V. (1985). *Memoirs of a Computer Pioneer.* Cambridge, MA: MIT Press.

Wilkes, M.V. (1986). "The Genesis of Microprogramming," *Annals of the History of Computing*, 3, 2, pp. 116–126.

Wilkes, M.V. and Renwick, W. (1950). "The EDSAC." In: *Report on the Conference on High-Speed Automatic Calculating Machines.* Cambridge: University Mathematical Laboratory, pp. 9–11.

Wilkes, M.V., Wheeler, D.J. and Gill, S. (1951). *Preparation of Programs for an Electronic Digital Computer.* Cambridge, MA: Addison-Wesley.

Williams, F.C. and Kilburn, T. (1949). "A Storage System for Use in Binary Digital Computing Machines," *Proceedings, Institution of Electrical Engineers* (IEE), 96, Part 2, 30, 183ff.

Williams, R. (1963). *Culture and Society 1780–1850.* Harmondsworth: Penguin Books.

Wing, J.M. (2006). "Computational Thinking," *Communications of the ACM*, 49, 3, pp. 33–35.

Wing, J.M. (2008). "Computational Thinking and Rethinking about Computing," *Philosophical Transactions of the Royal Society*, Series A, 366, pp. 3717–3725.

Winograd, T. (1972). *Understanding Natural Language.* New York: Academic Press.

Winograd, T. (1980). "What Does It Mean to Understand Language?" *Cognitive Science*, 4, pp. 209–241.

Winograd, T. and Flores, F. (1987). *Understanding Computers and Cognition.* Reading, MA: Addison-Wesley.

Wirth, N. (1968). "PL360, A Programming Language for the 360 Computers," *Journal of the ACM*, 15, 1, pp. 34–74.

Wirth, N. (1971a). "The Programming Language PASCAL," *Acta Informatica*, 1, 1, pp. 35–63.

Wirth, N. (1971b). "The Design of a PASCAL Compiler," *Software—Practice and Experience*, 1, pp. 309–333.

Wirth, N. (1971c). "Program Development by Stepwise Refinement," *Communications of the ACM*, 14, 4, pp. 221–227.

Wirth, N. (1973). *Systematic Programming: An Introduction.* Englewood-Cliffs, NJ: Prentice-Hall.

Wirth, N. (1977). "Modula: A Language for Modular Programming," *Software—Practice & Experience*, 7, 1, pp. 3–35.

Wirth, N. (1985). "From Programming Language Design to Computer Construction," *Communication of the ACM*, 28, 2, pp. 159–164.

Wirth, N. and Hoare, C.A.R. (1966). "A Contribution to the Development of ALGOL," *Communications of the ACM*, 9, pp. 413–432.

Wirth, N. and Weber, H. (1966a). "EULER: A Generalization of ALGOL and Its Formal Definition, Part I," *Communications of the ACM*, 9, 1, pp. 13–25.

Wirth, N. and Weber, H. (1966b). "EULER: A Generalization of ALGOL and Its Formal Definition, Part II," *Communications of the ACM*, 9, 2, pp. 89–99.

Wölfflin, H. (1932). *Principles of Art History*. New York: Dover.

Wollheim, R. (1987). *Painting as an Art*. Princeton, NJ: Princeton University Press.

Wood, P. (1992). "The Scientific Revolution in Scotland." In: R. Porter and M. Teich (ed.). *Scientific Revolution in National Context*. Cambridge: Cambridge University Press, pp. 263–287.

Woodward, C.E. (1989). "Art and Elegance in the Synthesis of Organic Compounds: Robert Burns Woodward." In: D.B. Wallace and H.E. Gruber (ed.). *Creative People at Work*. New York: Oxford University Press, pp. 227–253.

Woolf, V. (1979). *Women and Writing* (M. Barrett, ed.). New York: Harcourt.

Wootton, D. (2015). *The Invention of Science*. New York: HarperCollins.

Wordsworth, W. (1916). "Poetry and Poetic Diction" (1800) In: E.D. Jones (ed.). *English Critical Essays. Nineteenth Century*. London: Oxford University Press, pp. 1–39.

Wright, F.L. (1979). *The Future of Architecture*. New York: New American Library.

Wulf, W.A. (1972). "A Case Against the GOTO," *Proceedings of the 1971 IFIP Congress, Volume 1*. Amsterdam: North-Holland, pp. 791–797.

Wulf, W.A., Russell, D.B. and Haberman, A.N. (1971). "BLISS: A Language for Systems Programming," *Communications of the ACM*, 14, 12, pp. 780–790.

Yeats, W.B. (1912.) "Introduction." In: R. Tagore. *Gitanjali (Song Offerings)*. London: The India Society, pp. vii–xvi.

Zamora, L.P. and Faris, W.B. ed. (1995). *Magical Realism*. Durham, NC: Duke University Press.

Zervos, C. (1985). "Conversation with Picasso." (Originally published 1935). In: B. Ghiselin. *The Creative Process*. Berkeley, CA: University of California Press, pp. 48–53.

INDEX